A Guidebook to
Virginia's Historical Markers
REVISED AND EXPANDED EDITION

A Guidebook to
Virginia's Historical Markers

REVISED AND EXPANDED EDITION

Compiled by

John S. Salmon

Prepared by the Virginia Department of Historic Resources

Published by the University Press of Virginia

Charlottesville and London

THE UNIVERSITY PRESS OF VIRGINIA
© 1994 by the Virginia Department of Historic Resources

Second printing 1996

For this second printing, asterisks have been removed in the text and indexes where markers have been replaced.

Library of Congress Cataloging-in-Publication Data

Salmon, John S., 1948–
    A guidebook to Virginia's historical markers / compiled by John S. Salmon. – Rev. and expanded ed.
        p. cm.
    " Prepared by the Virginia Department of Historic Resources."
    Rev. and expanded ed. of : A guidebook to Virginia's historical markers / compiled by Margaret T. Peters. 1985.
    Includes indexes.
    ISBN 0-8139-1491-4 (pbk.)
    1. Historical markers — Virginia — Guidebooks. 2. Virginia — History, Local.
3. Virginia — Guidebooks. I. Virginia. Dept. of Historic Resources. II. Peters,
Margaret T. Guidebook to Virginia's historical markers. III. Title.
F227.S25 1994
917.5504' 43—dc20   93-39963
                                                                              CIP

Printed in the United States of America

Contents

Preface

VIRGINIA DEPARTMENT OF HISTORIC RESOURCES

VIRGINIA'S HISTORIC LANDMARKS are an unparalleled and irreplaceable resource representing the culture and history of America from prehistoric times to the present. The preservation and commemoration of these tangible reminders of our cultural heritage is in the interest of all Virginians. The Commonwealth of Virginia has established policies that encourage the preservation, protection, and proper management of our significant historic resources.

Historic properties provide communities with a sense of identity and stability. Preserving these properties contributes significantly to the vitality of today's communities and ensures that tangible reminders of the past will remain for future generations. The Department of Historic Resources and its seven-member Board of Historic Resources are responsible for oversight of the state's historic preservation programs, including formally recognizing the most significant properties by listing them in the Virginia Landmarks Register.

The Virginia Department of Historic Resources traces its roots to 1966 legislation that created the Virginia Historic Landmarks Commission. That legislation formally began the state's efforts toward the identification and preservation of its historic resources. The Department also serves as the State Historic Preservation Office in the federal preservation system, and nominates significant properties to the National Register of Historic Places.

The Department's director and its Board of Historic Resources are appointed by the governor. The Department's professional staff is made up of architectural historians, architects, archaeologists, historians, and archivists. In addition to offices in Richmond, the Department has a regional preservation office in Roanoke to serve that area of the Commonwealth. The Department is committed to providing public education in the field of historic preservation and offers technical assistance to local governments, preservation groups, and owners of historic properties. The Department publishes *The Virginia Landmarks Register, Notes on Virginia* (an annual journal of its activities), *Footnotes* (a bimonthly newsletter), and occasional monographs on archaeology, preservation planning, and countywide resource surveys.

The Board of Historic Resources is also responsible for authorizing new historical highway markers to commemorate the important places, people, and events in Virginia history. The concept for the highway historical marker program in Virginia originated with Richard C. Wight, an amateur historian who was inspired by his interest in the state's history. He attempted to persuade Governor E. Lee Trinkle (1922–26), then Governor Harry F. Byrd Sr. (1926–30), to adopt his idea, which ultimately resulted in legislation enacted by Virginia's General Assembly in 1926. The 1926 act created the Conservation and Economic Development Commission and provided funds for advertising the advantages and resources of the state to a growing traveling public. The state's leaders concluded that a state as rich in history as Virginia, the scene of two major wars, needed to explain that rich history to visitors to the Commonwealth. Soon thereafter, Dr. H. J. Eckenrode was selected by the Conservation and Economic Development Commission to direct a program to ascertain the historic sites in Virginia and to mark them appropriately. Highlights of the activities of the American Revolution and the Civil War that took place in Virginia proved to be among the most popular sites selected for recognition; also included were historic homes, churches, and sites of other major events in Virginia's past. Prominent Virginia historians such as Douglas Southall Freeman, H. R. McIlwaine, and Lyon G. Tyler served on a History Advisory Committee to assist Eckenrode in the selection of sites to be marked as well as in the preparation of texts for those markers.

Markers were identified by a letter/numeral code. The letter indicated the highway, since at that time highways were only designated by letter. The numeral assigned served to distinguish the markers on any one highway and were assigned as each marker was erected. This system has been followed to some degree throughout the years; however, changes in highway routes, along with the addition of many markers, have made strict adherence to the original system all but impossible.

Markers were to be placed along major travel routes in order to reach the largest number of travelers. Care was taken to place markers so that they would not impede safe travel, but so that they could be easily read by motorists as they passed by. As automobile speeds increased, Dr. Eckenrode realized the need for a guidebook containing the inscriptions on the markers, so in 1930 the first highway-marker guidebook was published.

The number of markers increased steadily. By 1934, 1,200 markers were in place, with plans for an additional 400 as funds became available. During the depression years, efforts were made to provide "pull-offs" for the markers, so the motorist could stop safely and read the text of each marker.

The marker program was suspended during World War II and did not resume until 1946. Responsibility for the erection and maintenance of markers was subsequently transferred to the Virginia Department of Highways, while the responsibility for researching and approving new markers was assigned to the Virginia State Library. The State Library continued to have jurisdiction over the marker program until 1966, when the General Assembly transferred the program to the newly created Virginia Historic Landmarks Commission.

Between 1948 and 1976, some one hundred new markers were erected, and efforts were made to broaden and diversify the subjects included on them. Although a number of the new markers continued to identify sites associated with the Civil War, many explained some important events in Virginia's twentieth-century history, as well as lesser-known sites associated with colonial and antebellum Virginia. In 1976, the Virginia General Assembly curtailed state funding for new or replacement markers.

Today all funds for new markers come from private sources or local governments. Approximately twenty to twenty-five new markers are approved by the Virginia Board of Historic Resources each year. The Virginia Department of Transportation retains responsibility for the erection of new markers and the maintenance of existing ones.

The original intent of the marker program was to foster interest nationwide in Virginia's history and to encourage tourism in Virginia. While subsequent research may have cast doubt on the accuracy of some of the early markers, the markers remain a valuable source of information that enhances the appeal to those using Virginia's highways. This updated guide to the markers in the state system as of June 1993 is intended to make that information even more readily available to today's traveler.

This new edition of Virginia's marker guidebook builds upon

the excellent work of the compiler of the previous edition, Margaret T. Peters. She provided the present compiler with a great deal of useful advice, which he gratefully acknowledges. Much of the labor involved in assembling this new edition was carried out by Kenneth M. Shores, who spent many weeks at the computer. Finally, this edition would not have been possible without the interest and support of all the outdoor advertising staff in the district offices of the Virginia Department of Transportation.

How to Use the Guidebook

The marker guidebook has been arranged to accommodate contemporary travel patterns and to facilitate finding a specific marker. The texts of the markers are arranged by symbol and number, beginning with A-1 and continuing through XP-6. This arrangement generally follows the location of primary highways. Markers with no accompanying letter/numeral symbols are arranged alphabetically by title at the end of the listings.

Three separate indexing systems have been developed. The first is alphabetical by marker title. The second is arranged by subject, so that a reader may refer to all markers displaying information on a particular subject or marking buildings of a specific type. The large group of markers pertaining to the Civil War are arranged regionally in that index to assist the traveler in a particular area of the state. The final index is arranged alphabetically by county and independent city, with the text (if any) for each jurisdiction marker followed by the location of all markers in that particular jurisdiction.

Markers with an asterisk are no longer in place, but their inscriptions have been included together with their original locations. Distances have been measured from the closest village, town, or major intersection. The text of each marker has been reproduced as it appears on the face of the marker itself. The traveler should be aware that, while there may be other historical markers that resemble the state's in shape and design, only markers formally approved by the state are included in this book.

Virginia's Historical Markers

Virginia's Historical Markers

A-1 ACTION AT STEPHENSON'S DEPOT

Near this place on June 15, 1863, Confederate troops of General Edward "Allegheny" Johnson's Division attacked and routed General Robert Milroy's Union Army during its retreat from Winchester. The short, pre-dawn battle resulted in the capture of Milroy's wagon train and more than 2300 Union prisoners. From here, the Confederate Army advanced into Pennsylvania where it suffered defeat two weeks later at Gettysburg. *Frederick Co.: Rte. 11 at Rte. 664.*

A-1* ACTION AT STEPHENSON'S DEPOT

Near this place, Ewell, on June 15, 1863, captured wagon trains, cannon and several thousand men of Milroy's army, which had been driven from Winchester by Early. *Frederick Co.: Rte. 11, 4 miles n. of Winchester.*

A-2 ACTION OF RUTHERFORD'S FARM

Near here, the Confederate General Stephen D. Ramseur was attacked by General William W. Averell and pushed back toward Winchester, July 20, 1864. *Frederick Co.: Rte. 11, .19 mile e. of Rte. 661.*

A-2* ACTION OF CARTER'S FARM

Near here the Confederate General Ramseur was attacked by Averell and pushed back toward Winchester, July 20, 1864. *Frederick Co.: Rte. 11, .19 mile e. of I-66.*

A-3 CAPTURE OF STAR FORT

The fort on the hilltop to the southwest, known as Star Fort, was taken by Colonel Schoonmaker of Sheridan's army in the battle of September 19, 1864. *Frederick Co.: Rte. 11, .8 mile n. of Winchester.*

A-4 FORT COLLIER

Just to the east, a redoubt known as Fort Collier was built by Joseph E. Johnston in 1861. Early's left rested here during the Third Battle of Winchester, September 19, 1864. *Frederick Co.: Rte. 11, .1 mile s. of Rte. 764.*

A-4* FORT COLLIER

Just to the south was built by Joseph E. Johnston, 1861. Early's left rested here, Third Battle of Winchester, September 19, 1864. *Frederick Co.: Rte. 11, .1 mile s. of Rte. 764.*

A-5 FIRST BATTLE OF WINCHESTER

On May 24, 1862, Confederate forces under Major General Thomas J. "Stonewall" Jackson pursued Major General Nathaniel Banks' Union Army from Strasburg to Winchester. Banks made a stand south of Winchester, posting one of two infantry brigades on Bower's Hill, now known as Williamsburg Heights, and the other here in the plain below. In attacks the following day, Jackson routed the Union Army and drove it through the town towards Harper's Ferry. *Frederick Co.: Rte. 11, .1 mile s. of Handley Blvd.*

A-6* FIRST BATTLE OF WINCHESTER

On the morning of May 25, 1862, New England troops in Bank's army held this position, facing Jackson, who was advancing from the south. *Frederick Co.: Rte. 11, s. of Winchester.*

A-7 FIRST BATTLE OF WINCHESTER

Here Stonewall Jackson, in the early morning of May 25, 1862, halted his advance guard and observed the Union position. *Frederick Co.: Rte. 11, .6 mile s. of Winchester.*

A-8 SECOND BATTLE OF WINCHESTER

On June 14, 1863, Jubal A. Early moved west from this point to attack federal fortifications west of Winchester. *Frederick Co.: Rte. 11, .18 mile s. of Rte. 37.*

A-8* SECOND BATTLE OF WINCHESTER

Here Ewell, on June 14, 1863, detached Early to move around Milroy's flank and attack the works west of Winchester. *Frederick Co.: Rte. 11, .6 mile s. of Winchester.*

A-9 BATTLE OF KERNSTOWN

On the hill to the west, Stonewall Jackson, late in the afternoon of March 23, 1862, attacked the Union force under Shields holding Winchester. After a fierce action, Jackson, who was greatly outnumbered, withdrew southward, leaving his dead on the field. These were buried next day by citizens of Winchester. *Frederick Co.: Rte. 11, 5.3 miles n. of Stephens City.*

A-10 EARLY AND CROOK

Here Early, just returned from his raid to Washington, attacked a pursuing force under Crook and drove it back, July 24, 1864. *Frederick Co.: Rte. 11, 1 mile n. of Kernstown.*

A-11 FIRST BATTLE OF WINCHESTER

The main body of Stonewall Jackson's army halted here to rest in the early morning of May 25, 1862. *Frederick Co.: Rte. 11, 3.2 miles n. of Stephens City.*

A-12 HOUSE OF FIRST SETTLER

Springdale, home of Colonel John Hite, son of Joist Hite, leader of the first settlers in this section, was built in 1753. Just to the south are the ruins of Hite's Fort, built about 1734. *Frederick Co.: Rte. 11, 2.3 miles n. of Stephens City.*

A-12 STEPHENS CITY

General David Hunter ordered the burning of this town on May 30, 1864; but Major Joseph Stearns of the First New York Cavalry prevented it. *Frederick Co.: Rte. 11, .16 mile s. of Rte. T1017.*

A-13* STEPHENS CITY

General David Hunter ordered the burning of this town, on May 30, 1864; but Major Stearns, First New York cavalry, prevented it. *Frederick Co.: Rte. 11, center of Stephens City.*

A-14 END OF SHERIDAN'S RIDE

This knoll marks the position of the Union Army when Sheridan rejoined it at 10:30 A.M., October 19, 1864, in the battle of Cedar Creek. His arrival, with Wright's efforts, checked the Union retreat. *Frederick Co.: Rte. 11, 3.2 miles s. of Stephens City.*

A-15 BATTLE OF CEDAR CREEK

Near this point General Early, on the morning of October 19, 1864, stopped his advance, and from this position he was driven by Sheridan in the afternoon. *Frederick Co.: Rte. 11, .2 mile n. of Middletown.*

A-16 ENGAGEMENT OF MIDDLETOWN

Here Stonewall Jackson, on May 24, 1862, attacked Banks, retreating from Strasburg, and forced him to divide his army. *Frederick Co.: Rte. 11, at Middletown.*

A-17 TOMB OF AN UNKNOWN SOLDIER

On the highest mountain top to the southeast is the grave of an unknown soldier. The mountain top was used as a signal station by both armies, 1861–1865. *Frederick Co.: Rte. 11, 1 mile s. of Middletown.*

A-18 ABRAHAM LINCOLN'S FATHER

Four miles west, Thomas Lincoln, father of the President, was born about 1778. He was taken to Kentucky by his father about 1781. Beside the road here was Lincoln Inn, long kept by a member of the family. *Rockingham Co.: Rte. 11, at Lacey Spring.*

A-19 TRENCHES ON HUPP'S HILL

These trenches were constructed by Sheridan in the autumn of 1864 while campaigning against Early. *Shenandoah Co.: Rte. 11, .8 mile n. of Strasburg.*

A-20 FRONTIER FORT

This house, built about 1755, is the old Hupp homestead. It was used as a fort in Indian attacks. *Shenandoah Co.: Rte. 11, at Strasburg.*

A-21 BATTLE OF CEDAR CREEK

The breaking of this bridge in the evening of October 19, 1864, permitted Sheridan to retake most of the material captured in the morning by Early. *Shenandoah Co.: Rte. 11, at Strasburg.*

A-22* BATTLE OF FISHER'S HILL

Early took position here after the battle of Winchester, and here he was attacked by Sheridan, September 22, 1864, and forced to retire. *Shenandoah Co.: Rte. 11, 1.9 miles s. of Strasburg.*

A-23 BATTLE OF FISHER'S HILL

Here Early's Adjutant-General, A. S. Pendleton, while attempting to check Sheridan's attack, was mortally wounded, September 22, 1864. *Shenandoah Co.: Rte. 11, 3.1 miles s. of Strasburg.*

A-24 BANKS' FORT

The earthworks on the hilltop to the southwest were constructed by General Banks in the campaign of 1862. *Shenandoah Co.: Rte. 11, at Strasburg.*

A-25 ACTION OF TOM'S BROOK

Here Early's cavalry under Rosser and Lomax was driven back by Sheridan's cavalry under Torbert, October 9, 1864. *Shenandoah Co.: Rte. 11, .1 mile s. of Tom's Brook.*

A-26* CAVALRY ENGAGEMENT

Near this point the First Virginia Cavalry and the First New York Cavalry fought an engagement, November 17, 1863. *Shenandoah Co.: Rte. 11, 1 mile s. of Mount Jackson.*

A-27 RUDE'S HILL ACTION

Rude's Hill was reached by two divisions of Sheridan's Union cavalry following the Confederate General Jubal A. Early, on November 22, 1864. Early promptly took position on the hill to oppose them. The cavalry, charging across the flats, were repulsed in a sharp action and fell back northward. *Shenandoah Co.: Rte. 11, 3.7 miles n. of New Market.*

A-28 BATTLE OF NEW MARKET

On the hills to the north took place the battle of New Market, May 15, 1864. The Union Army, under General Franz Sigel, faced southwest. John C. Breckinridge, once Vice-President of the United States, commanded the Confederates. General Scott Shipp commanded the cadet corps of the Virginia Military Institute, which distinguished itself, capturing a battery. The battle ended in Sigel's retreat northward. *Shenandoah Co.: Rte. 11, .6 mile n. of New Market.*

A-29 CAVALRY ENGAGEMENT

Here, at Lacey's Springs, Rosser's Confederate cavalry attacked Custer's camp, December 20, 1864. Rosser and Custer (of Indian fame) had been roommates at West Point. *Rockingham Co.: Rte. 11, 7.5 miles n. of Harrisonburg.*

A-30 WHERE ASHBY FELL

A mile and a half east of this point, Turner Ashby, Stonewall Jackson's cavalry commander, was killed, June 6, 1862, while opposing Fremont's advance. *Rockingham Co.: Rte. 11, 1.5 miles s. of Harrisonburg.*

A-31 OLD PROVIDENCE CHURCH

Two and a half miles northwest. As early as 1748, a log meeting house stood there. In 1793 a stone church (still standing) was built. In 1859 it was succeeded by a brick church, which gave way to the present building in 1918. In the graveyard rest ancestors of Cyrus McCormick, inventor of the reaper, and fourteen Revolutionary soldiers. *Augusta Co.: Rte. 11, 1.4 miles n. of Steeles Tavern.*

A-32 SHERIDAN'S LAST RAID

Here was fought the engagement of Mount Crawford, March 1, 1865, in Sheridan's last raid. *Rockingham Co.: Rte. 11, .3 mile s. of Mount Crawford.*

A-33 HARRISONBURG

Here Thomas Harrison and wife deeded land for the Rockingham County public buildings, August 5, 1779. The same act established both Louisville, Ky., and Harrisonburg, May, 1780. Named for its founder, the town was also known as Rocktown. It was incorporated in 1849. In its vicinity battles were fought in 1862 and 1864. The present courthouse was built in 1897. Harrisonburg became a city in 1916. *Harrisonburg: Rte. 11.*

A-34 SEVIER'S BIRTHPLACE

Near here was born John Sevier, pioneer and soldier, September 23, 1745. He was a leader in the Indian wars and at the battle of King's Mountain, 1780. He was the only governor of the short-lived state of Franklin and the first governor of Tennessee. Sevier died in Georgia, September 24, 1815. *Shenandoah Co.: Rte. 11, .7 mile s. of New Market.*

A-35 END OF THE CAMPAIGN

Here Stonewall Jackson, retreating up the Valley before the converging columns of Fremont and Shields, turned at bay, June, 1862. A mile southeast Jackson's cavalry commander, Ashby, was killed, June 6. At Cross Keys, six miles southeast, Ewell of Jackson's army defeated Fremont, June 8. Near Port Republic, ten miles southeast, Jackson defeated Shields, June 9. This was the end of Jackson's Valley Campaign. *Rockingham Co.: Rte. 11, at Harrisonburg.*

A-36 FAIRFAX LINE

Here ran the southwestern boundary of Lord Fairfax's vast land grant, the Northern Neck. It was surveyed by Peter Jefferson, Thomas Jefferson's father, and others in 1746. *Shenandoah Co.: Rte. 11, .7 mile s. of New Market.*

A-37 OLD STONE FORT

One mile west is the Old Stone Fort, built about 1755. The northern end is loopholed for defense against Indians. *Frederick Co.: Rte. 11, at Middletown.*

A-38 HACKWOOD PARK

One mile east is the site of the Hackwood Estate House, built in 1777 by General John Smith. Documents reveal that the Hackwood House caught fire during the Third Battle of Winchester. Union troops used buildings on the site for a hospital, September 19, 1864. *Frederick Co.: Rte. 11, .19 mile e. of Rte. 661.*

A-38* HACKWOOD PARK

One mile east is Hackwood Park House, built in 1777 by General John Smith. It was used by Union troops as a hospital, September 19, 1864. *Frederick Co.: Rte. 11, 1.7 miles n. of Winchester.*

A-39 NEW PROVIDENCE CHURCH

This church, seven and a half miles west, was organized by John Blair in 1746. Five successive church buildings have been erected. The first pastor was John Brown. Samuel Brown, second pastor, had as wife Mary Moore, captured in youth by Indians and known as "The Captive of Abb's Valley." The synod of Virginia was organized here, 1788. *Augusta Co.: Rte. 11, at Steeles Tavern.*

A-40* FIRST SETTLER'S CAMP

Near here the first settler of Rockbridge County, John McDowell, pitched his first camp in the county, October, 1737. *Augusta Co.: Rte. 11, at Steeles Tavern.*

A-41 LAST INDIAN OUTRAGE

Here, in 1766, took place the last Indian outrage in Shenandoah County. Five Indians attacked two settler families fleeing to Woodstock. Two men were killed; the women and children escaped. *Shenandoah Co.: Rte. 11, 1.9 miles s. of Woodstock.*

A-42* RUFFNER'S HOME

Just to the west is Tribrook, home of W. H. Ruffner, first superintendent of public instruction of Virginia. He began, in 1870, the state's public school system. *Rockbridge Co.: Rte. 11, at Lexington.*

A-42* CHRISMAN'S SPRING

Four hundred yards northeast of this spring is the home of Jacob Chrisman, son-in-law of Joist Hite, built about 1753. *Frederick Co.: Rte. 11, 2 miles s. of Stephens City.*

A-43 MCDOWELL'S GRAVE

In this cemetery are the graves of Captain John McDowell and seven companions, who were killed by Indians near Balcony Falls, December 14, 1742. This fight began a war that lasted until 1744. *Rockbridge Co.: Rte. 11, 1.1 miles s. of Fairfield.*

A-44 LIBERTY HALL ACADEMY

This school, which was founded in 1777 and finally grew into Washington and Lee University, stood a short distance to the southwest of this point. *Rockbridge Co.: Rte. 11, 5.3 miles n. of Lexington.*

A-45* RED HOUSE ESTATE

This was the site of the home of Captain John McDowell, killed by the Indians in 1742, and the birthplace of Doctor Ephraim McDowell, pioneer in abdominal surgery. *Rockbridge Co.: Rte. 11, 1.1 miles s. of Fairfield.*

A-46 TIMBER RIDGE CHURCH

This Presbyterian Church was built in 1756, nineteen years after the first settlement in Rockbridge County. *Rockbridge Co.: Rte. 11, 5.3 miles n. of Lexington (at Sam Houston Wayside).*

A-47 CHERRY GROVE ESTATE

Here was born James McDowell, Governor of Virginia, 1843–46. *Rockbridge Co.: Rte. 11, .3 mile s. of Fairfield.*

A-48 AUDLEY PAUL'S FORT

Near here stood the stockade fort of Captain Audley Paul, noted colonial frontier soldier. He served in the Sandy Creek expedition against the Shawnees, 1756, at the battle of Point Pleasant, 1774, and in repelling Indian raids. In 1761, the fort was crowded with settlers' families seeking protection against marauding Shawnees. *Botetourt Co.: Rte. 11, 4.5 miles s. of Natural Bridge.*

A-49 THORN HILL ESTATE

Home of Colonel John Bowyer, an officer in the Revolutionary War, and of General E. F. Paxton, commander of the Stonewall Brigade, killed at Chancellorsville, May 3, 1863. *Rockbridge Co.: Rte. 251, .6 mile n. of Lexington.*

A-50 INDIAN MASSACRE

Near here was the Renick settlement, raided by the Shawnee Indians in 1757. Five settlers were killed and nine taken captive. *Botetourt Co.: Rte. 11, .9 mile n. of Buchanan.*

A-51 VIRGINIA INVENTORS

A mile and a half northwest, Cyrus H. McCormick perfected, in 1831, the grain reaper. In that vicinity, in 1856, J. A. E. Gibbs devised the chainstitch sewing machine. *Augusta Co.: Rte. 11, at Steeles Tavern.*

A-52 BIRTHPLACE OF SAM HOUSTON

In a cabin on the hilltop to the east Sam Houston was born, March 2, 1793. As commander-in-chief of the Texas army, he won the battle of San Jacinto, which secured Texan independence, April 21, 1836. He was President of Texas, 1836–1838, 1841–1844; United States Senator, 1846–1859; Governor, 1860–1861. He died, July, 1863. *Rockbridge Co.: Rte. 11, 5.3 miles n. of Lexington.*

A-53 BETHEL CHURCH

Two miles west. The first church was built by Colonel Robert Doak in 1779. Captain James Tate, an elder, led in the battles of Cowpens and Guilford Courthouse (1781) a company drawn mainly from this church. In the churchyard 23 Revolutionary soldiers are buried. The present building was erected in 1888. *Augusta Co.: Rte. 11, 2.1 miles n. of Greenville.*

A-54 FORT TRIAL

Near here stood Fort Trial, one of a chain of forts built in 1756, in the French and Indian War, as places of refuge in Indian attacks. Washington visited it soon after its erection. *Henry Co.: Rte. 57, 6 miles n. of Martinsville.*

A-55* FORT BOWMAN

The stone house to the south is Fort Bowman, or Harmony Hall, built about 1753. Here was born Major Joseph Bowman, second in command in George Rogers Clark's expedition for the conquest of the Northwest. *Shenandoah Co.: Rte. 11, 1.9 miles n. of Strasburg.*

A-56 BATTLE OF CEDAR CREEK

Here the Union army lay in an entrenched camp, October 19, 1864. Crook was in the valley to the east; the Nineteenth Corps on the hillside facing south. At dawn the Confederates attacked from the east and south, capturing the camp and driving the Unionists northward two miles and a half. Wright finally halted the retreat. *Frederick Co.: Rte. 11, 1.3 miles s. of Middletown.*

A-57 WILLIAM BYRD'S CAMP

Near here, on Matrimony Creek, William Byrd pitched his camp, November, 1728, while determining the Virginia–North Carolina boundary line. *Henry Co.: Rte. 220, 3.5 miles s.w. of Ridgeway.*

A-58 BUCHANAN

The town was established in 1811 and named for Colonel John Buchanan, pioneer and soldier. It was incorporated in 1833. Its importance consisted in its being the western terminus of the James River and Kanawha Canal, which reached the town in 1851. Hunter passed here moving to Lynchburg, June, 1864. The town was reincorporated in 1892. *Botetourt Co.: Rte. 11, at Buchanan.*

A-59 DR. JESSEE BENNETT (1769–1842)

Near Edom, Virginia, on January 14, 1794, in a heroic effort to save his wife, Elizabeth, and child, Dr. Jessee Bennett performed the first successful Caesarian section and oophorectomy to be done in America. *Rockingham Co.: Rte. 42. at Edom.*

A-60 ROCKY MOUNT

This place was established as the county seat when Franklin County was formed. The first court was held in March, 1786. The first (log) courthouse was replaced in 1831. In 1836 the town consisted of 30 dwellings and a number of business houses. General Jubal A. Early practiced law here. The town was incorporated in 1873. The present courthouse was built in 1909. *Franklin Co.: Rte. 220, at Rocky Mount.*

A-61 BIRTHPLACE OF WOODROW WILSON, U.S. PRESIDENT 1913–21

Three and one half miles south, on Coalter Street in Staunton, is the birthplace of Thomas Woodrow Wilson, 8th Virginia-born president of the U.S., Princeton University president, New Jersey governor, 28th President (World War I), he was chief author and sponsor of the League of Nations. Born Dec. 28, 1856, died in Washington, Feb. 3, 1924. The birthplace is maintained as an historic shrine. *Augusta Co.: Rte. 11, 3.5 miles n. of Rte. 275.*

A-62 BIRTHPLACE OF WOODROW WILSON, U.S. PRESIDENT 1913–21

One mile south, on Coalter Street in Staunton, is the birthplace of Thomas Woodrow Wilson, 8th Virginia-born president of the U.S., Princeton University president, New Jersey governor, 28th President (World War I), he was chief author and sponsor of the League of Nations. Born Dec. 28, 1856, died in Washington, Feb. 3, 1924. The birthplace is maintained as an historic shrine. *Staunton: Rte. 11, .05 mile n. of Rte. 261.*

A-62* BELLEFONT

The house on the hill to the north is Bellefont, home of John Lewis, first settler in this region, who came here from Pennsylvania in 1732. The building, which was half dwelling, half fort, is thought to be the oldest occupied in the Shenandoah Valley. *Augusta Co.: Rte. 254, 1 mile e. of Rte. 11.*

A-63 DR. ALEXANDER HUMPHREYS

Dr. Humphreys (1757–1802), an important teacher in 18th-century Virginia, received his M.D. from the University of Edinburgh. He practiced medicine in Augusta County and Staunton from 1783 to 1802 in an office facing the county courthouse. Among Dr. Humphreys' many students were Dr. Ephraim McDowell, the "Founder of Abdominal Surgery"; Dr. Samuel Brown, a pioneer in the use of smallpox vaccination; and President William Henry Harrison. Dr. Humphreys is buried in the churchyard of Trinity Episcopal Church. *Staunton: Augusta St. at Johnson St.*

A-64 DR. WILLIAM FLEMING

Physician, soldier, and statesman, Dr. William Fleming (1728–1795) studied medicine in his native Scotland before practicing in Staunton from 1763 to 1768. His home stood at the crossing of New Street and Lewis Creek. Dr. Fleming's career included periods as commander of the Botetourt Regiment, Commissioner for Kentucky, member of the Continental Congress, delegate to the Virginia Constitutional Convention, and Acting Governor when the Virginia General Assembly met in Staunton in June, 1781. *Staunton: Greenville Ave. at New St.*

A-72 NATURAL BRIDGE OF VIRGINIA

Legend says the Monocan Indians called it "The Bridge of God" and worshipped it. Thomas Jefferson was the first American owner, patenting it with 157 acres on July 5, 1774, "for twenty shillings of good and lawful money." Millions of years old, Natural Bridge is considered one of the seven natural wonders of the world. *Rockbridge Co.: Rte. 11, at Natural Bridge.*

A-79 HOLLINS COLLEGE

First chartered college for women in Virginia, established 1842. The estate was the pioneer home of William Carvin, who settled here before 1746. *Roanoke Co.: Rte. 11, 5.8 miles n. of Roanoke.*

A-80 COMING OF THE RAILROAD

Near here took place the historic meeting of John C. Moomaw and C. M. Thomas that led to the termination of the Shenandoah Valley Railroad at Big Lick (now Roanoke), April, 1881. This was the beginning of the city of Roanoke. *Botetourt Co.: Rte. 11, 4.2 miles n. of Troutville.*

A-81 OLD CAROLINA ROAD

This is the old road from Pennsylvania to the Yadkin Valley, over which in early times settlers passed going south. On it were the Black Horse Tavern and the Tinker Creek Presbyterian Church. *Botetourt Co.: Rte. 11, 8 miles n. of Roanoke.*

A-82 CLOVERDALE FURNACE

Here was situated Cloverdale Furnace, an early iron industry, developed by Carter Beverly, in 1808. *Botetourt Co.: Rte. 11, 8.2 miles n. of Roanoke.*

A-91 LOONEY'S FERRY

Looney's Ferry, established in 1742, was the first crossing over the James River in this region. On the other side of the river was Cherry Tree Bottom, home of Colonel John Buchanan, and above the mouth of this creek stood Fort Fauquier, 1758–1763. *Botetourt Co.: Rte. 11, .7 mile s. of Buchanan.*

A-92 CARTMILL'S GAP

Indian raiders going west passed through this gap after massacring settlers on Cedar Creek near Natural Bridge, 1757. *Botetourt Co.: Rte. 11, 1.4 miles n. of Buchanan.*

A-93 FORT BLACKWATER

Near here stood a stockade erected by Capt. Nathaniel Terry and garrisoned by men under his command. Washington made "Terry's Fort" a link in his chain of forts and inspected it in the fall of 1756. *Franklin Co.: Rte. 220, 3 miles n. of Rocky Mount.*

A-94 MARTINSVILLE

Named for Joseph Martin, pioneer, who settled here in 1773. In 1793 the courthouse of Henry County was moved here and the town was established. Patrick Henry, for whom the county was named, lived near here once. In 1865, Stoneman, moving south to join Sherman, captured Martinsville. It was incorporated as a town in 1873 and as a city in 1929. *Martinsville: Rte. 220 at Martinsville.*

A-95 BIRTHPLACE OF GENERAL JUBAL EARLY

Near this place, on land occupied since the 1780s by the Early family, Confederate General Jubal Early was born in 1816. The General practiced law in Franklin County and served in the Mexican War before the Civil War. Early fought in more battles than any other Confederate general and came closest to capturing Washington. Because of his undying devotion to the southern cause, he became known as "The Unreconstructed Rebel." *Franklin Co.: Rte. 116, 5.2 miles n. of Rte. 122.*

A-96 CAROLINA ROAD

Here through the Maggotty Gap, the Great Wagon Road from Philadelphia to Georgia, known locally as the Carolina Road, passes through the Blue Ridge. Originating as the Great Warrior Path of the Iroquois centuries before, the path was frequently used by the Iroquois before being ceded to the whites in 1744 to become one of the most heavily traveled roads in all Colonial America. *Franklin Co.: Rte. 220, .7 mile s. of Roanoke-Franklin Co. line.*

A-97 WASHINGTON IRON WORKS

Here stands the furnace and ironmaster's house of the Washington Iron Works, Franklin County's first industry. Originally established in 1773 by Col. John Donelson, father-in-law of President Andrew Jackson, the iron plantation was acquired in 1779 by Col. James Callaway and Jeremiah Early and expanded to 18,000 acres to become one of the last great iron plantations in Virginia. The Saunders family continued the operation until 1850, supplying iron locally and as far south as Georgia. *Franklin Co.: Rte. 220 Bus., .5 mile s. of Franklin County Courthouse in Rocky Mount.*

A-98 TAYLOR'S STORE

Here stood Taylor's Store, established in 1799 by Skelton Taylor, a lieutenant in the Bedford County militia during the Revolutionary War. After Franklin County was formed, he became a militia captain and overseer of the poor. His store and ordinary served travelers along the nearby Warwick Road, which linked the Southside Piedmont counties with Richmond. The store became the hub of a community known as Taylor's Store and functioned as a post office between 1818 and 1933. It was dismantled ca. 1970. *Franklin Co.: Rte. 122, 1.6 miles e. of Rte. 116.*

A-99 WILLOW SPOUT

Here stood, from the early 19th century until the mid-1900s, the tavern and stagecoach stop first owned by Peter Hanger. In 1848 its second proprietor, Samuel Harnsbarger, planted a willow tree in a spring here, across the newly-constructed Valley Turnpike from the tollhouse. Spring water flowed up the trunk and out a spout driven in its side, falling into a wooden trough. For more than a century, three successive "willow spouts" provided water for thirsty travelers, horses, and automobiles. *Augusta Co.: Rte. 11, .03 mile s. of Rte. 742.*

A-135 BELLEVIEW

Three miles southwest is Belleview, home of Major John Redd, a pioneer in this section. Redd served in the Indian wars and in the Revolution, being present at the siege of Yorktown in 1781. *Henry Co.: Rte. 220, 4 miles s. of Martinsville.*

AB-1   MEEM'S BOTTOM COVERED BRIDGE

Built in 1892 by Franklin Hiser Wissler to provide access to his apple orchards at Strathmore Farms, this is the longest remaining covered bridge in Virginia. A 200-foot single span located one-half mile northwest, the bridge is a Burr Truss design, a combination of arch with vertical and diagonal supports. All construction materials were obtained locally. Damaged by arsonists in 1976, the bridge was restored and reopened in 1979. *Shenandoah Co.: Rte. 11, .2 mile s. of Rte. 720.*

AL-5   GLEBE BURYING GROUND

On the hill to the west is the oldest burying ground in this vicinity. It contains the grave of Colonel John Wilson, member of the House of Burgesses, 1748–1773; graves of colonial and Revolutionary soldiers, and those of victims of early Indian massacres. *Augusta Co.: Rte. 876, 12 miles s.w. of Staunton.*

AS-1   FAIRY STONE STATE PARK

This park was developed by the National Park Service, Interior Department, through the Civilian Conservation Corps, in conjunction with the Virginia Conservation Commission. It covers 5,000 acres and was opened, June 15, 1936. It takes its name from the fairy, or lucky, stones found everywhere in this area. *Patrick Co.: Rte. 623, 6 miles s. of Franklin Co. line.*

B-2*   THE BRIARS

One mile to the north is the home of John Esten Cooke, soldier, historian and novelist. Born in 1830, he died here in 1886. Cooke moved to the place in 1869. *Clarke Co.: Rte. 50, 3 miles n.w. of Boyce.*

B-4*   SARATOGA

Built in 1782 by General Daniel Morgan and named for the battle of Saratoga, 1777. Hessian prisoners did the construction work. Lee had his headquarters here in June, 1863, on the way to Gettysburg. *Clarke Co.: Rte. 50, at Boyce.*

B-7   SIGNAL STATION

On the hilltop to the south stood an important signal station used by both armies, 1861–1865. *Clarke Co.: Rte. 50, .7 mile w. of Paris.*

B-11   CAMPAIGN OF SECOND MANASSAS

Stonewall Jackson, sent by Lee to move around Pope's retreating army at Centreville and cut it off from Alexandria, reached this place August 31, 1862. Here Jackson turned east toward Fairfax. *Loudoun Co.: Rte. 50, .44 miles w. of Fairfax Co. line.*

B-11   BATTLE OF CHANTILLY (OX HILL)

The Battle of Chantilly (Ox Hill) took place here 1 September, 1862. Union General John Pope's Army, retreating after defeat by Lee at Second Manassas, clashed with Jackson's divisions which were attempting to prevent Pope from reaching Washington. Although Union generals Kearny and Stevens were killed, Jackson's men were held off by the smaller Union forces. The battle ended the Second Manassas campaign and led to Lee's invasion of Maryland. *Fairfax Co.: Rte. 50, 1.6 miles w. of I-66.*

B-12 COLONEL JOHN SINGLETON MOSBY

This road, along which many of his skirmishes took place, is named for Colonel John Singleton Mosby, commander of the 43rd Battalion of Confederate Partisan Rangers. Their activities in this area helped keep the Confederate cause alive in Northern Virginia toward the end of the Civil War. *Fairfax Co.: Rte. 50, 4 miles w. of Fairfax near Rte. 645.*

B-13* ACTION OF OX HILL

Stonewall Jackson reached Ox Hill (Chantilly) on September 1, 1862, attempting to prevent Pope, at Centreville, from retreating to Alexandria. The Confederates came into contact with Union troops and there followed a fierce action, ended by storm and darkness. General Philip Kearny was killed. Pope fell back to Alexandria. *Fairfax Co.: Rte. 50, 6.9 miles w. of Fairfax.*

B-16 COLONEL JOHN SINGLETON MOSBY

This road, along which many of his skirmishes took place, is named for Colonel John Singleton Mosby, commander of the 43rd Battalion of Confederate Partisan Rangers. Their activities in this area helped keep the Confederate cause alive in Northern Virginia toward the end of the Civil War. *Frederick Co.: Rte. 50 at Rte. 723.*

B-17 WILLOW SHADE

This house, built in 1858, was the childhood home of novelist Willa Cather from 1874 to 1883, when she moved with her family to Nebraska. It was the setting of the final chapters of her novel *Sapphira and the Slave Girl.* Willa Cather was born December 7, 1873, one mile south in the community of Gore, then known as Back Creek Valley. *Frederick Co.: Rte. 50, .71 mile e. of Gore.*

B-18 WILLA CATHER BIRTHPLACE

Here Willa Sibert Cather, the novelist, was born December 7, 1873. This community was her home until 1883 when her family moved to Nebraska. Nearby on Back Creek stands the old mill described in her novel "Sapphira and the Slave Girl." *Frederick Co.: Rte. 50, at Gore.*

B-19 SECOND BATTLE OF WINCHESTER

Here Jubal A. Early, detached to attack the rear of Milroy, holding Winchester, crossed this road and moved eastward in the afternoon of June 15, 1863. *Frederick Co.: Rte. 50, 2.5 miles w. of Winchester.*

B-20 JACKSON'S BIVOUAC

Near here Jackson's men, going to First Manassas, sank down to rest, July 19, 1861, without placing pickets. Jackson said: "Let the poor fellows sleep, I will guard the camp myself." *Fauquier Co.: Rtes. 50 and 17, at Paris.*

B-21 DELAPLANE

On July 19, 1861, Stonewall Jackson's brigade of General Joseph E. Johnston's corps marched to this station from Winchester. They crowded into freight and cattle cars and travelled to the 1st Battle of Manassas. The use of a railroad to carry more than ten thousand troops to the Manassas battlefield gave striking demonstration of the arrival of a new era in military transport and contributed significantly to the Confederate victory there. *Fauquier Co.: Rte. 17, 6.5 miles s. of Paris.*

B-22* MILITARY MOVEMENTS

This road was used by both armies, 1861–1864. Cavalry engagements took place near Middleburg on March 28, 1862, and June 19, 1863. *Loudoun Co.: Rte. 50, at Middleburg.*

B-23* ASHBY'S TAVERN

The old house to the north was Ashby's Tavern. As early as 1753, Thomas Watts had a license to keep a tavern here. He was succeeded by the Ashbys. In October, 1781, British prisoners from Yorktown rested here on their way to Winchester. *Clarke Co.: Rte. 50, 2 miles n.w. of Paris.*

B-24* ANCIENT HIGHWAY

The road to the south is the road from Dumfries, on the Potomac, to the Shenandoah Valley. It was traveled in March, 1748, by George Washington, then a lad of sixteen on his way to Greenway Court to survey Lord Fairfax's land beyond the Blue Ridge. *Fauquier Co.: Rte. 17, 1 mile s. of Paris.*

B-25 MOSBY'S RANGERS

Here at Atoka (Rector's Crossroads), on June 10, 1863, Company "A," 43rd Battalion of Partisan Rangers, known as "Mosby's Rangers," was formally organized. James William Foster was elected captain; Thomas Turner, first lieutenant; W. L. Hunter, second lieutenant; and G. H. Whitescarver, third lieutenant. Shortly after, Brawner's company of Prince William cavalry joined the command. *Fauquier Co.: Rte. 50, 4 miles w. of Middleburg.*

B-26 MOSBY'S MIDNIGHT RAID

Mosby, entering the town in the night of March 8, 1863, captured the Union General Stoughton. *Fairfax City: Rte. 123, .34 mile s. of Rte. 236.*

B-27* BRADDOCK ROAD

Here the wagon trains of General Braddock, in his expedition against the French, turned northeast to Snicker's Gap, June, 1755. Braddock was waiting for the wagons in Winchester before moving west to Fort Duquesne. [*Removed as inaccurate, May 1939.*] *Loudoun Co.: Rte. 50, at Aldie.*

B-28 MERCER'S HOME

Aldie was the home of Charles Fenton Mercer (born 1778, died 1858), liberal statesman. Mercer was a congressman (1817–1839) and a member of the Virginia constitutional convention of 1829–30, in which he advocated manhood suffrage. His attempt in 1817 to establish a free school system in Virginia nearly succeeded. He was a leading advocate of the colonization of free blacks in Liberia. *Loudoun Co.: Rte. 50, at Aldie.*

B-28* MERCER'S HOME

Aldie was the home of Charles Fenton Mercer (born 1778, died 1858), liberal statesman. Mercer was a Congressman and member of the Virginia convention of 1829–30, in which he advocated manhood suffrage. His attempt to establish a free school system in Virginia nearly succeeded, 1817. He was a leading advocate of the colonization of free negroes in Liberia. *Loudoun Co.: Rte. 50, at Aldie.*

B-29 SHARPSBURG (ANTIETAM) CAMPAIGN

Here Lee turned north, on the Ox Road, and moved toward Dranesville and Leesburg, September 3, 1862. The army entered Maryland, September 5–6, 1862. *Fairfax City: Rte. 50, at w. city limits.*

B-30* STUART AND BAYARD

Near here Stuart attacked the Union cavalry under Bayard, October 31, 1862. Bayard withdrew in the night to Chantilly. *Loudoun Co.: Rte. 50, at Aldie.*

B-31 STUART AND GREGG

Near here the Union cavalry general Gregg attacked Stuart and forced him to retire, June 19, 1863. *Fauquier Co.: Rte. 50, .4 mile e. of Upperville.*

B-32* GETTYSBURG CAMPAIGN

Here Stuart, screening Lee's movement into Pennsylvania, was surprised by Duffie of Hooker's cavalry and driven out of Middleburg, June 17, 1863. That night Stuart returned and drove Duffie out. *Loudoun Co.: Rte. 50, at limits of Middleburg.*

B-33 A REVOLUTIONARY WAR HERO

Near here stood the home of Sergeant Major John Champe (1752–1798), Continental soldier. Champe faked desertion and enlisted in Benedict Arnold's British command for the purpose of capturing the traitor. Failing in his attempt, Champe rejoined the American army. His meritorious service was attested to by such patriots as General Henry (Light Horse Harry) Lee. *Loudoun Co.: Rte. 50, 1.1 miles w. of Aldie.*

B-36 STUART AND MOSBY

Here on the evening of August 22, 1862, General J. E. B. Stuart raided General Pope's headquarters. Unable to burn the railroad bridge because of a heavy thunderstorm, Stuart withdrew his troops as well as 300 federal prisoners and Pope's dispatch case. At nearby Warrenton Junction (Calverton) on May 3, 1863, Colonel John S. Mosby attacked the Federal 1st West Virginia Regiment, but was forced to flee when surprised by 1st Vermont and 5th New York Cavalry. *Fauquier Co.: Rte. 28, 3.1 miles w. of Prince William Co. line.*

BW-2 BURKE'S STATION RAID

Burke's Station, four miles south, was raided by Stuart's cavalry, December, 1862. Stuart telegraphed to Washington complaining of the bad quality of the mules he had captured—a famous joke. *Fairfax City: Rte. 236, 1 mile e. of Rte. 123.*

BW-3 BURKE STATION

Burke Station was raided in December, 1862, by Confederate General J. E. B. Stuart. It was from this site, originally the Burke Station Depot, that he sent his famous telegram to the Union quartermaster general complaining of the poor quality of the Union mules he had just captured. *Fairfax Co.: Rte. 645 at Rte. 652, 3.11 miles n.e. of Rte. 123.*

BX-2* BRENT TOWN

Here the first blockhouse in this part of Virginia for protection against the Indians was built about 1688. The town was named for George Brent, engaged in a scheme for bringing Hugenots [*sic*] here to settle. *Fauquier Co.: Rte. 806, 5 miles s. of Catlett.*

BX-7 NEAVIL'S ORDINARY

Near here stood George Neavil's Ordinary, built at an early date and in existence as late as 1792. George Washington and George William Fairfax on their way to the Shenandoah Valley stopped here in 1748. *Fauquier Co.: Rte. 670, 6.1 miles e. of Warrenton.*

C-1* CLAY AND RANDOLPH DUEL

Near here Henry Clay and John Randolph of Roanoke fought a duel April 8, 1826. Randolph had called Clay a "blackleg" in a speech. Both men were unhurt, but Randolph's coat was pierced by a bullet. *Arlington Co.: Rte. 123, near Fairfax Co. line.*

C-2 WORLD'S FIRST PUBLIC PASSENGER FLIGHT

On September 9, 1908, near this site, Orville Wright carried aloft in public his first passenger, Lt. Frank P. Lahm, for a flight lasting 6 minutes and 24 seconds. Three days later, he took Major George O. Squier on a flight of 9 minutes and 6 seconds duration. From this primitive beginning has evolved an air transportation system that today spans the globe. *Arlington Co.: Rte. 50 and Pershing Dr. at Fort Myer.*

C-3* CAVALRY ENGAGEMENT

Robertson, shielding Stonewall Jackson's rear, fought an engagement here with Union cavalry, June 30, 1862. *Page Co.: Rte. 211, at Luray.*

C-4 CAVALRY ENGAGEMENT

Near this place an engagement took place between Robertson's brigade and the First Maine Cavalry, July 5, 1862. *Rappahannock Co.: Rte. 211, at Sperryville.*

C-5 WASHINGTON, VIRGINIA, THE FIRST OF THEM ALL

Of the 28 Washingtons in the United States, the "records very conclusively disclosed" that this town, "the first Washington of all," was surveyed and platted by George Washington on the 24th day of July (old style) 1749. He was assisted by John Lonem and Edward Corder as chairmen. By the General Assembly of Virginia it was officially established as a town in 1796 and incorporated in 1894. *Rappahannock Co.: Rte. 211, at Washington.*

C-5* MCCLELLAN'S FAREWELL

Half a mile north of this spot General McClellan issued his farewell order to the Army of the Potomac, November 7, 1862. *Fauquier Co.: Rte. 211, 3 miles w. of Buckland.*

C-6 CAMPAIGN OF SECOND MANASSAS

Here Stonewall Jackson, on his march around Pope's army by way of Jeffersonton to Bristoe Station, turned north, August 25, 1862. *Rappahannock Co.: Rte. 211, 7.2 miles e. of Massies Corner.*

C-7 FIRST HEAVIER-THAN-AIR FLIGHT IN VIRGINIA

The first heavier-than-air flight in Virginia was made by Orville Wright at Fort Myers on 4 September, 1908. A United States Signal Corps log noted the flight spanned three miles at a height of 40 feet. The engine's condition following the flight of four minutes and fifteen seconds was described as "good." The engine ran a total of six minutes. *Arlington Co.: Rte. 50, at entrance to Fort Myer.*

C-8 STUART'S RIDE AROUND POPE

Stuart, starting here with his cavalry on August 22, 1862, rode around Pope's army to Catlett's Station. He destroyed supplies and army material and captured Pope's headquarters wagons. *Culpeper Co.: Rte. 613, 6 miles w. of Warrenton.*

C-18 SULLY PLANTATION

The dwelling house at Sully Plantation was built in 1794 by Richard Bland Lee on land that had been patented in 1725. Lee was the first congressman from Northern Virginia and an early member of Phi Beta Kappa. His vote brought the capital city to the banks of the Potomac. Lee was appointed by President Madison as one of three commissioners to superintend the restoration of federal buildings burned by the British in 1814. Born at Leesylvania in Prince William County in 1761, Lee died in Washington in 1827. *Fairfax Co.: Rte. 28, at milepost 350.*

C-19 BULL RUN BATTLEFIELDS

Ten miles west were fought the two battles of Manassas or Bull Run. *Fairfax City: e. of Rte. 236, at Fairfax.*

C-20 FIRST BATTLE OF MANASSAS

McDowell gathered his forces here, July 18, 1861, to attack Beauregard, who lay west of Bull Run. From here a part of the Union army moved north to cross Bull Run and turn the Confederate left wing, July 21, 1861. This movement brought on the battle. *Fairfax Co.: Rte. 29, .5 mile s. of Centreville.*

C-21 CONFEDERATE DEFENSES

Here Joseph E. Johnston built fortifications in the winter of 1861–62 while the Confederate army was camped at Centreville. These strong works led McClellan in the spring of 1862 to attack Richmond from the York-James peninsula instead of from the north. *Fairfax Co.: Rte. 29, .5 mile s. of Centreville.*

C-22 SECOND BATTLE OF MANASSAS

Here Pope gathered his forces, August 30–31, 1862. From this point he detached troops to check Jackson at Ox Hill while the Union army retreated to the defenses at Alexandria. *Fairfax Co.: Rte. 29, .5 mile s. of Centreville.*

C-23 THE STONE BRIDGE

The old stone bridge, just to the north, played a part in the battles of Manassas. Here rested the Confederate left in the early morning of July 21, 1861; over the bridge Pope's retreating army passed, August 30, 1862. *Prince William Co.: Rte. 211, 6 miles e. of Gainesville.*

C-26* BATTLE OF GROVETON

Stonewall Jackson, to prevent a junction of Pope and McClellan while he was awaiting Longstreet, brought on an action here with Gibbon, August 28, 1862. Jackson's position was a short distance north of this road and facing it. Gibbon retired after a fierce fight. *Prince William Co.: Rte. 211, 3.5 miles e. of Gainesville.*

C-27 SECOND BATTLE OF MANASSAS

The center of Lee's army rested here on August 30, 1862; Jackson was to the north of this road, Longstreet to the south. Late in the afternoon, after Jackson had repulsed Pope's assaults, Longstreet moved eastward, driving the Union forces facing him toward Henry Hill. Jackson advanced southward at the same time. *Prince William Co.: Rte. 211, 1.6 miles e. of Gainesville.*

C-28* CAMPAIGN OF SECOND MANASSAS

Stonewall Jackson, moving southward on his march around Pope, was here joined by Stuart with his cavalry, August 26, 1862. From Gainesville, Jackson moved on to Bristoe Station. *Prince William Co.: Rte. 211, at Gainesville.*

C-29 COLONIAL ROAD

This crossroad is the ancient Dumfries-Winchester highway. Over it William Fairfax accompanied George Washington, then a lad of sixteen, on his first visit to Lord Fairfax at Greenway Court. It was on this occasion that Washington assisted in surveying the Fairfax grant. *Fauquier Co.: Rte. 211, 2.6 miles e. of Warrenton.*

C-30 WHITE HOUSE

The old building just north of the road was built for a fort in 1760. It has long been a landmark in this valley. *Page Co.: Rte. 211, 4 miles w. of Luray.*

C-31 BULL RUN BATTLEFIELDS

Just to the east were fought the two battles of Manassas or Bull Run. *Prince William Co.: Rte. 211, .4 mile e. of Gainesville.*

C-31* FORT LONG

Six miles south, near Alma, is Fort Long, built about 1740. *Page Co.: Rte. 211, 2 miles w. of Luray.*

C-33* SECOND BATTLE OF MANASSAS

Half a mile north, along a railway cut, Stonewall Jackson held position, August 29–30, 1862, repulsing all of Pope's assaults. When ammunition gave out on a section of the Confederate line, the soldiers used stones as missiles. Late in the afternoon of August 30, when Longstreet attacked, Jackson swept southward, completing the victory. *Prince William Co.: Rte. 211, 3 miles e. of Gainesville.*

C-34 FIRST BATTLE OF MANASSAS

Henry Hill lies just to the south. Here the Confederates repulsed the repeated attacks of the Union army under McDowell, July 21, 1861. Here Jackson won the name "Stonewall," and from here began McDowell's retreat that ended at Washington. *Prince William Co.: Rte. 211, 4.7 miles e. of Gainesville.*

C-40 CAMPAIGN OF SECOND MANASSAS

Seven miles south is Manassas, where Jackson, on his turning movement around Pope, destroyed vast quantities of supplies, August 26–27, 1862. Hill and Ewell of Jackson's force, coming from Manassas, reached Centreville on their way to Jackson's position north of Groveton, August 28, 1862. *Fairfax Co.: Rte. 29, .5 mile s. of Centreville.*

C-42* FIRST BATTLE OF MANASSAS

In the afternoon of July 21, 1861, the bridge over Cub Run was jammed by the upsetting of a wagon. This turned the retreat of the Union forces into disorder; carriages, cannon and caissons were abandoned as civilians and soldiers escaped across the stream on foot on their way to Alexandria. *Fairfax Co.: Rte. 211, 1.8 miles w. of Centreville.*

C-44 FIRST BATTLE OF MANASSAS

On the Matthews Hill, just to the north, the Confederates repulsed the attack of the Unionists, coming from the north, in the forenoon of July 21, 1861. The Union force, reinforced, drove the Confederates to the Henry Hill, just to the south. There the latter reformed under cover of Stonewall Jackson. In the afternoon, McDowell vainly attempted to rally his retreating troops on the Matthews Hill after they had been driven down the Henry Hill. *Prince William Co.: Rte. 211, 4.7 miles e. of Gainesville.*

C-46 SECOND BATTLE OF MANASSAS

On the Henry Hill, Pope's rear guard, in the late afternoon of August 30, 1862, repulsed the attacks of Longstreet coming from the west. If the hill had been taken, Pope's army would have been doomed; but the Unionists held it while the rest of their troops retreated across Bull Run on the way to Centreville. *Prince William Co.: Rte. 211, 4.7 miles e. of Gainesville.*

C-48 CAMPAIGN OF SECOND MANASSAS

Here Taliaferro, of Jackson's force, came into the highway in the late night of August 27, 1862. He was marching from Manassas to the position about a mile and a half to the north held by Jackson in the Second Battle of Manassas. *Prince William Co.: Rte. 211, 4.7 miles e. of Gainesville.*

C-50 THOROUGHFARE GAP

Five miles northwest is Thoroughfare Gap in the Bull Run Mountains. Through this gap J. E. Johnston and Jackson came, July 19, 1861, on their way to the First Battle of Manassas. Through it Lee sent Jackson, August 26, 1862, and followed with Longstreet to take part in the Second Battle of Manassas. *Prince William Co.: Rte. 55, at Gainesville.*

C-54* CAMPAIGN OF SECOND MANASSAS

Eight miles southeast, near Bristoe, Stonewall Jackson destroyed a railroad bridge over this stream as he moved to the rear of Pope's army, August 26, 1862. Reaching Manassas, Pope's supply depot, he destroyed vast quantities of stores. *Fauquier Co.: Rte. 211, 4.5 miles w. of Gainesville.*

C-56 WILLIAM RANDOLPH BARBEE

Here stood "Hawburg" birthplace of the eminent sculptor William R. Barbee (1818–1868). He studied in Florence, Italy where he carved his famed "Coquette" and "The Fisher Girl." Returning to the United States in 1858 he was at work on a design for the pediment of the U.S. House of Representatives when the outbreak of the war brought his career to an end. He died at "The Bower" which stood not far away. *Rappahannock Co.: Rte. 211 and Skyline Drive, at Panoramo.*

C-56* FREDERICKSBURG CAMPAIGN

In this vicinity Burnside took command of the Army of the Potomac, November 7, 1862. He reorganized the army and turned it southward to the Rappahannock River at Fredericksburg. On November 19, his headquarters were near Falmouth. On December 13, the battle of Fredericksburg was fought. *Fauquier Co.: Rte. 211, 2.6 miles e. of Warrenton.*

C-57 BLACK HORSE CAVALRY

The Black Horse Cavalry was conceived at a gathering of Warrenton lawyers in 1858 and was among the local militia companies called to active duty by Governor Henry Wise in 1859. The Black Horse led a successful charge against Union forces at the First Battle of Manassas, winning the special praise of Confederate President Jefferson Davis. Known as Company H of the 4th Virginia Cavalry, the unit served as bodyguard, escort, and scout for generals Joseph E. Johnston and Stonewall Jackson. Following the war, a number of the men of the Black Horse became prominent leaders in the Commonwealth. *Fauquier Co.: Rte. 17/211 Bus. at Rte. 211, in Warrenton.*

C-58* CAMPAIGN OF SECOND MANASSAS

By this road Stuart came on his raid to Catlett's Station, August 22, 1862. At that time most of the Union troops were guarding the passages of the Rappahannock River. Crossing at Waterloo Bridge, Stuart moved around the right of Pope's army to its rear. This raid should have awakened Pope to his dangerous position. *Fauquier Co.: Rte. 211, 4 miles w. of Warrenton.*

C-60 CAMPAIGN OF SECOND MANASSAS

About two miles north is Waterloo Bridge, where J. E. B. Stuart began his raid to Catlett's Station in the rear of Pope's army, August 22, 1862. Some miles farther north is Hinton's Mill, where Stonewall Jackson crossed this river, August 25, 1862, on the march around Pope that resulted in the Second Battle of Manassas. *Fauquier Co.: Rte. 211, 5.1 miles w. of Warrenton.*

C-61 CAMPAIGN OF SECOND MANASSAS

Here J. E. B. Stuart, raiding around Pope's army, turned northeast, August 22, 1862. He passed through Warrenton and went on to Catlett's Station, where he captured some of Pope's wagons, in one of which were found Pope's order book and uniform. *Rappahannock Co.: Rte. 211, 9.5 miles e. of Massies Corner.*

C-90 THE FALLS CHURCH

The first church on this site was built in 1734 and was in Truro Parish. George Washington was elected a vestryman, October 3, 1763. In 1765 the church fell within the newly-created Fairfax Parish, of which Washington was chosen a vestryman. The present church was built in 1768. It was used as a recruiting station in the Revolution and as a stable by the Union troops, 1862–64. *Fairfax Co.: s. of Rte. 7, at Falls Church.*

CB-1 CAMPAIGN OF SECOND MANASSAS

Here Lee and Longstreet, on their way to join Jackson then at Bristoe Station, camped on August 26. 1862. *Fauquier Co.: Rte. 688, 12 miles w. of Warrenton.*

CB-2 ASHLAND FARM

The Holtzclaw family acquired Ashland through a grant issued by Lt. Gov. Alexander Spotswood in 1724, and lived on this land until the 1920s. While a portion of the house dates to about 1725, the main residence was completed by 1889, and was remodeled and enlarged by architect William Lawrence Bottomley in 1929. Between 1861 and 1864, the Union army stationed pickets at Ashland, as it was used as a Federal medical dressing station. Legend claims that a Union army payroll, hidden by a paymaster who died in 1862 at nearby Waterloo, Virginia, is still buried here. *Fauquier Co.: Rte. 211, 4.4 miles w. of Warrenton.*

CL-2 RUFFNER PUBLIC SCHOOL NUMBER 1

Named for Wm. H. Ruffner, Virginia's First Superintendent of Public Instruction, and opened as a public school on this site. Before free public schools were established by the Virginia Constitution of 1869, a one room free school was in operation with voluntary gifts. *Manassas: Rte. 28, .1 mile s. of Rte. 334.*

CL-3 JOHN MARSHALL'S BIRTHPLACE

About one half mile southeast, just across the railroad, a stone marks the site of the birthplace, September 24, 1755. He died at Philadelphia, July 6, 1835. Revolutionary officer, congressman, Secretary of State, he is immortal as Chief Justice of the United States Supreme Court. During his long term of office his wise interpretation of the U.S. Constitution gave it enduring life. *Fauquier Co.: Rte. 28, .8 mile e. of Midland.*

CL-4 MANASSAS

According to tradition the name Manassas was derived either from an Indian source or from Manasseh, a Jewish innkeeper at Manassas Gap (35 miles west). The community originated in 1852 at the junction of the Manassas Gap and Orange & Alexandria railroads, which linked northern Virginia and Washington, D.C., with the Shenandoah Valley and central Virginia. During the Civil War the junction's strategic importance led to the battles of First and Second Manassas (Bull Run), both Confederate victories. Manassas was incorporated as a town in 1873 and became a city in 1975. *Manassas: Rte. 28, 5.41 miles n. of Rte. 215.*

D-1 FORT HARRISON

Daniel Harrison settled about 1745 at the headwaters of Cook's Creek where it is believed he built the stone portion of the present house. During the decades 1750–1770, when this area was the frontier of the colony, the house served the settlers as a refuge from Indian attacks. Subsequent owners added the brick portion and enlarged the windows and doors. The Harrison family had large land holdings in present Augusta and Rockingham counties. *Rockingham Co.: Bus. Rte. 42 at corp. limits of Dayton.*

D-6 BATTLE OF CROSS KEYS

Three miles south, on Mill Creek, Jackson's rearguard, under Ewell, was attacked by Fremont, June 8, 1862. Trimble, of Ewell's command, counterattacked, driving the Unionists back. Jackson, with the rest of his army, was near Port Republic awaiting the advance of Shields up the east bank of the Shenandoah River. *Rockingham Co.: Rte. 33, 5 miles e. of Harrisonburg.*

D-7 FIRST CHURCH IN ROCKINGHAM COUNTY

The first church in Rockingham County was built on this site in 1747 on land owned by Captain Daniel Harrison of the colonial militia. Serving as a "Chapel of Ease" for Augusta Parish, the first building is believed to have been built of logs. The chapel was replaced by a larger frame building some 20 years later. Following the Revolutionary War, the church was used by a Methodist congregation; it was sold and functioned as a barn until it was torn down about 1900. *Rockingham Co.: Rte. 732, .2 mile w. of Rte. 290.*

D-10 KNIGHTS OF THE GOLDEN HORSESHOE

Here, it is believed, Governor Alexander Spotswood and his party crossed the mountains into the Shenandoah Valley, September 5, 1716. This expedition paved the way for the settlement of the West. On the return east, Spotswood gave his companions small golden horseshoes because their shoeless horses had to be shod for the mountain journey. *Rockingham Co.: Rte. 33, 7 miles s.e. of Elkton.*

D-11 RUCKERSVILLE

A descendant of the Huguenot immigrant Peter Rucker, John Rucker (d. 1794) settled east of here on Rippin's Run, and built Friendly Acres, the first of many Rucker family dwellings in the area. He founded the village of Ruckersville, naming it for his uncle, Captain John Rucker, who was instrumental in selecting the site for St. Mark's Parish Church just west of here in 1732. *Greene Co.: Rtes. 29 and 33, in Ruckersville.*

D-20 MONTEBELLO

Here was born Zachary Taylor, twelfth president of the United States, November 24, 1784. Taylor, commanding the American army, won the notable battle of Buena Vista in Mexico, 1847. *Orange Co.: Rte. 33, 3 miles w. of Gordonsville.*

D-22 BARBOURSVILLE

A short distance south are the ruins of Barboursville, built, 1814–1822, by James Barbour partly after plans made by Jefferson. It was burned, December 25, 1884. James Barbour, buried here, was Governor of Virginia, 1812–1815, United States Senator, Secretary of War, Minister to England. *Orange Co.: Rte. 33, at Barboursville.*

D-24 FORT LEWIS

Seven miles east stood a small stockade known first as Wilson's Fort. It was garrisoned in the fall of 1756 by a force under the command of Lt. Charles Lewis, younger brother of the famous Indian fighter, Andrew Lewis. *Bath Co.: Rte. 220, 11 miles n. of Warm Springs.*

D-26 FORT BRECKENRIDGE

Three miles west at the mouth of Falling Spring Creek was a post garrisoned by militia under Capt. Robert Breckenridge. Washington inspected it in 1756. It survived an attack by Shawnees under Cornstalk during Pontiac's war in 1763. *Alleghany Co.: Rte. 220, 3 miles n. of Covington.*

D-27 FORT YOUNG

George Washington, Commander of Virginia Defense Forces in the French and Indian War, inspected this post near here in 1756. A relief force from here, sent to the aid of Fort Breckenridge in 1763, was ambushed by Indians. *City of Covington: Rte. 154, on Durant Rd., n. of Jackson River.*

D-28 FINCASTLE

Miller's place here was selected as the county seat of Botetourt in 1770. In 1772 the town of Fincastle was established on land donated by Israel Christian and named for Lord Fincastle, eldest son of Governor Lord Dunmore. It was incorporated in 1828. In 1845 it had a population of 700. The present courthouse was erected about 1850. *Botetourt Co.: Rte. 220, at Fincastle.*

Captain William Preston built this post near here, and it was inspected by Colonel George Washington in 1756. It was attacked by Indians that October. Settlers in the area "forted up" here during Pontiac's War, 1763. *Botetourt Co.: Rte. 220, 3 miles s. of Fincastle.*

One mile west is Greenfield, home of William Preston, built before the Revolution. Preston was a member of the House of Burgesses for Augusta County, 1765–1768, and for Botetourt County, 1769–1771. He was an officer in the Indian wars and the Revolution, dying in 1783. *Botetourt Co.: Rte. 220, 5 miles s. of Fincastle.*

The (Roanoke) Valley Baptist Association was organized on 7 August 1841 at nearby Zion Hill Baptist Church. Seventeen congregations constituted the original fellowship of churches; during the next century and a half membership grew to more than seventy churches. *Botetourt Co.: Rte. 220, near Rte. 681.*

Near here is Santillane, one of Botetourt County's most distinguished properties. The Greek Revival house sits on a tract of land originally owned by Colonel George Hancock, a member of the United States Congress from 1793 to 1797. In 1808 Hancock's daughter, Judith, married General William Clark. Clark served from 1803 to 1806 as a leader of Thomas Jefferson's famous Lewis and Clark expedition which was instrumental in opening the West for American settlement. *Botetourt Co.: Rte. 220 at Rte. 1211, .25 mile s. of Fincastle.*

Here stand the earliest coke ovens of the Low Moor Iron Company (organized 1873). The ovens converted coal into coke to fuel the company's blast furnace. The company built more than a hundred such ovens in 1881. By 1923 the Low Moor Iron Company employed 1,600 workers in Virginia and West Virginia, could produce 75 tons of foundry iron a day, and supported the company town of Low Moor. The last survivor among Alleghany County's once-thriving ironworks, the company closed in 1926. *Alleghany Co.: Rte. 1101, .04 mile e. of Rte. 696.*

In 1676 this region was Bacon's "Quarter," or Plantation, the property of Nathaniel Bacon, who headed a rebellion that was a forerunner of the Revolution. *Richmond: Chamberlayne Ave.*

Here ran, east and west, the intermediate line of Richmond defenses during the Civil War. Near this spot on 1 March 1864 Union Brig. Gen. H. Judson Kilpatrick halted his raid that was intended to free Union prisoners and lower morale in the Confederate capital. A detachment led by Col. Ulric Dahlgren was defeated to the west of the city. On 2 March Dahlgren was killed; Southern morale soared. *Richmond: Laburnam and Chamberlayne aves.*

Here ran, east and west, the intermediate line of Richmond defenses, 1862–65. Kilpatrick on his raid came, March 1, 1864, nearly to this spot. *Richmond: Laburnum and Chamberlayne aves.*

E-3* WHERE SHERIDAN MOVED EAST

Sheridan, in his raid to Richmond on May 11, 1864, entered the outer defenses on the Brook Road. At this point he turned east to Mechanicsville. *Henrico Co.: Chamberlayne and Azalea aves.*

E-4* BROOK ROAD

By this road Lafayette came to Richmond, on April 29, 1781, to oppose the British invasion, and he retreated before Cornwallis on the same road on May 27, 1781. *Richmond: Brook Rd. and Rte. 1.*

E-5 FORK CHURCH

Fork Church was first housed in a 1722 frame building near the present church site. It was known as "The Chapel in the Forks" and derived its name from the nearby confluence of the North and South Anna rivers and the Little and Newfound rivers. The present building was erected between 1736 and 1740. Erected in Memory of Stuart Anderson Oliver, 1982. *Hanover Co.: Rte. 738, 4.5 miles w. of Rte. 1.*

E-6 OUTER FORTIFICATIONS

Here, east and west, ran the outer line of Richmond defenses, 1862–65. At this point Sheridan's cavalry, raiding to Richmond, broke through the line on May 11, 1864, after the fight at Yellow Tavern. *Henrico Co.: Rte. 1, .7 mile n. of Richmond.*

E-7* YELLOW TAVERN

This is the site of Yellow Tavern, an old inn of the Richmond road. In this vicinity a cavalry engagement took place, on May 11, 1864, between Sheridan raiding to Richmond and J. E. B. Stuart defending the city. Sheridan penetrated the outer defenses of Richmond but then turned off. *Henrico Co.: Rte. 1, 2.5 miles n. of Richmond.*

E-8 STUART

At this point J. E. B. Stuart had his headquarters and cavalry camp in December, 1862. *Spotsylvania Co.: Rte. 1, 5.4 miles s. of Falmouth.*

E-9 STUART'S MORTAL WOUND

One half mile to the east, on the Old Telegraph Road, is a monument marking the field where General J. E. B. Stuart was mortally wounded on May 11, 1864. The monument was erected by veterans of Stuart's Cavalry in 1888. *Henrico Co.: Rte. 1 at Rte. 677 (Francis Rd.).*

E-9* CAVALRY ENGAGEMENT

In this vicinity was fought the engagement of Yellow Tavern between Sheridan's cavalry raiding to Richmond and the Confederates, May 11, 1864. *Henrico Co.: Rte. 1, 6.25 miles n. of Richmond.*

E-10 GLEN ALLEN

Called Mountain Road Crossing when rail service began in 1836, the settlement which came to be known as Glen Allen took its name from the homestead of a local landowner, Mrs. Benjamin Allen. Its most noted resident was Captain John Cussons, a native Englishman, Confederate scout, author, and entrepreneur. Cussons made his residence here after the Civil War and founded a successful printing company. Later he built a fashionable resort hotel known as Forest Lodge adjacent to the railroad tracks. *Henrico Co.: Mountain Rd. at Glen Allen.*

E-11* BATTLES ON THE CHICKAHOMINY

Near this river and some miles to the east were fought the battles of Seven Pines, May 31–June 1, 1862; Mechanicsville, June 26, 1862; Gaines's Mill, June 27, 1862; Savage's Station, June 29, 1862; and Cold Harbor, June 3, 1864. *Hanover Co.: Rte. 1, 4.9 miles s. of Ashland.*

E-12* SMITH AND LAFAYETTE

On this stream some miles to the east, Captain John Smith was captured by the Indians in December, 1607. On it Lafayette and Cornwallis camped in 1781. *Hanover Co.: Rte. 1, 4.9 miles s. of Ashland.*

E-13 LEE'S TURN TO COLD HARBOR

Lee had his headquarters near here, May 27, 1864, while moving south from the North Anna River. Here Longstreet's (Anderson's) and Hill's corps of his army turned east to meet Grant at Cold Harbor, where a great battle was fought, June 3, 1864. *Hanover Co.: Rte. 1, 4.5 miles s. of Ashland.*

E-14* CAVALRY SKIRMISH

On this spot, on June 25, 1862, the Fourth Virginia Cavalry fought a skirmish with the Eighth Illinois Cavalry. *Hanover Co.: Rte. 1, 1 mile s. of Ashland.*

E-14* JACKSON'S MARCH TO GAINES'S MILL

Stonewall Jackson, coming from the Shenandoah Valley, moved east over the Ashcake Road to join Lee, confronting McClellan at Mechanicsville, June 26, 1862. Owing to many obstacles, Jackson did not join Lee until the next day, June 27, 1862, while the battle of Gaines's Mill was raging. His attack won the battle. *Hanover Co.: Rte. 1, .4 mile s. of Ashland.*

E-15 HENRY AT HANOVER COURTHOUSE

Six miles east still stands Hanover Courthouse, in which, December, 1763, Patrick Henry delivered his great speech in the "Parsons' Cause," when he denounced the British government for vetoing an act of the Virginia General Assembly. *Hanover Co.: Rte. 1, at Ashland.*

E-16* ASHLAND

Henry Clay was born a few miles to the east, and as a boy brought grain to a mill here. This place was raided by Stoneman, on May 3, 1863; by Kilpatrick, on March 1, 1864; and by Sheridan, on May 11, 1864. *Hanover Co.: Rte. 1, at Ashland.*

E-17* ELLETT'S BRIDGE

The wagon trains of Lee's army crossed the South Anna here on May 27, 1864. On the railroad bridge just to the east Longstreet's (Anderson's) and Hill's corps crossed the river on the same day on the way to Cold Harbor. *Hanover Co.: Rte. 1, 3 miles n. of Ashland.*

E-18* LAFAYETTE AND CORNWALLIS

Lafayette, commanding an American force, crossed the river west of this point, on May 29, 1781, while retreating before Cornwallis, who moved a few miles to the east. *Hanover Co.: Rte. 1, 3.6 miles n. of Ashland.*

E-19 LEE'S LEFT WING

On this stream, the Little River, and to the west, Lee's left wing rested while his army faced Grant along the North Anna, May 23–26, 1864. *Hanover Co.: Rte. 1, 5.2 miles n. of Ashland.*

E-20 LEE'S MOVEMENTS

A short distance east, at Taylorsville, Lee had his headquarters, May 24–26, 1864, as his army moved southeastward to intervene between Grant and Richmond. There Ewell's corps turned to Cold Harbor, May 27, 1864. *Hanover Co.: Rte. 1, 6.2 miles n. of Ashland.*

E-21* HANOVER JUNCTION

An important point because the junction of two railroads. The Virginia Central (C. & O.) was Lee's main line of supply in 1864 and was protected by the earthworks here. Lee camped here on May 22–23, 1864. *Hanover Co.: Rte. 1, 7.6 miles n. of Ashland.*

E-22* LAFAYETTE AND CORNWALLIS

Lafayette, commanding an American force, crossed this river, a few miles west, May 30, 1781. Cornwallis, the British commander, who had followed him from the James River, near here gave up the pursuit, June 1, and turned westward. Lafayette moved on to the Rapidan River, where he was joined by "Mad Anthony" Wayne. *Hanover Co.: Rte. 1, 3 miles s. of Carmel Church.*

E-23 LEE AND GRANT

Lee and Grant faced each other on the North Anna, May 23–26, 1864. Union forces crossed here and four miles to the west but found they could not dislodge Lee's center, which rested on the stream. Grant then turned east to Cold Harbor. *Caroline Co.: Rte. 1, 2.8 miles s. of Carmel Church.*

E-24 LONG CREEK ACTION

The earthworks in the angle between this stream and the North Anna River, held by a small Confederate force, were taken by Grant's troops moving southward on May 23, 1864. The Unionists then advanced to the river, on the south side of which was Lee's army. *Caroline Co.: Rte. 1, 2.4 miles s. of Carmel Church.*

E-25 GRANT'S OPERATIONS

Here, at Mount Carmel Church, on May 23, 1864, Hancock's (Second) Corps turned south to the North Anna River; Warren's (Fifth) Corps and Wright's (Sixth) Corps here turned west to Jericho Mills on the river. Grant had his headquarters in the church on May 24. On May 27, 1864, the four corps of Grant's army, returning from the North Anna, here turned east to Cold Harbor. *Caroline Co.: Rte. 1, at Carmel Church.*

E-26 DICKINSON'S MILL

Lee camped here, on May 21, 1864, on his way to the North Anna to oppose Grant moving southward. Ewell's and Longstreet's corps rested here that night. *Caroline Co.: Rte. 1, 2.2 miles s. of Ladysmith.*

E-27* BULL CHURCH

To the east, at Bull Church, a part of Warren's (Fifth) Corps camped on May 22, 1864, on the way to the North Anna River. *Caroline Co.: Rte. 1, at Ladysmith.*

E-28 NANCY WRIGHT'S

A little to the east, at Nancy Wright's, Warren's (Fifth) and Wright's (Sixth) Corps, coming from the east, on May 22, 1864, turned south. Wright camped here on May 22. *Caroline Co.: Rte. 1, 5.1 miles n. of Ladysmith.*

E-29* DOCTOR FLIPPO'S

Part of Warren's (Fifth) Corps, Army of the Potomac, camped at this place on May 22, 1864, on the way to the North Anna. *Caroline Co.: Rte. 1, 1.6 miles n. of Ladysmith.*

E-30 TURN IN SHERIDAN'S RAID

At this point in his Richmond raid, Sheridan, after a fight with Confederate cavalry commanded by General Williams C. Wickham, turned off the Telegraph Road to Beaver Dam, May 9, 1864. This change of route caused Sheridan to approach Richmond from the northwest instead of the north. *Spotsylvania Co.: Rte. 1, 1.8 miles s. of Thornburg.*

E-31 JERRELL'S MILL

Here, on May 9, 1864, Sheridan was attacked by Wickham's cavalry. Nearby, on May 22, 1864, Warren's (Fifth) Corps, moving to the North Anna, fought Rosser's cavalry. *Spotsylvania Co.: Rte. 1, 1.1 miles s. of Thornburg.*

E-32 MUD TAVERN

Mud Tavern was the old name of this place. Six miles east, at Guinea Station, Stonewall Jackson died, May 10, 1863. In the campaign of 1864, Ewell's and Longstreet's corps of Lee's army, coming from Spotsylvania Courthouse, here turned south, May 21, 1864. Lee fell back to the North Anna River as Grant swung around to the east. *Spotsylvania Co.: Rte. 1, at Thornburg.*

E-33* A RAID'S END

Here Gibbons and Hatch's Brigades, Army of the Potomac, raiding south from Fredericksburg, were attacked by Stuart's Cavalry, on August 6, 1862, and retreated northward. *Spotsylvania Co.: Rte. 1, 2 miles n. of Thornburg.*

E-34* WHERE BURNSIDE TURNED

Just to the east at Stanard's Mill, Burnside, on May 21, 1864, attempting to move south, found the river held by the Confederates in force and turned east to Guinea Station. *Spotsylvania Co.: Rte. 1, 1.3 miles n. of Thornburg.*

E-35* WHERE BURNSIDE CROSSED

Here, at Smith's Mill, Burnside's (Ninth) Corps, Army of the Potomac, crossed the Ny River, May 21, 1864, advancing southward. Repulsed at the Po River, it recrossed the Ny here and moved eastward. *Spotsylvania Co.: Rte. 1, 1.3 miles n. of Thornburg.*

E-36* UNION ARMY ROUTE

By this road the four corps of the Union army, coming from Spotsylvania, moved east to Guinea Station on May 21, 1864. *Spotsylvania Co.: Rte. 1, 3.8 miles n. of Thornburg.*

E-37* MASSAPONAX CHURCH

Grant's army, moving east from Spotsylvania on May 21, 1864, reached this road here and followed it as far as the road to Guinea Station. *Spotsylvania Co.: Rte. 1, 4.5 miles n. of Thornburg.*

E-38* LEE'S HEADQUARTERS

Lee's headquarters in the winter of 1862–63 were a mile down this road. *Spotsylvania Co.: Rte. 1, 5.4 miles s. of Falmouth.*

E-39   START OF SHERIDAN'S RAID

Here Sheridan, moving from camp, came into the Telegraph Road on his raid to Richmond, May 9, 1864, while Lee and Grant were fighting at Spotsylvania. The 10,000 Union cavalry filled the road for several miles. Turning from the road ten miles south, Sheridan came into it again at Yellow Tavern near Richmond May 11, 1864. *Spotsylvania Co.: Rte. 1, 5.3 miles s. of Falmouth.*

E-40*   GRANT'S SUPPLY LINE

This road to Spotsylvania Courthouse was Grant's line of supply in May, 1864, in the Wilderness campaign. *Spotsylvania Co.: Rte. 1, 4 miles s. of Fredericksburg.*

E-41   HISTORIC AQUIA CREEK

Giles Brent built a house here in 1647. After the Indian War of 1676 this creek was for ten years the northern frontier of Virginia. The Army of the Potomac, coming from the James, landed here in August, 1862. For campaigns in 1862–63 this stream was the supply base of the Union army. *Stafford Co.: Rte. 1, 3.6 miles n. of Stafford.*

E-41*   LONGSTREET'S HEADQUARTERS

Here Longstreet had his headquarters in the winter of 1862–63. *Spotsylvania Co.: Rte. 1, 3.5 miles s. of Fredericksburg.*

E-42*   EARLY'S LINE OF BATTLE

Here Jubal A. Early formed line of battle across the road on the afternoon of May 3, 1863, after being driven from Fredericksburg by Sedgwick. *Spotsylvania Co.: Rte. 1, 3.5 miles s. of Fredericksburg.*

E-43*   LEE'S POSITION

On this hill, a little to the east, Lee watched the battle of Fredericksburg, December 13, 1862. *Spotsylvania Co.: Rte. 1, 1 mile s. of Fredericksburg.*

E-44*   BATTLES OF FREDERICKSBURG

The hill here is Marye's Heights, occupied by the Confederates in the battles of December 13, 1862, and May 3, 1863. In the first battle all attempts of the Union troops to take it failed. In the second battle (the Chancellorsville campaign) the Union troops carried the position, which was held by a small force. *Spotsylvania Co.: Rte. 1, at s. entrance of Fredericksburg.*

E-45*   FREDERICKSBURG

A settlement was made here at an early period. The town was established in 1727 and was named for Prince Frederick, father of George III. *Stafford Co.: Rte. 1, at n. entrance of Fredericksburg.*

E-46*   COLONIAL FORT

A fort was built at the falls here in 1676 to protect the settlers from the Indians, who were raiding the settlements. *Spotsylvania Co.: Rte. 1, at n. entrance of Fredericksburg.*

E-46-a   FREDERICKSBURG

Captain John Smith was here in 1608; Lederer, the explorer, in 1670. In May 1671 John Buckner and Thomas Royster patented the Lease Land Grant. The town was established in 1727 and lots were laid out. It was named for Frederick, Prince of Wales, father of George III. The court for Spotsylvania County was moved here in 1732 and the town was enlarged in 1759 and 1769. Fredericksburg was incorporated as a town in 1781, as a city in 1879, and declared a city of the first class in 1941. *Spotsylvania Co.: Alt. Rte. 1, 2 miles s. of Falmouth.*

E-46-b FREDERICKSBURG

Captain John Smith was here in 1608; Lederer, the explorer, in 1670. In May 1671 John Buckner and Thomas Royster patented the Lease Land Grant. The town was established in 1727 and lots were laid out. It was named for Frederick, Prince of Wales, father of George III. The court for Spotsylvania County was moved here in 1732 and the town was enlarged in 1759 and 1769. Fredericksburg was incorporated as a town in 1781, as a city in 1879, and declared a city of the first class in 1941. *Spotsylvania Co.: Rte. 1, 2 miles s. of Falmouth.*

E-47 HISTORIC FALMOUTH

Founded in 1727 as a trading center for the Northern Neck, Hunter's iron works here were an objective in the Virginia campaign of 1781. The Army of the Potomac camped here from November, 1862, to June, 1863, and moved hence to Chancellorsville and Gettysburg. *Stafford Co.: Rte. 1, .95 mile n. of Rte. 17.*

E-48 POTOMAC CREEK

Near the mouth of this creek, several miles east, was the Indian Village "Petomek," where Pocahontas was kidnapped by Captain Samuel Argall in 1613. There, travelers landed from steamers to take the stage to Fredericksburg, early railroad terminus. *Stafford Co.: Rte. 1, 3.8 miles n. of Falmouth.*

E-48* SMITH AND POCAHONTAS

At the mouth of this stream Captain John Smith in 1608 found an Indian "King's house" called "Petomek." The river takes its name from this. Here the Indian Princess, Pocahontas, was kidnapped by the English in June, 1612. *Stafford Co.: Rte. 1, 1.5 miles n. of Falmouth.*

E-48* POTOMAC CREEK

Near the mouth of this creek, several miles east, explorers in 1608 found an Indian village called "Petomek," from which the river took its name. There the Indian princess, Pocahontas, was kidnapped by Captain Argall in 1613. There travelers landed from steamers to take the stage to Fredericksburg, early railroad terminus. Charles Dickens landed there, going to Richmond, and returned the same way, March, 1842. *Stafford Co.: Rte. 1, 3 miles n. of Falmouth.*

E-49-a and E-49-b "FALL HILL"

On the heights one mile to the west, the home of the Thorntons from about 1736. Francis Thornton 2nd was a justice, a Burgess 1744–45, and Lieutenant Colonel of his Majesty's militia for Spotsylvania County. He and two of his brothers married three Gregory sisters, first cousins of George Washington. "Fall Hill" is still (1950) owned and occupied by direct Thornton descendants. *Spotsylvania Co.: Rte. 1, at Fredericksburg.*

E-49* ANCIENT IRON FURNACE

Here on Accokeek Run were iron mines and a furnace in which Augustine Washington, father of George Washington, began to smelt iron in 1727. *Stafford Co.: Rte. 1, 2 miles s. of Stafford Court House.*

E-50* INDIAN TRAIL

Here ran the original Indian trail. In 1664 a road was opened here and in 1666 it was extended to Aquia Creek. In 1750 this became a post road. In September, 1781, Washington passed over this road on the way to Yorktown, and over it the French army later marched north. *Stafford Co.: Rte. 1, .3 mile n. of Stafford.*

E-52*   CHOPAWAMSIC

Settlement began here in 1651. Samuel Matthews, Governor of Virginia, 1659–60, patented land here. On December 27, 1862, Fitz Lee, raiding from Fredericksburg, struck the road here and moved northward, capturing wagons. *Prince William Co.: Rte. 1, 4.3 miles s. of Dumfries.*

E-53   CAMPAIGN OF 1781

Lafayette, coming to Virginia to take command, moved by this road, April 1781. Here passed Washington and Rochambeau going to Yorktown, September, 1781. *Prince William Co.: Rte. 1, at n. entrance of Dumfries.*

E-53*   EARLY LAND PATENTS

Here on Quantico Creek, land was first patented by Richard Hawkins in 1653. *Prince William Co.: Rte. 1, s. of Dumfries.*

E-54*   ANCIENT ROAD TO VALLEY

Opened in 1731, this road by 1759 extended across the Blue Ridge Mountains, via Ashby's Gap. *Prince William Co.: Rte. 1, s. of Dumfries.*

E-55   HISTORY OF DUMFRIES

A tobacco warehouse was built here in 1730; the town was established in 1749 and became a noted port. In 1774 it elected one of the first Revolutionary committees of correspondence. Washington came to Dumfries frequently. On December 12, 1862, Wade Hampton here surprised a Union force, capturing some wagons; and, on December 27, 1862, J. E. B. Stuart had a skirmish with the Union troops holding the place. *Prince William Co.: Rte. 1, at Dumfries.*

E-56*   EARLY LAND PATENTS

Here on Marumsco Creek land was first patented by Thomas Burbage in 1653. *Prince William Co.: Rte. 1, 1.1 miles s. of Woodbridge.*

E-57*   EARLY LAND PATENTS

Land here on Powell's Run was first patented in 1757, at which time the stream was known as Yosococomico. *Prince William Co.: Rte. 1, 4 miles n. of Dumfries.*

E-58*   EARLY IRON FURNACE

Iron was mined on this stream before 1738 and John Tayloe had a furnace near by. A few miles to the east was "Leesylvania," home of Robert E. Lee's grandfather. *Prince William Co.: Rte. 1, 3.2 miles n. of Dumfries.*

E-59*   THE OCCOQUAN

Near here in 1608 Captain John Smith found the "King's House" of the Doeg Indians. In 1729 "King" Carter built a landing here to ship copper ore. A town called Colchester was established here in 1753. Occoquan, to the west, was founded in 1804. On December 27, 1862, Wade Hampton raided Occoquan. *Prince William Co.: Rte. 1, at Woodbridge.*

E-60*   EVENTS ON POHICK CREEK

Here on Pohick Creek the second George Mason settled in 1690. Here the Iroquois Indians, by a treaty of 1722, agreed to deliver up runaway slaves. The fourth George Mason wished to build Pohick Church on the creek, but was overruled by George Washington. *Fairfax Co.: Rte. 1, 3.2 miles n. of Woodbridge.*

E-61 OCCOQUAN WORKHOUSE

In the nearby Occoquan Workhouse, from June to December, 1917, scores of women suffragists were imprisoned by the District of Columbia for picketing the White House demanding their right to vote. Their courage and dedication during harsh treatment aroused the nation to hasten the passage and ratification of the 19th Amendment in 1920. The struggle for woman's suffrage had taken 72 years. *Fairfax Co.: Rte. 123, at Lorton Penitentiary Youth Center.*

E-62 OLD TELEGRAPH LINE

One of the first telegraph lines in the world, a part of the Washington–New Orleans Telegraph Company, was built from Washington to Petersburg in 1847. From this the road took its name. *Fairfax Co.: Rte. 1, 4.1 miles n. of Woodbridge.*

E-63* EARLY LAND PATENTS

Land was first patented on Accotink Creek in 1657. *Fairfax Co.: Rte. 1, 5.6 miles n. of Woodbridge.*

E-64* FORT HUMPHREYS

Here stood "Belvoir" built by William Fairfax in 1741. In it Lawrence Washington was married in 1743. It was for many years the office of the Northern Neck proprietor. In the World War, 1918, camp for training engineers stood here. *Fairfax Co.: Rte. 1, .7 mile n. of Woodbridge.*

E-65 GUNSTON HALL

Gunston Hall, four miles to the east, is one of the most noted colonial places in Virginia. The land was patented in 1651 by Richard Turney, who was hanged for taking part in Bacon's Rebellion in 1676. In 1696 the second George Mason acquired it. The house was built in 1755–1758 by the fourth George Mason, Revolutionary leader and author of the Virginia Declaration of Rights and the first Constitution of Virginia. *Fairfax Co.: Rte. 1, 2.4 miles n. of Woodbridge.*

E-66* WOODLAWN

The estate was inherited by Nellie Custis from George Washington. The house was built in 1805. A century later it became the home of Senator Oscar W. Underwood. *Fairfax Co.: Rte. 1, 7.4 miles s. of Alexandria.*

E-67* HISTORY ON DOGUE RUN

Land on this stream, first patented in 1657, was later owned by William Dudley, one of Bacon's supporters in the rebellion of 1676. Rankin's Point near by was bombarded by British ships in 1814. *Fairfax Co.: Rte. 1, 7.1 miles s. of Alexandria.*

E-68* MOUNT VERNON ESTATE

Two miles to the east. The original house was built in 1743 by Lawrence Washington. George Washington came into possession in 1752. From here he set out, in April, 1775, to take his seat in the Continental Congress. On December 24, 1783, he returned from the army and here he died on December 14, 1799. *Fairfax Co.: Rte. 1, 4.5 miles s. of Alexandria.*

E-69* LITTLE HUNTING CREEK

Margaret Brent, secretary to Lord Baltimore, the first woman in America to demand a vote, patented land here in 1663. Augustine Washington lived here from 1734 to 1739, and here George Washington passed most of his infancy. *Fairfax Co.: Rte. 1, 4.5 miles s. of Alexandria.*

E-70* COLONIAL FORT

Here on Hunting Creek, Governor Berkeley in 1676, built a fort for defense against the Susquehannock Indians in the troubles that led to Bacon's Rebellion. *Fairfax Co.: Rte. 1, at Alexandria.*

E-71* HISTORIC ALEXANDRIA

Land was first patented here in 1657. In 1731 a warehouse was built on Hunting Creek about which grew up the village of Belhaven. The town of Alexandria was established in 1749 and became one of the main colonial trading centers. It was a part of the original District of Columbia but was returned to Virginia in 1847. *Alexandria: Rte. 1, at s. entrance to city.*

E-71 LEWIS CHAPEL / CRANFORD
        MEMORIAL METHODIST CHURCH

This church is a combination of several structures built on the site of the first Pohick Church (1730–1774), making this one of the earliest sites of a religious institution in Fairfax County. Lewis Chapel, named after a Methodist Circuit rider, was built in 1857 and moved from a site nearby in 1972. Cranford Memorial, the main portion of the complex, was constructed in 1900. *Fairfax Co.: Rte. 242 at Rte. 611, .7 mile e. of Rte. 1.*

E-72 POHICK CHURCH

This building was begun in 1769 and completed by 1774, succeeding an earlier church two miles to the south. It was the lower church of Truro Parish, established in 1732, the parish of Mount Vernon and Gunston Hall. George William Fairfax, George Washington and George Mason, vestrymen, were members of the building committee under which the church was constructed. *Fairfax Co.: Rte. 1, 4.3 miles n. of Woodbridge.*

E-72* OLD ROAD TO WEST

Washington traveled by this road on his mission to Fort Duquesne in 1753. In 1754 he marched over it in command of the Virginia regiment. In 1755 a brigade of Braddock's army moved by it to the defeat near Pittsburg. *Fairfax Co.: Rte. 50 at n. entrance of Alexandria.*

E-73 WASHINGTON'S MILL

Just to the left is the restored mill operated by George Washington for years. (Restoration made by the State Commission on Conservation and Development—1932.) *Fairfax Co.: Rte. 1, 7.4 miles s. of Alexandria at Rte. 235.*

E-74 STUART'S RIDE AROUND McCLELLAN

Near here, on Winston's Farm, J. E. B. Stuart, advancing north, camped on June 12, 1862. Stuart was scouting to find the position of the right wing of McClellan's army besieging Richmond. At this point he turned east to Hanover Courthouse. Stuart made a complete circuit of the Union army. *Hanover Co.: Rte. 1, 1.9 miles n. of Ashland.*

E-75 MARLBOROUGH

In 1691, Marlborough, the Port Town in Stafford County, was laid off. Houses were built and the county court was held there for some years. The town did not develop. Nearby was the Indian Town where Pocahontas was sold in 1613 by the Indian Chief Japasaws to Captain Samuel Argall, 8 Miles East. *Stafford Co.: Rte. 1, 3.8 miles n. of Falmouth.*

E-76 FIRST ROMAN CATHOLIC
SETTLEMENT IN VIRGINIA

The crucifix by sculptor Georg J. Lober was erected in 1930 and commemorates Spanish Jesuits who were martyred nearby in 1571. It also honors the first English Roman Catholic settlers, Giles Brent and his half-sister Margaret, who emigrated from Maryland in 1647. Brent constructed his house, which he named "Peace," on land granted by King James II. Many members of the Brent family are buried in the nearby cemetery. *Stafford Co.: Rte. 1, near Rte. 637.*

E-77 GOLD MINING IN STAFFORD COUNTY

Near here are located ten of the nineteenth-century gold mines of Stafford County. The best-known were the Eagle, Rattlesnake (Horse Pen), Lee, New Hope, and Monroe mines. The Eagle Gold Mining Company, Rappahannock Gold Mine Company of New York, Rapidan Mining and Milling Company of Pennsylvania, United States Mining Company, and Stafford Mining Company operated here between the 1830s and the early twentieth century. Mining activities gradually ceased because of declining profits. *Stafford Co.: Rte. 17, .5 mile n. of Hartwood Post Office.*

E-78 MASSAPONAX BAPTIST CHURCH

Massaponax Baptist Church, built in 1859, served a congregation founded in 1788. On 21 May 1864 Lt. Gen. Ulysses S. Grant and his commanders conferred on pews in the churchyard as the Union army marched from the Spotsylvania Court House battlefield to the North Anna River. Photographer Timothy O'Sullivan hauled his heavy stereo camera to the balcony of the church and recorded this conference in a unique series of candid images showing a war council in progress. *Spotsylvania Co.: Rte. 608 near Rte. 1.*

E-79 PEYTON'S ORDINARY

In this vicinity stood Peyton's Ordinary. George Washington, going to Fredericksburg to visit his mother, dined here, March 6, 1769. On his way to attend the House of Burgesses, he spent the night here, October 31, 1769, and stayed here again on September 14, 1772. Rochambeau's army, marching north from Williamsburg in 1782, camped here. *Stafford Co.: Rte. 1, 1.8 miles n. of Stafford.*

E-80* INDIAN MASSACRE

To the east, in Dogue Neck, Piscataway Indians attacked the house of Thomas Barton, killing eight persons, June 16, 1700. George Mason (2nd) described this as the "horriblest murder that ever was in Stafford." *Fairfax Co.: Rte. 1, 8.25 miles s. of Alexandria.*

E-81* DEFENSES OF WASHINGTON

Just to the north lie Forts O'Rorke, Weed, Farnsworth, and Lyon. To the east is Fort Willard. These fortifications constituted the extreme southern defense line of the city of Washington, 1862–65. *Fairfax Co.: Rte. 1, .8 mile s. of Alexandria.*

E-90 AQUIA CHURCH

Here is Aquia Church, the church of Over-wharton Parish, formed before 1680 by the division of Potomac Parish. It was built in 1757, on the site of an earlier church, in the rectorship of Reverend John Moncure, who was the parish minister from 1738 to 1764. The communion silver was given the parish in 1739 and was buried in three successive wars, 1776, 1812 and 1861. *Stafford Co.: Rte. 1, 2.7 miles n. of Stafford.*

E-91 LEE'S BOYHOOD HOME

Robert E. Lee left this home that he loved so well to enter West Point. After Appomattox he returned and climbed the wall to see "if the snowballs were in bloom." George Washington dined here when it was the home of William Fitzhugh, Lee's kinsman and his wife's grandfather. Lafayette visited here in 1824. *Alexandria: 607 Oronoco St.*

E-92 SITE OF THE FIRST SYNAGOGUE OF BETH EL HEBREW CONGREGATION

On this site stood Beth El Hebrew Congregation's synagogue, the first structure built as a Jewish house of worship in the Washington metropolitan area. Founded in 1859, Beth El, the first reform Jewish congregation in the Washington area, is northern Virginia's oldest Jewish congregation. Beth El built the synagogue here in 1871 and worshipped in it until 1954. A new synagogue on Seminary Road, Alexandria, was dedicated in 1957. *Alexandria: 206 North Washington St.*

E-93 LEE-FENDALL HOUSE

"Light Horse Harry" Lee, Revolutionary War officer, owned this land in 1784. The house was built in 1785 by Philip Fendall, a Lee relative. Renovated in 1850 in the Greek Revival style, the house remained in the Lee family until 1903. John L. Lewis, labor leader and president of the United Mine Workers of America and the Congress of Industrial Organizations, was the last resident owner, from 1937 to 1969. *Alexandria: 614 Oronoco St.*

E-94 GUM SPRINGS

Gum Springs, an African-American community, originated here on a 214-acre farm bought in 1833 by West Ford (ca. 1785–1863), a freed man, skilled carpenter, and manager of the Mount Vernon estate. The freedman's school begun here in 1867 at Bethlehem Baptist Church encouraged black settlement. In 1890 the Rev. Samuel K. Taylor, William Belfield, Lovelace Brown, Hamilton Gray, Robert D. King, Henry Randall, and Nathan Webb formed the Joint Stock Company of Gum Springs and sold lots. Gum Springs has remained a vigorous black community. *Fairfax Co.: Rte. 626, .27 mile e. of Rte. 1.*

E-95 SILAS BURKE HOUSE

Here lived Lt. Col. Silas Burke (b. 1796–d. 1854) and his wife, Hannah Coffer. Burke, for whom Burke's Station on the Orange & Alexandria Railroad was named, served as a director of the railroad and the Fairfax Turnpike Company. An innkeeper and farmer, Burke was elected president of the Fairfax Agricultural Society in 1850. He held many county offices with distinction, including road surveyor, commissioner of public buildings and schools, county court justice, presiding justice, and sheriff. *Fairfax Co.: Rte. 645, 2.5 miles n. of Rte. 123.*

EA-1   NORTH ANNA RIVER CAMPAIGN,
       21–26 MAY 1864

Approaching Richmond from the north
after the Wilderness Campaign, Lt. General U. S. Grant sought to cross the North
Anna River and capture the critical rail
center at Hanover Junction (Doswell).
General R. E. Lee ordered the construction of a complex web of earthworks here
to defend the river crossing and junction.
The Union army probed the defenses and
captured some of them but soon abandoned the effort and moved east toward
Cold Harbor. *Hanover Co.: Rte. 1, .65
mile s. of Hanover-Caroline Co. line.*

EA-1   MEADOW FARM

The land comprising Meadow Farm was
first patented by William Sheppard in
1713. In 1800, Sheppard family slaves
thwarted plans for a well-organized slave
uprising known as Gabriel's Insurrection.
The farmhouse was built in 1810. Dr. John
Mosby Sheppard practiced medicine at
Meadow Farm between 1840 and 1877.
The last private owner of Meadow Farm,
Major General Sheppard Crump, was a
founding member of the American Legion
and Adjutant General of Virginia from
1956–1960. Until 1960, the Sheppard
family farmed the land, growing a variety
of grains and tobacco. *Henrico Co.:
Courtney and Old Mountain rds., at entrance to Crump Memorial Park.*

EA-2   WALKERTON

Constructed in 1825 for John Walker,
Walkerton served travellers along the
Mountain Road, once a major route between Richmond and the Western Piedmont of Virginia. The tavern, the largest
and only brick structure among the 19th-
century taverns still standing in Henrico
County, is notable for a hinged, swinging,
two-segment partition that was used to en-
large an upstairs room to accomodate tavern guests. *Henrico Co.: Mountain Rd.
at Glen Allen.*

EA-3   LAUREL HISTORIC DISTRICT

Laurel, first named Hungary Station, was
the location of a spur railroad line to the
coal fields in western Henrico County.
During the Civil War the station here was
burned, and Colonel Ulrich Dahlgren's
body was secretly buried here in March
1864 and later reinterred in Philadelphia.
Nearby stood the first public school in
Henrico County. In 1890 the Laurel Industrial School for Boys was established here
as an alternative to imprisonment. Several
nearby buildings served the institution,
later called the Virginia Industrial School;
during 1920–1922 the school was moved
to Beaumont in Powhatan County. *Henrico Co.: Hungary Rd. and Hungary
Springs Rd.*

EA-4   ATTACK AT OX FORD, 24 MAY 1864

A half mile north, a brigade of Union infantry commanded by Brig. Gen. James H.
Ledlie struck the center of Lee's army,
which blocked Grant's approach to Richmond. Formidable earthworks hastily
erected by Brig. Gen. William H. Mahone's division anchored the Confederate
battle line at Ox Ford on the North Anna
River. Although instructed to use "utmost
caution," Ledlie, fortified with alcohol, ordered a charge. His men were bloodily
repulsed and suffered more than 200 casualties, while Mahone lost about 50. On 27
May Grant withdrew toward Totopotomoy
Creek. *Hanover Co.: Rte. 684, 2.43
miles w. of Rte. 1.*

EH-8 ASBURY'S DEATHPLACE

A short distance southeast is the site of the George Arnold house where Bishop Francis Asbury died, March 31, 1816. Asbury, born in England in 1745, came to America in 1771 and labored here until his death. He was ordained one of the first two bishops of the Methodist Episcopal Church in America at the Baltimore Conference of December, 1784. *Spotsylvania Co.: Rte. 738, 5.5 miles s. of Spotsylvania Court House.*

EM-1 FREDERICKSVILLE FURNACE

Charles Chiswell established the ironmaking community of Fredericksville near this point of Douglas Run, a tributary of the North Anna River. The furnace had been in blast for about five years when William Byrd in 1732 toured the site in the company of Chiswell and his iron-master, Robert Durham. An archaeological investigation of the furnace was financed by Virginia Electric and Power Company in 1970. *Spotsylvania Co.: Rte. 208, 100 yards s.w. of furnace.*

EM-2 ENGAGEMENT AT HARRIS FARM
(BLOOMSBURY)

On 19 May 1864 Confederate forces commanded by Lt. Gen. Richard S. Ewell attacked Brig. Gen. Robert O. Tyler's heavy artillery division on the Union right flank near the Harris farm, Bloomsbury, about one-quarter mile northwest. Newly arrived from the forts protecting Washington, D.C., the inexperienced "heavies" fought as infantry and stubbornly held their ground. At dark Ewell withdrew, ending the last major engagement of the Battle of Spotsylvania Court House. The Confederates suffered 900 casualties at the Harris farm, the Federals about 1,500. Two days later, the Union army marched to the North Anna River as Grant maneuvered south toward Richmond. *Spotsylvania Co.: Rte. 208, .25 mile w. of Rte. 628.*

EP-8 BIRTHPLACE OF MADISON

At this place, Port Conway, James Madison, Fourth President of the United States and Father of the Constitution, was born, March 16, 1751. His mother was staying at her paternal home, Belle Grove, 400 yards east, when her son was born. Madison's father, James Madison, Senior, lived in Orange County. The President had his home at Montpelier in that county. *King George Co.: Rte. 301, .4 mile n. of Port Royal.*

EP-9 CLEYDAEL

This T-shaped house was built in 1859 by Dr. Richard Stuart as a summer residence for his family. On Sunday afternoon, April 23, 1865, John Wilkes Booth and three companions came to this house seeking medical assistance from Dr. Stuart. Suspicious of his visitors and aware of Lincoln's assassination, Dr. Stuart refused to aid them and sent them away after dinner. *King George Co.: Rte. 206, 1.35 miles w. of Rte. 218.*

EP-20 JOHN WILKES BOOTH

This is the Garrett place where John Wilkes Booth, assassin of Lincoln, was cornered by Union soldiers and killed, April 26, 1865. The house stood a short distance from this spot. *Caroline Co.: Rte. 301, 9.1 miles n.e. of Bowling Green.*

EP-21 BIRTHPLACE OF GOVERNOR WISE

Here stood the birthplace of Henry Alexander Wise (1806–1876), Governor of Virginia (1856–1860) and General in the Confederate States Army. A talented orator and debator in an age of great orators, Wise was elected to six terms in Congress. He served as a delegate at the Virginia Conventions of 1850 and 1861, and as United States Minister to Brazil (1844–1847). *Accomack Co.: Bus. Rte. 13, town of Accomac.*

EP-22 MARY NOTTINGHAM SMITH HIGH SCHOOL

The first high school for blacks in Accomack County was dedicated on this site in 1932. It was named in honor of Mary Nottingham Smith (1892–1951), a black educator who dedicated her life to educating all young people. In 1956, the school was renamed for T. C. Walker, an attorney from Gloucester County. It was demolished in 1987. A second Mary N. Smith High School was built on another site in 1953. *Accomack Co.: Bus. Rte. 13, .5 mile e. of Rte. 13.*

F-1 BATTLE OF BALL'S BLUFF

One mile east occurred the battle of Ball's Bluff, October 21, 1861. A Union force, which had crossed the river at this point, was driven back over it by the Confederates. *Loudoun Co.: Rte. 15, .9 mile n. of Leesburg.*

F-2 POTOMAC CROSSINGS

Here Lee turned east to the Potomac, crossing at White's Ford, September 6, 1862, in his invasion of Maryland. Jubal A. Early, returning from his Washington raid, crossed the river at White's Ford, July 14, 1864. *Loudoun Co.: Rte. 15, 6.9 miles n. of Leesburg.*

F-3 GREENWOOD

Home of Judge William Green. Judge Green entertained Lafayette here on August 22, 1825. *Culpeper Co.: Rte. 15, .8 mile s. of Culpeper.*

F-4 OAK HILL

The house to the northwest is Oak Hill, home of President James Monroe, who built it about 1818. Lafayette was entertained here in 1824. Monroe lived here most of the time from his retirement in 1825 to his death in 1831. *Loudoun Co.: Rte. 15, 3 miles n. of Aldie.*

F-5 WAYNE'S CROSSING

Three miles southeast, at Noland's Ferry, "Mad Anthony" Wayne, on his way to join Lafayette, crossed the Potomac River, May 31, 1781. He passed through Leesburg, June 3, and joined Lafayette near the Rapidan River, June 10. *Loudoun Co.: Rte. 15, 7.2 miles n. of Leesburg.*

F-6 SHARPSBURG (ANTIETAM) CAMPAIGN

Near here Stonewall Jackson bivouacked on the march into Maryland, September 4, 1862. *Loudoun Co.: Rte. 15, 2.7 miles n. of Leesburg.*

F-7 GOOSE CREEK CHAPEL

A short distance west is the site of the "Chapel above Goose Creek," built by the vestry of Truro Parish in 1736. Augustine Washington, father of George Washington, was a member of the vestry at the time. This was the first church on the soil of Loudoun County, erected as a chapel of ease for the benefit of early settlers. *Loudoun Co.: Rte. 15, 2 miles n. of Leesburg.*

F-8 COLONIAL HOME

Seven miles west is Roanoke Bridge, colonial homestead of Joseph Morton. The land was patented in 1746 and settled in 1755. Joseph Morton, one of the leading pioneers of this section, was a justice, a surveyor, and a founder of Briery Presbyterian Church. *Charlotte Co.: Rte. 15, 2.4 miles n. of Keysville.*

F-9 CAMPAIGN OF SECOND MANASSAS

Here Jackson, on his march around Pope to Bristoe Station, turned to the southeast, August 26, 1862. *Fauquier Co.: Rte. 55, at The Plains.*

F-10 WHERE PELHAM FELL

Four miles southeast, at Kelly's Ford, Major John Pelham, commanding Stuart's horse artillery, was mortally wounded, March 17, 1863. *Culpeper Co.: Rte. 15, at Elkwood.*

F-11 BATTLE OF BRANDY STATION

In this vicinity was fought one of the greatest Cavalry Battles of the Civil War. On June 9, 1863 Union forces under Pleasonton attacked Stuart, who was screening Lee's Northward movement toward Pennsylvania. After heavy fighting Pleasonton withdrew. *Culpeper Co.: Rte. 29, 1 mile n. of Brandy.*

F-11 BATTLE OF BRANDY STATION

This was the scene of many cavalry actions. A great cavalry battle took place here, on June 9, 1863, between Stuart, screening Lee's move to Gettysburg, and the cavalry of Hooker's army. *Culpeper Co.: Rtes. 15 and 29, .7 mile n.e. of Brandy.*

F-12* BETTY WASHINGTON

Two miles south of this spot is the grave of Betty Lewis, sister of George Washington. She died March 31, 1797. *Culpeper Co.: Rte. 15, 3.1 miles n.e. of Culpeper.*

F-13 OPENING OF GETTYSBURG CAMPAIGN

On this plain Lee reviewed his cavalry, June 8, 1863. The next day the cavalry battle of Brandy Station was fought. On June 10, Ewell's Corps, from its camp near here, began the march to Pennsylvania. *Culpeper Co.: Rte. 15, .5 mile s.w. of Brandy.*

F-14 SIMON KENTON'S BIRTHPLACE

Near Hopewell Gap, five miles west, Simon Kenton was born, 1755. Leaving home in 1771, he became an associate of Daniel Boone and George Rogers Clark in Indian fighting. He won fame as a scout and as one of the founders of Kentucky. Kenton died in Ohio in 1836. *Prince William Co.: Rte. 15, 6.9 miles s. of Gilberts Corner.*

F-15 MOTHER OF STONEWALL JACKSON

In this vicinity (and according to tradition two miles east at Peach Orchard) was born Julia Beckwith Neale, mother of Stonewall Jackson, February 29, 1798. She married Jonathan Jackson in 1818 and died, October 1831. *Loudoun Co.: Rte. 15, .9 mile s. of Gilberts Corner.*

F-15* SIGNAL STATION

The lone peak to the northeast, Mount Pony, was used by Pope as a signal station, 1862. *Culpeper Co.: Rte. 15, 2 miles s. of Culpeper.*

To the south is Clark's Mountain, behind which Lee's army was gathered, August 17, 1862. From a signal station on the mountain top Lee looked down on Pope's army, which he wished to attack. Pope, realizing his danger, retired northward. *Culpeper Co.: Rte. 15, 4.7 miles s. of Culpeper.*

A mile south is the grave of James Lawson Kemper, who led his brigade of Virginia troops in Pickett's charge at Gettysburg, July 3, 1863, and fell desperately wounded. He became a major-general in 1864. Kemper was governor of Virginia, 1874–1878. *Orange Co.: Rte. 15, 2.7 miles n. of Orange.*

Thomas Jefferson stated in NOTES ON THE STATE OF VIRGINIA (1782) that he found gold bearing rock weighing approximately four pounds near this site. Among the 19 gold mines that have been in operation since then in the area, the Franklin and the Liberty were the most productive with the Franklin producing 6259 ounces of gold as recently as 1936. *Fauquier Co.: Rte. 17, at Goldvein.*

Here Stonewall Jackson halted his advance late in the afternoon of August 9, 1862, having driven Banks back from Cedar Mountain. *Culpeper Co.: Rte. 15, 3 miles s. of Culpeper.*

Near here Jackson formed line of battle and received the attack of Banks' Corps of Pope's army. From here he attacked in turn, driving the Union forces northwest. *Culpeper Co.: Rte. 15, 6.1 miles s. of Culpeper.*

This church was organized in 1772. Among its first pastors was Thomas Ammon, who had once been imprisoned for preaching. In 1789, the first meeting of the Orange Association was held at this church. *Culpeper Co.: Rte. 15, 9.7 miles s. of Culpeper.*

Here at Locust Dale, Stonewall Jackson's army crossed the river moving north to the battle of Cedar Mountain, August 9, 1862. The battle was fought a few hours later. *Madison Co.: Rte. 15, 7.6 miles n. of Orange.*

Near here was the church of James Waddel, the blind Presbyterian preacher. Waddel, who had been a minister in the Northern Neck and elsewhere, came here about 1785 and died here in 1805. William Wirt, stopping in 1803 to hear a sermon, was impressed by Waddel's eloquence. He made it the subject of a classic essay. *Orange Co.: Rte. 15, .5 mile n. of Gordonsville.*

F-24   WOODBERRY FOREST SCHOOL

Two miles northeast is Woodberry Forest School, a college preparatory school for boys, founded in 1889 by Robert Stringfellow Walker, a captain with Mosby's Rangers. The school was named for the estate on which it stands, formerly owned by William Madison, brother of President James Madison. *Madison Co.: Rte. 15, 6 miles n. of Orange.*

F-24*   WOODBERRY FOREST SCHOOL

One mile east is Woodberry Forest School, a college preparatory school for boys founded in 1889 by Robert Stringfellow Walker, a captain in Mosby's Rangers. The school is named for the estate on which it stands, formerly owned by William Madison, brother of President James Madison. *Orange Co.: 1.5 miles n. of Orange.*

F-25   MITCHELLS PRESBYTERIAN CHURCH

This Gothic Revival church, built in 1879, contains an elaborate example of trompe-l'oeil fresco painting done in 1888. Joseph Dominick Phillip Oddenino, an Italian immigrant artist, painted to deceive the eye into believing that his plaster murals of Gothic arches, Renaissance-styled cornices, and embellished Corinthian columns were three dimensional. Oddenino decorated the ceilings at Mitchells Church and Hebron Lutheran Church in Madison with geometric designs. *Culpeper Co.: Rte. 652, .28 mile e. of Rte. 615.*

F-25A   MITCHELLS PRESBYTERIAN
         CHURCH

Built in 1879, this Gothic Revival church stands two miles south of this location. It contains an elaborate example of trompe-l'oeil fresco painting done in 1888. Joseph Dominick Phillip Oddenino, an Italian immigrant artist, painted to deceive the eye into believing that his plaster murals of Gothic arches, Renaissance-styled cornices, and embellished Corinthian columns were three dimensional. The ceiling is decorated with geometric designs. *Culpeper Co.: Rte. 522 at Rte. 615, .25 mile s. of Winston.*

F-26   MONTPELIER AND MADISON'S TOMB

Five miles southwest is Montpelier, the home of James Madison, "Father of the American Constitution" and fourth President of the United States, 1809–1817. Near the house is the tomb of Madison, who died at Montpelier on June 28, 1836. *Orange Co.: Rte. 15, at Orange.*

F-27   CATOCTIN RURAL HISTORIC
        DISTRICT

The surrounding area of about 25,000 acres has been a cohesive agricultural community since the mid-1700s, when it was settled largely by former Tidewater Virginia planters attracted by its streams and fertile soils. Bordered by Catoctin Mountain (west) and the Potomac River (north and east), the district includes well-preserved farmsteads, historical road networks, and crossroad communities. These resources date from the late 1700s to the early 1900s and enhance the picturesque rural landscape. *Loudoun Co.: Rte. 15, 4.5 miles s. of Maryland line.*

F-32 CAMPAIGN OF SECOND MANASSAS

Near here Stonewall Jackson camped, August 13–15, 1862, just after the Cedar Mountain engagement. *Orange Co.: Rte. 15, 3.2 miles s. of Orange.*

F-40 CAMPAIGN OF 1781

Lafayette, moving west to protect stores in Albemarle from Tarleton, passed near here, June, 1781. *Louisa Co.: Rte. 15, 3.3 miles s. of Boswell's Tavern.*

F-49 FLUVANNA COUNTY COURTHOUSE

The Fluvanna County Courthouse is one of the few in the state to retain its original configuration. Fluvanna County was formed from part of Albemarle County in 1777 with the county seat located on the southeast side of the Rivanna River. In 1828 Palmyra was selected as the new county seat, and the present courthouse was erected in 1830 by the Reverend Walker Timberlake and John Hartwell Cocke of nearby Bremo. Cocke also prepared the plans for the stone jail, built in 1828, which now houses the Fluvanna County Historical Society's museum. *Fluvanna Co.: Rte. 15, at the courthouse.*

F-50 POINT OF FORK

Four miles southeast is Point of Fork, near which an Indian village stood in 1610. In the Revolution a state arsenal was there. In June, 1781, Simcoe, sent by Cornwallis with a small force to destroy the stores there, succeeded in making Baron Steuben, the American commander, believe the whole British army to be near. Steuben retreated, leaving the stores to be destroyed. *Fluvanna Co.: Rte. 15, at Dixie.*

F-51 "TEXAS JACK" OMOHUNDRO BIRTHPLACE

J. B. "Texas Jack" Omohundro was born at Pleasure Hill Farm about 1 mile west of here on July 26, 1846. At age 17 he served as a scout under the command of General J. E. B. Stuart. Later he was renowned as a scout and heroic plainsman of the old west. Texas Jack with his friend W. F. "Buffalo Bill" Cody started the first "Wild West" shows in America. He died in Leadville, Colorado, June 28, 1880. *Fluvanna Co.: Rte. 15, 1 mile s. of Palmyra.*

F-52 BREMO

To the west is Bremo, built by John Hartwell Cocke after plans made by Thomas Jefferson and completed about 1819. Two other houses once owned by Cocke, Lower Bremo and Recess, are in the vicinity. Cocke, one of the prominent men of his time and associated in the founding of the University of Virginia, was an early temperance advocate. *Fluvanna Co.: Rte. 15, 3.2 miles s. of Fork Union.*

F-53 CARTER G. WOODSON 1875–1950

Three miles east is the birthplace of the noted teacher, educator and historian, Dr. Carter G. Woodson. He was the founder of the association for the study of negro life and history, originated negro history week and authored more than a dozen important works dealing with his race in the United States. *Buckingham Co.: Rte. 15, 10 miles n. of Dillwyn.*

F-54 FEMALE COLLEGIATE INSTITUTE

Two miles east is the site of the first college for women in Virginia, the Female Collegiate Institute. Opened in 1837, it failed in 1843. Reopened in 1848, it survived until 1863. The school building has been destroyed but the "President's Cottage" still stands. *Buckingham Co.: Rte. 15, 5 miles n. of Dillwyn.*

F-55　GOLD MINES

This was the most notable gold-mining region in the country before the California gold rush in 1849. The Morrow Mine here, opened before 1835, was one of the earliest gold mines in which underground mining was employed. Profitably worked for a number of years, it was finally closed. Many other now unworked mines are near by. *Buckingham Co.: Rte. 15, at Dillwyn.*

F-56　OLD BUCKINGHAM CHURCH

The original, or southwest, wing was erected, circa 1758, as a church for the newly-formed Tillotson Parish. Abandoned soon after the Disestablishment (1784), the property was acquired by the Baptists during the next quarter century. It has since served continuously as the meeting house of Buckingham Baptist Church, which was itself constituted May 7, 1771. *Buckingham Co.: Rte. 15, .75 mile s.w. of Rte. 610.*

F-57　CARTER G. WOODSON BIRTHPLACE

Carter Godwin Woodson was born about three miles east on 19 December 1875. As a youth he mined coal near Huntington, W.Va. He earned degrees at Berea College (B.L., 1903), University of Chicago (B.A. and M.A., 1908), and Harvard (Ph.D., 1912)—one of the first blacks awarded a doctorate by Harvard. In 1915 he organized the Association for the Study of Negro Life and History and in 1916 established the *Journal of Negro History.* Known as the Father of Afro-American History, Woodson founded Negro History Week—now Afro-American History Month—in 1926. He died in Washington, D.C., on 3 April 1950. *Buckingham Co.: Rte. 15 at Rte. 670.*

F-59　MARCH TO APPOMATTOX

Part of Lee's army passed here retreating westward, April 8, 1865. The Sixth (Wright's) Corps of Grant's army passed here, in pursuit, in the afternoon of the same day, moving on toward Appomattox. *Buckingham Co.: Rte. 15, 8.8 miles s. of Sprouses.*

F-60　EVE OF APPOMATTOX

Part of Lee's army passed here, April 8, 1865, retreating westward. The Second (Humphrey's) Corps of Grant's army passed, in pursuit, in the afternoon of the same day. Grant spent the night here, receiving early in the morning of April 9 a note from Lee in regard to surrender. He sent a reply and then went on to Appomattox. *Buckingham Co.: Rte. 15, 11.3 miles s. of Sprouses.*

F-61　NEW STORE VILLAGE

Four miles west is the site of New Store Village, in early times an important stop on the Stage Coach Road between Richmond and Lynchburg. Philip Watkins McKinney, Governor of Virginia 1890–1894, was born here in 1832. Peter Francisco, Revolutionary War hero, grew to maturity at nearby Hunting Towers, home of Judge Anthony Winston, an uncle of Patrick Henry. *Buckingham Co.: Rte. 15, 11.3 miles s. of Sprouses.*

F-65　OLD WORSHAM

A short distance south stands the colonial jail of Prince Edward County, built about 1755; the courthouse was near by. The British cavalryman, Tarleton, raided here in July, 1781. Here Patrick Henry made a great speech against the ratification of the United States Constitution, 1788. Washington was here on his southern tour, June 7, 1791. *Prince Edward Co.: Rte. 15, 5.6 miles s. of Farmville.*

F-66* SLATE HILL PLANTATION

A mile west is Slate Hill, home of Nathaniel Venable, who was a member of the Prince Edward Committee of Safety in the Revolution and a charter trustee of Hampden-Sydney College. Tarleton's British cavalry raided this place in 1781, seeking to capture Venable and army supplies stored here. *Prince Edward Co.: Rte. 15, 6.5 miles s. of Farmville.*

F-69 RANDOLPH-MACON MEDICAL
       SCHOOL

Just to the west was the medical school of John Peter Mettauer, which became a branch of Randolph-Macon College in 1847. It was discontinued, probably in 1861. Dr. Mettauer, one of the leading surgeons of the day, practiced until his death in 1875. *Prince Edward Co.: Rte. 15, 5 miles s. of Farmville.*

F-70 KINGSVILLE

Here, before the Revolution, stood King's Tavern. The British cavalryman, Tarleton, raiding, camped here in 1781. In the same year sick and wounded French soldiers were brought to this place from Yorktown; seventy of them are buried here. Nearby is the site of the colonial church of which Archibald McRoberts was minister. *Prince Edward Co.: Rte. 15, 4.5 miles s. of Farmville.*

F-71 PROVIDENCE

Two miles east is the glebe house where the Rev. Archibald McRoberts lived during the Revolution. Tarleton, raiding through this section in July, 1781, set fire to the house, but a timely rain put out the flames. Accordingly, the place was named "Providence." *Prince Edward Co.: Route 5, 5.6 miles s of Farmville.*

F-72 CAMPAIGN OF 1781

Tarleton, sent by Cornwallis to destroy supplies at Bedford, passed here going west, July, 1781. *Prince Edward Co.: Rte. 15, 5.6 miles s. of Farmville.*

F-73 HIGH BRIDGE

One mile north stood the Southside Railroad Bridge, spanning the 75-foot-wide Appomattox River. On 6 April, 1865, nine hundred Union soldiers attempting to burn the 2500-foot-long, 126-foot-high structure were captured by Confederate cavalry. Crossing on 7 April, retreating Confederates burned four spans but failed to destroy the lower wagon bridge thus allowing Union soldiers to cross and attack at Cumberland Church north of Farmville. *Prince Edward Co.: Rte. 619 at Rte. 688, 2.25 miles n. of Rte. 460.*

F-75 OLD BRIERY CHURCH

Just to the north stands Briery Church, organized in 1755 following the missionary work of Presbyterian Minister Samuel Davies. The first church was built about 1760 and was replaced in 1824. The present Gothic Revival church was built about 1855 to designs of Robert Lewis Dabney. *Prince Edward Co.: Rte. 15, 2.4 miles n. of Keysville.*

F-77 EARLY EXPLORATION

Batts, Fallam and Thomas Wood, sent by Abraham Wood to explore Western Virginia, passed near here, September, 1671. *Charlotte Co.: Rte. 15, .2 mile n. of Keysville.*

F-78 CAMPAIGN OF 1781

Tarleton, British cavalryman, returning from his raid to Bedford, passed near here, July, 1781. *Charlotte Co.: Rte. 15, at s. entrance of Keysville.*

F-80 ROANOKE PLANTATION

Nine miles west is Roanoke, home of John Randolph, a member of the House of Representatives for many years, and Senator. Randolph at first was Jefferson's lieutenant and later on an opponent and critic, but he never lost the love of his constituents. He died in Philadelphia, May 24, 1833, and was buried here; later his remains were removed to Richmond. *Charlotte Co.: Rte. 15, at Wyliesburg.*

F-82 STAUNTON BRIDGE ACTION

The railroad bridge over Staunton River, nine miles west, was held by a body of Confederate reserves and citizens from Halifax, Charlotte and Mecklenburg counties against Union cavalry raiding to destroy railroads, June 25, 1864. When the Unionists attempted to burn the bridge, they were repulsed. Meanwhile Confederate cavalry attacked from the rear. Thereupon the raiders retreated to Grant's army at Petersburg. *Charlotte County: Rte. 15, at Wyliesburg.*

F-95 PRESTWOULD PLANTATION

The second William Byrd obtained land here about 1730 and named the place "Blue Stone Castle." The estate extended ten miles along Roanoke River. Before the Revolution Sir Peyton Skipwith came into possession and built the present house, which he named "Prestwould." *Mecklenburg Co.: Rte. 15, 3 miles n. of Clarksville.*

F-98* OCCANEECHEE ISLAND

Just to the west lies Occaneechee Island, former home of the Occaneechee Indians. It was visited by Abraham Wood in 1650. Bacon, the Rebel, following a band of savages ravaging the frontier, overtook them here and persuaded the Occaneechees to attack them. When the Occaneechees refused him food, Bacon turned on them, May 16, 1676. *Mecklenburg Co.: Rte. 15, near state line.*

FA-1* CAMPAIGN OF SECOND MANASSAS

Lee and Longstreet, moving eastward to join Jackson at Manassas, found this gap held by a Union force, August 28, 1862. They forced the gap, after some fighting, and moved on toward Manassas, August 29, 1862. *Prince William Co.: Rte. 55, 5 miles s.e. of The Plains.*

FB-2 JOHN MARSHALL'S HOME

The land was bought by Thomas Marshall, the Chief Justice's father, who built the old part of the house in 1773. John Marshall lived here until he entered the army in 1775. Years later he built the new house for his eldest son. *Fauquier Co.: Rte. 55, 4 miles w. of Marshall.*

FB-4 CAMPAIGN OF SECOND MANASSAS

Near here Stonewall Jackson, after a march of twenty-six miles on his way to Bristoe Station, halted for a few hours to rest his men, August 25–26, 1862. *Fauquier Co.: Rte. 55, at Marshall.*

FF-2 STATE FISH HATCHERY

One mile south. This fish cultural station was established in 1933 for hatching and rearing smallmouth bass and other species of sunfish for the stocking of the public waters of Virginia. *Warren Co.: Rte. 55, 5 miles w. of Riverton.*

FF-4* GETTYSBURG CAMPAIGN

General R. E. Lee established his head-quarters here, June 17, 1863. Ewell's advance had crossed the Potomac; Long-street was near Snicker's Gap; Stuart in contact with the Union cavalry near Aldie; A. P. Hill moving to Chester Gap. The Army of Northern Virginia was about to invade the North. *Fauquier Co.: Rte. 55, at Markham.*

FF-5* LEE'S ESCAPE

Near here Robert E. Lee and staff, moving to join Jackson for the battle of Second Manassas, narrowly escaped capture by the Ninth New York cavalry August 27, 1862. The staff, forming in line confronted the Unionists, who withdrew without charging. *Fauquier Co.: Rte. 55, 2 miles w. of Marshall.*

FF-8 McCLELLAN RELIEVED FROM COMMAND

At Rectortown, four miles north, General George B. McClellan received the order relieving him from command of the Army of the Potomac, November 7, 1862. As Burnside, his successor, was present, McClellan immediately turned over the command to him. *Fauquier Co.: Rte. 55, at Marshall.*

FF-9 MANASSAS GAP

The name Manassas—after Manasseh, a local Jewish innkeeper, according to one tradition published in 1861, or from an un-identified Indian word, according to another—first appeared as "Manasses Run" on a 1737 map. Manassas Gap, at about 950 feet the lowest in the Blue Ridge, initially was named Calmes's Gap for county justice Marquis Calmes, then renamed for Manassas Run. The Manassas Gap Rail-road, built through the gap in the 1850s, linked Washington, D.C., with the Shen-andoah Valley. *Fauquier Co.: Rte. 55, .57 mile e. of Linden.*

FL-8 ASH LAWN

Home of James Monroe, fifth President of the United States, from 1799 until Oak Hill was built. The house was designed by Thomas Jefferson; the rear part was constructed under his plans, 1794–1799. The place was in a neighborhood that included Monticello and the homes of other such noted men as William Short and Philip Mazzei. *Albemarle Co.: Rte. 695, 4 miles s. of Charlottesville.*

FR-3 RED HOUSE

This old tavern was built by Martin Hancock about 1813 on the site of his earlier cabin. It was a noted stopping place and trade center on the old south road to the West. *Charlotte Co.: Rte. 727, at Red House.*

FR-6 EDGEHILL

Three miles north is Edgehill, home of Clement Carrington. He ran away from Hampden-Sydney College to join the Revolutionary army, served in Lee's Legion, 1780–81, and was wounded at Eutaw Springs, September 8, 1781. *Charlotte Co.: Rte. 40, 2 miles e. of Charlotte.*

FR-7 GREENFIELD

Half a mile north is Greenfield, built in 1771 by Isaac Read. Read was a member of the House of Burgesses, 1769–1771, and of the Virginia conventions of 1774 and 1775. He served as an officer in the Revolutionary War, dying of wounds in 1777. *Charlotte Co.: Rte. 40, 2 miles e. of Charlotte.*

FR-8*   COLONIAL HOME

Seven miles west is Roanoke Bridge, colonial homestead of Joseph Morton. The land was patented in 1746 and settled in 1755. Joseph Morton, one of the leading pioneers of this section, was a justice, a surveyor, and a founder of Briery Presbyterian Church. *Charlotte Co.: Rte. 40, 2 miles e. of Charlotte Court House.*

FR-10   HENRY AND RANDOLPH'S DEBATE

Here, in March, 1799, took place the noted debate between Patrick Henry and John Randolph of Roanoke on the question of States' Rights. Henry denied the right of a state to oppose oppressive Federal laws. Randolph affirmed that right. This was Henry's last speech and Randolph's first. Henry died three months later. *Charlotte Co.: Rte. 40, at Charlotte.*

FR-12   CAMPAIGN OF 1781

At Cole's Ferry on Staunton River, twelve miles southwest, Steuben halted his southward march, June 10, 1781. *Charlotte Co.: Rte. 40, at Charlotte.*

FR-14   CUB CREEK CHURCH

Six miles south is Cub Creek Presbyterian Church, the oldest church in this section. The neighborhood was known as the Caldwell Settlement for John Caldwell, grandfather of John C. Calhoun of South Carolina. About 1738 he brought here a colony of Scotch-Irish and obtained permission to establish a church. *Charlotte Co.: Rte. 40, 2 miles e. of Phenix.*

FR-15   ROUGH CREEK CHURCH

A chapel was built here in 1765–1769 by order of the vestry of Cornwall Parrish. Following the disestablishment and a brief period of irregular use, the property passed to the Republican Methodists, a denomination then active in the South. It was received under the care of Hanover Presbytery in 1822, and the present building was erected in 1838 on the original site. Rough Creek is the mother church of Madisonville, Oak View, and Phenix Presbyterian churches organized 1907–1914. *Charlotte Co.: Rte. 727, n. of Phenix.*

FR-16   HAT CREEK CHURCH

Four and a half miles north stands Hat Creek Presbyterian Church, founded by John Irvin and associates (first settlers) about 1742. William Irvin, son of John, and the noted blind preacher, James Waddel, were among its pastors. The first log building was replaced in 1788, and two other churches have been built on the original site. *Campbell Co.: Rte. 40, 2.1 miles e. of Brookneal.*

FR-25   PATRICK HENRY'S GRAVE

Five miles southeast of Red Hill, last home and resting place of Patrick Henry. He moved here in 1796 and died here, June 6, 1799. *Campbell Co.: Rte. 40, 2.5 miles e. of Brookneal.*

FR-26   ST. JOHN'S LUTHERAN CHURCH

German settlers formed a congregation here that was a center of Lutheranism in Virginia throughout the 19th century. The church built around 1800 was replaced by the present structure in 1854. The cemetery has distinctive stones dating from 1804 to the present. St. John's became a part of Holy Trinity, Wytheville, in 1924. *Wythe Co.: Rte. 21, at Wytheville.*

Lt. Gen. Lewis Andrew Pick was born here on November 18, 1890. Educated at Rustburg and at VPI (where he was a member of the Corps of Cadets), General Pick served in two world wars and in the Korean conflict. Best known as the builder of the 1,030-mile long Ledo Road, used to supply American and Chinese troops in the China-Burma-India Theatre during World War II, Pick also served as chief of the Army Corps of Engineers before his death in 1956. *Campbell Co.: Rte. 40, in Brookneal.*

G-2   LEETON FOREST

Half a mile east is the site of Leeton Forest, latter-day home of Charles Lee, Attorney General in Washington's and Adams' cabinets, 1795–1801. The tract was patented by Thomas Lee, of Stratford, in 1718 and descended to his son, Richard Henry Lee, Revolutionary leader. The latter's daughter Anne married Charles Lee, who obtained title to the property in 1803, and who died here in June, 1815. *Fauquier Co.: Rte. 802, .5 mile s. of Warrenton.*

G-3   ST. JAMES UNITED CHURCH OF CHRIST

Formerly St. James Evangelical and Reformed Church, this is the oldest active congregation of the German Reformed tradition in Virginia. Lovettsville, a German settlement, was founded by settlers of the Reformed Faith in 1733. Early records indicate that Elder William Wenner, the first leader of the Lovettsville congregation, arrived in the area as early as 1720. *Loudoun Co.: Rte. 673, .1 mile e. of Rte. 287.*

G-9   CAMPAIGN OF SECOND MANASSAS

Here Lee and Jackson had their headquarters. Here, August 24, 1862, they formed the plan to attack Pope's line of supply and bring him to battle before McClellan could join him. *Culpeper Co.: Rte. 211, 7 miles n.w. of Warrenton.*

G-9   LITTLE FORK CHURCH

One-half mile east stands Little Fork Episcopal Church, begun 1753, destroyed by fire in 1773. Present structure completed in 1776. *Culpeper Co.: Rte. 229, 6 miles s. of Rte. 211.*

G-10   GENERAL EDWARD STEVENS

Here is buried General Edward Stevens, who served at Brandywine, Camden, Guilford Courthouse and Yorktown. He died on August 17, 1820. *Culpeper: Rte. 229, at n. entrance of Culpeper.*

G-11   CAVALRY ENGAGEMENT AT JACK'S SHOP

First known as Jack's Shop for a blacksmith shop that stood nearby, Rochelle was the scene of a cavalry skirmish on 22 September 1863. While Confederate cavalry under Major General J. E. B. Stuart engaged Union Brigadier General John Buford's troops, the cavalry of Brigadier General H. Judson Kilpatrick rode to Buford's support and attacked the rear of Stuart's force. Stuart's horse artillery and his cavalry fired and charged in both directions. They broke through Kilpatrick's lines and escaped. *Madison Co.: Rte. 231, 6.5 miles s. of Madison.*

G-11*   CAVALRY ENGAGEMENT

Near here J. E. B. Stuart, while fighting the Union cavalryman, Buford, was attacked in the rear by another cavalry force under Kilpatrick. Stuart, turning on Kilpatrick, cut his way out, September 22, 1863. Buford pursued him to the Rapidan River. *Madison Co.: Rte. 231, 5.5 miles s. of Madison.*

G-12   JOSEPH EARLY HOME

One mile west was the home of Joseph Early, Revolutionary soldier. Washington, in going West and reforming, stopped at Early's overnight. His diary for October 2, 1784, shows that he spent the night before at "Widow Early's." *Madison Co.: Rte. 29, 3 miles s. of Madison.*

G-15   HENRY HOUSE

These are the grounds of the Henry House, where occurred the main action of the First Battle of Manassas, July 21, 1861, and the closing scene of the Second Battle of Manassas, August 30, 1862. *Prince William Co.: Rte. 234, 5.1 miles n.w. of Manassas.*

G-16   JAMES ROBINSON HOUSE

To the south stood the farmhouse of James Robinson, a former slave freed by Landon Carter. There, during the First Battle of Manassas on 21 July 1861, Col. Wade Hampton's Legion covered the Confederates falling back to Henry Hill, where Jackson stood "like a stone wall." The house survived that battle, and during the Second Battle of Manassas in August 1862 served the Union troops as a field hospital. Congress later authorized compensation to Robinson for property damages. The present house stands partially on the foundation of the original. *Prince William Co.: Rte. 29, .27 mile n. of Rte. 234.*

G-17   SECOND PRINCE WILLIAM COUNTY
         COURTHOUSE

In 1743, the second Prince William County Courthouse was built near here along Cedar Run, replacing the first county courthouse in Woodbridge. After the creation of Fairfax County, the Cedar Run location, owned by Philemon Waters, became the center of Prince William County. The court remained here only until 1759, when it moved to Dumfries after the creation of Fauquier County. Henry Lee, father of Governor Henry ("Lighthorse Harry") Lee, and grandfather of General Robert E. Lee, practiced law here. The building, like its predecessor, no longer stands. *Prince William Co.: Rte. 646, 3.55 miles w. of Rte. 234.*

G-25*   GENERAL SUMTER'S BOYHOOD

Thomas Sumter, Revolutionary soldier in South Carolina for whom Fort Sumter was named, lived for a time in his youth at Sumter's Mill, five miles southeast. *Albemarle Co.: Rte. 29, 5 miles s. of Ruckersville.*

G-26   RIO MILLS

The 19th-century mill village of Rio Mills stood 600 yards west of here, where the former Harrisonburg-Charlottesville Turnpike crossed the South Fork of the Rivanna River. Following the Battle of Rio Hill on 29 February 1864, Union General George Armstrong Custer burned the covered bridge and gristmill at Rio Mills. Immediately rebuilt under the direction of Abraham L. Hildebrand, the gristmill continued to grind wheat and corn for the Confederacy. The milling operation apparently closed down soon after 1900. *Albemarle Co.: Rte. 29, 5.75 miles n. of Charlottesville.*

GA-32 POINT OF FORK

Here was an important supply depot and arsenal of the Virginia government in 1781, and here Baron von Steuben, commanding the American forces, trained recruits for Greene's army in the South. Threatened by Cornwallis's approach, Stueben moved stores across James River. On June 4, 1781, Colonel Simcoe, with his cavalry, made Steuben believe that the whole British army was at hand. Steuben retreated, leaving stores to be destroyed. *Fluvanna Co.: Rte. 6, .8 mile w. of Columbia.*

GA-33 FORK UNION ACADEMY

First classes of Fork Union Academy were held here October 15, 1898, in the residence of Susan Payne Cooper. Established as a coeducational English and classical school, it became Fork Union Military Academy for boys in 1903. Organized by ten guarantors who were members of Fork Church, the Academy was sustained mainly by private contributions from the Fork Union Community until 1913 when it became affiliated with the Baptist denomination. *Fluvanna Co.: Rte. 6 at Rte. 15.*

GA-34 RASSAWEK

Rassawek, a town of the Monacan Indians, stood near here at the time of the settlement in 1607. The Monacans, a Siouan tribe, were decimated by repeated attacks of the Iroquois from the north, and finally moved westward. *Fluvanna Co.: Rte. 6, .8 mile w. of Columbia.*

GA-35 BARCLAY HOUSE AND SCOTTSVILLE MUSEUM

Here stands the Barclay House, built about 1830, later the home of Dr. James Turner Barclay, inventor for the U.S. Mint and missionary to Jerusalem. He founded the adjacent Disciples Church in 1846 and served as its first preacher. It is now the Scottsville Museum. *Albemarle Co.: Rte. 6, at Scottsville.*

GA-36 HISTORIC SCOTTSVILLE

In 1745 Old Albemarle County was organized at Scott's landing, its first county seat, here on the Great Horseshoe Bend of the James River. In 1818 the town was incorporated as Scottsville. Beginning in 1840 it flourished as the chief port above Richmond for freight and passenger boats on the James River and Kanawha Canal. It played a vital role in the opening up of the west. The 1840s and '50s were its golden era. *Albemarle Co.: Rte. 20, at Rte. 6 in Scottsville.*

GA-37 HATTON FERRY

James A. Brown began operating a store and ferry at this site on rented property in the late 1870s. In 1881 he bought the land from S. P. Gantt at which time the store became a stop on the Richmond and Alleghany Railroad. Two years later, Brown was authorized to open a post office in his store, which was named Hatton for the young federal postal officer who signed the authorizing documents. The ferry is one of only two poled ferries still functioning in the continental United States. *Albemarle Co.: Rte. 625, 5.75 miles w. of Scottsville.*

GA-38 HATTON FERRY

Five miles southwest of here is the Hatton Ferry on the James River which began operating in the 1870s. James A. Brown established the ferry and a store on land first rented and then purchased from S. P. Gantt in 1881. In 1883 when a post office was approved for the store, it was named Hatton for the young federal postal officer who signed the authorizing documents. The ferry is one of only two poled ferries still functioning in the continental United States. *Albemarle Co.: Rte. 6, at Rte. 726, .38 mile n.w. of Scottsville.*

HD-1 COLONEL ABRAM PENN

200 yards south is "Poplar Grove," Penn's old home and burial place. At age 21, he "won his spurs," leading a company under General Lewis at Point Pleasant. During 1780–81 he organized the first Revolutionary troops from Henry and adjoining counties, and led his regiment to aid General Greene in the battles of Guilford Court House and Eutaw Springs. He helped organize Patrick County. *Patrick Co.: Rte. 58, 1.86 miles s.e. of Henry Co. line.*

I-1 VIRGINIA MILITARY INSTITUTE— A NATIONAL HISTORIC LANDMARK

The nation's first state military college, VMI was founded in 1839 on the concept of the citizen-soldier. The Corps of Cadets fought as a unit in the 1864 Battle of New Market. Confederate General "Stonewall" Jackson and oceanographer Matthew Fontaine Maury were among its faculty. George C. Marshall, a 1901 graduate, served as Army Chief of Staff in W.W. II, and later as Secretary of State, devising the Marshall Plan to rebuild Europe. He was awarded the Nobel Peace Prize. *Lexington: Letcher Ave. at entrance to VMI, .15 mile w. of Rte. 11.*

I-1 VIRGINIA MILITARY INSTITUTE

A state military, engineering and arts college, founded in 1839. Graduates of it have taken a prominent part in every war since the Mexican War, 2,000 of them serving in the World War. The cadets fought as a corps at New Market in 1864. Among the members of the faculty were Stonewall Jackson and the noted scientists, Matthew F. Maury and John M. Brooke. *Rockbridge Co.: Rte. 11, at Lexington.*

I-2 SOUTHWEST VIRGINIA MUSEUM

Originated by Mrs. Janie Slemp Newman and developed by her brother, C. Bascom Slemp, as a neighborhood museum. It contains books by local authors, portraits of citizens, implements, machines, furniture, household utensils, furnishings and costumes. It presents a representative picture of the life of Southwestern Virginians of the past. The collection of museum pieces was bequeathed to Virginia by will of C. Bascom Slemp and accepted by the State in 1946. *Wise Co.: Alt. Rte. 58, at Big Stone Gap.*

I-2-a VIRGINIA POLYTECHNIC INSTITUTE

Nine miles north is the Virginia Polytechnic Institute, a state college of agriculture, engineering and business, established in 1872, as a land-grant college, on the site of the Draper's Meadows massacre of 1755. Its founding marked the beginning of scientific agricultural and industrial instruction in Virginia. The college includes agricultural and engineering experiment stations. *Montgomery Co.: Rte. 11, .6 mile e. of Christiansburg.*

I-2-b VIRGINIA POLYTECHNIC INSTITUTE

Nine miles north is the Virginia Polytechnic Institute, a state college of agriculture, engineering and business, established in 1872, as a land-grant college, on the site of the Draper's Meadows massacre of 1755. Its founding marked the beginning of scientific agricultural and industrial instruction in Virginia. The college includes agricultural and engineering experiment stations. *Montgomery Co.: Rte. 11, at w. entrance of Christiansburg.*

I-2-c VIRGINIA POLYTECHNIC INSTITUTE

A state college of agriculture, engineering and business, established in 1872, as a land-grant college, on the site of the Draper's Meadows massacre of 1755. Its founding marked the beginning of scientific agricultural and industrial instruction in Virginia. The college includes agricultural and engineering experiment stations. *Montgomery Co.: Rte. 460, at Blacksburg.*

I-3 UNIVERSITY OF VIRGINIA

This institution was founded by Thomas Jefferson. The cornerstone of the first building was laid, on October 6, 1817, in the presence of three Presidents of the United States, Jefferson, Madison and Monroe, all members of the board of visitors. It became the state university in 1819 and was opened to instruction in 1825. The university was conducted by the faculty until 1904, when the first president was elected. *Charlottesville: Rte. 29, at Charlottesville.*

I-4 CATAWBA SANATORIUM

This institution, one mile northeast, stands on the site of the old Roanoke Red Sulphur Springs, which by 1859 was a noted summer resort. The sanatorium was established by the General Assembly of Virginia in 1908 for the treatment of persons suffering with incipient tuberculosis. It opened its doors on July 30, 1909. The location was selected for its bracing and healthy climate. *Roanoke Co.: Rte. 311, at Catawba.*

I-5* STATE COLONY

One mile southeast is the state colony for epileptics and feebleminded, chartered by the General Assembly, February 20, 1906, opened to patients in May, 1911. In its grounds are earthworks erected in June, 1864, to defend Lynchburg against Sheridan's advance from the east. Sheridan, defeated by Hampton at Trevillians, did not reach here. *Amherst Co.: Rte. 29, 1 mile n. of Lynchburg.*

I-6 CENTRAL STATE HOSPITAL

Established in 1869 in temporary quarters at Howard's Grove near Richmond. In 1870 it came under control of the State. In 1885 it was moved to the present location, the site of "Mayfield Plantation," which was purchased and donated to the State by the City of Petersburg. The first hospital in America exclusively for the treatment of mental disease in the Negro. *Dinwiddie Co.: Rte. 1, .4 mile w. of Petersburg.*

I-7 EMORY AND HENRY COLLEGE

One mile north is Emory and Henry College, founded in 1836, the first institution of higher learning in Southwest Virginia. It was named for Bishop John Emory of the Methodist Church and Patrick Henry, the orator of the Revolution. Four bishops of the Methodist Church, three governors, and one United States Senator are among its alumni. *Washington Co.: Rte. 11, 8.3 miles e. of Abingdon.*

I-8 WASHINGTON AND LEE UNIVERSITY

Founded 1749, as Augusta Academy, near Greenville; reestablished at Timber Ridge, May, 1776, as Liberty Hall Academy; moved to Lexington and chartered as a college, 1782; endowed by George Washington, 1796, and named for him. Under presidency, 1865–1870, of Robert E. Lee (buried in the university chapel), whose name after death was incorporated in the official title. *Rockbridge Co.: Rte. 11, at Lexington.*

I-9 HAMPDEN-SYDNEY COLLEGE

Formed in 1776 (six months before the Declaration of Independence) and named for John Hampden and Algernon Sydney, English patriots, it was brought into being by the love of liberty. Patrick Henry and James Madison were on the first board of trustees. President William Henry Harrison was a member of the class of 1791. The college is one of the leading educational institutions of the Presbyterian Church. *Prince Edward Co.: Rte. 692, at Hampden Sydney.*

I-10-a RANDOLPH-MACON COLLEGE

Three blocks west is Randolph Macon College for men, the oldest Methodist college in America. It was chartered in 1830 and was named for John Randolph of Roanoke and Nathaniel Macon of North Carolina. Originally situated at Boydton in southside Virginia, it was moved to present location in 1868. *Hanover Co.: Rte. 1, at Ashland.*

I-10-b* RANDOLPH-MACON COLLEGE

A liberal arts college for men, chartered February 3, 1830. Named for John Randolph and Nathaniel Macon. The oldest Methodist college in America. *Hanover Co.: Rte. 54, at Ashland.*

I-11-a ROANOKE COLLEGE

Five miles west is the birthplace of Virginia Institute, founded in 1842 by David F. Bittle, assisted by Christopher C. Baughman. Chartered on January 30, 1845, as Virginia Collegiate Institute, the school was moved to Salem, Virginia, in 1847, and was chartered as Roanoke College, March 14, 1853. *Augusta Co.: Rte. 340, 2.1 miles n. of Greenville.*

I-11-b ROANOKE COLLEGE

At Salem is a liberal arts institution for men and women. Founded in Augusta County in 1842 as Virginia Institute, it was chartered in 1845 as Virginia Collegiate Institute; moved to Salem in 1847; chartered as Roanoke College in 1853, and was in operation throughout 1861–65. The students formed a company in the Confederate Army, Virginia Reserves, September 1, 1864. *Roanoke Co.: Rte. 11, .2 mile w. of Salem.*

I-13 BRIDGEWATER COLLEGE

Located two miles southwest in the town of Bridgewater, this liberal arts college is affiliated with the Church of the Brethren. It grew out of the Spring Creek Normal School and Collegiate Institute, founded in 1880, and became Bridgewater College nine years later. It has been coeducational from the beginning. *Rockingham Co.: Rte. 11 at Rte. 257 (Mount Crawford).*

I-13-a BRIDGEWATER COLLEGE

Founded near this site in 1880, the college is now located 4.3 miles east in the town of Bridgewater. This liberal arts college is affiliated with the Church of the Brethren. It grew out of the Spring Creek Normal School and Collegiate Institute and became Bridgewater College nine years later. It has been coeducational from its founding. *Rockingham Co.: Rtes. 613 and 748 at Spring Creek.*

I-15 STATE TEACHERS COLLEGE AT FARMVILLE

The college opened here in October 1884 as a "State Female Normal School." In 1914 the name was changed to "State Normal School for Women at Farmville;" in 1924 to "State Teachers College at Farmville." In 1916 conferring the B.S. degree was authorized and later the B.A. degree. William H. Ruffner, first State Superintendent of Public Instruction, was the first president. The fourth, J. L. Jarman, served from 1902 to 1946, succeeded by Dabney S. Lancaster. *Prince Edward Co.: Rte. 15, at Farmville.*

I-15-a* LONGWOOD COLLEGE

The college, on High Street in Farmville, opened in 1884 as a "State Female Normal School." In 1914 the name was changed to "State Normal School for Women at Farmville"; in 1924 to "State Teachers College at Farmville;" in 1949 to "Longwood College." Conferring the B.S. degree was authorized in 1916, and later the B.A. degree. William H. Ruffner, first State Superintendent of Public Instruction, was the first president. The fourth, J. L. Jarman, served from 1902 to 1946. *Prince Edward Co.: Rte. 460, at Farmville.*

I-16 THE VIRGINIA SCHOOL FOR THE DEAF AND THE BLIND—FOUNDED 1839

A State residential school created by an act of the General Assembly of the Commonwealth of Virginia on March 31, 1838 for the purpose of educating the deaf and the blind children of the state. *Staunton: Rte. 11 Bypass, just e. of the school.*

I-17 MARY BALDWIN COLLEGE

The oldest college for women related to the Presbyterian Church, U.S. Founded 1842 by Rufus W. Bailey as Augusta Female Seminary; renamed in 1895 to honor Mary Julia Baldwin, pioneer woman, educator and principal, 1863–1897. *Staunton: E. Frederick St., at Mary Baldwin College.*

I-18 WOODROW WILSON REHABILITATION CENTER

In 1947 the Woodrow Wilson Rehabilitation Center became the first state comprehensive rehabilitation center in the United States. Operated by the Virginia Department of Rehabilitative Services, this residential facility offers various programs for individuals with a wide range of physical, emotional, and mental disabilities to help them live more independently. *Augusta Co.: Rte. 250 at Rte. 358, .88 mile w. of Fishersville.*

I-19 PRESBYTERIAN SEMINARY

The first Presbyterian seminary in the South was established here in 1812 as the Theology Department of Hampden-Sydney College. It became independent of the college in 1822. After the synods of Virginia and North Carolina assumed joint ownership in 1827, it was called Union Theological Seminary; several of its buildings still stand. When the seminary moved to Richmond in 1898, its property on the south side of this road was purchased by Maj. Richard M. Venable, of Baltimore, and donated to the college. *Prince Edward Co.: Rte. 1001, on campus of Hampden-Sydney College.*

I-20 SOLITUDE

The earliest portion of Solitude was constructed about 1801 on land owned by Philip Barger, who sold the property in 1803 to James Patton Preston, governor of Virginia (1816–1819). Governor John Floyd (1830–1834), Preston's brother-in-law, lived at Solitude about 1814–1815. Preston's son, Col. Robert Preston, enlarged the house from a simple log dwelling to a central-passage-plan, Greek Revival-style house about 1851. Col. Preston sold Solitude in 1872 to secure the location of Virginia's first land-grant university, Virginia Polytechnic Institute and State University. *Montgomery Co.: At VPI&SU on West Campus Dr., .4 mile s. of Rte. 412.*

I-21 STUART HALL

Chartered on 13 January 1844 as the Virginia Female Institute, Stuart Hall is Virginia's oldest college preparatory school for girls. The Rev. Dr. Richard H. Phillips headed the school from 1848 until 1880. Flora Cooke Stuart, "Mrs. General" J. E. B. Stuart, for whom the school was renamed in 1907, was principal from 1880 until 1899. Two of General Robert E. Lee's daughters attended Stuart Hall, and Lee served as president of the school's board of visitors from 1865 until 1870. *Staunton: W. Frederick and St. Clair sts.*

J-1* A RAID OF MOSBY'S

Here Mosby attacked Sheridan's supply train, August 13, 1864, capturing 600 horses and mules and 200 prisoners. *Clarke Co.: Rte. 340, 1 mile n. of Berryville.*

J-1-a BUCK MARSH BAPTIST CHURCH

Organized near this spot by Wm. and Daniel Fristoe in 1772. Constituted by Elders John Marks and John Garrand, the latter serving as its Pastor. James Ireland served as Pastor from 1778–1806 and is buried here. *Clark Co.: Rte. 340, n. of Berryville.*

J-2* BUCK MARSH

Near here, in 1744, Joseph Hampton and his two sons, while pioneering, lived in a hollow sycamore tree for some months. *Clarke Co.: Rte. 340, 1.5 miles n. of Berryville.*

J-3 THIRD BATTLE OF WINCHESTER

Here Confederate forces under General Jubal A. Early, facing east, received the attack of Sheridan's army at noon on September 19, 1864. Early repulsed the attack and countercharged, breaking the Union line. Only prompt action by General Emory Upton in changing front saved the Union forces from disaster. At 3 P.M. Sheridan made a second attack, driving Early back to Winchester. *Frederick Co.: Rte. 7 at Rte. 656.*

J-3* THIRD BATTLE OF WINCHESTER

Here Early, facing east, received the attack of Sheridan's army, at noon on September 19, 1864. Early repulsed the attack and countercharged, breaking the Union line. Only Upton's prompt action in changing front saved the Unionists from disaster. At 3 P.M., Sheridan made a second attack, driving Early back to Winchester. *Frederick Co.: Rte. 522 at e. entrance of Winchester.*

J-4 THIRD BATTLE OF WINCHESTER

Near here Early, facing east, took his last position on September 19, 1864. About sundown he was attacked and driven from it, retreating south. Presidents Rutherford B. Hayes and William McKinley served in this engagement on the Union side. *Winchester: Rte. 522 at national cemetery.*

J-5 GEORGE WASHINGTON CARVER REGIONAL HIGH SCHOOL

George Washington Carver Regional High School was founded in 1948 to serve the educational needs of black students in Culpeper, Madison, Orange, and Rappahannock counties. Secondary schools for blacks in those counties were either nonexistent or inadequate for collegiate preparation. The regional high school was established as an economical solution to these problems. In 1968 the school was renamed the Piedmont Technical Education Center. *Culpeper Co.: Rte. 15, 8 miles s. of Culpeper.*

J-6* JOHN S. BARBOUR'S BIRTHPLACE

Just to the south stood "Catalpa," birthplace of John Strode Barbour, December 29, 1820. Barbour was a member of the House of Representatives; chairman of the state Democratic committee 1883–90; United States Senator, March 4, 1889 until his death on May 14, 1892. *Culpeper Co.: Rte. 522, at w. entrance of Culpeper.*

J-7 THE McKAY HOME

A short distance west, at Cedarville, stands the old home of the pioneer Robert McKay. Built of walnut logs, it is one of the oldest houses in the Valley. In 1731, Joist Hite, Robert McKay and others received a grant of 100,000 acres. Hite settled on the Opequon and McKay at this place on Crooked Run. These men opened the Valley to succeeding settlers. *Warren Co.: Rte. 340, at Cedarville.*

J-8 CAPTURE OF FRONT ROYAL

Stonewall Jackson, moving against Banks, captured this town from a Union force under Colonel Kenly, May 23, 1862. *Warren Co.: Rte. 340, at Front Royal.*

J-9 MOSBY'S MEN

Near this spot several of Mosby's men were executed by order of General Custer, September 23, 1864. On the following November 6 Colonel Mosby, in retaliation, ordered the execution of an equal number of Custer's men near Berryville. *Warren Co.: Rte. 340, .5 mile n. of Front Royal.*

J-10 CULPEPER MINUTE MEN

On the hill to the south the famous Culpeper Minute Men were organized, 1775. John Marshall, later Chief Justice of the Supreme Court, was a lieutenant. *Culpeper: Rte. 522, at w. entrance of Culpeper.*

J-11* GUARD'S HILL AFFAIR

General Fitz Lee's cavalry, supported by a brigade of Kershaw's infantry, detached from Anderson's Corps at Front Royal, near here attacked Merritt of Sheridan's cavalry, August 16, 1864. Merritt, on being reinforced, drove the Confederates back across the river. He then withdrew towards Charlestown. *Warren Co.: Rte. 340, .2 mile n. of Riverton.*

J-12 RECREATIONAL CENTER OF FRONT ROYAL

The lands in this part were presented to the people of this community by Mr. and Mrs. William E. Carson and the park facilities were developed under the supervision of the National Park Service of the Department of the Interior by enrollees of the Civilian Conservation Corps. *Warren Co.: Rte. 340, 1.1 miles n. of Riverton.*

J-13 THIRD BATTLE OF WINCHESTER

On a hill, approximately one-half mile to the west, Philip H. Sheridan established his final position on September 19, 1864. General Jubal A. Early held the ground one-half mile further to the west. At 4 P.M., Sheridan advanced with massed cavalry and infantry and broke Early's line. *Frederick Co.: Rte. 7, .41 mile e. of Rte. 716.*

J-13* THIRD BATTLE OF WINCHESTER

On this hill, Sheridan, facing west, took his final position, September 19, 1864. Early held position a half mile to the west. At 4 P.M. Sheridan, massing his cavalry and infantry, advanced on Early, whose line was broken by the assault. *Frederick Co.: Rte. 50, at Winchester.*

J-14* GETTYSBURG CAMPAIGN

Lee and Longstreet, on their way to Gettysburg, camped here, June 18–19, 1863. *Clarke Co.: Rte. 340, 1 mile n. of Berryville.*

J-15 SIGNAL STATIONS

The hilltop northeast of this spot is Cole's Hill. The mountain to the west is Mount Pony. Both were used by Pope as signal stations, 1862. *Culpeper Co.: Rte. 3, 3.6 miles e. of Culpeper.*

J-16 DEFENSES OF WINCHESTER

The fort on the hilltop to the north is one of a chain of defenses commanding the crossings of the Opequon. It was constructed by Milroy in 1863. *Frederick Co.: Rte. 522, 4 miles s. of Winchester.*

J-17 BROTHER AGAINST BROTHER

The first Maryland Regiment, U.S.A., was a part of the force holding this town when it was attacked by Stonewall Jackson, May 23, 1862. With Jackson was the First Maryland Regiment, C.S.A. The two regiments were arrayed against each other. *Warren Co.: Rte. 340, at Front Royal.*

J-25 GETTYSBURG CAMPAIGN

Ewell's Corps of Lee's army passed here going north, June 11–12, 1863; Hill's Corps, June 19. *Rappahannock Co.: Rte. 522, 5 miles s. of Front Royal.*

J-26 ALBERT GALLATIN WILLIS

A ministerial student, aged 20, of Mosby's command, he was hanged nearby October 14, 1864 by U.S. 2nd Cavalry (W. Va.) in reprisal for alleged murder of U.S. soldier by Mosby's men. Of two captured, one was to be hanged. Willis was offered chaplain's exemption, but refused to doom his companion, a married man. Professing his Christian readiness to die, he prayed for his executioners. *Rappahannock Co.: Rte. 522, 5.5 miles n. of Flint Hill.*

J-29* POPE'S ARMY OF VIRGINIA

Here was organized, from the troops of Fremont, Banks and McDowell, the Union army of Virginia, June 26, 1862. *Rappahannock Co.: Rte. 522, at Sperryville.*

J-30* ANDERSON AND CROOK

Near here R. H. Anderson, on his march to join Lee, then hard pressed at Petersburg, met Crook's Army of West Virginia. Anderson attacked, driving Crook back on Sheridan's main army, September 4, 1864. *Clarke Co.: Rte. 7, .7 mile w. of Berryville.*

J-33 OPENING OF THE WILDERNESS CAMPAIGN

Near here the Second Corps of Grant's army camped in the winter of 1863–64. To this point came Sheridan's cavalry, the Sixth Corps from Brandy Station, and the Fifth Corps from Culpeper. The Union army moved hence to Germanna and Ely's Fords on the Rapidan River, May 4, 1864, to open the Wilderness Campaign. *Culpeper Co.: Rte. 3, at Stevensburg.*

J-34 GERMANNA

Here Governor Alexander Spotswood established a colony of Germans in 1714. At that time the Rapidan River was the frontier of Virginia. On August 29, 1716, Spotswood left from this place with his Knights of the Golden Horseshoe on his exploring expedition across the mountains. The German colony later moved to Fauquier County. Spotswood lived for some years at Germanna where he was visited in 1732 by William Byrd who called his house "Spotswood's Enchanted Castle." *Orange Co.: Rte. 3, 4.8 miles w. of Wilderness.*

J-34* GERMANNA

Here Governor Alexander Spotswood planted a colony of Germans in 1714. At that time this river was the frontier of Virginia. On August 29, 1716, Spotswood left this place with his Knights of the Golden Horseshoe on his exploring expedition across the mountains. The German colony moved hence to Fauquier County. Spotswood lived here for some years and was visited here by William Byrd in 1732. *Orange Co.: Rte. 3, 4.8 miles w. of Wilderness.*

J-35 GERMANNA FORD

One of the principal crossings of the Rapidan River from colonial times. Here a part of the Army of the Potomac crossed the river, April 30, 1863, preceding the battle of Chancellorsville. Here a part of Meade's army crossed on the way to Mine Run, November 26, 1863. Here the Fifth and Sixth corps of Grant's army crossed, May 4–5, 1864, to open the Wilderness campaign. *Orange Co.: Rte. 3, 4.8 miles w. of Wilderness.*

J-37 JACKSON'S AMPUTATION

Near here stood the hospital tent to which the wounded "Stonewall" Jackson was brought during the Battle of Chancellorsville. In that tent his left arm was amputated on May 3, 1863. He died seven days later at Guinea. *Spotsylvania Co.: Rte. 3, e. of Rte. 20.*

J-38 ELY'S FORD

On this hill, May 3, 1863, Confederate General J. E. B. Stuart was notified that General Stonewall Jackson had been wounded at Chancellorsville and that he was to take command of Jackson's Corps. Moments before, Stuart had ordered his 1,000 men from North Carolina and Virginia to attack the 3,400 Pennsylvanians under General A. W. Averell at Ely's Ford. After ordering three volleys of musket fire at the Union troops below, Stuart canceled the attack and left to assume his command at Chancellorsville. (Erected 1981 by the Spotsylvania Historical Association.) *Spotsylvania Co.: Rte. 610, .54 mile e. of Culpeper Co. line.*

J-39* WOUNDING OF JACKSON

Stonewall Jackson, coming from the west, surprised Howard's Corps of the Army of the Potomac, May 2, 1863. Howard retreated along this road toward Chancellorsville, pursued by the Confederates. Here, Jackson, in the early evening, moving in front of his line of battle to reconnoitre, fell, mortally wounded by his own men. *Spotsylvania Co.: Rte. 3, .9 mi w. of Chancellorsville.*

J-40 BATTLE OF CHANCELLORSVILLE

Hooker reached this point, April 30, 1863; next day he entrenched, with his left wing on the river and his right wing on this road several miles west. That wing was surprised by Jackson and driven back here, May 2. The Confederates stormed the position here, May 3. The Union army withdrew northward, May 5–6, 1863. *Spotsylvania Co.: Rte. 3, at Chancellorsville.*

J-42 SPOTSWOOD'S FURNACE

Four miles north on this side road is the site of an ancient iron furnace established about 1716 by Governor Alexander Spotswood, the first fully equipped iron furnace in the colonies. Iron was hauled along this road to the Rappahannock River for shipment. William Byrd visited the furnace in 1732 and described it. *Spotsylvania Co.: Rte. 3, 5.4 miles w. of Fredericksburg.*

J-60 CHATHAM

Here is Chatham, built about 1750 by William Fitzhugh. Here Robert E. Lee came to court his wife. In the battle of Fredericksburg, December 13, 1862, the house was occupied by General Sumner. It was General Hooker's headquarters for a time, 1863. *Stafford Co.: Rte. 3, .2 mile east of Fredericksburg.*

J-61 WASHINGTON'S BOYHOOD HOME

At this place, George Washington lived most of the time from 1739 to 1747. Here, according to tradition, he cut down the cherry tree. Washington's father died here in 1743; the farm was his share of the paternal estate. His mother lived here until 1771. *Stafford Co.: Rte. 3, 1.1 miles e. of Fredericksburg.*

J-62 LAMB'S CREEK CHURCH

This old church was probably built before 1750. The stepping stone at the door bears the date 1782. Near here Kilpatrick's Union cavalry, on a raid to destroy gunboats at Port Conway, fought a skirmish, September 1, 1863. *King George Co.: Rte. 3, 5.5 miles w. of King George.*

J-63 MARMION

Two miles north is Marmion, probably built by John Fitzhugh early in the eighteenth century and later named for Scott's poem. About 1785 it passed from Philip Fitzhugh to George Washington's favorite nephew, who died there. The place has come down in the Lewis family in direct line from him. The richly decorated interior is one of the best in Virginia. *King George Co.: Rte. 3, 2.3 miles w. of King George.*

J-64 BRISTOL IRON WORKS

On the river a short distance south is the site of the Bristol Iron Works, which were projected by John King and Company of Bristol, England, and established in 1721 by John Tayloe, John Lomax and associates. The works, which were on the Foxhall's Mill property owned in 1670 by Major Underwood, were in operation in 1729 and later. *Westmoreland Co.: Rte. 3, 2.6 miles w. of Oak Grove.*

J-65 ST. PAUL'S CHURCH

Eight miles northeast is St. Paul's Church, built about 1766. The building was in a ruinous condition in 1812 but was repaired by the State and used both as a church and as a schoolhouse. About 1828 it once more became exclusively a church. *King George Co.: Rte. 3, 1.5 miles w. of King George.*

J-66* HISTORIC PORT CONWAY

Six miles southeast is Port Conway on the Rappahannock. At the Conway place there, James Madison, fourth President of the United States, was born, 1751. There Kilpatrick's Union cavalry shelled two gunboats captured by the Confederates, September 1, 1863. There John Wilkes Booth, assassin of Lincoln, crossed the river, April 24, 1865. *King George Co.: Rte. 3, 2.7 miles e. of King George.*

J-67 HISTORY AT OAK GROVE

Here George Washington, while living at Wakefield with a brother, went to school, 1744–1746. Here Union cavalry came on a raid through the Northern Neck, May, 1863. Several miles north of this place, James Monroe, fifth President of the United States, was born, 1758. *Westmoreland Co.: Rte. 3, at Oak Grove.*

J-68 WESTMORELAND ASSOCIATION

At Leedstown, seven miles south, an association was formed to resist the enforcement of the Stamp Act, February 27, 1766. The resolutions, drafted by the Revolutionary leader Richard Henry Lee, were one of the first protests against the Stamp Act and influenced public opinion in all the Colonies. *Westmoreland Co.: Rte. 3, at Oak Grove.*

J-68* LEEDSTOWN

Six miles south on the Rappahannock River. An Indian village stood here in 1608; a settlement was made at the place in 1683. In February, 1766, a public meeting was held there at which resolutions were adopted denouncing the Stamp Act. *Westmoreland Co.: Rte. 3, s. of Colonial Beach.*

J-69* THE WASHINGTON HOME

John Washington settled at Wakefield in 1665. Augustine Washington, father of George Washington, was born here in 1694. George Washington was born here, February 22, 1732. In 1734 Washington's father moved away, but George Washington lived here again in 1744–46. Here at Wakefield are the tombs of the early Washingtons. *Westmoreland Co.: Rte. 3, 2.8 miles s.e. of Oak Grove.*

J-69-a POPES CREEK EPISCOPAL CHURCH

On this site, a part of "Longwood," stood Popes Creek Episcopal Church, built about 1744 on land given by the McCarty family. The Lees and Washingtons worshipped here. About 1826 it fell into disuse and was burned as being unsafe. *Westmoreland Co.: Rte. 3, 4.8 miles s.e. of Oak Grove.*

J-69-b WASHINGTON'S BIRTHPLACE

Two miles north, on Pope's Creek, stood the house where George Washington was born, February 22, 1732. It was completed by his father, Augustine, about 1726. The present Memorial House is in the style of the original, which burned about 1779. *Westmoreland Co.: Rte. 3, 2.8 miles s.e. of Oak Grove.*

J-70* LEE'S BIRTHPLACE

Two miles east is Stratford, built about 1727 by Thomas Lee. There January 20, 1732, was born Richard Henry Lee, who introduced the resolution in the Continental Congress for the Declaration of Independence. There Robert E. Lee was born, January 19, 1807. *Westmoreland Co.: Rte. 3, 4 miles n.w. of Montross.*

J-71 OLD WESTMORELAND COURTHOUSE

At a public meeting here, on June 22, 1774, resolutions of Richard Henry Lee offering aid to Boston, whose port had been closed by the British government, were adopted. Here, on May 23, 1775, the Westmoreland Committee of Safety passed resolutions denouncing the royal governor, Lord Dunmore, for seizing the colony's powder supply at Williamsburg. *Westmoreland Co.: Rte. 3, at Montross.*

J-72 NOMINI HALL

The house was built about 1730 and burned in 1850. It was not rebuilt. Only some poplar trees remain. A fine colonial mansion, it was the home of the celebrated "Councilor" Robert Carter. Philip Fithian, tutor at Nomini Hall, 1773–74, wrote his well-known "Journal" there. *Westmoreland Co.: Rte. 3, at Templemans Cross Roads.*

J-73 MENOKIN

Near here is Menokin, home of Francis Lightfoot Lee, signer of the Declaration of Independence. Lee was a member of the Continental Congress from 1775 to 1779 and died at Menokin in 1797. *Richmond Co.: Rte. 690, 4.1 miles north of Warsaw.*

J-74* CHANTILLY

One mile beyond Stratford is Chantilly, the home of Richard Henry Lee, a leader in the American Revolution and the proposer of the Declaration of Independence. Lee moved there about 1764 and died there in 1794. The house, which was named for a chateau in France, was destroyed many years ago. *Westmoreland Co.: Rte. 3, 4 miles n.w. of Montross.*

J-75 WESTMORELAND STATE PARK

This park was developed by the National Park Service, Interior Department, through the Civilian Conservation Corps, in conjunction with the Virginia Conservation Commission. It covers 1300 acres and was opened June 15, 1936. It was originally included in "Clifts Plantation," patented by Nathaniel Pope about 1650, and became a part of Stratford estate when purchased by Thomas Lee in 1716. *Westmoreland Co.: Rte. 3, 4.7 miles n.w. of Montross.*

J-76 STRATFORD AND CHANTILLY

Two miles east of Stratford, built about 1725 by Thomas Lee (1690–1750). President of the Virginia Council and father of Richard Henry Lee & Francis Lightfoot Lee, both signers of the Declaration of Independence. Here also was born Robert Edward Lee (1807–1870). Three miles east of Stratford stood Chantilly, the home of Richard Henry Lee in his later years. *Westmoreland Co.: Rte. 3, 4 miles n.w. of Montross.*

J-77 NORTH FARNHAM CHURCH

This is the church of North Farnham Parish, built about 1737. In 1814, a skirmish was fought here between raiders from Admiral Cockburn's British fleet and Virginia militia; bullet holes are still visible in the walls. The church was used as a stable by Union soldiers, 1863–65. It was restored in 1872, damaged by fire in 1887 and restored again in 1924. *Richmond Co.: Rte. 692, at Farnham.*

J-78 CYRUS GRIFFIN'S BIRTHPLACE

Four and a half miles southwest was born Cyrus Griffin, July 16, 1748. Educated in England, he served in the Virginia House of Delegates, 1777–8, 1786–7. He was a member of the Continental Congress, 1787–1788, in which last year he was president of the body. Griffin was president of the court of admiralty, commissioner to the Creeks, 1789, and a United States district judge, He died at Yorktown, December 14, 1810. *Richmond Co.: Rte. 2, 2.8 miles s.e. of Farnham.*

J-79 NOMINI BAPTIST CHURCH

Nomini Baptist Church was established on 29 April 1786 with 17 members. By 1809 it was reputedly the largest Baptist church in Virginia with 875 members. The original meetinghouse, built nearby in 1790 on land donated by a charter member, Captain Joseph Pierce, was replaced in 1858–59 by the present brick church. During the past two centuries Nomini Baptist Church has had 27 ministers, beginning with Elder Henry Toler, and is considered the mother church of ten congregations in three counties. *Westmoreland Co.: Rte. 3 at Rte. 202.*

J-80 BIRTHPLACE OF WASHINGTON'S MOTHER

Seven-tenths mile west is Epping Forest. The land was patented by Colonel Joseph Ball, who died there in 1711. His daughter, Mary Ball, mother of George Washington, was born there in 1707/8. The house incorporates parts of the original structure. *Lancaster Co.: Rte. 3, 9.3 miles e. of Farnham.*

J-80* EPPING FOREST

In 1704 Colonel Joseph Ball obtained land here. Here, in 1707, was born Mary Ball, George Washington's mother. The old house burned some years ago, but the cook house and coach house remain. *Lancaster Co.: Rte. 3, 12 miles e. of Warsaw.*

J-81 BEWDLEY

About three miles southeast, on the north bank of the Rappahannock River. Bewdley was one of the most unusual houses in Virginia, with two rows of dormer windows. It was built by Major James Ball, cousin of Washington's mother, about 1750. The first steamboat on the river touched at its wharf. The house burned in 1917; only one chimney remains. *Lancaster Co.: Rte. 354, 2.13 miles e. of Rte. 3.*

J-82 ST. MARY'S WHITE CHAPEL

Three miles southwest. A church was built there in 1669, and the tablets are of that date. The present church was built in 1741 and was later remodeled. St. Mary's White Chapel parish was united with Christ Church parish in 1752. The tombs of the Balls, ancestors and relatives of George Washington, are there. *Lancaster Co.: Rte. 3, at Lively.*

J-83 WHITE MARSH CHURCH

This church, founded in 1792, was the mother church of Methodism in the Northern Neck of Virginia. The first camp meeting in this section was held here. Bishops Enoch George and David S. Doggett were members of this church. Bishop Joshua Soule, author of the constitution of the General Conference of the American Methodist Church, preached at meetings here. *Lancaster Co.: Rte 3.6 miles n.w. of Kilmarnock.*

J-85 COROTOMAN

This place was three miles south. Little remains of the house. John Carter obtained patents for a large grant here before 1654, but the place is better known as the home of his son, Robert ("King") Carter. In April, 1814, the British, raiding in the Chesapeake region, pillaged the plantation. *Lancaster Co.: Rte. 646, .66 mile w. of Rte. 3.*

J-86 CHRIST CHURCH

Christ Church was built in 1732, on the site of an older church by Robert ("King") Carter, who reserved one quarter of it for seating his tenants and servants. It is one of the very few colonial churches in America that have [*sic*] never been altered, a typical early eighteenth-century structure. Robert Carter is buried here. *Lancaster Co.: Rte. 646, .66 mile w. of Rte. 3.*

J-87 WINDMILL POINT

Troops were stationed here in November, 1813. Here, April 23, 1814, the British made a landing and pillaged a vessel. They were driven off by militia stationed across the creek. *Lancaster Co.: Rte. 695, 6.5 miles e. of Rte. 3 in Whitestone.*

J-88 DITCHLEY AND COBBS

Ditchley, five miles northeast, was patented in 1651 by Colonel Richard Lee. The first house dated from 1687; the present house was built by Kendall Lee in 1752. Cobbs Hall, near by, was acquired by Richard Lee, probably before 1651. A house was built there by Charles Lee in 1720; the present house is modern. *Northumberland Co.: Rte. 200, 1.4 miles n. of Kilmarnock.*

J-89 FIRST AMERICAN WOMAN MISSIONARY TO CHINA

Here was born, October 28, 1817, Henrietta Hall (daughter of Colonel Addison Hall), first American woman missionary to China. She married Rev. J. Lewis Shuck, and was sent with him to China by the Baptist Board of Foreign Missions, arriving there in September, 1836. She died at Hong Kong, November 27, 1844. *Lancaster Co.: Rte. 3, at Kilmarnock.*

J-90 BARFORD

Located one mile south on land lying between the eastern and western branches of the Corotoman River, is the site of Barford, the dwelling of Captain Thomas Carter who was living there by 1674. A gift from his father-in-law, Edward Dale, the property remained in the Carter family until 1782 when it was sold to Colonel James Gordon, Jr. by Edward Carter, great-grandson of Captain Thomas Carter. *Lancaster Co.: Rte. 604 at Rte. 611.*

J-91 A. T. WRIGHT HIGH SCHOOL

Albert Terry Wright (1871–1944) was born in Hanover County, Virginia. He taught in the black schools of Richmond and, by 1908, at White Stone in Lancaster County. By 1921 Wright was principal of the county's first high school for blacks, which was constructed largely with funds raised by black residents. Named in his honor, A. T. Wright High School served black students until 1959, when the county opened Brookvale High School. The history of the man and his school exemplified the struggle for education by Virginia's rural blacks. *Lancaster Co.: Rte. 637, .19 mile w. of Rte. 3.*

JD-1 BELLE BOYD AND JACKSON

Near here Stonewall Jackson was met by the spy, Belle Boyd, and informed of the position of the Union troops at Front Royal, May 24, 1862. Jackson was advancing northward, attempting to get between Banks' army and Winchester. *Warren Co.: Rte. 340, 3 miles s.w. of Front Royal.*

JD-2 WILLIAM E. CARSON

William E. Carson, of Riverton, was the first chairman of the Virginia Conservation Commission, 1926–34. As such he was a pioneer and leading spirit in the establishment of the Shenandoah National Park and Skyline Drive; the Colonial National Historical Park; the state parks, and the state system of historical markers. *Warren Co.: Rte. 340, at Front Royal.*

JD-8 FIRST SETTLER (GREEN MEADOW)

To the west was the home of Adam Miller (1703–1783) one of the first Europeans to settle in the Valley. Property remained in the Miller (originally Mueller) family from the 1740s through 1936. *Rockingham Co.: Rte. 340, .5 mile n. of Elkton.*

JD-10 BATTLE OF PORT REPUBLIC

The cross road here roughly divides the Confederate and Union lines in the battle of June 9, 1862. Jackson attacked Shields, coming southward to join Fremont, but was repulsed. Reinforced by Ewell, Jackson attacked again and drove Shields from the field. At the same time he burned the bridge at Port Republic, preventing Fremont from coming to Shields' aid. *Rockingham Co.: Rte. 340, 3 miles n. of Grottoes.*

JD-14 JARMAN'S GAP

Five miles east is Jarman's Gap, formerly known as Woods' Gap. Through this pass Michael Woods, his three sons and three sons-in-law (Andrew, Peter, William Wallace), coming from Pennsylvania via Shenandoah Valley, crossed into Albemarle County in 1734—pioneers in settling this section. In 1780–81 British prisoners taken at Saratoga went through the gap en route to Winchester. In June 1862 part of Jackson's army, moving to join Lee at Richmond, crossed the mountain here. *Augusta Co.: Rte. 340, 1.2 miles n. of Waynesboro.*

JD-15 JOHN COLTER

John Colter, born in Stuart's Draft about 1775, was a member of the northwest expedition led by Meriwether Lewis and William Clark (1804–1806). During his subsequent, solitary explorations of the West, Colter traversed the area now comprising Yellowstone National Park and discovered several passes through the Rocky Mountains suitable for wagon trains. His escape from the Blackfeet Indians following a footrace for his life has become a legend of the West. Colter died in Missouri in 1813. *Augusta Co.: Rte. 340, 2.5 miles s. of I-64.*

JE-1 JACKSON'S MARCH TO FREDERICKSBURG

Stonewall Jackson, on his march from Winchester to Fredericksburg, preceding the battle of Fredericksburg, camped here, November 26, 1862. *Madison Co.: Rte. 231, at Madison.*

JE-2 KNIGHTS OF THE GOLDEN HORSESHOE

Near here Governor Alexander Spotswood and his troop of gentlemen, Knights of the Golden Horseshoe, on their way to explore the land beyond the mountains, camped on August 31, 1716. *Madison Co.: Rte. 15, 3.3 miles n. of Orange.*

JE-3 JAMES L. KEMPER RESIDENCE

This Greek Revival–style house was built about 1852 for state senator Thomas N. Welch. In 1868 James Lawson Kemper (1823–1895) purchased it from his mother-in-law, Mrs. Belfield Cave. Kemper, an attorney, represented Madison County in the House of Delegates (1853–1863), served as speaker (1861–1863), led a brigade in the Civil War, was wounded in Pickett's Charge at Gettysburg, and served as governor of Virginia (1874–1878). In 1882 he moved from Madison to Walnut Hills in Orange County. *Madison Co.: Bus. Rte. 29, .1 mile s. of Madison.*

JE-4 HEBRON CHURCH

One mile south stands Hebron Church, the oldest Lutheran church in the South, built about 1740. The first communion service bears the date, May 13, 1727; another the date, March 28, 1737. The organ was built in 1800. *Madison Co.: Rte. 231, 9.5 miles n. of Madison.*

JE-6 MAURY'S SCHOOL

Just north was a classical school conducted by the Rev. James Maury, Rector of Fredericksville Parish from 1754 to 1769. Thomas Jefferson was one of Maury's students. Matthew Fontaine Maury, the "Pathfinder of the Seas," was Maury's grandson. *Albemarle Co.: Rte. 231, 4.5 miles s.e. of Gordonsville.*

JE-15 A CAMP OF STONEWALL JACKSON'S

Just to the north, on the night of November 25, 1862, Stonewall Jackson, with his corps, camped. He was on his way to join Lee at Fredericksburg. *Madison Co.: Rte. 670, 1 mile n. of Criglersville.*

JE-35 LEE'S STOPPING PLACE

Here at Flannagan's (Trice's) Mill, Robert E. Lee spent the night of April 13–14, 1865, on his journey from Appomattox to Richmond. *Cumberland Co.: Rte. 690 at Rte. 612, 8.8 miles s. of Columbia.*

JE-36 CLIFTON

One mile north; home of Carter Henry Harrison, land patented, 1723. Harrison, as a member of the Cumberland Committee of Safety, wrote the instructions for independence (adopted April 22) presented by the county delegates to the Virginia convention of May, 1776. Apparently this was the first of such declarations publicly approved. The convention declared for independence. *Cumberland Co.: Rte. 690 at 605, 11 miles s. of Columbia.*

JF-15 WALNUT GROVE

Archibald Stuart—Revolutionary soldier, legislator, and judge was born here March 19, 1757, at the home of his grandfather and namesake, an early settler. The property was acquired by William A. Pratt in 1868 and G. Julian Pratt in 1900. *Augusta Co.: Rte. 340, .3 miles s. of Waynesboro city limits.*

JJ-2* LEE'S HEADQUARTERS

Half a mile west Robert E. Lee had his headquarters from December, 1863, to May, 1864, while his army held the line of the Rapidan River. Lee left this place to begin the Wilderness Campaign early in May, 1864. *Orange Co.: Rte. 20, 1.6 miles e. of Orange.*

JJ-4 BLOOMSBURY

A mile north is Bloomsbury, estate of the pioneer, James Taylor, ancestor of Presidents James Madison and Zachary Taylor. He was a member of Spotswood's expedition over the mountains in 1716. *Orange Co.: Rte. 20, 3.3 miles e. of Orange.*

JJ-6 CAMPAIGN OF SECOND MANASSAS

Two miles north, near Pisgah Church, Jackson, Ewell, and A. P. Hill camped, August 15–20, 1862, awaiting Longstreet. *Orange Co.: Rte. 20, 5.7 miles e. of Orange.*

JJ-10 MINE RUN CAMPAIGN

Meade, advancing south from the Rapidan River to attack Lee, found him in an entrenched position here on November 28, 1863. Heavy skirmishing went on until December 1. Then Meade, thinking Lee's lines too strong to assault, retired across the Rapidan in time to avoid a counter-attack by the Confederates. *Orange Co.: Rte. 20, 6.6 miles e. of Unionville.*

JJ-12* STUART'S ESCAPE

Near here, early morning, August 18, 1862, General J. E. B. Stuart narrowly escaped capture. *Orange Co.: 4.1 miles e. of Unionville.*

JJ-15 ROBINSON'S TAVERN

Near here stood ancient Robinson's Tavern. Here Meade wished to concentrate his army in the Mine Run Campaign, November, 1863, but one corps, coming up late, disarranged his plans. Here Ewell, moving east from Orange in the Wilderness Campaign, camped on May 4, 1864. *Orange Co.: Rte. 20, at Locust Grove.*

JJ-20 BATTLE OF THE WILDERNESS

Ewell's Corps, the left wing of Lee's army, moving down this road from Orange, came into conflict near here with Warren's Corps of Grant's army, May 5, 1864. The fight moved to and fro until Ewell finally drove Warren back and entrenched here. Late the next afternoon, May 6, Ewell attacked the Unionists. Meanwhile, two miles south on the Orange Plank Road, the right wing of Lee's army was engaged with Grant's left wing. *Orange Co.: Rte. 20, 2.9 miles e. of Locust Grove.*

JJ-24 CAMPAIGN OF 1781

Lafayette, marching southward from Raccoon Ford, camped here, June 8–9, 1781. *Orange Co.: Rte. 20, 2.6 miles e. of Unionville (at Rhodesville).*

JJ-25 GASPAR TOCHMAN

A mile south is the unmarked grave of Gaspar Tochman (1797–1880), a major in the Polish army who participated in the failed 1830 revolt against Russia. Exiled, in 1837 he immigrated to the United States, where he practiced law, wrote, and lectured. During the Civil War he recruited the Polish Brigade (14th and 15th Louisiana regiments) of Jackson's Corps. A colonel in the Confederate army, he sought unsuccessfully the rank of brigadier general. Tochman settled here in 1866 and served as the European agent for the Virginia Board of Immigration. *Spotsylvania Co.: Rte. 621, .25 mile s. of Rte. 611.*

JP-6 BIRTHPLACE OF MONROE

In this vicinity stood the Monroe home where James Monroe, fifth President of the United States, was born, April 28, 1758. His father was Spence Monroe and his mother, Elizabeth Jones. He left home at the age of sixteen to enter William and Mary College and left college to enter the army. *Westmoreland Co.: Rte. 205, 1.8 miles s. of Colonial Beach.*

JQ-1 LEESYLVANIA STATE PARK

This 508-acre park was donated to the Commonwealth in 1978 by Daniel K. Ludwig and was opened on June 17, 1989. The park, whose name means "Lee's Woods," is the ancestral home of the famous Lee family of Virginia. The land, which was patented in 1658, was the home of Henry Lee II and Henry "Light Horse Harry" Lee III, father of General Robert E. Lee. Nearby Freestone Point was the site of a Confederate artillery emplacement which successfully blockaded the Potomac River during the Civil War. *Prince William Co.: Rte. 610, 1.53 miles e. of Rte. 1.*

JT-2 NOMINY CHURCH

One of the two churches of Cople Parish. It was built in 1704 on land given by Youell Watkins, and was replaced in 1755 by a brick church on the same site. George Washington attended services here twice in 1768. The last colonial church was burned (1814) by the British Admiral Cockburn, who carried off the church silver. The present building was erected about 1852. The first Nominy Church of 1655 stood on the north side of the river opposite this place. *Westmoreland Co.: Rte. 202, 3.7 miles e. of Templemans Cross Roads.*

JT-3 THE GLEBE

Five miles north is the home of the rectors of Cople Parish, one of whom, Walter Jones, married Washington's parents, March 6, 1731. Here lived Thomas Smith, rector of the parish, 1764–1799, and chairman of the county Committee of Safety, 1775. He entertained Washington, May 25, 1771. The house is possibly the oldest in the Northern Neck. *Westmoreland Co.: Rte. 202, 4.4 miles e. of Templemans Cross Roads.*

JT-4 WASHINGTON'S MOTHER

At Sandy Point, seven and a half miles east, Mary Ball, Washington's mother, spent her youth in the home of her guardian, George Eskridge. There she was married to Augustine Washington, March, 1731. She is supposed to have named her eldest son for George Eskridge. *Westmoreland Co.: Rte. 202, 4.8 miles n.w. of Callao.*

JT-5 BUSHFIELD

A mile and a half east. This was the home of John Augustine Washington, younger brother of George Washington, who visited here. Here was born, in 1762, Bushrod Washington, who became a justice of the United States Supreme Court in 1798, and died in 1829. He inherited Mount Vernon. *Westmoreland Co.: Rte. 202, 4.4 miles e. of Templemans Cross Roads.*

JT-6 RICHARD HENRY LEE'S GRAVE

A mile and a half north, in the Lee burying ground, is the grave of Richard Henry Lee, who died, June 19, 1794. Lee was one of the first leaders of the American Revolution. On June 7, 1776, he introduced a resolution in the Continental Congress for a declaration of independence, and argued for it, June 7–10. The declaration was signed, July 4, 1776. *Westmoreland Co.: Rte. 202, 8.8 miles s.e. of Templemans Cross Roads.*

JT-7 YEOCOMICO CHURCH

Two miles east. Built in 1655 of oak timbers sheathed with clapboards. Rebuilt of brick in 1706. In this vicinity Mary Ball lived under the tutelage of Colonel George Eskridge, of Sandy Point, from 1721 until her marriage to Augustine Washington in 1730, and attended church here. In 1906 an association was formed to preserve the church. *Westmoreland Co.: Rte. 202, 8.1 miles n.w. of Callao.*

Two miles east, on picturesque Yeocomico River, is Kinsale, the founding of which the Assembly ordered in 1705. The town was established in 1784. Near by at the old home of the Bailey family, "The Great House," is the tomb of Midshipman James B. Sigourney, who in command of the sloop "Asp" fell in an engagement with the British in Yeocomico River, June 14, 1813. *Westmoreland Co.: Rte. 202, 4.8 miles n.w. of Callao.*

JT-9*   COAN RIVER

This is a head stream of the Coan River, which flows into the Potomac. On this river Captain John Smith had an encounter with Indians in 1608. Marylanders made the first settlement in this region about 1640. In October, 1814, a force of British troops came up the Coan River and marched to Heathsville. *Northumberland Co.: Rte. 360, 2.2 miles w. of Heathsville.*

JT-12   NORTHUMBERLAND HOUSE AND
        MANTUA

Five miles northeast is the site of Northumberland House, built by the third Peter Presley, who was murdered in 1750. He was the last male descendant of the first William Presley, who settled there and who was a burgess as early as 1647. Mantua, near by, was built by James Smith, who died in 1832. It is a good house of the old Virginia type. *Northumberland Co.: Rte. 360, 1 mile e. of Heathsville.*

JT-15   LEEDSTOWN

Here at the then thriving port of Leedstown on February 27, 1766, ten years before the Declaration of Independence, the Leedstown Resolutions (or Westmoreland Association) were drawn. This association, a protest against the Stamp Act and a pledge of mutual aid in event of its execution, was signed by 115 men from Westmoreland and surrounding counties. *Westmoreland Co.: Rte. 637, at Leedstown.*

JT-16   SANDY POINT

Here at Sandy Point, Mary Ball, George Washington's Mother, spent her youth in the home of her Guardian, Colonel George Eskridge. Here she married Augustine Washington in March 1731. She is supposed to have named her eldest son, George, for Colonel Eskridge. *Westmoreland Co.: Rte. 604, at Sandy Point.*

JX-5   MORATTICO BAPTIST CHURCH

On the hill is Morattico church, organized in 1778, the mother Baptist Church of the Northern Neck. The present building was erected in 1856. Lewis Lunsford, first pastor, is buried here. *Northumberland Co.: Rte. 200, 2.8 miles n. of Kilmarnock.*

K-1   CUMBERLAND GAP

This pass was long the gateway to the West. On April 13, 1750, Dr. Thomas Walker reached the gap, which he named for the Duke of Cumberland, son of George II. A few years later Daniel Boone and numberless pioneers passed through it on the way to Kentucky. In August, 1863, Cumberland Gap was captured by a Union army under General Ambrose E. Burnside. *Lee Co.: Rte. 58, at Cumberland Gap.*

K-3 INDIAN MOUND

The knoll a short distance to the north is an Indian burial mound. The Cherokees were the principal tribe inhabiting this region. *Lee Co.: Rte. 58, 2 miles w. of Rose Hill.*

K-4 COLONIAL FORT

Near here Joseph Martin established a fort in 1768. It consisted of five or six cabins surrounded by a strong stockade. Indians soon forced the settlers to abandon this fort. *Lee Co.: Rte. 58, at Rose Hill.*

K-5 INDIAN MASSACRE

In this valley, in June, 1785, Indians led by the notorious half breed, Benge, massacred the family of Archibald Scott, killing the father and five children and taking the mother into captivity. She later escaped. *Lee Co.: Rte. 58, at Stickleyville.*

K-6 THOMPSON SETTLEMENT CHURCH

This Baptist church, a mile southeast, is the oldest church in Lee County. It was organized in 1800; the original site was on Powell's River, a short distance west. James Kinney was the first pastor. The church was removed to the present site in 1822. *Lee Co.: Rte. 758, 10.2 miles s.w. of Jonesville.*

K-7 HANGING ROCK

The cliffs to the north were a familiar landmark along the Wilderness road which was blazed by Daniel Boone in March, 1775, and which was the principal route from Virginia to Kentucky. They are part of the Cumberland Mountains. *Lee Co.: Rte. 58, .25 mile w. of Ewing.*

K-8 DOCTOR STILL'S BIRTHPLACE

Andrew Taylor Still, physician and founder of osteopathy, was born two miles southwest, near the Natural Bridge of Lee County, August 6, 1828. Dr. Still served in the War between the States. He established the first American school of osteopathy in 1892 at Kirksville, Missouri. He died there, December 12, 1917. *Lee Co.: Rte. 58, at w. entrance of Jonesville.*

K-9 JONESVILLE METHODIST CAMP GROUND

This Camp Ground was established in 1810 as a place for religious services for the Methodists of Lee County on lands given by Elkanah Wynn. In June 1827, Rev. Abraham Still, Daniel Dickenson, George Morris, Evans Peery, Henry Thompson, Elkanah Wynn and James Woodward were appointed trustees and the present auditorium was built in 1827–28. The massive oak columns were hewn by Henry Woodward, David Orr, Robert Wynn and Rev. Joseph Haskew. *Lee Co.: Rte. 58, 1 mile w. of Jonesville.*

K-10 JONESVILLE

This town was established in 1794 as the county seat of Lee County and was named for Frederick Jones. Here on January 3, 1864, General William E. Jones, assisted by Colonel A. L. Pridemore, defeated a Union force, capturing the battalion. Union troops burned the courthouse in 1864. The present courthouse was erected in 1933. The town was incorporated in 1834, and reincorporated in 1901. *Lee Co.: Rte. 58, at Jonesville.*

K-11 GATE CITY

The town was laid off in 1815 as the county seat of Scott County. The original name of Winfield, for General Winfield Scott, was changed to Estillville for Judge Benjamin Estill. In 1886, the name was changed to Gate City because of its situation in Moccasin Gap, through which the old Wilderness Road to the West passed. It was incorporated, 1892. *Scott Co.: Rte. 71 and Rte. 23, at Gate City.*

K-12 FARIS STATION

Near by stood the home and tavern of Elisha Faris, an early station on the Boone trail to Kentucky. Indians led by Chief Benge here massacred members of the Faris family in 1791. *Scott Co.: Rte. 71 and Rte. 23, at Gate City.*

K-13 FORT BLACKMORE

Ten miles north, on Clinch River near the mouth of Stony Creek, stood Fort Blackmore, the first settlement in Scott County, established about 1771. It was attacked by Indians several times but was never captured. *Scott Co.: Rte. 71 and Rte. 23, at Gate City.*

K-14 McCONNELL'S BIRTHPLACE

Four miles south was born John Preston McConnell, noted educator. He taught in Milligan College, the University of Virginia and Emory and Henry College. He was president of the Radford State Teachers' College, 1913–1937. Dr. McConnell was president of Southwestern Virginia, Incorporated, and was associated with many cultural agencies. He was active in every phase of educational work, writing several books and many articles. *Scott Co.: Rte. 23 and Rte. 58, at Weber City.*

K-15 BIG MOCCASIN GAP

In March, 1775, Daniel Boone made a road through this gap to Boonesboro, Kentucky. It followed the original Indian path and was known as the Wilderness Road. For a long time it was the main route to Kentucky from the East. *Scott Co.: Rte. 23 and Rte. 58, at Weber City.*

K-16 DONELSON'S INDIAN LINE

John Donelson's line, surveyed after the treaty of Lochaber with the Indians, 1770, crossed the road here. This line separated Indian territory from land open to settlement. Violations of the line by settlers contributed to Dunmore's War, 1774. *Scott Co.: Rte. 23 and Rte. 58, at Weber City.*

K-17 HOUSTON'S FORT

The first settlement in what is now Scott County was established on this site by Thomas McCulloch in 1769. In 1771, the settlement was abandoned in fear of Indian attack. William Houston, assignee of Thomas McCulloch, constructed a fort here in 1774. During an attack on the fort by a large force of Cherokee Indians in 1776, Samuel Cowan, a messenger, was killed and scalped. *Scott Co.: Rte. 613, 6.8 miles s. of Rte. 71.*

K-18 PATRICK PORTER

Patrick Porter was among the early pioneer settlers in present Scott County. Nearby on Fall Creek is the site of Porter's Mill, built by Porter in 1774, the earliest licensed mill on waters of the Clinch River. Porter is also credited with the erection of a fort house in the same year to protect residents from Indian attacks. His son Samuel travelled with Daniel Boone to Kentucky in 1773 and in 1778 answered Boone's request for assistance in defending Boonsborough. *Scott Co.: Rte. 65, .5 mile e. of Rte. 72, in Dungannon.*

K-19   SEVEN MILE FORD

The place takes its name from the highway ford on the Holston, seven miles west of Royal Oak. The land here belonged to General William Campbell, hero of King's Mountain, 1780. It descended to the wife of John M. Preston. The town originated as a railroad station. It was occupied in Stoneman's raid of December, 1864. *Smyth Co.: Rte. 11, 2.9 miles e. of Chilhowie.*

K-20   WILLIAM CAMPBELL'S GRAVE

A short distance north are the home site and grave of William Campbell, noted Indian fighter and commander of troops at the battle of King's Mountain, 1780. Later he was with Lafayette in eastern Virginia until his death, August 22, 1781, shortly before the siege of Yorktown. *Smyth Co.: Rte. 11, 2 miles e. of Chilhowie.*

K-21   FARTHEST WEST, 1750

Near here, in 1750, Dr. Thomas Walker, on his first journey southwest, assisted Samuel Stalnaker in building his cabin. At that time this was the farthest west settlement. *Smyth Co.: Rte. 11, at Chilhowie.*

K-22   CHILHOWIE

An Indian name meaning "Valley of Many Deer." Land was patented here by Colonel James Patton, 1746; Samuel Stalnaker, first settler, built a home here in 1750. In 1804 Robert Gannaway came here and in 1815 opened Chilhowie Springs. When the railroad came the town was called Greever's Switch, later changed to Chilhowie. It was incorporated, 1913. *Smyth Co.: Rte. 11, at Chilhowie.*

K-23*   A COLONIAL SOLDIER'S HOME

Five miles north was the home of Walter Crockett, a captain in the Point Pleasant Indian expedition of 1774 and the suppressor of a Tory rising in 1779. He was county lieutenant and clerk of Wythe County. *Wythe Co.: Rte. 11, at e. entrance of Wytheville.*

K-24*   EARLY CHURCH

Two hundred yards south is the site of the Old Upper Congregation Presbyterian Church, organized in 1776. *Smyth Co.: Rte. 11, .6 mile e. of Marion.*

K-25   NEW RIVER

This stream was reached by the explorers, Batts and Fallam, September, 1671. The expedition was sent out by Abraham Wood, who lived at Fort Henry (Petersburg). The river was known as Wood's River until renamed New River. *Pulaski Co.: Rte. 11, .5 mile n.w. of Radford.*

K-26   BATTLE OF MARION

Here, on December 17–18, 1864, General Stoneman, raiding to Saltville, fought an engagement with John C. Breckinridge, Confederate commander in southwest Virginia. *Smyth Co.: Rte. 11, at Marion e. corp. limits.*

K-27   SITE OF COLONIAL HOME

Royal Oak, home of Arthur Campbell, Indian fighter and Revolutionary leader, who settled here in 1769, stood three hundred yards south. The house was a neighborhood fort and in it, in 1832, the first court of Smyth County was held. *Smyth Co.: Rte. 11 at Rte. 16, in Marion.*

K-28 SALTVILLE HISTORY

William King built salt works there in 1795. In October, 1864, Union troops, raiding Saltville, were driven off; but in December, 1864, the works were destroyed by General Stoneman. *Smyth Co.: Rte. 107, 1 mile s. of Saltville.*

K-29 FIRST SETTLEMENT

About five miles southwest is Dunkard Bottom, where Dr. Walker found [sic] a settlement in 1750. The fort there was built about 1756 and was the first fort in Virginia west of New River. The first store and first mill were also there. *Pulaski Co.: Rte. 11, 1.9 miles w. of Radford.*

K-30 EARLY SETTLERS

Stephen Holstein (Holston), coming here before 1748, gave his name to the river and valley. James Davis settled on this place, "Davis' Fancy," in 1748 and his home became a neighborhood fort. *Smyth Co.: Rte. 11, 8.5 miles e. of Marion.*

K-31 SITE OF MOUNT AIRY

A German settlement of colonial times had its center here. One of its leading men, Robert Doak, was a member of the House of Burgesses for Fincastle County, 1773–1775. *Wythe Co.: Rte. 11, 12.9 miles w. of Wytheville.*

K-32* DEATH OF BOONE'S SON

Near here, October 10, 1773, James Boone, son of Daniel Boone, and Henry Russell, members of Boone's party on the way to Kentucky, were surprised and killed by Indians. *Lee Co.: Rte. 58, 1 mile e. of Stickleyville.*

K-32 DEATH OF BOONE'S SON

On nearby Indian Creek, then known as Walden's Creek, James Boone, Henry Russell, and four other youths were killed by Shawnee Indians, 10 October 1773. Witnessed by a negro slave, this tragic event forced Daniel Boone to abandon his first attempt to settle Kentucky. *Lee Co.: Rte. 58 at Rte. 684, 11 miles e. of Cumberland Gap.*

K-33 HUNGRY MOTHER STATE PARK

This park was developed by the National Park Service, Interior Department, through the Civilian Conservation Corps, in conjunction with the Virginia Conservation Commission. It covers 2150 acres and was opened, June 15, 1936. It takes its name from a legend of an Indian raid in which a woman was carried off with her infant. *Smyth Co.: Rte. 16, at entrance to park, 3.75 miles n. of Rte. 11.*

K-34 MARION

The community center here was known as Royal Oak, home of Arthur Campbell, frontiersman. The place became the county seat when Smyth County was formed and was named for Francis Marion, Revolutionary hero. It was incorporated in 1832; the courthouse was built in 1834; the railroad came in 1856. A cavalry action was fought here, December 1864, in Stoneman's raid. *Smyth Co.: Smyth Co. Courthouse, at Marion.*

K-35 WYTHEVILLE

When Wythe County was formed, this place became the county seat under the name of Evansham. It was incorporated in 1839 as Wytheville. The old Wilderness Road to Cumberland Gap passed here. In July, 1863, Toland's raiders captured the town. In May, 1864, Averell passed here on a raid; the town was again occupied by Union troops in December, 1864, and April, 1865. *Wythe Co.: Rte. 11, at Wytheville.*

K-36 ANCHOR AND HOPE PLANTATION

One mile north is a plantation that was surveyed in March, 1748, and patented, in June, 1753, by Colonel John Buchanan and named by him "Anchor and Hope." There in 1792 an academy was established to teach oratory. The pioneer educator, Thomas E. Birch, was instructor and minister for the settlement. *Wythe Co.: Rte. 52, at Fort Chiswell.*

K-37 INGLESIDE

Home of Colonel R. E. Withers, Confederate officer, Lieutenant Governor of Virginia, United States Senator and Consul at Hong Kong. *Wythe Co.: Rte. 11, at e. entrance of Wytheville.*

K-38* BATTLE OF CLOYD'S MOUNTAIN

Five miles north, at Cloyd's Mountain, General George Crook, raiding south to destroy the Virginia and Tennessee railroad (N & W), met and repulsed General A. G. Jenkins in a fierce action, May 9, 1864. Jenkins was mortally wounded. *Pulaski Co.: Rte. 100, at Dublin.*

K-38 BATTLE OF CLOYD'S MOUNTAIN

In April 1864 Grant ordered Brig. Gen. George Crook to cut the Virginia & Tennessee RR in Southwest Virginia. Near Cloyd's Mountain, five miles north of Dublin, on 9 May Crook battled Confederate defenders commanded by Brig. Gen. Albert G. Jenkins. Attacking Jenkins's right flank, Crook drove him from his earthworks after a sharp engagement with heavy casualties on both sides. Jenkins was mortally wounded and lost 538 of 2,400 men (23 percent). Crook severed the railroad at Dublin and withdrew on 11 May. *Pulaski Co.: Rte. 100, 1.4 miles n. of Rte. 627.*

K-39 LEAD MINES

Nine miles south on New River. Discovered in 1756 by Colonel John Chiswell. These mines supplied lead for the patriots in the Revolutionary War. Tories attempted to seize them in 1780 but were suppressed. *Wythe Co.: Rte. 52, at Fort Chiswell.*

K-40 DRAPER'S VALLEY

To the south and west lies Draper's Valley, named for John Draper, who settled here in 1765. He moved hence from Draper's Meadows (Blacksburg), where his wife was captured by the Indians in the massacre of 1755. Six years later Draper ransomed her. He served as an officer in the Point Pleasant Indian expedition of 1774. *Pulaski Co.: Rte. 11, 1.9 miles s. of Pulaski.*

K-41 PULASKI

The town sprang up at the coming of the railroad and was first known as Martin's Tank. Governor John Floyd lived near by. The county seat was moved here from Newburn in 1894. The town, like the county, was named for Count Casimir Pulaski, killed in the siege of Savannah, 1779. It was incorporated in 1886. Zinc and iron were early industries. *Pulaski Co.: Rte. 11, at Pulaski.*

K-42 BRISTOL, VIRGINIA

The Sapling Grove tract (Bristol) was surveyed for John Tayloe, 1749. It was owned by Isaac Baker and Evan Shelby, who built a post about 1770. The Virginia tract was bought by John Goodson, whose son founded the town of Goodson, incorporated in 1856. In 1863 and 1865 it was raided by Unionists and partly burned. in 1890 it was named Bristol when incorporated as a city. *Bristol: Rte. 11, at n. corp. limits of Bristol.*

K-43 HISTORIC BRISTOL

Evan Shelby, noted Indian fighter, settled here about 1765 on a tract called "Sapling Grove." His home was a neighborhood fort, the refuge of settlers in Indian attacks. Bristol grew around this place and became an early railroad center. *Bristol: Randall Expwy. and State St., at train station.*

K-45 PAGE'S MEETING HOUSE

One mile to the north stood this Methodist Chapel, an early one in the New River area. It was built on land given in 1795 by Alexander Page. Bishop Francis Asbury preached in the Chapel in 1802 and again in 1806. *Pulaski Co.: Rte. 11, 1.25 miles w. of Radford.*

K-46 SHERWOOD ANDERSON

A prolific author whose works influenced Faulkner, Hemingway, and other writers of the American School of Realism, Anderson lived in this area from 1925 until his death in 1941. He built his home "Ripshin" near Troutdale (22 mi. S.E.) and was for a time publisher of two Smyth County weekly newspapers. He is buried here in Round Hill Cemetery. *Smyth Co.: Rte. 11, at e. corp. limits of Marion.*

K-47 KING'S MOUNTAIN MEN

From this vicinity went forth a force of Virginians, under the command of Colonel William Campbell, to fight against the British in the Carolinas, 1780. The Virginia troops played an important part in the victory of King's Mountain, South Carolina, won by the Americans over Patrick Ferguson, October 7, 1780. *Washington Co.: Rte. 11, at w. entrance of Abingdon.*

K-48 SITE OF BLACK'S FORT

The fort, built in 1776, stood a short distance to the south. Here the first court of Washington County was held, January 28, 1777. *Washington Co.: Rte. 11, at Abingdon.*

K-49 ABINGDON

First known as Wolf Hills, land was patented here by Dr. Thomas Walker in 1750. Black's Fort was built, 1776. The town of Abingdon was established in 1778 as the county seat of Washington County. A courthouse, built about 1800, was replaced in 1850. In 1862 the church bells were melted for cannon. In Stoneman's raid, December, 1864, the town was partly burned. A new courthouse was built, 1869. *Washington Co.: Rte. 11, Abingdon.*

K-64 FOUNDING OF THE FUTURE FARMERS OF VIRGINIA

The Future Farmers of Virginia (FFV) was founded on the campus of Virginia Polytechnic Institute by four members of the Agricultural Education Department in September, 1925. Developed as a statewide organization for boys enrolled in high school vocational agriculture, the FFV was used as a model for establishing the Future Farmers of America. The four founders were Walter Newman, Henry Groseclose, Edmund Magill, and Harry Sanders. *Montgomery Co.: Rte. 314 at VPI&SU, .25 mile e. of Rte. 460 Bypass.*

K-65 RADFORD

It originated as a railroad town in 1856 and was known as Central. In 1862–65 this section was in the range of Union raids; Confederates burned the bridge at Ingles Ferry to retard raiders. Incorporated in 1887 as a town, the place was incorporated as a city in 1892 and named Radford, for Dr. John B. Radford, prominent citizen. Radford State Teachers College was established here, 1913. *Radford: Rte. 11, at Radford.*

K-66 STATE TEACHERS COLLEGE AT RADFORD

A state college for women established in 1910. Opened 1913. Empowered by legislature in 1916 to grant degrees in education and in the arts and sciences. Present name authorized in 1924. The John Preston McConnell Library, named for the first president of the college, contains a valuable collection on the history of Southwest Virginia. *Radford: Rte. 11, at Radford.*

K-67 "FOTHERINGAY"

To the east is the home of Colonel George Hancock (1754–1820), Revolutionary soldier, Congressman, and father-in-law of explorer William Clark. In this vicinity George Washington and two companions escaped being ambushed by Shawnee Indians in October, 1756. *Montgomery Co.: Rte. 11, 4.5 miles w. of Roanoke County.*

K-68 CHRISTIANSBURG INDUSTRIAL INSTITUTE

In 1866, Captain Charles S. Schaeffer, a Freedmen's Bureau agent, organized a school for blacks on the hill just to the southeast. Charles L. Marshall of Tuskegee Institute became principal of the school in 1896. Under his guidance and with support from Philadelphia Quakers, a library, dormitories, classrooms, shops, and barns were constructed. Both academic and industrial classes were offered at the institute until 1947 when it became a public high school. In 1966, the institute graduated its last class, and its property was sold at public auction. *Montgomery Co.: Rte. 460 Bus., 1 mile w. of Rte. 11, in Christiansburg.*

K-70 INGLES FERRY ROAD

Ingles Ferry, several miles west, was the first rendezvous of Colonel William Byrd's expedition against the Cherokees, 1760. There Indians returning from their last foray in the New River region, 1763, were attacked by William Ingles and a party of settlers. *Montgomery Co.: Rte. 11, 1.4 miles e. of Radford.*

K-71 LEWIS-MCHENRY DUEL

In this town occurred the duel between Thomas Lewis and John McHenry in May 1808. This was the first duel with rifles known to have taken place in Virginia. It resulted in the death of both men. Dr. John Floyd, later Governor of Virginia and member of Congress, was the attending surgeon. This affair contributed to the passage in January, 1810, of the Barbour Bill outlawing dueling in Virginia. *Montgomery Co.: Rtes. 11 and 460, at Christiansburg.*

K-72 CHRISTIANSBURG

Christiansburg, originally known as "Hans' Meadows," was established in 1792 and named for Colonel William Christian, noted Colonial and Revolutionary Indian fighter. It became an important place on the route to the West. On May 10, 1864, Averell raided the town on an expedition into southwest Virginia. On April 5, Stoneman raided it while destroying railroads. *Montgomery Co.: Rte. 11, .6 mile e. of Christiansburg.*

K-73 FORT VAUSE

The fort stood on this hill. It was attacked and burned by French and Indians in June, 1756. It was rebuilt by Captain Peter Hogg, and visited by George Washington in October, 1756. *Montgomery Co.: Rte. 11, .3 mile w. of Shawsville.*

K-74 COLONIAL MANSION SITE

The home of James Campbell, a prominent colonial pioneer, who settled here in 1742, stood on this site. On his land Fort Lewis was built in 1756. *Roanoke Co.: Rte. 11, 2.5 miles w. of Salem.*

K-75 GENERAL ANDREW LEWIS

Richfield, home of Andrew Lewis, famous colonial and Revolutionary soldier, is marked by the knoll and locust trees a half mile east of this spot. *Salem: Rte. 11, at College Ave. and Eighth St.*

K-76 OLD LUTHERAN CHURCH

Tradition has it that the church near by was built where Moravian and Lutheran missionaries preached soon after the Revolution. Here, in 1796, Lutherans held services and, a little later, organized their first congregation in this section. In 1828, the Lutheran synod of North Carolina met here and consecrated the church. *Roanoke Co.: Rte. 11, .8 mile w. of Roanoke.*

K-77 GENERAL ANDREW LEWIS' GRAVE

This famous pioneer, patriot, statesman, and soldier, is buried here on part of his 625 acre estate. Member of House of Burgesses, 1772–1775; defeated Indians at battle of Point Pleasant, 1774; drove Lord Dunmore from Virginia, 1776. Died 1781. *Salem: Rte. 460, at Park Ave. and Main St.*

K-78 SGT. JAMES WALTON, SALEM FLYING ARTILLERY, C.S.A.

Here at East Hill Cemetery is buried Sgt. James Walton (1838–1875). A gunner in Capt. Charles B. Griffin's Battery (Salem Flying Artillery), Walton fired one of the last artillery shots by Gen. Robert E. Lee's Army of Northern Virginia at Appomattox Court House. Stationed in the yard of the George Peers house at the northeastern end of the village, Griffin's battery fired at Union cavalry until ordered to stop. Walton had just loaded powder into a gun when the order arrived; he discharged the cannon to clear it and saved the primer as a souvenir. *Salem: Main St. at entrance to East Hill Cemetery.*

K-88 OLD SALEM INNS

Salem, founded in 1803, was a notable stopping place on the route to the West. The inns located near this spot were the Bull's Eye, Ye Olde Time Tavern, the Globe, the Indian Queen, and the Mermaid. *Roanoke Co.: Rte. 11, .2 mile w. of Salem.*

K-95 ROANOKE

The first village here, at Pate's Mill and Tavern on Evans' Mill Creek, was called Big Lick for nearby salt marshes. In 1839 it was laid off as the town of Gainesborough. After the coming of the Virginia and Tennessee Railroad (later N & W) in 1852, another village sprang up about the old Stover House that was also named Big Lick. Gainesborough became known as Old Lick. *Roanoke: East Bullit and South Jefferson sts.*

K-95 ROANOKE

In June, 1864, General Hunter passed here retreating from Lynchburg. In 1874 Big Lick was incorporated. In 1881, with the junction of the new Shenandoah Valley Railroad with the N. & W., rapid growth began. In 1882 the name was changed to Roanoke; in 1884 it was incorporated as a city. In 1909 the Virginian Railroad operated its first train. In recent years Roanoke became the third city of Virginia. *Roanoke: East Bullit and South Jefferson sts.*

K-96 ROANOKE CITY MARKET

The Roanoke farmers' market is one of the oldest such markets in continuous use in Virginia. In 1882, licenses were issued to twenty-five hucksters. The City of Roanoke's first charter formally authorized a municipally owned market in 1884, and the first permanent market building was completed in 1886. This formed the core of a continuing curb market in and around the Market Square. The present market building was erected in 1922 to replace the original market structure. *Roanoke: Campbell Ave. adjacent to Center in the Square.*

K-116 A COLONIAL FORD

Tosh's Ford and Evans' Mill, located on the river near this crossing, were the base of supplies for military expeditions of colonial days in all this region. *Roanoke: Franklin Rd. S.W. between Naval Reserve and Brandon aves.*

K-119* INDIAN REMAINS

The large knoll three hundred yards to the east is an Indian mound. It is supposed to have been built by some tribe of the Siouan race which later was driven westward. [*Removed as inaccurate.*] *Bedford Co.: Rte. 460, 12 miles w. of Bedford.*

K-121* COLONIAL FORT

Near here stood a fort, or blockhouse, built for protection against Indian attacks. In this fort Mrs. William Ingles took refuge after her escape from captivity among the Indians in the spring of 1756. *Bedford Co.: Rte. 460, 11 miles w. of Bedford.*

K-130   HUNTER'S BIVOUAC

Near here General Hunter, on his retreat from Lynchburg, halted for the night of June 18, 1864. He resumed his retreat early in the morning of June 19. *Bedford Co.: Rte. 460, 3 miles w. of Bedford.*

K-132   HOME OF JOHN GOODE

Here is the home of John Goode, political leader, born 1829, died, 1909. Goode was a member of the secession convention of 1861; of the Confederate Congress and of the United States Congress; Solicitor General of the United States; president of the Virginia constitutional convention of 1901. *Bedford Co.: Rte. 460, at Bedford.*

K-133   RANDOLPH-MACON
ACADEMY—LIBERTY ACADEMY

Randolph-Macon Academy, a Methodist preparatory school for boys, occupied a building on this site from 1890 until 1934 when the school was consolidated with the Randolph-Macon Academy at Front Royal. In 1936, the property was purchased by Bedford County. Liberty Academy, a public and consolidated elementary school, occupied the building until 1964. The large and imposing Romanesque-style structure designed by W. M. Poindexter of Washington, D.C., was later demolished. *Bedford Co.: College St. near Bedford Primary School, in Bedford.*

K-134   BEDFORD

This place became the county seat of Bedford when it was moved from New London in 1782. First called Liberty (incorporated in 1839), the town changed its name to Bedford City in 1890 and to Bedford in 1912. A third courthouse, built in 1834, was replaced by the present building in 1930. The Union General Hunter, with his army, passed here in June, 1864, on his way to Lynchburg, and repassed on his retreat. *Bedford Co.: Rte. 460, at Bedford.*

K-136   PEAKS OF OTTER ROAD

This road was followed by General Hunter when he crossed the Blue Ridge at the Peaks of Otter and came to Bedford en route to Lynchburg, June 16, 1864. *Bedford Co.: Rte. 460, at Bedford.*

K-138   POPLAR FOREST

A mile and a half south is Poplar Forest, Thomas Jefferson's Bedford estate. He came here in June, 1781, after his term as governor expired, and while here was thrown from a horse and injured. During his recovery he wrote his "Notes on Virginia." *Bedford Co.: Rte. 460, 6.5 miles w. of Lynchburg.*

K-139   NEW LONDON

This place, on the old stage road, was the first county seat of Bedford; the first courthouse, built in 1755, was standing until 1856. In 1781, New London was raided by the British cavalryman, Tarleton, seeking military stores. It came into Campbell County in 1782. An arsenal here was afterward removed to Harper's Ferry. *Campbell Co.: Rte. 858, 4 miles w. of Lynchburg.*

K-139   NEW LONDON

At New London, Patrick Henry made one of his most famous speeches. John Hook, a Tory, brought suit for two steers impressed for the American army in 1781. Henry, the opposing counsel, so pictured the sufferings of the patriots in that critical year and their joy at Cornwallis's surrender, and so ridiculed Hook, that the case was laughed out of court. *Campbell Co.: Rte. 858, 4 miles w. of Lynchburg.*

K-140   ST. STEPHEN'S CHURCH

Half a mile north, is St. Stephen's Church, built about 1825 under Rev. Nicholas Cobb, later Bishop of Alabama. In the old cemetery here many members of early families of the community are buried. *Bedford Co.: Rte. 460, 8 miles w. of Lynchburg.*

K-141   NEW LONDON ACADEMY

Chartered by the state in 1795, this is the oldest secondary school in Virginia in continuous operation under its own charter. Conducted for many years as a private school for boys, it began to receive public funds in 1884. It now operates as a public school. *Bedford Co.: Rte. 460, at New London Academy.*

K-142*   JOHN DANIEL'S HOME

Half a mile west is Westerly, once the home of Colonel Peyton Leftwick, War of 1812 soldier. Later it was the home of Judge William Daniel and of his son, John Warwick Daniel, Confederate soldier and for many years United States Senator from Virginia. *Lynchburg: 720 Court St.*

K-142   JOHN DANIEL'S HOME

This Federal-style mansion was built by John Marshall Warwick in 1826. It was the birthplace of John Warwick Daniel, grandson of the builder, whose father was Judge William Daniel, resident of nearby Point of Honor. John W. Daniel was known as the "Lame Lion of Lynchburg" due to extensive wounds suffered in the Civil War. He later served in the Virginia Assembly as both delegate and senator and for sixteen years in the United States Congress as congressman and senator. *Lynchburg: 720 Court St.*

K-146*   CHESTNUT HILL

Two miles north is Chestnut Hill, home of Charles Lynch, Sr., father of John Lynch, founder of Lynchburg, and of Charles Lynch, Revolutionary soldier. Charles Lynch, Sr., died in 1753 and is supposed to be buried at Chestnut Hill. *Campbell Co.: Rte. 501, 4 miles e. of Lynchburg.*

K 148*   MOUNT ATHOS

Two miles north are the ruins of Mount Athos, or Buffalo Lick Plantation. The house was built in 1796 by William J. Lewis, who commanded a corps of mountain riflemen at the siege of Yorktown in 1781. *Campbell Co.: Rte. 460, 6 miles e. of Lynchburg.*

K-150*   OXFORD FURNACE

Across the stream stood Oxford Furnace, conducted in the Revolution by James Calloway to supply military materials. Iron mines were near by. The furnace was operated until 1875, the mill until 1900. *Campbell Co.: Rte. 460, 2.5 miles e. of Lynchburg.*

K-152   CONCORD STATION

The first railroad train passed this station in 1854. In 1864, the station building and the Confederate commissary here were burned by the Union General Hunter. This was the extreme eastern limit of Hunter's raid. *Campbell Co.: Rte. 460, at Concord.*

K-156 THE LAST FIGHT

Two miles north, at sunrise of April 9, 1865, Fitz Lee and Gordon, moving westward, attacked Sheridan's position. The attack was repulsed, but a part of the Confederate cavalry under Munford and Rosser broke through the Union line and escaped. This was the last action between the Army of Northern Virginia and the Army of the Potomac. *Appomattox Co.: Rte. 460 at Rte. 131 in Appomattox.*

K-157 SURRENDER AT APPOMATTOX

At the McLean house at Appomattox, two miles north, took place the meeting between Lee and Grant to arrange terms for the surrender of the Army of Northern Virginia. This was at 1:30 P.M. on Sunday, April 9, 1865. *Appomattox Co.: Rte. 460 at Rte. 131 in Appomattox.*

K-158* APPOMATTOX COURTHOUSE— NEW AND OLD

This building, erected in 1892 when the county seat was moved to this location, should not be mistaken for the original, built in 1846 and destroyed by fire in 1892. Three miles northeast is Old Appomattox Court House and the McLean House where Lee surrendered to Grant on April 9, 1865, thus ending the War Between the States. The village of Old Appomattox Court House is now preserved as a national shrine by the Federal Government. *Appomattox Co.: Rte. 131, at Appomattox.*

K-158 APPOMATTOX COURTHOUSE— NEW AND OLD

The first courthouse for Appomattox County, erected in 1846, was destroyed by fire in 1892. It was located three miles northeast in the village of Old Appomattox Court House where Lee surrendered to Grant on April 9, 1865, signalling the end of the Civil War. The village of Appomattox Court House is preserved as a national shrine by the National Park Service of the United States Department of the Interior. This building was erected in 1892 when the county seat was moved to this location. *Appomattox Co.: Rte. 131, at Appomattox.*

K-159 BATTLE OF APPOMATTOX STATION—1865

Near this building stood the station of the South Side Rail Road where, on April 8th, 1865, three trains unloading supplies for the Army of Northern Virginia were captured by units of Sheridan's Union Cavalry under General George Custer. Significant for its relationship to the surrender by General Robert E. Lee at Appomattox Court House, this action also marked the last strategic use of rail by Confederate forces. *Appomattox Co.: Main and Church sts. in Appomattox.*

K-170 NOTTOWAY COURTHOUSE

Near here the Confederate cavalryman, W. H. F. Lee, interposed between Wilson and Kautz raiding to Burkeville and fought a sharp action, June 23, 1864. Wilson then started on his return to Grant's army. Grant passed here with a part of his army in pursuit of Lee, April 5, 1865. Here he received word from Sheridan that the latter was at Jetersville across Lee's line of retreat. *Nottoway Co.: Rte. 460, .2 mile w. of Nottoway.*

K-172 BLACKSTONE

A tobacco center, originally known as "Black's and White's" for rival tavern-keepers. The Union General Wilson passed here on the raid of June, 1864. General Ord, with a corps of Grant's army, spent the night of April 5–6, 1865, here. The name of the town was changed to Blackstone about 1885; it was incorporated in 1888. Blackstone College for girls is here. *Nottoway Co.: Rte. 460, at Blackstone.*

K-173 FORT PICKETT

Named in honor of Confederate Maj. Gen. George Edward Pickett upon its creation in 1942, Camp Pickett was dedicated to the cause of a "reunited nation at war." Established as a 46,000-acre World War II Army installation, Camp Pickett was home to eight combat divisions, seven infantry divisions, and one armored division, during both the European and the Pacific campaigns. The famed "Cross of Lorraine" 79th Infantry Division trained here before the invasion at Normandy. The post was redesignated Fort Pickett and became a full-time training facility in 1974. *Nottoway Co.: Rte. 40, 1 mile s. of Rte. 460.*

K-203 COLONEL THOMAS LYGON

Colonel Thomas Lygon, who came to the Virginia colony in the early 1640s from Worcestershire, England, patented several large parcels of land on the north bank of the Appomattox River in an area known as The Cowpens, near Mount My Lady, which was then part of Henrico County. It is likely that he lived in this area with his wife Mary Harris and their five children. Lygon served in the House of Burgesses from Henrico County in 1656, as a colonel in the county militia, and as surveyor of the county until his death in 1675. *Chesterfield Co.: Rte. 10, 1 mile w. of Hopewell.*

K-204 ETTRICK

The site of an Appomattox Indian village burned in 1676 in Bacon's Rebellion, the present town of Ettrick stands on land that belonged to "Ettrick Banks" and "Matoax," the boyhood plantation of John Randolph of Roanoke. In 1810 Campbell's Bridge connected Ettrick with Petersburg, hastening the development of mills on the river. Virginia State University, formerly known as the Virginia Normal and Collegiate Institute, was established here in 1882. *Chesterfield Co.: Rte. 36, .2 mile w. of Petersburg.*

K-205 CITY POINT AND HOPEWELL

City Point is five miles northeast. There Governor Sir Thomas Dale made a settlement in 1613. In April, 1781, the British General Phillips landed there. Grant had his base of operations there in the siege of Petersburg, 1864–1865. Lincoln was there in April, 1865. In the World War the city of Hopewell grew up near by. *Prince George Co.: Rte. 36, .7 mile e. of Petersburg.*

K-206* BAILEY'S CREEK

Named for Temperance Bailey, who owned land here in 1626. *Prince George Co.: Rte. 106, 5.5 miles e. of Petersburg.*

K-207 HISTORY AT PRINCE GEORGE COURTHOUSE

Lord Cornwallis, going toward the James in pursuit of Lafayette, passed here, May 24, 1781. A part of Grant's army passed here on the way to Petersburg, June, 1864. The place was occupied by Union troops in 1864–65. *Prince George Co.: Rte. 106, at Prince George.*

K-208 JORDAN'S POINT

Five miles north on James River. There, in 1619, Samuel Jordan established a place, Jordan's Journey. Near there, in April, 1676, the settlers in arms against the Indians chose Bacon as their leader. The Revolutionary leader, Richard Bland, had his home there, and near by the great agriculturist, Edmund Ruffin, lived. *Prince George Co.: Rte. 106, 2.9 miles e. of Prince George.*

K-209 MERCHANT'S HOPE CHURCH

Half a mile south. This church was built about 1657 and is, therefore, one of the oldest churches in Virginia. The first Prince George Courthouse was near it. The parish, that of Martin's Brandon, was one of the earliest established in Charles City County. *Prince George Co.: Rte. 10, 8.3 miles n.w. of Burrowsville.*

K-210 COGGIN'S POINT

Four miles north on James River. When Benedict Arnold fell back down the James after his raid to Richmond, Baron Steuben, at Coggin's Point, observed his fleet, January 10, 1781. From the bluff General D. H. Hill bombarded McClellan's camp on the north side of the river, July 31, 1862. *Prince George Co.: Rte. 10, 8.3 miles n.w. of Burrowsville.*

K-211 THE CATTLE RAID

Just to the north of the road here, at old Sycamore Church, Wade Hampton, coming from the south, attacked the Union cavalry guarding Grant's beef cattle, September 16, 1864. The Unionists were overpowered; Hampton, rounding up 2,500 beeves, succeeded in escaping with them across the Blackwater and into Lee's lines. *Prince George Co.: Rte. 106, 6.8 miles e. of Prince George.*

K-211* UPPER CHIPPOKES CREEK

In 1610 an Indian chief, Chopoke [*sic*], lived near the mouth of this creek. In 1637 the first Benjamin Harrison obtained a land grant on the stream. *Surry Co.: Rte. 10, 13.5 miles w. of Surry.*

K-212 POWELL'S CREEK

The creek nearby was named for Nathaniel Powell, acting governor in 1619. Weyanoke Indian town was here. Nearby is the site of an old mill, known in the Revolution as Bland's, and later, Cocke's Mill. The British General Phillips passed here, May, 1781. Here Grant's army, after crossing the James, turned towards Petersburg, June, 1864. *Prince George Co.: Rte. 10, 5.3 miles n.w. of Burrowsville.*

K-213 MAYCOCK'S PLANTATION

Six miles north on James River. The place was patented about 1618 by Samuel Maycock, slain in the massacre of 1622. In 1774, David Meade became the owner. There Cornwallis crossed the river, May 24, 1781. Anthony Wayne crossed there, August 30, 1781. *Prince George Co.: Rte. 10, 5.3 miles n.w. of Burrowsville.*

K-214 FLOWERDEW HUNDRED

Four miles north. Governor Sir George Yeardley patented land there in 1619, and in 1621 built at Windmill Point the first windmill in English America. The place was named for Temperance Flowerdew, Yeardley's wife. Near there Grant's army crossed the James in June, 1864. *Prince George Co.: Rte. 10, 5.3 miles n.w. of Burrowsville.*

Four miles north on James River. There, on January 3, 1781, Benedict Arnold, ascending the river, was fired on by cannon. On January 10, Arnold, returning, sent ashore there a force that was ambushed by George Rogers Clark. Fort Powhatan stood there in the War of 1812. *Prince George Co.: Rte. 10, at Burrowsville.*

Named for John Ward, who patented land here in 1619. The plantation was represented in the first General Assembly, 1619. *Prince George Co.: Rte. 10, at Burrowsville.*

This place, five miles northeast, has been owned by the Harrison family for two centuries. John Martin patented the land in 1617. Nathaniel Harrison bought it in 1720. The present house was built about 1770. The British General Phillips landed at Brandon, May 7, 1781. A mile farther is Upper Brandon. *Prince George Co.: Rte. 10, at Burrowsville.*

A village was here as early as 1689. Here Baron Steuben gathered militia in January, 1781, to resist Benedict Arnold's invasion, and here General Muhlenberg, watching Arnold at Portsmouth, had his headquarters. *Surry Co.: Rte. 10, 4 miles n.w. of Spring Grove.*

This is six miles north. William Rookings patented land there in 1636. His son, William Rookings, was one of the leaders in Bacon's Rebellion, 1676. *Surry Co.: Rte. 10, 4 miles n.w. of Spring Grove.*

This place, seven miles north, was settled by Richard Pace in 1620. On the night before the Indian massacre of March 22, 1622, an Indian, Chanco, revealed the plot to Pace, who reached Jamestown in time to save the settlers in that vicinity. *Surry Co.: Rte. 10, 3.5 miles w. of Surry.*

The Quiyoughcohannock Indian village nearby was first visited by English settlers in May, 1607. The first land patent at Claremont was 200 acres granted to George Harrison in 1621. Arthur Allen, who built the house now known as Bacon's Castle, first purchased land here in 1656. The estate was called "Cleremont" by William Allen by 1793, and Claremont Manor was probably built by him after 1754. Situated on land that had been part of the Allen estate, the town of Claremont was incorporated in 1886. *Surry Co.: Rte. 613, at Claremont.*

Four miles north. The village of the Quioughcohanock [*sic*] Indians nearby was first visited by English settlers in May, 1607. The estate was patented in 1649; the house was built some years later by Arthur Allen, rumored to be a prince. There is an underground passage to the river. A place of great romantic interest. Railroad iron from there was used to armor the Confederate battleship "Merrimac." *Surry Co.: Rte. 10, 4 miles n.w. of Spring Grove.*

Five miles north is Wakefield, owned by the first Benjamin Harrison as early as 1635. Seven miles northeast is Pipsico, named for a noted Indian chief. In 1608 an Indian village was in that vicinity. *Surry Co.: Rte. 10, at Spring Grove.*

K-227   PLEASANT POINT

Four miles north is Pleasant Point on
James River. William Edwards patented
land there in 1657; the house is ancient.
Edwards was clerk of the general court
and a member of the House of Burgesses.
Surry Co.: Rte. 10, 1.3 miles s.e. of Surry.

K-228*   GLEBE HOUSE

Built before 1724, this was the glebe
house of Southwark Parish. *Surry Co.:
Rte. 10, 4.7 miles w. of Surry.*

K-229   SOUTHWARK CHURCH

Four miles northeast are the ruins of this
church, built before 1673. *Surry Co.:
Rte. 10, 3.5 miles w. of Surry.*

K-230   BELL FARM (COLONEL
        MICHAEL BLOW)

One mile south stood Bell Farm, home of
Michael Blow. Colonel Blow was the first
Chairman of the Committee of Safety of
Sussex County, member of the House of
Burgesses, member of the First Virginia
Convention (1774), County Justice, and
colonel in the Revolutionary Army. *Sus-
sex Co.: Rte. 460 at Rte. 628.*

K-230*   SETTLEMENT ON GRAY'S CREEK

First called Rolfe's Creek for Thomas
Rolfe, son of Pocahontas, who was an
early landowner here. Later it was named
for Thomas Gray, who patented land here
in 1639. *Surry Co.: Rte. 10, 2 miles n.w.
of Surry.*

K-231   SWANN'S POINT

Ten miles northeast is Swann's Point on
James River. In 1635 William Swann patented land there. The English commissioners investigating Bacon's Rebellion
met at Swann's Point in 1677. William
Swann's tomb, dated 1680, is there.
Surry Co.: Rte. 10, at Spring Grove.

K-232*   CYPRESS CHURCH

Eight miles southwest are the ruins of Cypress Church, built in 1753.   *Surry Co.:
Rte. 10, 1 mile s. of Surry.*

K-233   SMITH'S FORT PLANTATION

Two miles north is the Thomas Warren
House, one of the oldest in Virginia.
Erected during 1651–1652 some of the
land had descended to Thomas Rolfe, son
of Pocahontas, from her father, the Indian
chief Powhatan. Earlier on this tract Captain John Smith and the colonists built a
fort for the protection of Jamestown, just
across the river. *Surry Co.: Rte. 10, at
Surry.*

K-234*   HISTORY ON CROUCH'S CREEK

Originally called Tappahannock Creek. In
1625 the poet, George Sandys, treasurer
of the colony, had a settlement here and a
building for raising silk worms. In 1638
Thomas Crouch patented land on this
stream. *Surry Co.: Rte. 10, at Surry.*

K-235   BACON'S CASTLE

This house, just to the north, was built by
Arthur Allen in 1655. In Bacon's Rebellion, 1676, the house was seized by a party
of rebels and fortified. On December 29,
1676, it was captured by sailors from a
ship in James River who were engaged in
putting down the rebellion. *Surry Co.:
Rte. 10, at Bacon's Castle.*

K-236 ORGANIZATION OF THE CHRISTIAN CHURCH

At "Old Lebanon Church" here, the Christian Church was established under the leadership of James O'Kelly, August, 1794. O'Kelly had withdrawn from the Methodist Church, 1792. *Surry Co.: Rte. 10, 1.5 miles w. of Surry.*

K-237 HOG ISLAND

On this point, in James River nine miles northeast, the settlers kept their hogs in 1608. When abandoning Jamestown in June, 1610, they stopped at the island for a night. The next morning, proceeding down the river, they met a messenger from Governor Lord Delaware, who had just arrived, and returned to Jamestown. *Surry Co.: Rte. 10, at Bacon's Castle.*

K-238 OLD TOWN

Half a mile north, stood the Warrascoyack Indian village. Captain John Smith obtained corn there for the starving colonists in 1608. The Warrascoyacks took part in the massacre of 1622 and their village was destroyed in 1623. In 1680, Old Town was established. *Isle of Wight Co.: Rte. 621, .1 mile e. of Rte. 10.*

K-239 LAWNE'S CREEK

Named for Christopher Lawne, who settled at the mouth of the creek in 1619. In 1634 the plantations hereabouts became the county of Warrascoyack. In 1637 the name was changed to Isle of Wight. *Isle of Wight Co.: Rte. 10, 8.1 miles n.w. of Smithfield.*

K-240* WRENN'S MILL SITE

Two miles south, on Pagan Creek, stood Wrenn's Mill as early as 1646. About 1685 George Hardy operated a mill there. On this site, which has seen several mill structures, a mill is still running. *Isle of Wight Co.: Rte. 10, 4.5 miles n.w. of Smithfield.*

K-240-b WRENN'S MILL

About one mile south, on Pagan Creek, stands a mill which was in operation by 1650. Once known as "Green's Mill," it was purchased by Charles Wrenn in 1821. A skirmish was fought there, April 14, 1864. *Isle of Wight Co.: Rte. 10, 4.5 miles w. of Smithfield.*

K-241* BENNETT'S PLANTATION

This place, two miles north, was settled by Edward Bennett in February, 1622. Houses were being built in March, 1622, when the Indians massacre occurred. More than fifty of the settlers perished; others, resisting, drove off the savages. *Isle of Wight Co.: Rte. 10, 2 miles n.w. of Smithfield.*

K-242* BASSE'S CHOICE

This place, three miles north, was settled by Nathaniel Basse in 1621. In the massacre of 1622, the Indians killed twenty settlers there. *Isle of Wight Co.: Rte. 10, 2 miles n.w. of Smithfield.*

K-243 SMITHFIELD

The town was established in 1752. The Masonic Hall was built in 1753. Benedict Arnold occupied the town, January 15, 1781. At Cherry Grove Landing near by, skirmishing took place on April 13–15, 1864, and the Confederates made a daring capture of a Union vessel on December 5, 1864. *Isle of Wight Co.: Rte. 10, at Smithfield.*

K-244 PAGAN POINT

Two miles north. There stood an Indian village named Mokete. "Pagan" refers to the heathenism of the Indians. *Isle of Wight Co.: Rte. 10, .4 mile w. of Smithfield.*

K-245 SAINT LUKE'S CHURCH

To the east is the venerable "Old Brick Church." By tradition it is dated 1632. It is the nation's only original Gothic house of worship surviving from colonial times and may also be the oldest church in the United States. *Isle of Wight Co.: Rte. 10, 4.25 miles s.e. of Smithfield.*

K-245* ST. LUKE'S CHURCH

The church, bricks of which bear the date of 1632, is one of the oldest churches in the United States. It was abandoned in 1830 and restored about 1890. Tarleton's British cavalry camped here in 1781. *Isle of Wight Co.: Rte. 10, .25 mile n.w. of Benn's Church.*

K-246 BENN'S CHURCH

This Methodist church was known in 1804 as Benn's Chapel. Bishop Asbury preached here in 1804. *Isle of Wight Co.: Rte. 10, 4.2 miles s.e. of Smithfield.*

K-247* MACCLESFIELD

Seven miles north. It was the home of Colonel Josiah Parker, Revolutionary officer. In 1781, British cavalry under Tarleton raided the place in the effort to capture Parker. A militia camp was at Macclesfield in the War of 1812. *Isle of Wight Co.: Rte. 10, 4.2 miles s.e. of Smithfield.*

K-248 CHUCKATUCK

A colonial church is here. In July, 1781, the British cavalryman Tarleton was at Chuckatuck. On May 3, 1863, a skirmish took place here between Union and Confederate forces as Longstreet withdrew from the siege of Suffolk. *Suffolk ("old" Nansemond Co.): Rte. 10, 9.2 miles n.w. of Suffolk proper.*

K-249 DUMPLING ISLAND

One mile east in Nansemond River. There, in 1608, the English settlers were attacked by Indians in canoes. The savages jumped overboard when the English fired their guns and later ransomed the canoes for corn. In 1609, the colonists sought to seize the Indians' corn on the island but were driven off. *Suffolk ("old" Nansemond Co.): Rte. 10, 6 miles n.w. of Suffolk proper.*

K-250 REID'S FERRY

The village of the Nansemond Indians stood near here, 1608, when the region was first explored by the English settlers. These savages took part in the massacre of 1622, and in the war that followed their town was destroyed by Sir George Yeardley. *Suffolk ("old" Nansemond Co.): Rte. 10, 5.5 miles n.w. of Suffolk proper.*

K-251* EARLY HISTORY OF SUFFOLK

A warehouse was established here in 1730 on land of the Widow Constance. The town was established in 1742. Robert Howe occupied it with Virginia and North Carolina troops in February, 1776. It was burned by a British raiding force under General Matthews, May 13, 1779. Lafayette visited it in February, 1825. Suffolk was destroyed by fire in 1837 but soon rose from its ashes. *Suffolk ("old" Nansemond Co.): Rte. 10, 1.5 miles n.w. of Suffolk proper.*

K-252 SIEGE OF SUFFOLK

The town was occupied by Union Troops from May, 1862, until the end of the Civil War. Confederate forces under Longstreet unsuccessfully besieged Suffolk, from April 11, to May 3, 1863, when they withdrew across the James on Lee's orders. *Suffolk: Rte. 460, .5 mile w. of old city limits.*

K-253* DISMAL SWAMP

The swamp, just to the south, was visited by William Byrd in 1728 while surveying the Virginia–North Carolina Line. In 1763, George Washington made explorations in it, and organized the Dismal Swamp Company to drain it. The company acquired 40,000 acres of land in the swamp. *Suffolk: ("old" Nansemond Co.): Rte. 58, 4.7 miles e. of Suffolk proper.*

K-254* REVOLUTIONARY CAMP

Here the Nansemond militia under Colonel Willis Riddick, opposing a British raid, camped on May 11, 1779. *Suffolk ("old" Nansemond Co.): Rte. 337, 6.2 miles n.e. of Suffolk proper.*

K-255 YEATES SCHOOL

Before 1731 John Yeates established two free schools in this neighborhood, one on each side of Bennett's Creek. By his will, September 18, 1731, he left his property for the use of these schools. They continued until 1861 and were sold in 1866 under an act of legislature. *Suffolk ("old" Nansemond Co.): Rte. 337, at Driver.*

K-255* HISTORIC CLAREMONT

Claremont is four miles north. There stood the village of the Quioughcohanock Indians, visited by the first settlers in May, 1607. An English settlement was made there about 1632; the manor house is a colonial dwelling. Rails from a railroad there were used to armor the Confederate warship Merrimac. *Surry Co.: Rte. 10, at Spring Grove.*

K-256 SLEEPY HOLE FERRY

Three miles east, Benedict Arnold, returning from his Richmond raid, crossed the river there, January 16, 1781; Cornwallis, going to Portsmouth, crossed there in July, 1781. *Suffolk ("old" Nansemond Co.): Rte. 337, at Driver.*

K-257 BENNETT'S HOME

On this stream, Bennett's Creek, stood the home of Richard Bennett. He was one of the commissioners to "reduce" Virginia after the victory of Parliament in the civil war in England, 1651, and the first governor under the Cromwellian domination, 1652–55. *Suffolk ("old" Nansemond Co.): Rte. 337, at Driver.*

K-258 GLEBE CHURCH

Built in 1738. In 1775 the parish minister, Parson Agnew, was driven from the church for preaching loyalty to the king. The building was repaired in 1854. *Suffolk ("old" Nansemond Co.): Rte. 337, at Driver.*

K-259 SIEGE OF SUFFOLK

Across the road here ran the main line of Confederate works, built by Longstreet besieging Suffolk, April 1863. He abandoned the siege and rejoined Lee at Fredericksburg. *Suffolk ("old" Nansemond Co.): Rte. 10, 1.5 miles n.w. of Suffolk proper.*

K-261* PIG POINT

Eight miles north, at the mouth of Nansemond River. A Confederate battery there had an engagement with the Union ship, Harriet Lane, June 5, 1861. *Suffolk ("old" Nansemond Co.): Rte. 460, 8 miles w. of Portsmouth.*

K-262 CRANEY ISLAND

This island in the Elizabeth River is about four miles northeast. British forces moving on Norfolk attacked American fortifications there June 22, 1813, but were repulsed. The Confederate Ironclad "Virginia" (MERRIMAC) was destroyed by her crew there May 11, 1862. *Chesapeake ("old" Norfolk Co.): Rte. 17, w. of Churchland bypass.*

K-262* CRANEY ISLAND

Seven miles northeast on Elizabeth River. The fortifications on the island were attacked, June 22, 1813, by the British, who were repulsed with loss. The Portsmouth artillery served with distinction. Here, May 11, 1862, the Confederates destroyed the iron-clad Merrimac. *Chesapeake ("old" Norfolk Co.): Rte. 337, 2.8 miles w. of Portsmouth.*

K-263* HODGES FERRY

Near here stood a colonial church, built about 1762. William Braidforth, a Scotchman who sided with the colonists in the Revolution, was chaplain here through the war period. *Chesapeake ("old" Norfolk Co.): Rte. 337, 2.3 miles w. of Portsmouth.*

K-264* DALE POINT

A short distance north, birthplace of Commodore Richard Dale, born 1756, Lieutenant on Bon Homme Richard in the fight with British ship Serapis, 1779. First Commandant Norfolk Navy Yard, 1794, commanded squadron against Barbary Pirates, 1801. *Chesapeake ("old" Norfolk Co.): Rte. 460, .25 mile w. of Portsmouth.*

K-265* FORT NELSON

In Portsmouth (Naval Hospital) stood Fort Nelson, built in the Revolution to protect the Norfolk area. In May, 1779, a British fleet under Sir George Collier, carrying troops under General Matthews, took the fort, which was abandoned by the garrison. The British destroyed ships, tobacco and supplies. The point was fortified again in 1861. *Chesapeake ("old" Norfolk Co.): Rte. 337, near w. city limits of Portsmouth.*

K-270* HARGROVE'S TAVERN

Nearby is the site of Hargrove's Tavern, known as the Halfway House, which was built before the Revolution. Here Captains King and Davis of the Virginia militia were surprised by the British, May, 1781, and Davis was killed. *Suffolk ("old" Nansemond Co.): .8 mile e. of Driver.*

Three miles east is Kempsville. There Lord Dunmore, royal governor, attacked a party of militia, November 16, 1775, and dispersed it. The place was Princess Anne County Courthouse from 1778 to 1822. Kempsville was established as a town in 1783. *Virginia Beach ("old" Princess Anne Co.): Rte. 165, at Kempsville.*

K-273*   NEW TOWN

Two miles south, on the Eastern Branch, is the site of New Town, laid out in 1697 and established as a town in 1740. Princess Anne County Courthouse was there from 1753 to 1778. Norfolk people refugeed [*sic*] there after the burning of Norfolk, January 1, 1776. The British cavalryman Simcoe was stationed there in March, 1781. *Virginia Beach ("old" Princess Anne Co.): Rte. 58, 3 miles e. of Norfolk.*

K-275*   GREAT BRIDGE

Eight miles south is Great Bridge, which at the time of the Revolution was a causeway through a marsh. Lord Dunmore, the royal governor, had a British garrison here to protect this approach to Norfolk. On December 9, 1775, an action was fought there between the British and the Virginia troops, in which the former were defeated. This fight forced Dunmore to evacuate Norfolk. *Chesapeake ("old" Norfolk Co.): Rte. 17, 3 miles s. of Portsmouth.*

K-276*   DONATION CHURCH AND
          WITCH DUCK

Two and three-tenths miles north is Donation Church, first built before 1694. Nearby is the site of Princess Anne County Courthouse, 1730–1753. One mile north of this place is "Witch Duck," where Grace Sherwood, accused of being a witch, was tested. She was put in water "above man's depth" to "try her how she swims therein." *Virginia Beach ("old" Princess Anne Co.): Rte. 58, 5 miles e. of Norfolk.*

K-277*   FIRST EASTERN SHORE CHAPEL

About one mile northwest of this point near the head of Wolfsnare Creek stood the first Eastern Shore Chapel of Lynhaven Parish, built before 1689. Adjoining it was built in this year a secondary courthouse for Lower Norfolk County, which became the first courthouse of Princess Anne County upon its formation in 1691. Near the chapel also stood in 1693 the first recorded Presbyterian meeting-house in Virginia, founded by the Rev. Josias Mackie. *Norfolk: Rte. 58, 2.2 miles w. of Virginia Beach.*

K-278*   EASTERN SHORE CHAPEL

One mile south is Eastern Shore Chapel. The land on which it stands, patented by William Cornick in 1657, was given to Lynnhaven Parish by his heirs. Two wooden buildings occupied the site; the present church was built in 1754. The communion service, which bears the date, 1759, was buried in a hen house, 1861–65, to save it from raiders. The chapel was abandoned in war time but was later reoccupied. *Virginia Beach ("old" Princess Anne Co.): Rte. 58, 2.2 miles w. of beachfront.*

K-279 CHIPPOKES PLANTATION

This plantation, four miles to the northeast, was established in 1619 by Captain William Powell of Jamestown. Structures and artifacts on the property reflect plantation life from the early 17th century to the present. Donated to the Commonwealth by Mrs. Victor Stewart in 1967 for use as a state park, Chippokes is noted for its 350 years of continuous agricultural production and its modern recreational facilities. *Surry Co.: Rte. 10, 1.3 miles s.e. of Surry.*

K-300 LAWNES CREEK CHURCH

Approximately six miles to the north, near Hog Island Creek, is the site of Lawnes Creek Church. Authorized in 1629 as a "chapel of ease" for the settlers in the area by the Council and General Court of Colonial Virginia, the church was the site of a meeting in 1673 to protest unjust taxation and government without representation and to manifest a spirit of religious independence. *Surry Co.: Rte. 10, 7.2 miles s.e. of Surry.*

K-301 JAMES RIVER FERRY

Near this site on February 26, 1925, the ferry *Captain John Smith* began the first automobile ferry service crossing the James River. Captain Albert F. Jester was the inaugurator and owner/operator until it was sold to the Commonwealth of Virginia in 1945. This ferry system provided an important link for the Maine-to-Florida traveler through Surry County to Jamestown Island, the site of the first permanent English settlement in America. *Surry Co.: Rte. 31, at Scotland Wharf.*

K-304 SALLIE JONES ATKINSON

Sallie Jones Atkinson, prominent educator and community leader in Dinwiddie County and her husband, John Pryor Atkinson, gave the land on which Sunnyside High School was built in 1911. By her vision, tireless industry, and determination, the school became the first eight-month rural school accredited in Virginia. Mrs. Atkinson also served on the state committee that worked to secure Governor Montague's approval for women's suffrage. *Dinwiddie Co.: Rte. 40, 2.5 miles w. of McKenney.*

K-305* LEE'S RETREAT

Here the Confederates, under General Heth, made a gallant stand, April 2, 1865, but were finally overwhelmed. The loss of this point cut Lee's railway connection with Danville. On April 3, Grant and Meade camped here in pursuit of Lee. *Dinwiddie Co.: Rte. 460, .2 mile e. of Sutherland.*

K-306 EARLY PEANUT CROP

One mile northwest Dr. Matthew Harris grew the first commercial crop of peanuts in the United States, according to tradition, in or soon after 1842. *Sussex Co.: Rte. 460, 4 miles s.e. of Waverly.*

K-307 BATTLE OF FIVE FORKS

Four miles south is the battlefield of Five Forks. To that point Pickett retired from Dinwiddie Courthouse in the night of March 31, 1865. Sheridan, following, attacked him in the afternoon of April 1, 1865. The Confederates, outnumbered and surrounded, were overwhelmed. This defeat broke Lee's line of defense around Petersburg and forced him to retreat. *Dinwiddie Co.: Rte. 460, 4.9 miles w. of Sutherland.*

K-308 MILES B. CARPENTER

Miles B. Carpenter (1889–1985) moved to a Sussex County peanut farm from Pennsylvania in 1902. He entered the lumber business in 1912 with a planing mill and sawmill. When business slowed during World War II, he whittled figures but did not carve in earnest until the 1960s, when his watermelons, peanut men, and whimsical monsters earned him a national reputation as a folk artist. Carpenter's woodcarvings reflected the influence of Sussex County's two major industries: lumber and peanuts. *Sussex Co.: Rte. 460 in Waverly, .11 mile n. of Rte. 40.*

K-310 JAMES BOWSER PLANTATION

James Bowser, the only negro from Nansemond County to fight in the American Revolution, enlisted as a private in the Virginia Continental Line and was honorably discharged in 1782. Bowser returned to the county at the close of the Revolution and built his own business as a farmer and horse-breeder on land granted as bounty for his services to the Commonwealth. He married and reared a large family of freeborn citizens. *Suffolk ("old" Nansemond Co.): 1 mile n. of Rtes. 629 and 337.*

K-311 JAMES RIVER

The James River flows about 340 miles from the junction of the Jackson and Cowpasture rivers in Botetourt County to Hampton Roads at the Chesapeake Bay. In 1607 the first permanent English settlement in the New World was established on its banks at Jamestown. The colonists used the river as a path for exploration. With modern cities and shipyards as well as ancient plantations lining its banks, the James River remains one of Virginia's most important natural resources. *Isle of Wight Co.: Rte. 17, at s. end of James River Bridge.*

KA-7 CARTER'S FORT

Near here stood a fort first known as Crissman's Fort, and later as Carter's or Rye Cove Fort, and by militia officers as Fort Lee. Built by Isaac Crissman, Sr. in 1774, it was acquired by Thomas Carter (1731–1803) after Crissman's death at the hands of Indians in 1776. The fort was rebuilt in 1777 by Col. Joseph Martin and his militia troops who occupied it until at least 1794. The fort was under the command of Captain Andrew Lewis, Jr. from 1792 to 1794. *Scott Co.: Rte. 23, .5 miles w. of Rte. 871.*

KA-8 DONELSON'S INDIAN LINE

John Donelson's line, surveyed after the treaty of Lochaber with the Indians, 1770, crossed the road here. This line separated Indian territory from land open to settlement. Violations of the line by settlers contributed to Dunmore's War, 1774. *Lee Co.: Rte. 23, 5 miles s. of Big Stone Gap.*

KA-9 KILGORE FORT HOUSE

The Kilgore Fort House was built in 1786 by Robert Kilgore whose family were early settlers in this area. It was one of the twelve forts between Castlewood and Cumberland Gap providing ready refuge for settlers from Indian attacks in the late 18th century. Kilgore later was a preacher in the Primitive Baptist Church, often holding religious services at the Fort House. He married Jane Porter Green, daughter of Patrick Porter who built Porter's Fort on Fall Creek. *Scott Co.: Rte. 71, 1.2 miles w. of Nickelsville.*

KA-10 CARTER'S FORT

Three miles east, in Rye Cove, stood Carter's Fort, built by Thomas Carter in 1784. It was a station on the old Wilderness Road from North Carolina to Kentucky. *Scott Co.: Rte. 871, 1 mile e. of Sunbright.*

KA-11 BIG STONE GAP

Big Stone Gap, originally known as Three Forks, received its charter February 23, 1888. A postoffice was established April 12, 1856. In the early nineties it became the center of iron and coal development. It was the home and workshop of John Fox, Jr., novelist, and author of "Trail of the Lonesome Pine." *Wise Co.: Rte. 23, at Powell River bridge in Big Stone Gap.*

KA-15 FIRST COURT OF SCOTT COUNTY

The monument in the field to the east marks the site of Benjamin T. Hollins' home, in which was held the first court of this county, February 14, 1815. *Scott Co.: Rte. 23 and Rte. 58, at Weber City.*

KA-16 PATRICK HAGAN AND DUNGANNON

Patrick Hagan (1828–1917) emigrated from Dungannon, Ireland, about 1844 and joined his uncle, Joseph Hagan, in Scott County. He read law, was admitted to the bar, and became one of the state's foremost land lawyers. Hagan amassed large holdings of coal and timber lands, including Osborne's Ford, as it had been called since 1786 when Stephen Osborne obtained a land grant. The community, which Hagan renamed for his birthplace, grew rapidly after the Clinchfield Railroad built a depot in 1912. Hagan also designed the town plan, and Dungannon was incorporated in 1918. *Scott Co.: Rte. 65, at Dungannon.*

KB-6 SALTVILLE

The land, patented by Charles Campbell in 1753, passed to the wife of General Francis Preston. General William Russell began saltmaking here in 1788; Thomas Madison directed the work in 1790. William King greatly enlarged the works. In 1861–64 the Confederate government obtained salt here. In October, 1864, Stoneman destroyed the salt works. The town was incorporated in 1894. *Smyth Co.: Rte. 91, at Saltville.*

KB-56 EGGLESTON'S SPRINGS

Near here Adam Harmon, probably in 1750, established what is believed to be the first settlement in Giles County. Here, in 1755, he found Mary Ingles as she was making her way back to Draper's Meadows after her escape from the Indians. *Giles Co.: Rte. 730, at Eggleston.*

KB-65* LINCOLN'S VIRGINIA ANCESTORS

Thomas Lincoln, the father of the president, was born just west of here in 1778. He was a grandson of John Lincoln who settled here about 1767, and whose house stood to the east. The Lincoln family graveyard is nearby. *Rockingham Co.: Rte. 42, 2.5 miles n. of Edom.*

KB-75 FORT DICKINSON

The site was about one-half mile north of the river. This was one of a chain of frontier forts ordered erected by the Virginia Legislature early in 1756. The chain extended from Hampshire County (now West Virginia) to Patrick Co. on the North Carolina border. These forts were established under the supervision of Colonel George Washington, who made an inspection tour of the chain. This Fort was attacked by Indians at least once in 1756 and again the next year. *Bath Co.: Rte. 42, 3 miles s.e. of Milboro Springs.*

KC-1 BLAND

The community center was first known as Crab Orchard. The place became the county seat of Bland County when it was formed in 1861 under the name of Seddon, which was later changed to that of the county. At Rocky Gap a skirmish was fought in Crook's raid against the Virginia and Tennessee Railroad, May, 1864. *Bland Co.: Rte. 52, .35 mile s. of Rte. 98.*

KC-2* A GREAT PREACHER

Some miles to the east was born William Elbert Munsey, July 13, 1833, and near here he preached his first sermon. Ordained to the Methodist ministry in 1855, Munsey was a noted preacher in several States. He died, October 23, 1877. *Bland Co.: Rte. 52, 2 miles s. of Rocky Gap.*

KC-3 ONE OF THE "BIG FOUR"

Here is the home of S. H. Newberry, who, with three others, composed the "Big Four" in the Virginia Senate. These four men united to defeat objectionable measures of the Readjuster movement. *Bland Co.: Rte. 52, 7 miles s. of Bland.*

KC-4 TOLAND'S RAID

Over this pass, Union cavalry under Colonel John T. Toland raided to Wytheville to destroy the Virginia and Tennessee Railway (N. & W.), July 1863. Mary Tynes, a girl of the neighborhood, rode ahead to warn the people. When the raiders reached Wytheville, they were repulsed by home guards and Toland was killed. *Wythe Co.: Rte. 52, at Bland Co. line.*

KC-10 CATY SAGE

Two miles to the southwest was the home of James and Lovis Sage. From it their five-year-old daughter Caty was abducted in 1792. Fifty-six years later a brother found her in Eastern Kansas, living with Wyandot Indians. *Grayson Co.: Rte. 21, 4 miles s. of Wythe Co. line.*

KD-5 SEAT OF FINCASTLE COUNTY

Three miles southwest, on New River, was the seat of Fincastle County, which from 1772 to 1776 embraced Southwestern Virginia, including Kentucky. There are the ancient lead mines, visited and described by Thomas Jefferson. *Wythe Co.: Rte. 52, 5.5 miles s.e. of Fort Chiswell.*

KD-6 JACKSON'S FERRY AND OLD SHOT TOWER

Here on New River, Captain William Herbert, before the Revolution, established a ferry, later called Jackson's Ferry, that was in operation until 1930. The old tower across the river was built about 1820 for the manufacture of shot. *Wythe Co.: Rte. 52, 7.7 miles s.e. of Fort Chiswell.*

KD-8 AUSTIN'S BIRTHPLACE

Near Austinville, five miles west, was born Stephen F. Austin, "Father of Texas," November, 1793. He began his colonization work in 1821. *Wythe Co.: Rte. 52, at Poplar Camp.*

KD-12 HILLSVILLE

This place became the county seat when Carroll County was formed. The first court was held here, 1842; A. W. C. Nowlin was the first judge. The courthouse, built in 1872, was remodeled some years ago. The town was incorporated in 1900 and rechartered in 1940. *Carroll Co.: Rte. 52, at Hillsville.*

KE-5 BATTLE OF CLOYD'S MOUNTAIN

Just to the west took place the battle of Cloyd's Mountain, May 9, 1864. The Union General Crook, raiding to destroy the Virginia and Tennessee Railroad (N. & W.), met and repulsed General A. G. Jenkins, who was mortally wounded. *Pulaski Co.: Rte. 100, 5 miles n. of Dublin.*

KG-2 STUART'S BIRTHPLACE

A short distance west is the site of the home of Archibald Stuart, Jr., a statesman of a century ago. There was born, February 6, 1833, his son, James Ewell Brown Stuart, who became Major-General commanding the cavalry of the Army of Northern Virginia and whose fame is a part of the history of that army. Stuart closed his career by falling in the defense of Richmond, May 11, 1864. *Patrick Co.: Rte. 103, 4 miles s. of Friends Mission.*

KG-5 FLOYD

This place became the county seat when Floyd County was formed in 1831. First called Jacksonville for Andrew Jackson, its name was changed to that of the county. The courthouse was built on land given by the Phlegar family. The town was incorporated in 1892 and rechartered in 1936. Here was born Admiral Robley D. Evans, hero of the Spanish-American War. *Floyd Co.: Rte. 8, at Floyd.*

KG-8 COLONEL WILLIAM PRESTON

One mile west is "Smithfield," old home of Col. William Preston, who materially guided the destiny of the Virginia frontier from the French and Indian War through the Revolution. On this estate two Virginia governors were born: James P. Preston, 1816–19; John B. Floyd, 1849–52. The latter was the son of another Virginia governor, John Floyd, 1830–34, who while in office advocated before the legislature abolition of slavery in Virginia. *Montgomery Co.: Rte. 460, at Blacksburg.*

KG-10 DRAPER'S MEADOW MASSACRE

Here a settlement was made by the Ingles and Draper families in 1748. It was attacked in July, 1755, about the time of Braddock's Defeat, by Indians, who killed or captured every person found. Colonel James Patton was among the slain. Mrs. Draper and Mrs. William Ingles were carried into captivity. *Montgomery Co.: Rte. 460, at s. entrance of Blacksburg.*

KG-12 MONTGOMERY WHITE SULPHUR SPRINGS

Near here stood Montgomery White Sulphur Springs, popular resort area of 19th century America. During the Civil War the resort was converted into a military hospital staffed by Catholic nuns. Several hundred victims of smallpox including nurses and soldiers are buried nearby. The Southern Historical Society was reorganized here in August, 1873, when Jefferson Davis delivered the principal address. *Montgomery Co.: I-81, .75 mile n. of Exit 128 at rest area, northbound lane.*

KG-14   CAMP JOHN J. PERSHING, CIVILIAN
         CONSERVATION CORPS COMPANY
         1370-2386

Near here is the original site of C.C.C. Company 1370–2386, known as Camp John J. Pershing, from 1933 to 1935, when it was moved to Nottoway County. Among the most popular New Deal programs, the Civilian Conservation Corps was designed to encourage conservation of natural resources and employment training during the Great Depression. C.C.C. Company 1370–2386 built roads, fire trails, and fire towers, and carried out extensive reforestation efforts in this county. *Giles Co.: Rte. 460 at Rte. 1404, in Pembroke.*

KG-15   MOUNTAIN EVANGELIST

The Reverend Robert Sayers Shelley (1820–1902), although one of a kind as to style and personality, was a Methodist Circuit Rider in the classic frontier tradition. Celebrated for the intensity of his faith and prayer, as well as for his eccentricities, Sheffey's authority was recognized throughout this region. He is buried nearby, in Wesley Chapel Cemetery, beside his second wife, Elizabeth Stafford Shelley. *Giles Co.: Rte. 100 at Rte. 730.*

KG-16   OLD-FASHIONED CAMP MEETING

Adjacent to and named for this stream, Wabash Campground was exemplary of a religious and social institution, indeed of a way of life, which flourished during the 19th century. Hundreds of families would camp for two weeks or more while attending the revival meetings first held here in 1834. The campground functioned until the early 1900's, when the large shed used during worship and many family shelters were destroyed by fire. *Giles Co.: Rte. 100, .6 mile n. of Rte. 659.*

KG-17   SNIDOW'S FERRY

In this vicinity Christian Snidow, pioneer, established a ferry over the river in 1786, and built a house in 1793. *Giles Co.: Rte. 460, 3 miles e. of Pearisburg.*

KG-19   DISCOVERY OF NEW RIVER

Abraham Wood, who lived at Fort Henry (Petersburg), possibly visited this stream in 1654. It was reached by Batts and Fallam, sent by Wood, on September 13, 1671. Long known as Wood's River, it came to be called New River. *Giles Co.: Rte. 460, 3 miles e. of Pearisburg.*

KG-20   FIRST COURT OF GILES COUNTY

About a mile north, in what is now Bluff City, was held the first court of Giles County, May 13, 1806. Near by stood the home of George Pearis, the first settler in this section. *Giles Co.: Rte. 460, 1 mile n. of Pearisburg.*

KG-21   PEARISBURG

The town was laid off in 1806 when Giles County was formed, and named for Captain George Pearis, early settler. Established in 1808, it was first incorporated in 1835, and reincorporated in 1914. Here, in May 1862, Union troops under Colonel Rutherford B. Hayes were defeated by Confederates under General Henry Heth. The present courthouse was erected in 1836. *Giles Co.: Rte. 460, at Pearisburg.*

KG-22 NARROWS

Named for the narrows in New River. The place was occupied by Confederate troops under French and Jackson in May, 1864. Combining with McCausland, they forced the Union General Crook to evacuate Blacksburg. Crook passed here on his way to West Virginia. The Norfolk and Western Railroad came in 1884; the Virginian in 1910. The town was incorporated in 1904. *Giles Co.: Rte. 460, at Narrows.*

KG-23 PITTSYLVANIA COURT HOUSE

This Greek Revival building was erected in 1853 as the third Court House of Pittsylvania County. The county, formed in 1767, and the Town of Chatham were named for William Pitt, First Earl of Chatham. The present Court House replaced a structure built in 1783 one block west where the old offices of the clerk still stands. The court was removed to this locality from Callands in 1777. *Pittsylvania Co.: Rte. 29 in front of courthouse.*

KH-1 GOVERNOR FLOYD'S GRAVE

A short distance across the State line is the grave of John Floyd, Governor of Virginia, 1830–34. Floyd while in Congress led in taking measures to secure Oregon for the United States. He died in 1837. *Alleghany Co.: Rte. 311, just s. of Sweet Chalybeate.*

KH-2 GREAT EASTERN DIVIDE— ELEVATION 2704 FEET

This point marks a spot along the geographical feature known as the Great Eastern Divide. From here water of Sinking Creek flows southwest into the New River. The New River, probably the oldest stream in eastern North America, becomes the Kanawha before joining the Ohio, the Mississippi, and eventually the Gulf of Mexico. From this spot water of Meadow Creek flows northeast to New Castle where it joins Craigs Creek, which in turn flows into the James River and ultimately into the Atlantic Ocean. *Craig Co.: Rte. 42, 8.1 miles w. of Rte. 311.*

KH-4 NEW CASTLE

This place became the county seat when Craig County was formed in 1851. The courthouse was built in 1851 and remodeled in 1935. General Averell passed through New Castle in his raid of December, 1863, and General Hunter in June, 1864. The town was incorporated in 1890. *Craig Co.: Rte. 311, at New Castle.*

KH-7 HANGING ROCK

On June 31, 1864 General Hunter, retreating from defeat at Lynchburg by General Early, met confederate forces led by General John McCausland. After losing some of his artillery here, Hunter continued his withdrawal northwest through New Castle to Lewisburg. *Roanoke Co.: Rte. 311, n. of Salem at Rte. 116.*

KM-5 QUAKER BAPTIST CHURCH

A Quaker meeting was established on Goose Creek in 1757, and a meeting house built. Fear of Indians caused most of the Quakers to move elsewhere though some of them returned. Unsuccessful attempts were made to reestablish the Goose Creek meeting. Before 1824 a church was established near here, known as Difficult Creek Baptist Church. The present Church (Quaker Baptist), built in 1898, stands near the site of the old building. *Bedford Co.: Rte. 24, 3 miles e. of Rtes. 122 and 24.*

KN-1 HOSPITAL OF ST. VINCENT DEPAUL

Founded in 1855, the Hospital of St. Vincent depaul was Norfolk's first civilian hospital. Located two blocks south at the corner of Church and Wood streets, the hospital was opened in the home of Ann Plume Herron by eight Daughters of Charity during a yellow fever epidemic. It was incorporated March 3, 1856, and later named dePaul Hospital when moved to the present site at Kingsley Lane and Granby Street. *Norfolk: Kingsley Ln. and Granby St.*

KN-2 NORFOLK BOTANICAL GARDENS

These gardens were conceived by City Manager Thomas Thompson during the Great Depression. His idea was executed by city gardener Frederic Heutte; noted landscape architect Charles F. Gillette served as a consultant. In 1938 about 200 black women were paid with Works Progress Administration funds to clear and plant the first 25 acres. The first phase of the gardens, which now occupy 175 acres and include landscaped vistas, arboretums, and special display areas, were their creation. *Norfolk: Rte. 192, at entrance to gardens.*

KN-3 BANK STREET BAPTIST CHURCH

The Bank Street Baptist Church was built on this site in 1802 as a Presbyterian church. In 1840 it was purchased by a group of free blacks to serve them as a Baptist church. Because it had one of the first church bells in Norfolk, the building was known as the Bell Church. The church continued to serve the black community until its demolition in 1967 when the congregation moved to its new location on Chesapeake Boulevard. *Norfolk: St. Paul's Blvd. and Charlotte St.*

KO-1 ST. JOHN'S CHURCH

Founded about 1643 and formerly known as Chuckatuck Church. The present building, the third on or near the site, was built in 1755 and is the second oldest church building in Nansemond County. Renamed St. John's Church in 1828. *Suffolk ("old" Nansemond Co.): Rte. 125, 1 mile e. of Chuckatuck.*

KO-2 NANSEMOND COLLEGIATE INSTITUTE

Here stood the Nansemond Collegiate Institute, founded in 1890 as the Nansemond Industrial Institute by Rev. William W. Gaines to provide local black children with an education, because free public schools were closed to them. Eventually the institute offered elementary, secondary, and normal school courses of instruction. In 1927 a public school for black students was opened; competition for students and a series of disastrous fires forced the institute to close in 1939. *Suffolk: E. Washington St. near Fifth St.*

KP-4* BOOKER WASHINGTON'S BIRTHPLACE

Nearby was born Booker Taliaferro Washington, probably in 1858, the son of a slave woman. He graduated at Hampton Institute, 1875, and became an instructor there. In 1881, he was appointed principal of the later famous Tuskegee Institute, Alabama. Recognized as an orator and the leader of the Negroes in America, he used his influence to promote harmony between the races and to advance the colored people educationally and economically. He died, November 14, 1915. *Franklin Co.: Rte. 122, just w. of Hales Ford Church.*

KP-4 BOOKER T. WASHINGTON BIRTHPLACE

Booker T. Washington was born a slave on the nearby Burroughs plantation on April 5, 1856. He was graduated from Hampton Institute in 1875 where he became an instructor. Because of his achievements as an educator, he was selected to establish a normal school for blacks in Alabama which later became the Tuskegee Institute. Recognized as an orator and author of *Up From Slavery,* he exerted great influence both in the Republican party and as a humanitarian for the benefit of his fellow blacks. He died November 14, 1915. *Franklin Co.: Rte. 122, just w. of Hales Ford Church.*

KV-1 FIRST FLIGHT SHIP TO SHORE

On 14 November, 1910, Eugene Ely in a Curtiss built "Hudson Flyer," utilizing a specially constructed platform with an up-tilt at the end, took off from the cruiser Birmingham anchored off Fort Monroe and landed at Willoughby Spit, 2 1/2 miles distant, thus completing the first flight from ship to shore and the first flight to utilize the "Ski Jump" deck. This was the birth of Naval aviation. *Norfolk: Fourth View St. and I-64, at visitors center.*

KV-4 SEASHORE STATE PARK

This park was developed by the National Park Service, Interior Department, through the Civilian Conservation Corps, in conjunction with the Virginia Conservation Commission. It covers 3400 acres and was opened, June 15, 1936. Two miles west is Lynnhaven Bay, in or near which there were naval actions in 1672 and 1700, and naval movements in 1781 and 1813. *Virginia Beach ("old" Princess Anne Co.): Rte. 60, 1 mile e. of Rte. 615.*

KV-5 LANDING OF WOOL AND SURRENDER OF NORFOLK

Near here Major-General John E. Wool, on May 10, 1862, landed with 6,000 Union troops. President Lincoln, Salmon P. Chase, Secretary of the Treasury, and Edwin M. Stanton, Secretary of War, watched the movement from a ship in Hampton Roads. As the Confederate troops had withdrawn, Wool marched to Norfolk, which was surrendered to him by Major W. W. Lamb that afternoon. *Norfolk: W. Ocean View Ave. near Mason Creek Rd.*

KV-6 SARAH CONSTANT SHRINE

This shrine commemorates the name of Captain Christopher Newport's flagship, the "Sarah Constant." The "Sarah Constant," with the two other ships, the "Godspeed," Captain Bartholomew Gosnold, and the "Discovery," Captain John Ratcliffe, first came to anchor in Virginia waters near here, April 26, 1607. *Norfolk: W. Ocean View Ave. near Fourth View St.*

KV-7 OPERATION TORCH, 1942

The first major amphibious action of World War II was planned near here in the Nansemond Hotel, Hdq. of Amphibious Force U.S. Atlantic Fleet. An Army-Navy staff under Adm. H. K. Hewitt met with General G. S. Patton to plan the movement of Task Force "A" from Hampton Roads to North Africa. *Norfolk: 350 ft. e. of Rte. 60 and Tidewater Dr.*

KV-15 FIRST LANDING

Near here the first permanent English settlers in North America first landed on American soil, April 26, 1607. From here they went on to make the settlement at Jamestown. The brick lighthouse was built in 1791. *Virginia Beach ("old" Princess Anne Co.): Rte. 60, .85 mile w. of Rte. 305, at Cape Henry.*

KW-16* OLDEST BRICK HOUSE
    IN VIRGINIA

One mile east stands the house of Adam Thoroughgood, built in 1636, the oldest brick residence in Virginia. Nearby is the site of the first church of Lynnhaven Parish, erected before 1640. *Virginia Beach ("old" Princess Anne Co.): Rte. 500, 7 miles e. of Norfolk.*

KY-4* BATTLE OF GREAT BRIDGE

A short distance east was a stockade fort built by the British to command a causeway and bridges over the swamp. Lord Dunmore, the royal governor, held this fort with a force of British regulars, tories and Negroes. On December 9, 1775, the regulars, led by Captain Fordyce, tried to cross the causeway to attack the Americans. Most of the British were killed or wounded, and Dunmore withdrew to his fleet. *Chesapeake ("old" Norfolk Co.): Rte. 170, at Great Bridge.*

KY-5 BATTLE OF GREAT BRIDGE

In this vicinity, in 1775, was the southern end of a causeway, with bridges, by which the swamp and stream were crossed. Here William Woodford's Virginia riflemen defended the passage. When Lord Dunmore's British regulars attempted to cross the swamp, on December 9, 1775, they were cut to pieces by the fire of the riflemen. This defeat forced Dunmore to evacuate Norfolk. *Chesapeake ("old" Norfolk Co.): Rte. 168, at Great Bridge.*

L-3 DOUTHAT STATE PARK

This park was developed by the National Park Service, Interior Department, through the Civilian Conservation Corps, in conjunction with the Virginia Conservation Commission. It covers nearly 4,500 acres and was opened, June 15, 1936. It lies in a region once extensively devoted to iron smelting. *Alleghany Co.: Rte. 60, 1.5 miles e. of Clifton Forge.*

L-5 LUCY SELINA FURNACE

This furnace was built in 1827 by Ironmasters John Jordan and John Irvine and was named for their wives. During the Civil War, iron produced here was used in the manufacture of Confederate Munitions. *Alleghany Co.: Rte. 60, at Longdale.*

L-8 NEW MONMOUTH CHURCH AND
    MORRISON'S BIRTHPLACE

This is the site of the first church, built 1746. Just northeast was the birthplace of William McCutchan Morrison, born, 1867, died, 1918. A missionary to the Belgian Congo, he translated the Bible into native languages and exposed conditions there. Buried at Luebo, Congo. *Rockbridge Co.: Rte. 60, 2 miles w. of Lexington.*

L-10 FIRST INDIAN FIGHT

The first clash between settlers and Indians in Rockbridge County occurred near here, December 18, 1742. Captain John McDonald led the settlers; the Indians were the Iroquois. *Rockbridge Co.: Rte. 130, at Glasgow.*

L-11 MOOMAW'S LANDING

Here was Moomaw's Landing on the North River Canal. In May 1863 the Packet Marshall passed here bearing the body of Gen. Thomas J. (Stonewall) Jackson to Lexington. Mrs. Robert E. Lee used the canal in 1865 to join her husband at Washington College (now Washington & Lee University) in Lexington. *Rockbridge Co.: Rte. 60, w. end of Buena Vista.*

L-12 SHADY GROVE

Two miles east is Shady Grove, built by Patrick Henry for his son, Spotswood Henry. *Campbell Co.: Rte. 501, at Gladys.*

L-20 QUAKER MEETING HOUSE

The first Quaker meeting house here was built in 1757; it was remodeled in 1765. Sarah Lynch, mother of Charles and John Lynch, founder of Lynchburg, gave the land for the church. This church is now the Quaker Memorial Presbyterian Church. *Lynchburg: Fort Ave. at Quaker Pkwy.*

L-21 MONTVIEW

Montview was constructed in 1923 as the home of Senator and former Secretary of the U.S. Treasury, Carter Glass. Glass served in the House of Representatives and Senate from 1902 to 1946 and was known as the "Father of the Federal Reserve System" in recognition of which his likeness appears on the $50,000 Treasury note. Glass was a co-sponsor of the Glass-Steagall Act of 1933. In 1941, he was sworn in as President Pro-Tem of the U.S. Senate on the sun porch of Montview. *Lynchburg: University Blvd., at entrance to Liberty University.*

L-22 SANDUSKY

In the grove to the northwest is Sandusky, built by Charles Johnston in 1797 and named for the city in Ohio, then a trading post, where Johnston stayed after escaping from the Indians. Here the Union General Hunter had his headquarters, June 17–18, 1864. Presidents Rutherford B. Hayes and William McKinley, then officers under Hunter, roomed together in this house. *Lynchburg: Fort Ave. at Quaker Pkwy.*

L-30* ORIGIN OF LYNCH LAW

A hundred yards west stands a walnut tree under which Colonel Charles Lynch, William Preston, Robert Adams, Jr., James Callaway and others held an informal court for the trial of tories and criminals, 1780. Punishment usually consisted of whipping. From this rude justice the term "Lynch Law" was evolved. *Campbell Co.: Rte. 29, 1 mile n. of Alta Vista.*

L-32 CLEMENT HILL

The house on the hill three hundred yards to the west was the home of Captain Benjamin Clement, who was one of the first makers of gunpowder in Virginia, 1775. The land grant was made in 1741. *Pittsylvania Co.: Rte. 29, 1 mile s. of Alta Vista.*

L-48 WHITMELL P. TUNSTALL

One mile east stands Belle Grove, the home of Whitmell Pugh Tunstall (1810–1854). Educated at Danville Academy and the University of North Carolina, Tunstall was admitted to the bar in 1832. He served in the House of Delegates (1836–1841; 1845–1848) and the Senate of Virginia (1841–1842). As a delegate representing Pittsylvania County, he fought for a decade to charter the Richmond and Danville Railroad (part of the present-day Norfolk Southern Railway). He served as the company's first president from 1847 until his death. Tunstall is buried at Belle Grove. *Pittsylvania Co.: Rte. 29 at Rte. 703.*

L-49 CLAUDE A. SWANSON

A native of Pittsylvania County, Claude Augustus Swanson (1862–1939), practiced law in Chatham until he won election to Congress in 1892. He served seven terms in the House of Representatives (1893–1906); was governor of Virginia (1906–1910) and United States senator (1910–1933); and served as secretary of the navy under President Franklin D. Roosevelt (1933–1939). As governor, Swanson persuaded the General Assembly to reform the public school system, improve rural roads, and create the position of state health commissioner. His last home in the county was at nearby Eldon. *Pittsylvania Co.: Rte. 29, .5 mile n. of Bus. Rte. 29.*

L-50* PEYTONSBURG

This place, fifteen miles east, was a village in 1752, when Halifax County was formed. It was established as a town in 1759, and fell within Pittsylvania when that county was formed in 1767. Canteens were made there for Greene's army in 1780–81. Washington stopped there on his Southern tour, June 4, 1791. *Pittsylvania Co.: Rte. 29, at Chatham.*

L-52 MARKHAM

Some miles northeast is the site of Markham, where was born Rachel Donelson, wife of President Andrew Jackson, 1767. Her father, John Donelson, leaving Virginia, became one of the first settlers of Tennessee. Fort Donelson was named for him. *Pittsylvania Co.: Rte. 29 Bypass, at Chatham, .25 mile s. of Rte. 685 exit.*

L-53 SAPONI RELIGIOUS BELIEFS EXPLAINED

On 12–15 October 1728 Col. William Byrd II and his party camped .6 mile west while surveying the Virginia–North Carolina boundary. Bearskin, Byrd's Saponi hunter and guide, described his tribe's religious beliefs, which, wrote Byrd in his diary, contained "the three Great Articles of Natural Religion: The Belief of a God; the Moral Distinction betwixt Good and Evil; and the Expectation of Rewards and Punishments in Another World." Bearskin's religion also included a Hindu-like belief in reincarnation. *Danville: Rte. 29 at North Carolina line.*

L-61 BEAVERS TAVERN

The house to the east was Beavers Tavern, 1800–1840. This was the muster ground of the county militia and a popular stage station. John C. Calhoun was a frequent visitor here. *Pittsylvania Co.: Rte. 29, 5 miles n. of Danville.*

LT-1   CALLANDS

Pittsylvania was cut off from Halifax in 1767 and the courthouse built here. In 1769 a town named Chatham was established here on land of James Roberts. A few years later Samuel Calland opened a store and the town took his name. In 1777 Henry County was cut off from Pittsylvania, and the county seat moved to Competition, more centrally located. The name Competition became Chatham in 1874. *Pittsylvania Co.: Rte. 57, at Callands.*

M-1*   ROBERT RUSSA MOTON
         HIGH SCHOOL

On this site 4–23–51, the students staged a strike protesting inadequate school facilities. Led by Rev. L. Francis Griffin, these students' actions became a part of the 1954 U.S. Supreme Court's Brown v. Board of Education decision, which ruled racial segregation in public schools unconstitutional. To avoid desegregation, the Prince Edward County public schools were closed 6–4–59 and remained closed until 9–2–64. *Prince Edward Co.: Rte. 15 and Ely St. in Farmville.*

M-1   ROBERT RUSSA MOTON
        HIGH SCHOOL

On this site 4–23–51, the students staged a strike protesting inadequate school facilities. Led by Rev. L. Francis Griffin, these students' actions became a part of the 1954 U.S. Supreme Court's Brown v. Board of Education decision, which ruled racial segregation in public schools unconstitutional. To avoid desegregation, the Prince Edward County public schools were closed until 9–2–64. *Prince Edward Co.: Rte. 15 and Ely St. in Farmville.*

M-7   TRABUE'S TAVERN

This was the home of Lt. John Trabue, Revolutionary War soldier and patriot, and of his descendants well into the 20th century. Trabue witnessed the surrender of the British forces at Yorktown in 1781 and later became an original member of the Society of the Cincinnati in Virginia. The Trabues were among the principal coalmine proprietors in the Midlothian area and here maintained a tavern that was patronized both by travelers and by workers from mines in the vicinity. *Chesterfield Co.: Rte. 677, .6 mile w. of Rte. 147.*

M-8   EPPINGTON

Two and one-third miles south stands Eppington, built in the late 1760s by Francis Eppes and his wife Elizabeth Wayles Eppes, half-sister to Martha Wayles Jefferson. Thomas Jefferson frequently visited Eppington. Lucy Jefferson, his daughter, died and was presumably buried at Eppington in 1786. Mary Jefferson, another daughter, was married to John Wayles Eppes, the son of Francis and Elizabeth Wayles Eppes, in 1797, and subsequently resided at Eppington. *Chesterfield Co.: Rte. 602, 4.5 miles e. of Amelia Co. line.*

M-9   PAUL CARRINGTON

Member of House of Burgesses 1765–1775, of Virginia conventions, 1774–1788, including Constitutional Conventions, of first Supreme Court of Appeals of Virginia. A founder of Hampden-Sydney College. Lived and is buried at Mulberry Hill nearby. *Charlotte Co.: Rte. 360, at Rte. 607 in Wylliesburg.*

M-10 GOODE'S BRIDGE

Here Anthony Wayne took station in July, 1781, to prevent the British from moving southward. Here, April 3, 1865, Longstreet's, Hill's and Gordon's corps of Lee's army, retreating from Petersburg toward Danville, crossed the river. *Chesterfield Co.: Rte. 360, 7.8 miles e. of Amelia.*

M-11 LEE'S RETREAT

Lee's army reached Amelia, April 45, 1865, moving southward. Here it was delayed by having to forage for food. In the afternoon of April 5, Lee advanced toward Jetersville. *Amelia Co.: Rte. 360, at Amelia.*

M-12 LEE'S RETREAT

Near here Lee, moving south toward Danville in the afternoon of April 5, 1865, found the road blocked by Sheridan. He then turned westward by way of Amelia Springs, hoping to reach the Southside (Norfolk and Western) Railroad. *Amelia Co.: Rte. 360, 4.8 miles s.w. of Amelia.*

M-13* LEE'S RETREAT

Near here, April 6, 1865, Meade, who was advancing northward on Amelia Courthouse, learned that Lee had turned westward. Meade sent the Second Corps on the Deatonsville Road, the Fifth Corps on the Paineville Road, and the Sixth Corps on a parallel route. *Amelia Co.: Rte. 360, 5.3 miles s.w. of Amelia.*

M-14 LEE'S RETREAT

Sheridan reached here on April 4, 1865, with cavalry and the Fifth Corps, and entrenched. He was thus squarely across Lee's line of retreat to Danville. On April 5, Grant and Meade arrived from the east with the Second Corps and the Sixth Corps. *Amelia Co.: Rte. 360, .7 mile s.w. of Jetersville.*

M-15 LEE'S RETREAT

From here Union cavalry moved north on April 5, 1865, to ascertain Lee's whereabouts. On the morning of April 6, the Second, Fifth and Sixth corps of Grant's army advanced from Jetersville toward Amelia Courthouse to attack Lee. *Amelia Co.: Rte. 360, at Jetersville.*

M-16 LEE'S RETREAT

The Union General Ord reached this place in the night of April 5, 1865, to head off Lee. On April 6, Ord sent a cavalry force from here to burn the bridges near Farmville and then moved westward with the Twenty-fourth Corps. *Nottoway Co.: Rte. 360, at Burkeville.*

M-17 HISTORIC BURKEVILLE

Tarleton's British cavalry, raiding west, stopped here in July, 1781. When railroads were built, the place was known as Burke's Junction. The Union cavalryman Kautz destroyed the railways here in June, 1864. Jefferson Davis passed through Burkeville, going south, April 3, 1865. Grant's headquarters were here, April 6, 1865. *Nottoway Co.: Rte. 360, at Burkeville.*

M-18 FRANCISCO'S FIGHT

A few miles east Peter Francisco, a soldier in the Virginia service, defeated, singlehanded, nine of Tarleton's British dragoons, July 1781. Francisco weighed two hundred and sixty pounds and was considered the strongest man in Virginia. After the Revolution he became doorkeeper of the House of Delegates. He died in 1836. *Nottoway Co.: Rte. 360, 6 miles n.e. of Burkeville.*

M-19 LEE'S RETREAT

Three miles north is Amelia Springs, once a noted summer resort. There Lee, checked by Sheridan at Jetersville and forced to detour, spent the night of April 5–6, 1865. *Amelia Co.: Rte. 360, at Jetersville.*

M-20 T. O. SANDY (FIRST COUNTY AGENT)

First Farm Demonstration Agent in Virginia lived one mile south. Appointed State Agent in 1907. Under his able leadership programs in Farm and Home Demonstration work, Boys Corn Clubs and Girls Canning Clubs were developed. In 1914 the Agency was transferred to the Virginia Polytechnic Institute and became the Extension Service now embracing mens and womens work and 4-H clubs. *Nottoway Co.: Rte. 460, 2.1 miles e. of Burkeville.*

M-21 CIVILIAN CONSERVATION CORPS COMPANY 1370

Near here is the site of Civilian Conservation Corps Company 1370 from 1935–1940. Among the most popular New Deal programs, the CCC was designed to encourage conservation of natural resources and employment training during the Great Depression. CCC 1370 enrollees were actively involved in soil erosion control and extensive reforestation efforts in this county. *Nottoway Co.: Rte. 460, at Crewe e. corp. limits.*

M-24 LEE'S RETREAT

Two miles north are the battlefields of Sailor's Creek, April 6, 1865. There Grant captured more men than were captured in any other one day's field engagement of the war. *Prince Edward Co.: Rte. 307, 3 miles e. of Rice.*

M-25 BATTLE OF SAILOR'S CREEK

Six miles north took place the battle of Sailor's Creek, April 6, 1865. Lee's army, retreating westward from Amelia Courthouse to Farmville by way of Deatonsville, was attacked by Sheridan, who surrounded Ewell's Corps. After a fierce action the Confederates were overpowered. Ewell, eleven other generals, and several thousand men were captured. This was the last major engagement between Lee's and Grant's armies. *Prince Edward Co.: Rte. 460, at Rice.*

M-26 BATTLE OF SAILOR'S (SAYLER'S) CREEK

This is the Hillsman House, used by the Unionists as a hospital in the engagement of April 6, 1865. From the west side of the creek the Confederates charged and broke through the Union infantry, but were stopped by the batteries along the hillside here. A mass surrender followed, including a corps commander, Gen. R. S. Ewell, several other generals, many colonels, about 7000 rank and file, and several hundred wagons. It was the largest unstipulated surrender of the war. *Amelia Co.: Rte. 617, 5 miles n.e. of Rice.*

M-26 BATTLE OF SAILOR'S (SAYLER'S) CREEK

At the same time another engagement took place two miles north, on the main Sailor's (Sayler's) Creek, where Gen. John B. Gordon repulsed pursuing Union troops. He lost most of his wagons but saved the majority of his men. At this time Gen. Robert E. Lee was retreating from Petersburg toward Danville, closely followed by Gen. Grant. Lee lost half of his troops in these two memorable rearguard actions, which foreshadowed the surrender at Appomattox three days later. *Amelia Co.: Rte. 617, 5 miles n.e. of Rice.*

M-30* ACTION OF HIGH BRIDGE

Three miles north took place the engagement of High Bridge, April 7, 1865. Lee's rear guard at the bridge head on the west bank of the Appomattox was driven off by the Second Corps of Grant's army after setting fire to the bridge. *Prince Edward Co.: Rte. 460, at Rice.*

M-33* LONGWOOD ESTATE

Birthplace, and until 1811, residence of Peter Johnston, Lieutenant in Lee's Legion in the Revolution; and birthplace of his son, Joseph E. Johnston, Brigadier General U.S.A., and General C.S.A. *Prince Edward Co.: Rte. 460, at Farmville.*

M-60 LYNCHBURG DEFENSES

The earthwork on the hilltop two hundred yards to the east was thrown up as a part of the system of defenses for Lynchburg, 1861–65. The city was an important supply base and railroad center. *Lynchburg: Rte. 501, e. entrance of Lynchburg.*

M-66 ELDON

Three miles north is Eldon, birthplace and home of Henry D. "Hal" Flood (1865–1921). A member of the United States House of Representatives (1901–1921), and Chairman of the Committee on Foreign Affairs (1913–1919), he drafted the Resolution declaring war on Germany and Austria, April 6, 1917. *Appomattox Co.: Rte. 460 at 131, in Appomattox.*

M-66* ELDON

Three miles north is Eldon, birthplace and home of Hal D. Flood, for many years a member of the United States House of Representatives. He was chairman of the Committee on Foreign Affairs, January, 1913–March, 1919, and the author of the resolution declaring war on Germany and Austria, April, 1917. He died in Washington, December 8, 1921. *Appomattox Co.: Rte. 24, 1.1 miles n. of Appomattox.*

M-66 INVENTOR OF THE BANJO

Nearby is buried Joel Walker Sweeney (circa 1810–1860), musician and developer of the five-string banjo. In 1831 Sweeney launched himself and his two brothers, Sam and Dick, on a series of minstrel tours that continued until his death twenty-nine years later. *Appomattox Co.: Rte. 24, 3.2 miles e. of Appomattox.*

M-66 MARLFIELD

A mile and a half west is the site of Marlfield, an eighteenth-century dwelling built by the Buckner family. It was purchased in 1782 by William Jones, who gave the house its name. Jones was among the first Virginia planters to use marl in his agricultural practices. His descendants sold Marlfield in 1906 but retained ownership of the nearby family cemetery. Marlfield had fallen into ruins by the mid-twentieth century. *Gloucester Co.: Rte. 17 at Rte. 613.*

M-67 CLAY SMOKING PIPES

For many years, residents of the vicinity made clay smoking pipes. Products of this industry were distributed to all parts of America during the nineteenth century. More recently, smoking pipes were factory produced in Pamplin City. *Appomattox Co.: Rte. 460, at Pamplin.*

MG-1 APPOMATTOX COURT HOUSE
　　　CONFEDERATE CEMETERY

Here were buried eighteen Confederate soldiers who died April 8 and 9, 1865 in the closing days of the War Between the States. The remains of one unknown Union soldier found some years after the war are interred beside the Confederate dead. About 500 yards east of this cemetery is the McLean House where Lee and Grant signed the surrender terms. *Appomattox Co.: Rte. 24, .2 mile e. of Appomattox.*

MG-2* THE LAST POSITIONS

Lee, retreating from Petersburg, reached the hills to the northeast, only to find Grant in position here across his line of retreat, April 8, 1865. The Confederates made an attack early in the morning of April 9. John B. Gordon broke through the opposing cavalry but was stopped by the infantry. Some hours later Lee rode along this road to meet Grant for surrender. *Appomattox Co.: Rte. 24, 2 miles n. of Appomattox.*

MG-3 WILDWAY

Three miles north is Wildway, home of Thomas S. Bocock, member of the United States Congress and only speaker of the Confederate House of Representatives. He was born, May 18, 1815, and died, August 25, 1891. *Appomattox Co.: Rte. 24, at Vera.*

MJ-1 BIZARRE

Near here is the site of Bizarre, owned in 1742 by Richard Randolph of Curles. In 1781, his grandson, John Randolph of Roanoke, took refuge at Bizarre with his mother on account of Arnold's invasion. John Randolph lived here until 1810, when he moved to Roanoke in Charlotte County. *Cumberland Co.: Rte. 45, at n. entrance of Farmville.*

N-3 THE GALLANT PELHAM

Here Major John Pelham, commanding Stuart's Horse Artillery, executed a stunning flank attack on advancing Union troops during the Battle of Fredericksburg on 13 December 1862. Reduced to one cannon, the 24-year-old Pelham halted the Federals for almost two hours by employing the flying artillery tactics that he had perfected. Observing from a nearby hilltop, Lee exclaimed, "It is glorious to see such courage in one so young!" Lee's battle report commended "the gallant Pelham." The Alabamian was fatally wounded three months later at Kelly's Ford on the upper Rappahannock River. *Spotsylvania Co.: Rte. 17, .02 mile s. of Rte. 608.*

N-4* FREDERICKSBURG CAMPAIGN

Here passed part of the Army of the Potomac, under General Burnside, on the way from Warrenton to Fredericksburg, November, 1862. The battle of Fredericksburg was fought, December 13, 1862. *Stafford Co.: Rte. 17, 4.1 miles n.w. of Falmouth.*

N-5 CAVALRY AFFAIRS

Near here Wade Hampton with a small cavalry force surprised and captured 5 officers and 87 men of the Third Pennsylvania Cavalry, November 28, 1862. At that time Burnside was moving toward Fredericksburg. On February 25, 1863, Fitz Lee, on a reconnaissance, attacked Union cavalry here, driving it back on Falmouth where the Union army was encamped. *Stafford Co.: Rte. 17, 8 miles n.w. of Falmouth.*

N-6* THE MUD MARCH

Here passed a part of the Army of the Potomac moving westward toward the fords of the Rappahannock, January 20–21, 1863. Burnside, commanding, sought to get in the rear of Lee, who was at Fredericksburg. A storm, making the roads deep in mud, forced the abandonment of the movement. *Stafford Co.: Rte. 17, 4.1 miles n.w. of Falmouth.*

N-8 LEDERER EXPEDITION

The explorer, John Lederer, and his companions started near here in August, 1670 on their way to the Blue Ridge Mountains. Lederer was one of the first to explore the Piedmont north of the James River. *Caroline Co.: Rte. 17, 12.5 miles s.e. of Fredericksburg.*

N-9 EARLY SETTLEMENT

Two miles east near the river, Richard Coleman planted a frontier settlement and trading post in 1652. By 1660 a church was built to which every man was required to come armed for protection against the Indians. *Essex Co.: Rte. 17, 7 miles n.w. of Caret.*

N-10 COLONIAL POST OFFICE

Here was Newpost, headquarters of Alexander Spotswood (Governor of Virginia, 1710–22), deputy postmaster general for the colonies, 1730–39. Spotswood also had an iron furnace here. *Spotsylvania Co.: Rte. 17, .4 mile n.w. of New Post.*

N-11 JACKSON'S HEADQUARTERS

In an outhouse, here at Moss Neck, Stonewall Jackson had his headquarters, December, 1862–March, 1863. He was engaged in guarding the line of the Rappahannock with his corps of Lee's army. *Caroline Co.: Rte. 17, 5.7 miles s.e. of New Post.*

N-12 WINDSOR

This is the ancient Woodford estate. Governor Spotswood and the Knights of the Golden Horseshoe stopped here on their way to the mountains, August, 1716. Here General William Woodford was born, October 6, 1734. He defeated Governor Lord Dunmore at the Great Bridge, December, 1775, and took an important part in the Revolutionary War. *Caroline Co.: Rte. 17, 6.9 miles s.e. of New Post.*

N-13 SKINKER'S NECK

Two miles north on the Rappahannock River. There Jubal A. Early, in December, 1862, confronted Burnside's army on the other side of the river. His alertness prevented a crossing and battle at this point. *Caroline Co.: Rte. 17, 6.9 miles s.e. of New Post.*

N-14 HAZELWOOD

Here was the home of John Taylor of Caroline, Jefferson's chief political lieutenant and a leading advocate of States Rights. He died here in 1824. *Caroline Co.: Rte. 17, 12.7 miles s.e. of New Post.*

N-15 RAPPAHANNOCK ACADEMY

On this site colonial Mount Church, built about 1750. In 1808 the parish glebe was sold and the proceeds were used to establish a school; the church building was turned into Rappahannock Academy, one of the most noted schools in Virginia. *Caroline Co.: Rte. 17, 10 miles s.e. of New Post.*

N-16 WHERE BOOTH DIED

On this road two miles south is the Garrett place. There John Wilkes Booth, Lincoln's assassin, was found by Union cavalry and killed while resisting arrest, April 26, 1865. *Caroline Co.: Rte. 301, at Port Royal Cross Roads.*

N-17 OLD PORT ROYAL

The town was established in 1744 and was one of the principal shipping points on the Rappahannock River in colonial times. In December, 1862, Burnside, commanding the Army of the Potomac, considered crossing the river here but finally moved up to Fredericksburg. Union gunboats, attempting to pass up the river at that time, were driven back by D. H. Hill. *Caroline Co.: Rte. 1002, in Port Royal.*

N-18 OLD RAPPAHANNOCK COURTHOUSE

About half a mile northeast stood the old courthouse and clerk's office of Rappahannock County, 1665–1693. To this courthouse Thomas Goodrich and Benjamin Goodrich, ordered to appear with halters around their necks, came to express their penitence for taking part in Bacon's Rebellion in 1676. *Essex Co.: Rte. 17, at Caret.*

N-19 PORTOBAGO INDIAN TOWNS

On the river two and a half miles north and two miles northeast were the two principal towns of the Portobago Indians. In 1669 these Indians had sixty bowmen and hunters. *Essex Co.: Rte. 17, 11.8 miles n.w. of Caret.*

N-20* FONTHILL

A mile and a half west is Fonthill, home of R. M. T. Hunter, United States Senator, Confederate Secretary of State, and Confederate Senator. The place was raided by Union troops in 1863. In 1865, Hunter was arrested here and taken to prison in Fort Pulaski. *Essex Co.: Rte. 17, 3 miles n.w. of Caret.*

N-20 FONTHILL

A mile and a half west stands Fonthill, built in 1832 by Robert Mercer Taliaferro Hunter. He served variously as United States senator, Confederate secretary of state, Confederate States senator, and as a member of the peace commission that met with Union representatives near Fort Monroe in February 1865. Imprisoned briefly at the end of the war, Hunter soon resumed his public career, serving as treasurer of Virginia from 1874 to 1880. *Essex Co.: Rte. 17, 3 miles n.w. of Caret.*

N-21 HISTORIC TAPPAHANNOCK

The town was founded in 1680 under the name of Hobbs His Hole. In 1682, a port was established here and called New Plymouth. In 1808, the name was changed to Tappahannock. The British Admiral Cockburn shelled the town, December 1, 1814. An old customs house and a debtors' jail are here. *Essex Co.: Rte. 360, at Tappahannock.*

N-22 RITCHIE'S BIRTHPLACE

Here was born Thomas Ritchie, November 5, 1778. In 1804, he established the Richmond Enquirer, which ran until 1877, the most noted of Virginia newspapers. Ritchie was a political leader in Virginia and an editor of national fame. In 1845, he became editor of the Washington Union. He retired in 1851 and died, July 3, 1854. *Essex Co.: Cross St., at Tappahannock.*

N-23 VAUTER'S CHURCH

This was the upper church of St. Anne's Parish, formed in 1693. The northern half of the structure was built about 1719, the southern wing in 1731. The church still has a communion service set presented by Queen Anne. *Essex Co.: Rte. 17, 10.7 miles n.w. of Caret.*

N-24 FORT LOWRY—CAMP BYRON

Located two miles N.E. on Rappahannock River at Lowry's Point was a Confederate eight gun "water battery" constructed in 1861. Here at Dunnsville was located Camp Byron, home of Company F (Essex Light Dragoons), Ninth Cavalry, C.S.A.; the company moved to Fort Lowry in October 1861 to assist in the fort's defense and to conduct scouting missions. *Essex Co.: Rte. 17 at Rte. 611.*

N-25 ANCIENT INDIAN TOWN

Two hundred yards northeast on the river stood an early Indian town, seemingly the one known as "Appamatuck" to Captain John Smith in 1607. *Essex Co.: Rte. 17, 1.75 miles w. of Tappahannock.*

Just to the east stood Mann Meeting House, the first Methodist Episcopal Church in this region. It was built before 1794 and abandoned about 1880. The site is now occupied by the Macedonia Colored Baptist Church. *Essex Co.: Rte. 17, 12.4 miles s.e. of Tappahannock.*

Just east of here was the seat of the Waring family, members of which served the colony and our fledgling nation in elected and appointed offices and as officers in the county militia and the Continental Line. Thomas Waring II (ca. 1690–1754), Burgess 1736–1754, built a mansion here in 1733. His son Francis (1717–1771) Burgess 1758–1769, was an organizer of the Sons of Liberty and a signer of the Leedstown Resolves. The house, having survived three wars, burned in the late 19th century. *Essex Co.: Rte. 17, 2.27 miles s. of Caret.*

In the forest west of this point the Rappahannock Indians built a wooden fort as a defense against hostile Northern Indians. From the shore just to the northeast the Rappahannocks were transported thirty-five miles up the river, February 4, 1684. *Essex Co.: Rte. 17, 2.8 miles n.w. of Tappahannock.*

Here in 1861 Confederates constructed an eight gun "water battery" principally for the defense of Fredericksburg. The guns were manned by the 55th Infantry Regiment located 500 yards N.W. The cannons were moved and the fort abandoned March 1862 after Northern Neck troop withdrawal left unit [*sic*] defenseless. On April 14, 1862, six Union gun boats bombarded and burned the installation. Thereafter, the fort functioned in limited capacity until the war ended. *Essex Co.: Rte. 646 at fort site.*

This church was constituted in 1772 by the noted Baptist preacher, John Waller. The first building stood on the old glebe overlooking the Rappahannock River; hence the name Glebe Landing. The present building was erected in 1839. *Middlesex Co.: Rte. 17, 12.1 miles n.w. of Saluda.*

Three miles east is Hewick, built about 1678 by Christopher Robinson, clerk of Middlesex County. It was the birthplace of John Robinson, Speaker of the House of Burgesses and Treasurer of Virginia, 1738–1766, the leading man of the colony. *Middlesex Co.: Rte. 17, 3.1 miles n.w. of Saluda.*

Half a mile east is Christ Church, Middlesex. The first building was erected about 1666; the present one in 1712. About 1840 the church was restored. The colonial governor, Sir Henry Chicheley, is buried there. *Middlesex Co.: Rte. 33, 2.4 miles s. of Urbanna.*

N-49 TOMB OF PULLER

In Christ Churchyard immediately to north lies buried Lt. Gen. Lewis Burwell Puller, USMC. He led Marines in 19 campaigns from Haiti and Nicaragua through the Korean War receiving 53 decorations and the admiration and affection of those he led. He was a Marine's Marine and is a tradition of Virginia and our nation's history. *Middlesex Co.: Rte. 33, 3 miles e. of Saluda.*

N-50 LOWER METHODIST CHURCH

Built 1717, this was the second lower chapel of Christ Church Parish, Middlesex County. It occupies the site of the first lower chapel of this parish, built before 1661 as the church of Piankatank Parish. Bartholomew Yates was the first minister of the present church. After 1792 the church was unused, except by the Methodists or Baptists. In 1857 Robert Healy bought the church from the parish and gave it to the Methodists, who have worshipped here ever since. *Middlesex Co.: Rte. 33, 9.3 miles s.e. of Saluda.*

N-58* THE SERVANTS' PLOT

On this Poropotank Creek, in 1663, the indentured servants of Gloucester County, weary of their hard lot, plotted an insurrection. The plot was matured, but it was betrayed by one Birkenhead, a servant at Purton, who thereby probably prevented a massacre. He was freed and given a present of tobacco. Mary Johnston's novel, "Prisoners of Hope," uses this incident. *King and Queen Co.: Rte. 14, 1.1 miles w. of Adner.*

N-61 POPLAR SPRING CHURCH

This is the site of Poplar Spring Church of Petsworth Parish. In 1694, old Petsworth Church was abandoned in favor of this church. It was considered the finest church of colonial Virginia. In 1676, the followers of Bacon, the Rebel, interred here a casket supposed to contain his remains, but in reality filled with stones. The body was buried secretly. *Gloucester Co.: Rte. 17, 5 miles n.w. of Gloucester.*

N-66 MARLFIELD

A mile and a half west is Marlfield, home of John Buckner, clerk of Gloucester County, who brought the first printing press into Virginia. Buckner printed the laws of 1680 without license, for which he was reproved in 1682 by Governor Lord Culpeper and his printing was prohibited. *Gloucester Co.: Rte. 17, 4.5 miles n.w. of Gloucester.*

N-77 STINGRAY POINT

Eight miles east, where the Rappahannock River joins Chesapeake Bay. Near there, in June, 1608, Captain John Smith, the explorer, was hurt by a stingray while fishing in the river. The point took its name from this incident. *Middlesex Co.: Rte. 33, 8.6 miles w. of Deltaville.*

N-84 CAPTAIN SALLY L. TOMPKINS, C.S.A., 1833–1916

Sally Tompkins, born at Poplar Grove 3 miles south of here, was the only woman granted a commission in the Army of the Confederacy. "Captain Sally" founded and directed Robertson Hospital in Richmond where over 1300 Confederate soldiers were cared for between 1861 and 1865. Her grave and monument are located in Christ Church Cemetery on Williams Wharf Road two miles to the south. *Mathews Co.: Rte. 611, 2 miles w. of Mathews Court House.*

On the shore here General Andrew Lewis, commanding the Virginia forces, erected a battery facing a stockaded camp on Gwynn's Island established by Governor Lord Dunmore, July, 1776. The fire from this point, Cricket Hill, damaged the camp and the British ships and forced the evacuation of the island. A little later Dunmore put out to sea. *Mathews Co.: Rte. 223, 4 miles n. of Mathews.*

N-86 FITCHETT'S WHARF

Fitchett's Wharf was a center of commercial activity for this area of Mathews County from 1845 until the early 20th century. It also served as a major port of call for vessels plying the Chesapeake Bay until 1932. An important shipyard, owned and operated by Lewis Hudgins, stood here until it was burned by Union forces in 1864. Several well-known brig and schooner class commercial ships were built here, including the Victory and the Conquest. The shipbuilder's house still stands nearby, and the wharf store has been restored as a residence. *Mathews Co.: Rte. 642, at Moon Post Office.*

N-87 KINGSTON PARISH GLEBE

Just south, between Put In Creek and Woodas Creek, lies the former glebe of Kingston Parish of the Church of England (now the Protestant Episcopal Church). In 1665 the parish acquired the first parcel (455 acres) of glebe land to support its minister. After the Revolution and subsequent disestablishment of the Church of England, parishes gradually relinquished their property. In 1802 the General Assembly ordered all glebes sold. Kingston Parish auctioned off its glebe in 1810 to help the poor. *Mathews Co.: Rte. 621 near Rte. 611.*

N-88 MATHEWS COUNTY COURTHOUSE SQUARE

Mathews County was formed in 1790 from Gloucester County and named for Thomas Mathews, of Norfolk, a soldier of the Revolution who was then Speaker of the Virginia House of Delegates. A local builder, Richard Billups, constructed the courthouse between 1792 and 1795. Other early buildings in the square include a jail (ca. 1795) and clerk's office (1859). The courthouse square is listed in the Virginia Landmarks Register and the National Register of Historic Places. *Mathews Co.: Rte. 611, .2 mile w. of Rte. 14.*

ND-3 NEWMARKET

Newmarket stood on the Little River near Verdon in northern Hanover County until 1987, when to preserve it Robert W. Cabaniss moved it to this site. The seat of the Doswell family for whom the town of Doswell was named, the house is the sole survivor of a large plantation complex that once included a gristmill, tanyard, and cotton factory. James Doswell, a Revolutionary War veteran, probably built Newmarket in the late eighteenth century. *Hanover Co.: Rte. 615, 1.2 miles n. of Rte. 606.*

ND-4 PATRICK HENRY'S BIRTHPLACE

Seven miles east, at Studley, May 29, 1736, was born Patrick Henry, the orator of the Revolution. *Hanover Co.: Rte. 2, 8.9 miles s. of Hanover.*

ND-5 EDMUND PENDLETON'S HOME

Six miles southeast is the site of Edmundsbury, home of Edmund Pendleton. Pendleton, born September 9, 1721, was in the House of Burgesses; a delegate to the Continental Congress; chairman of the Virginia Committee of Safety, 1775–6; president of the May 1776 convention and the convention that ratified the United States constitution, 1788; president of the Virginia supreme court. He died, October 26, 1803, and was buried there but was later removed to Williamsburg. *Caroline Co.: Rte. 2, 2.5 miles s. of Bowling Green.*

ND-6 CLAY'S BIRTHPLACE

Three miles northwest is Clay Spring, where Henry Clay was born, April 12, 1777. He passed most of his early life in Richmond, removing to Kentucky in 1797. His career as a public man and as a peacemaker between North and South is an important part of American history. *Hanover Co.: Rte. 2, 4.5 miles s. of Hanover.*

ND-7 CAMPAIGN OF 1781

Lafayette, marching from Head of Elk, Maryland, to Richmond, camped here the night of April 27, 1781. *Caroline Co.: Rte. 2, at Bowling Green.*

ND-8 THE DEPOT AT BEAVER DAM

The first railroad depot at Beaver Dam was built ca. 1840 to serve the farmers of Hanover and Louisa counties. Its strategic location during the Civil War made it the target of many Union raids. The July 20, 1862, raid saw the depot burned and Colonel John S. Mosby, the Gray Ghost, captured as he awaited a train to take him to General Stonewall Jackson. Rebuilt after this raid, the depot was again burned by Union troops on February 29, 1864, and May 9, 1864, the last time by the cavalry of General George A. Custer. The existing depot was rebuilt and rededicated in 1866. *Hanover Co.: Rte. 739, at Beaverdam.*

ND-9 CORNWALLIS'S ROUTE

Lord Cornwallis, marching northward in pursuit of Lafayette's American force, camped near here, May 30, 1781. He entered this road from the east on his way from Hanover Town to the North Anna at Chesterfield Ford (Telegraph Bridge). *Hanover Co.: Rte. 2, 1.3 miles s. of Hanover.*

ND-10 MEADOW FARM—BIRTHPLACE OF SECRETARIAT

This famous horsebreeding farm was established in 1936 by Christopher T. Chenery and continued under the management of his daughter, Helen "Penny" Chenery until 1979. Secretariat (1970–1989), also known as "Big Red," was born and trained here. A bright chestnut stallion with a white star and narrow stripe, he was a horse of uncommon excellence as he proved when he captured the Triple Crown in 1973. His win at the Belmont Stakes by 31 lengths won him the love and admiration of the nation. Other notable Thoroughbreds such as Riva Ridge, Hill Prince and First Landing also were raised at Meadow Farm. *Caroline Co.: Rte. 301, .4 mile e. of Hanover Co. line.*

NN-3 JOHN CLAYTON, BOTANIST

One and a half miles north is the site of his home "Windsor" where he developed an excellent botanical garden. He was the first president, Virginia Society for the promotion of Useful Knowledge, and clerk of Gloucester County from 1722 until his death in 1773. His herbarium specimens, some still preserved in the British Museum, were the basis of "Flora Virginia," compiled by Gronovius with the collaboration of Linnaeus and originally published at Leyden in 1739. *Mathews Co.: Rte. 14 e. of Gloucester Co. line.*

NP-1 CHARLES CHURCH

About one mile east, on north (lefthand) side of road (see stone marker and old foundations) stood the last colonial church of Charles Parish, built about 1708 and burned a century later, on the site of two earlier churches of the parish, built about 1636 and 1682. This parish was first known as New Poquoson Parish in 1635 and was renamed Charles Parish in 1692. *York Co.: Rtes. 134 and 17, at Tabb.*

NP-3 SEAFORD

Settlement began here in 1636, when John Chisman patented 600 acres on Crab Neck, a peninsula bounded by Chisman Creek and Back Creek, a tributary of York River. The neck then lay in Charles River Parish in York County, one of the eight original shires created in 1634. A Confederate fortification stood near the narrowest part of the neck in 1862, and during the Civil War Union troops destroyed Zion Methodist Church here. Crab Neck post office was established in 1889; its name was changed to Seaford in 1910. *York Co.: Rte. 622, at Seaford.*

NP-12 GOODWIN NECK

This area, locally known as Dandy, was part of the land granted to John Chew July 6, 1636, and was sold by his heirs to James Goodwin, a member of the House of Burgesses from Jamestown, August 27, 1668. The area was strategically important both to British General Charles Cornwallis and to Confederate General John B. Magruder, who erected earth redoubts at the heads of several creeks on Goodwin Neck. *York Co.: Rte. 173, 3.5 miles e. of Rte. 17.*

NW-1 GLOUCESTER COURTHOUSE

The courthouse was built in 1766. The debtor's prison is also old. A skirmish occurred near here between Confederate and Union cavalry, January 29, 1864. *Gloucester Co.: Rte. 17, at Gloucester.*

NW-2 WARE CHURCH

A mile east is Ware Church, built about 1693. Near by is Church Hill, another relic of colonial days. Not far distant is White Hall, a colonial mansion built by the Willis family. *Gloucester Co.: Rte. 17, at e. entrance of Gloucester.*

NW-3 TO GWYNN'S ISLAND

Two miles east is Toddsbury, home of the Todd family, built in 1722. Farther east, in Mathews County are the old homes, Green Plains, Auburn, and Midlothian. Some miles beyond them is Gwynn's Island, where General Andrew Lewis drove the last royal governor, Lord Dunmore, from Virginia soil, July, 1776. *Gloucester Co.: Rte. 17, at e. entrance of Gloucester.*

NW-4 WARNER HALL

Three miles east is Warner Hall. The estate was patented about 1650 by Augustine Warner, who built the first house in 1674. Bacon, the Rebel, was here for a time in 1676. The later house, built about 1740 and burned in 1849, has been beautifully restored. *Gloucester Co.: Rte. 17, 4.2 miles s. of Gloucester.*

NW-5 ABINGDON CHURCH

This is the third church of Abingdon Parish and was erected in 1755 on the site of an earlier one. The parish, established between 1650 and 1655, had its first church near the river. *Gloucester Co.: Rte. 17, 6.2 miles s. of Gloucester.*

NW-6 WHITE MARSH AND REED'S BIRTHPLACE

Near here is White Marsh, a fine old house with terraced garden. Five miles west is the birthplace of Dr. Walter Reed, of the United States army, who first proved that yellow fever is conveyed by mosquitoes. *Gloucester Co.: Rte. 17, 5.3 miles s. of Gloucester.*

NW-7 TARLETON'S LAST FIGHT

Here, at the Hook, Tarleton, commanding the cavalry of Cornwallis's army, fought an action with Choisy's French force and Virginia militia, October 3, 1781. The Duke de Lauzun's cavalry charged Tarleton, who retired to Gloucester Point. There he was blockaded by the French and by Virginia militia. *Gloucester Co.: Rte. 1216, 2.1 miles n. of Gloucester Point.*

NW-8 ROSEWELL AND WEROWOCOMOCO

Several miles west is Rosewell, built about 1750, home of the Page family, and the largest of colonial Virginia houses. On York River, probably at Purtan Bay some miles west of Rosewell, was Werowocomoco, chief town of the Indian ruler Powhatan in 1607. *Gloucester Co.: Rte. 17, 5.3 miles s. of Gloucester.*

NW-9 GLOUCESTER POINT

Known first as Tyndall's Point. The colonists built a fort here in 1667. In 1676 Bacon led his rebels across the river here. Tarleton and Dundas occupied the place in October, 1781, in the siege of Yorktown. Cornwallis planned to break through the blockade here, but a storm kept him from crossing the river. The point was fortified by the Confederates in 1861 and occupied by Union troops in 1862. *Gloucester Co.: Rte. 17, at Gloucester Point.*

NW-10 EARLY LAND PATENT

Argoll Yeardley patented 4,000 acres of land, known as Tyndall's Neck, here on the north side of Charles (now York) River, October 12, 1640. This was one of the first land patents north of the York River. *Gloucester Co.: Rte. 17, at Gloucester Point.*

NW-11 THOMAS CALHOUN WALKER
(1862–1953)

Here lived Thomas Calhoun Walker, the first black to practice law in Gloucester County and a civil rights spokesman who vigorously advocated education and land ownership for blacks. Mr. Walker was elected for two terms to Gloucester's Board of Supervisors, serving from 1891 to 1895. President William McKinley appointed him the Commonwealth's first black collector of customs in 1893. He became the only black to hold statewide office in President Roosevelt's Works Project Administration when he was appointed Consultant and Advisor on Negro Affairs in 1934. *Gloucester Co.: Rte. 17, .1 mile n. of Rtes. 3 and 14.*

NW-12 ROBERT RUSSA MOTON

Robert Russa Moton was born in Amelia County, Virginia, on 26 August 1867, and was educated in a local freedman's school and at Hampton Institute (now Hampton University). He served as an administrator at the institute from 1890 to 1915, when he succeeded Booker T. Washington as president of Tuskegee Institute. There Moton led the school to full collegiate accreditation. An advisor to five U.S. presidents and a founder of the Urban League, he retired to Holly Knoll (10 miles northwest) in 1935. Moton died on 31 May 1940. Holly Knoll was designated a National Historic Landmark in 1981. *Gloucester Co.: Rte. 17, .04 mile s. of Rte. 614.*

NW-13 UNITED NEGRO COLLEGE FUND

Dr. Frederick D. Patterson founded the United Negro College Fund in 1944. He and the presidents of the member colleges of the Fund began meeting in 1946 at Holly Knoll, the retirement home of the late Robert Russa Moton. Patterson had established Holly Knoll Associates in 1945 to serve as a conference center for black educators. Their meetings contributed to the growth and reputation of the United Negro College Fund, which aids more than 40 historically black colleges, and provides student scholarships and faculty grants. The fund is known for its motto, "A mind is a terrible thing to waste." *Gloucester Co.: Rte. 17, .04 mile s. of Rte. 614.*

NW-15* DISMAL SWAMP CANAL

This canal, which connects Chesapeake Bay and Albemarle Sound, was charted by Virginia in 1787 and by North Carolina in 1790. It was opened to local traffic in 1806. The canal is now part of the inland waterway. *Chesapeake: Rte. 17, 1 mile s. of Rte. 104.*

NW-15 DISMAL SWAMP CANAL

This canal, which connects Chesapeake Bay and Albemarle Sound, was chartered by Virginia in 1787 and North Carolina in 1790. It opened to traffic in 1806 and is now part of the inland waterway. The area was visited by William Byrd II when he was surveying the boundary between Virginia and North Carolina. In 1763, George Washington explored the area and organized the Dismal Swamp Company to drain it for farmland. The Great Dismal Swamp is now a National Wildlife Refuge. *Chesapeake: Rte. 17, 1 mile s. of Rte. 104.*

O-5 OUTER FORTIFICATIONS

On the hilltops here ran the outer line of Richmond fortifications, 1862–1865. *Henrico Co.: Rte. 360, 1.4 miles s.w. of Mechanicsville.*

O-6* SEVEN DAYS' BATTLES

Longstreet's and D. H. Hill's divisions of Lee's army crossed the river here, in the afternoon of June 26, 1862, to attack the Union force at Mechanicsville. It was the opening of the Seven Days' Battles. *Hanover Co.: Rte. 360 at Henrico Co. line.*

O-7* SEVEN DAYS' BATTLES

By this road the Confederates moved to attack McClellan's fortified position at Ellerson's Mill on Beaver Dam Creek, June 26, 1862. Beyond is the field of Gaines's Mill, fought on June 27, 1862. *Hanover Co.: Rte. 156, .5 mile s. of Mechanicsville.*

O-8* SHERIDAN'S RAID

Sheridan, moving around Richmond, reached this point on May 12, 1864, after a fight, and passed on to the James River near Shirley. *Hanover Co.: Rte. 360, e. entrance of Mechanicsville.*

O-9 SEVEN DAYS' BATTLES

Here the Confederates attacked the force holding McClellan's fortified position on the east bank of Beaver Dam Creek, June 26, 1862. *Hanover Co.: Rte. 360, .2 mile n.e. of Mechanicsville.*

O-11 BATTLE OF COLD HARBOR

The left of Lee's line at Cold Harbor, June 3, 1864, crossed the road here. The main battle took place to the east, where Grant attacked Lee's trenches without success. *Hanover Co.: Rte. 360, 3.6 miles n.e. of Mechanicsville.*

O-12* BETHESDA CHURCH

This is the site of Old Bethesda Church. Here, on May 30, 1864, a part of Warren's (Fifth) Corps of Grant's army, advancing southward, was attacked by Early. On June 2, 1864, Early here attacked Burnside's (Ninth) Corps. *Hanover Co.: Rte. 360, 4.6 miles n.e. of Mechanicsville.*

O-13* CORNWALLIS'S ROUTE

Lord Cornwallis, in the pursuit of Lafayette that led him to the North Anna River, passed near here, May 30, 1781. *Hanover Co.: Rte. 360, 10.6 miles n.e. of Mechanicsville.*

O-14* GRANT'S CROSSING

Some miles west of this spot the four corps of Grant's army crossed the river, May 28–29, 1864, moving toward Richmond. This move was followed by the battle of Cold Harbor. *Hanover Co.: Rte. 360, 11.8 miles n.e. of Mechanicsville.*

O-15 HENRY'S CALL TO ARMS

One mile east on the river was Newcastle. There, on May 2, 1775, Patrick Henry put himself at the head of the Hanover volunteers and marched against the royal governor, Lord Dunmore, who had seized the colony's powder. *Hanover Co.: Rte. 360, 11.8 miles n.e. of Mechanicsville.*

O-16 RUMFORD ACADEMY

Two miles east was Rumford Academy, established in 1804. It was one of the most noted Virginia schools of its time. *King William Co.: Rte. 360, at Central Garage.*

O-17* OLD PLACES

About twelve miles to the east are Mount Pleasant, built about 1734; and Sweet Hall, built about 1720, one of the quaintest old houses in Virginia. A little beyond is Romancoke, once the home of Lee's son, R. E. Lee, Jr., and visited by General Lee. *King and Queen Co.: Rte. 631, 2 miles n. of Manquin.*

O-18 CAVALRY RAIDS

Kilpatrick, coming from the east, burned Confederate stores here, May 5, 1863. Dahlgren, coming from Richmond, crossed the Mattapony here March 2, 1864. Sheridan, returning from his Richmond raid, was here, May 22–23, 1864, and on his Trevillian raid passed here, June 7, 1864. *King William Co.: Rte. 360, at Aylett.*

O-20 CLARK HOME

About twelve miles east is the site of the original home of the family of George Rogers Clark, conqueror of the Northwest. The family moved from here to Albemarle County. *King and Queen Co.: Rte. 360, at Saint Stephens Church.*

O-21* WHERE DAHLGREN DIED

Colonel Ulric Dalgren, returning from his raid to Richmond, was killed by Confederate soldiers and home guards about twelve miles to the southeast, March 2, 1864. *King and Queen Co.: Rte. 360, at Saint Stephens Church.*

O-22 MATTAPONY INDIAN TOWN

Three miles north, on Piscataway Swamp, the Mattapony Indians settled after the massacre of 1644. Here they lived in peace until 1668, when they moved west to the Mattapony River. *Essex Co.: Rte. 360, at Millers Tavern.*

O-23 BACON'S NORTHERN FORCE

At Piscataway, near here, the northern followers of Bacon the Rebel assembled in 1676. On July 10, 1676, an action was fought with Governor Berkeley's supporters, some of whom were killed and wounded. Several houses were burned. Passing here, the rebels marched south to the Pamunkey River, where they joined their leader, Bacon. *Essex Co.: Rte. 360, at Millers Tavern.*

O-24 EDMUND RUFFIN'S GRAVE

Here at Marlbourne (named for marl) is the grave of Edmund Ruffin, one of the greatest of American agriculturists. Ruffin moved here in 1843 and here carried on many of the experiments that made him famous. An ardent secessionist, he fired the first gun at Fort Sumter, April, 1861, and served in the Confederate army until incapacitated by age. He died in June, 1865. *Hanover Co.: Rte. 360, 8.9 miles n.e. of Mechanicsville.*

O-25 DUNLORA ACADEMY

Two and a half miles north, on Dunlora plantation then owned by Mrs. Ann Hickman, the Virginia Baptist Education Society established, in 1830, a school for ministers. This school, under the principalship of Rev. Edward Baptist, M.A., was known locally as Dunlora Academy. Edward Baptist resigned in 1832, and the school was removed to Henrico County and then to Richmond. From it developed Richmond College and later, the University of Richmond. *Powhatan Co.: Rte. 60, 5.7 miles w. of Powhatan.*

O-25* MONTVILLE ESTATE

This typical plantation house was built by a member of the Aylett family in 1803 on the site of an older house. *King William Co.: Rte. 360, 1 mile s.w. of Aylett.*

O-26 MATTOAX

Mattoax was located to the south on the Appomattox River. John Randolph, Sr., built a house there in the 1770s that burned after 1810; it was the boyhood home of his son, John Randolph of Roanoke. Mattoax also was the residence of St. George Tucker, a noted jurist, and his sons: Henry St. George Tucker, lawyer and legislator, and Nathaniel Beverley Tucker, novelist and law professor. In 1854 Sylvester J. Pearce built a second house on the site that stood until the 1930s. *Chesterfield Co.: Rte. 36, 1.9 miles w. of Ettrick.*

O-27* BETHLEHEM BAPTIST CHURCH

Formerly Spring Creek Church. Organized, July 25, 1790. Benjamin Watkins, founder and first pastor, 1790–1831. Located four miles northwest, 1790–1855. Then four miles southwest, 1855–1897. Moved to this location, 1897. Home church of Nannie Bland David, Missionary to Africa, 1880–1885. Her dying words: "Never give up Africa." *Chesterfield Co.: Rte. 60, 5.4 miles w. of Richmond.*

O-28 HUGUENOT SETTLEMENT

In this vicinity Huguenots, refugees from the tyranny of Louis XIV, settled in 1700 under the leadership of the Marquis de la Muce. The region had been deserted by its former occupants, the Monacan Indians, and the Huguenot settlement centered at the site of their village, called "Manakin Town." Later parties of Huguenots settled on both sides of James River and elsewhere. *Chesterfield Co.: Rte. 60, 1.7 miles e. of Midlothian.*

O-29 SALISBURY

Two miles north stood Salisbury, built in the eighteenth century as a hunting lodge. There Patrick Henry lived during his fourth and fifth terms as Governor of Virginia, 1784–1786. The Confederate General Edward Johnson lived there in his later years and died there. *Chesterfield Co.: Rte. 60, at Midlothian.*

O-30 DERWENT

Ten miles north is "Derwent" where Robert E. Lee lived in the summer of 1865 as the guest of Mrs. E. R. Cocke. Lee arrived at "Derwent" early in July. While there he was offered the presidency of Washington College, Lexington, which he accepted on August 24, 1865. On September 15, he left "Derwent" for Lexington. *Powhatan Co.: Rte. 13, 2 miles e. of Tobaccoville.*

O-31 GILES'S HOME

Five miles southwest is the Wigwam, the home of William B. Giles, Jefferson's chief lieutenant; United States Senator, 1804–1815, and Governor of Virginia, 1827–1830, an orator and famous political leader. Giles died there, December 4, 1830. *Powhatan Co.: Rte. 60, 1.7 miles w. of Powhatan.*

O-32 POWHATAN COURTHOUSE

The first courthouse was built about 1777. The village that grew up around it was long known as Scottsville for General Charles Scott, Revolutionary soldier, who lived in this county. A skirmish occurred here, January 25, 1865. Nearby is a tavern of the Revolutionary period. *Powhatan Co.: Rte. 13, at Powhatan.*

O-33 HUGUENOT SETTLEMENT

Huguenots, the largest single group of French Protestant refugees to come to Virginia, settled near here on the site of a deserted Monacan Indian village during the period 1700–1701. In 1700, the Virginia General Assembly established King William Parish, also known as Huguenot Parish. The Huguenots established a church at this site now known as the Manakin Episcopal Church. *Powhatan Co.: Rte. 711, 2.55 miles w. of Chesterfield Co. line.*

O-34 BLACK HEATH

Half a mile north is Black Heath, originally owned by John Heth, Revolutionary soldier. Here Major-General Henry Heth of the Confederate army was born, 1825. The best coal in Virginia was long found in the Black Heath mine. *Chesterfield Co.: Rte. 60, 1.7 miles e. of Midlothian.*

O-35* MIDLOTHIAN COAL MINES

A mile south are the Midlothian Coal Mines, probably the oldest coal mines in America. Coal was first mined here before 1730 and a railway was built from the mines to James River before 1830. Operations went on continuously until 1865, and the coal used in cannon casting at the Tredegar Iron Works, Richmond, was obtained here. *Chesterfield Co.: Rte. 60, at Midlothian.*

O-35 MIDLOTHIAN COAL MINES

South of here are the Midlothian Coal Mines, probably the oldest coal mines in America. Coal was first mined here before 1730, and during the Revolution, coal from these mines supplied the cannon foundry at Westham. The first railroad in Virginia was built from the Midlothian mines to the town of Manchester in 1831. The mines produced coal that was used in casting cannon at the Tredegar Iron Works in Richmond during the Civil War. Mining operations ceased in 1923. *Chesterfield Co.: Rte. 60, at Midlothian.*

O-36 HUGUENOT SPRINGS CONFEDERATE CEMETERY

Approximately 250 unidentifed Confederate soldiers, who died at nearby Huguenot Springs Confederate Hospital, are buried in unmarked graves about a mile and a half southwest of here. Burial records have never been located. The former Huguenot Springs Hotel Resort/Spa, opened in 1847, was converted to a convalescent hospital during the Civil War. The building was burned about 1890. *Powhatan Co.: Rte. 711, 2.13 miles w. of Chesterfield Co. line.*

O-37 PROVIDENCE UNITED METHODIST CHURCH

Established by 1807, the Providence Church congregation of the Methodist Episcopal Church became one of the first Methodist congregations in Chesterfield County to build a permanent house of worship when it constructed a meetinghouse here before 1813. The congregation included both whites and blacks. During the Civil War, soldiers from both sides used the church for shelter. In 1896 the congregation built a Gothic Revival church here; it was replaced in 1958. *Chesterfield Co.: Rte. 678, .86 mile s. of Rte. 60.*

O-38 MILLBROOK—HOME OF JOHN
WAYLES EPPES

Approximately 2 miles east stood Mill-brook (1811–1866), home of U.S. Senator John Wayles Eppes (1772–1823). He attended the University of Pennsylvania, was graduated from Hampden-Sydney College, and was admitted to the Bar in 1794. He married Maria, daughter of Thomas Jefferson, in 1797. His second wife was Martha Burke Jones. Eppes served in the Virginia House of Delegates and the Congress of the United States. It is believed that Jefferson advised Eppes on the design and landscaping of Mill-brook. The house burned in 1866. *Buckingham Co.: Rte. 15, 6.5 miles s. of Rte. 60.*

O-39 GEOGRAPHICAL CENTER OF
VIRGINIA

About two miles south and one-half mile west is the geographical center of the state. Latitude: 37 degrees 30.6' north, Longitude: 78 degrees 37.5' west. *Buckingham Co.: Rtes. 60 and 24 at Mount Rush.*

O-40* BELLONA ARSENAL

Five miles north are the ruins of Bellona Arsenal, established by the United States government in 1816. It was used as an arsenal and barracks until 1835. A foundry was also here and cannon were cast. In 1853 the arsenal was sold; in 1861 it was taken over by the Virginia government and served the Confederate cause. *Chesterfield Co.: Rte. 60, 5.7 miles w. of Richmond.*

O-40 BELLONA ARSENAL

In 1810 Major John Clarke and noted Richmond lawyer, William Wirt, established a weapons factory for the U.S. War Department on the south bank of the James River five miles north of here. Bellona Arsenal, (named for the Roman goddess of war,) [sic] was erected in 1816. After five years of disuse, it was leased to Thomas Mann Randolph in 1837 (for use as a silk worm farm.) [sic] Junius L. Archer bought the property in 1856, and on January 1, 1863, he leased both the arsenal and foundry to the Confederate government. Bellona Arsenal became one of Virginia's leading producers of arms. *Chesterfield Co.: Rte. 60, 3.22 miles w. of Richmond.*

O-41* PISCATAWAY CHURCH

Five miles north is Mt. Zion Church, successor of Piscataway Church, organized in 1774, the mother Baptist church of the vicinity. In 1813 the congregation occupied a colonial Episcopal church, which was not far from the present Mt. Zion Church. *King and Queen Co.: Rte. 360, 1.6 miles s.w. of Millers Tavern.*

O-42 AFTER APPOMATTOX

Just to the south a monument marks the spot where the tent of Robert E. Lee stood the night of April 12–13, 1865. *Buckingham Co.: Rte. 60, 1.1 miles e. of Buckingham.*

O-44 CAMPAIGN OF 1781

Steuben, both on his retreat from Simcoe and on his return north to join Lafayette, passed near here, June, 1781. *Cumberland Co.: Rte. 60, 1.8 miles w. of Cumberland.*

A mile and a half southeast is Sabine Hall, built in 1730 for Landon Carter, son of Robert ("King") Carter, and one of the noted colonial homes. In 1861, the estate passed to Elizabeth Carter, wife of Dr. Armistead N. Welford. [*Removed as inaccurate.*] *Richmond Co.: Rte. 360, .3 mile west of Warsaw.*

O-46 WARSAW

When Richmond County was formed in 1692, this place became the county seat and was known as Richmond (County) Courthouse. The present courthouse building was erected in 1748–49. The village was renamed Warsaw about 1846 in sympathy with the Polish struggle for liberty. It was the home of Congressman William A. Jones, advocate of Philippine independence. *Richmond Co.: Rte. 360, at Warsaw.*

O-49 ST. STEPHEN'S PARISH

Formed in 1653 as Chickacone Parish and renamed Fairfield in 1664. The upper part was known locally as Bowtracy Parish. When St. Stephen's Parish was formed in 1698, Fairfield became its lower part and Bowtracy its upper part. *Northumberland Co.: Rte. 360, at Heathsville.*

O-50 BETHEL BAPTIST CHURCH

In 1799 the local Baptist Society acquired this land and soon built a meetinghouse. The Bethel congregation worshiped in the meetinghouse and was constituted as a church in 1817. About 1820 the members built a brick church here—the first in Chesterfield County. The present sanctuary, which replaced it in 1894, was then the most elaborate rural church in the county, having Gothic buttresses, fine exterior detailing, and a rib-vaulted chancel. In the churchyard are buried soldiers of virtually every war from the Revolution through Vietnam. *Chesterfield Co.: Rte. 607, .1 mile n. of Rte. 60.*

O-51 REEDVILLE

Elijah W. Reed, a New England ship captain, established the town in 1874 after building a factory here to process menhaden, a small bony fish rich in oil. Reedville soon became the center of the industry and home port to the Atlantic menhaden fleet. By the early 20th century the town, which resembled a New England fishing village, reputedly had one of the highest per capita incomes in the country. Its historic district contains early fishermen's houses and Victorian mansions. The oldest dwelling is the Walker House (1875). *Northumberland Co.: Rte. 360 at Rte. 726.*

OB-2 BRUINGTON CHURCH

This is Bruington Church, organized in 1790. Here Robert Semple, one of the most noted Baptist ministers in Virginia, long served and here he is buried. *King and Queen Co.: Rte. 14, 6.2 miles n.w. of Stevensville.*

OB-3 MATTAPONY CHURCH

This is the ancient colonial Mattapony Church, used by the Baptists since 1824. Here are tombs of members of the family of Carter Braxton, signer of the Declaration of Independence. *King and Queen Co.: Rte. 14, 4.1 miles n.w. of King and Queen Courthouse.*

OB-5 HILLSBORO

This house, four miles south, was built by Colonel Humphrey Hill about 1722. It is of quaint architecture having brick ends and frame front and rear. The place was raided by the British during the Revolution. *King and Queen Co.: Rte. 14, 4.7 miles n.w. of Stevensville.*

OB-6 WHERE DAHLGREN DIED

Colonel Ulric Dahlgren, Federal officer, met death in the early morning, March 2, 1864, three hundred yards to the north. After the raid on Richmond, his force bivouacked here and, in breaking camp he fell to the fire of Confederate detachments and Home Defense forces who had gathered during the night. *King and Queen Co.: Rte. 631, 2.5 miles n.w. of King and Queen Court House.*

OB-9 NEWTOWN

Newtown began as a pre-Revolutionary tavern crossroads on the intercolonial King's Highway. The settlement prospered in the antebellum period, becoming King and Queen's largest post village and supporting several fine academies and schools. In June 1863 Newtown witnessed the last tactical action of General George Pickett's Division before its long march to Gettysburg. *King and Queen Co.: Rtes. 625 and 721.*

OB-10 NEWINGTON

A mile south on the Mattapony River is the site of Newington, birthplace of Carter Braxton (born September 10, 1736), signer of the Declaration of Independence. In earlier times, Colonel Jacob Lumpkin, supporter of Governor Berkeley in Bacon's Rebellion, 1676, lived there. *King and Queen Co.: Rte. 14, 1 mile n.w. of King and Queen Court House.*

OB-11 APPLE TREE CHURCH

About two miles south stood the colonial church known as the Apple Tree Church or St. Clement's Church. First authorized by the House of Burgesses in 1710, it served as the upper church of St. Stephen's Parish until after the Revolution. It was then abandoned and later destroyed by fire. *King and Queen Co.: Rte. 360, .4 mile e. of Rte. 14.*

OB-12 CORBIN'S CHURCH—THE NEW CHURCH

The New Church, also known as Corbin's Church, stood to the east of this road. Councillor Richard Corbin, who also served as Receiver-General of the colony, donated "Goliath's Old Field" for the church, which was completed in 1768 to replace two older Anglican churches in Stratton Major Parish. The New Church measured 50 by 80 feet and was 27 feet high with galleries. According to the parish vestry book, 275 persons were initially assigned pews in the church. *King and Queen Co.: Rte. 14, 1 mile n. of Rte. 33.*

OB-16 LANEVILLE

A mile and a half southwest stood Laneville, built by Richard Corbin, receiver general (treasurer), about 1760 on the site of an earlier house. There Patrick Henry sent, May, 1775, to obtain money in payment for the colony's powder seized by Lord Dunmore. Laneville was one of the largest and finest houses in Virginia. *King and Queen Co.: Rte. 14, 10 miles s.e. of King and Queen Courthouse.*

OB-18 COLONIAL CHURCH

This church, the new church of Stratton Major Parish, was built in 1767. Rev. William Robinson, the Bishop of London's commissary, came to the parish in 1744 and was the first minister of the new church. It fell into disuse after the Revolution but later became a Methodist church. *King and Queen Co.: Rte. 14, 8.5 miles s.e. of King and Queen Court House.*

OB-50 POROPOTANK CREEK

Land was patented on this creek as early as 1640. In 1653, John Lewis settled here. John Lewis, Jr., was living here in 1676 when Bacon's troops were encamped near by. He suffered from the depredations of the rebels. *King and Queen Co.: Rte. 14, 1.1 miles w. of Adner.*

OC-14 PAMUNKEY RESERVATION

Eight miles south is the reservation where live descendants of the ancient tribe of Pamunkey Indians. It has always been Indian property, all that remains of the domain of Powhatan, who at the time of the first settlement (1607) ruled over the tribes of eastern Virginia and Maryland. *King William Co.: Rte. 30, .6 mile s.e. of King William.*

OC-15 MATTAPONY RESERVATION

Two miles east is the Mattapony Indian Reservation. The Mattaponies were one of the tribes ruled by the great Chief, Powhatan. The reservation is governed by the chief and the council, which make the tribal laws. *King William Co.: Rte. 30, 4.9 miles s.e. of King William.*

OC-18 ST. JOHN'S CHURCH

This was the parish church of St. John's Parish, formed in 1680. It was built in 1734. Earlier churches stood at West Point and about one mile north of this site. Carter Braxton, Revolutionary Statesman, was a vestryman. Preserved by joint effort. *King William Co.: Rte. 30, 8.9 miles n.w. of West Point.*

OC-20 MANGOHICK CHURCH

Referred to by William Byrd in 1732 as the New Brick Church, Mangohick Church was built circa 1730 as a chapel of ease for those who lived in remote areas of St. Margaret's Parish. Distinguished by its fine Flemish bond brickwork, Mangohick became the Upper Church of St. David's when that parish was formed in 1774. It became a free church for use by any denomination following disestablishment of the Church of England in Virginia. It now serves the Mangohick Baptist congregation. *King William Co.: Rte. 30 near Rte. 671.*

OC-22*   CAMPAIGN OF 1781

About one mile south Lafayette placed in camp his Light Infantry consisting of Muhlenberg's and Febiger's commands, August 13, 1781. The troops had just been brought across the Pamunkey at Ruffins's Ferry, from New Castle, to observe Cornwallis, then entrenching at Yorktown. Within six weeks the Yorktown Campaign, in which these troops took part, opened. *King William Co.: Rte. 30, 6.6 miles n.w. of West Point.*

OC-25   CAMPAIGN OF 1781

About a mile to the east, August 13, 1781, Lafayette, then commanding American forces in Virginia, placed in camp his militia, consisting of Campbell's, Stevens's and Lawson's brigades. Wayne was at Westover; Muhlenberg and Febiger were in camp on the Pamunkey four miles northwest. The campaign of Yorktown was about to open; these troops were later engaged there. *King William Co.: Rte. 30, 3.4 miles n.w. of West Point.*

OC-26   CHERICOKE (HOME OF SIGNER)

Carter Braxton, Signer of the Declaration of Independence, lived at West Point 1777–1786 after fire destroyed his plantation Chericoke, upriver on the Pamunkey. The Town House no longer stands. From West Point Braxton channeled war goods to Patriot Troops. *King William Co.: Rte. 33, at West Point.*

OC-35   ROSEGILL

A short distance east is Rosegill. The house was built about 1650 by the first Ralph Wormeley; it became the summer home of the colonial governors, Sir Henry Chicheley and Lord Howard of Effingham. In 1776, the owner, the fifth Ralph Wormeley, was put under restraint as a Tory. In 1781, Rosegill was plundered by British privateersmen. *Middlesex Co.: Rte. 227, .7 mile s. of Urbanna.*

OC-36   CHRISTOPHER ROBINSON

In 1678, Christopher Robinson purchased 300 acres here that became Hewick, the Virginia seat of the Robinson family. Robinson's distinguished service to Virginia began as the clerk of Middlesex County Court from 1677 to 1688. He was elected to the House of Burgesses in 1691, and, in 1692, was appointed Councillor and Secretary of the Foreign Plantations by King William III of England. Robinson's final contribution to colonial Virginia came in 1693, when he served as a founding trustee of William and Mary College. *Middlesex Co.: Rte. 602, 100 ft. n. of Rte. 615, .5 mile w. of Urbanna.*

OC-40*   URBANNA CREEK

This creek, mentioned in an act of 1680 as "Wormeley's Creek," was earlier known as "Nimcock Creek." After Urbanna was named in 1705 for Queen Anne, the stream took the same name. British privateersmen entered the creek, June 5, 1781, and pillaged Urbanna and Rosegill. *Middlesex Co.: Rte. 227, at Urbanna.*

OC-40 URBANNA CREEK

First known as Nimcock Creek, this creek was mentioned in a legislative act of 1680 as "Wormeley's Creek." After the town of Urbanna was named in 1705 for Queen Anne, the stream was given the same name. British privateersmen entered the creek, June 5, 1781, and pillaged Urbanna and Rosegill, the plantation of Sir Ralph Wormeley. *Middlesex Co.: Rte. 227, at Urbanna.*

OH-10* LEE'S LAST CAMP

Here Robert E. Lee, returning from Appomattox, pitched his tent for the last time, April 14, 1865. He stopped here to visit his brother, Charles Carter Lee, who lived at nearby "Windsor." Fearing to incommode his brother, Lee camped by the roadside and the next day ended his journey at Richmond. *Powhatan Co.: Rte. 711, 9.5 miles n. of Powhatan.*

OH-10 LEE'S LAST CAMP

Here Robert E. Lee, riding from Appomattox to Richmond to join his family, pitched his tent for the last time on April 14, 1865. He stopped here to visit his brother, Charles Carter Lee, who lived nearby at Windsor. Not wishing to incommode his brother, Lee camped by the roadside and the next day ended his journey at Richmond. *Powhatan Co.: Rte. 711, 9.8 miles w. of Chesterfield Co. line.*

OL-10 LEE'S RETREAT

Near here Custer, commanding advance guard of the Army of the Potomac, struck and drove back Fitz Lee, left flank guard of Army of Northern Virginia, April 3, 1865. *Amelia Co.: Rte. 38, 7 miles e. of Mannboro.*

ON-5 CAMPAIGN OF 1781

At Carter's Ferry, near here, Steuben, marching northward to join Lafayette, crossed the James, June 16, 1781. *Cumberland Co.: Rte. 45, at Cartersville.*

ON-7 CAMPAIGN OF 1781

Two miles north, near the mouth of Willis River, Steuben camped, June 5–6, 1781, when driven from Point of Fork by Simcoe. *Cumberland Co.: Rte. 45, 1.8 miles s. of Cartersville.*

OQ-4 THOMAS MASSIE

One mile from here is "Level Green," the home of Major Thomas Massie (1747–1834). Commander of the Sixth Virginia Regiment of Infantry, later Aid to Governor Thomas Nelson at the siege of Yorktown, and one of first magistrates of Nelson County when it was formed in 1807. *Nelson Co.: Rtes. 56 and 666 at Massie's Mill.*

OQ-5 WILLIAM CABELL

Three miles southwest is Union Hill, home of William Cabell. He was born, March 30, 1730. Cabell was a burgess, signer of the Articles of Association, member of the Revolutionary conventions and of the ratifying convention of 1788. He died, March 23, 1798. *Nelson Co.: Rte. 56, at Wingina.*

PA-2 SEVENS DAYS' BATTLES— MECHANICSVILLE

Mechanicsville was held by Union outposts when, in the early afternoon of June 26, 1862, A. P. Hill reached it coming from the north. The Unionists were quickly driven back to their position on Beaver Dam Creek. Then D. H. Hill, followed by Longstreet, crossed the Chickahominy on this road and joined A. P. Hill. *Hanover Co.: Rte. 360, at Mechanicsville.*

PA-4   SEVEN DAYS' BATTLES—
        MECHANICSVILLE

Down this slope in the late afternoon of
June 26, 1862, A. P. Hill moved to attack
the Unionists holding the east side of Beaver Dam Creek. Pender's brigade was on
the left, Ripley's on the right. Exposed to
a terrible fire from entrenched troops,
Pender and Ripley were driven back,
though some men reached the stream.
*Hanover Co.: Rte. 156, .8 mile s. of Me-
chanicsville.*

PA-6   SEVEN DAYS' BATTLES—
        MECHANICSVILLE

This ridge was occupied by Porter's Corps
(facing west), which formed the right
wing of McClellan's army, June 26, 1862.
The strong position was strengthened by
earthworks and by an abatis along the
creek. When A. P. Hill attacked late in the
afternoon, the Confederates were driven
back with severe loss. *Hanover Co.: Rte.
156, 1.2 miles s. of Mechanicsville.*

PA-8   SEVEN DAYS' BATTLES—
        PORTER'S WITHDRAWAL

Along this road Fitz-John Porter withdrew
from Beaver Dam Creek in the early
morning of June 27, 1862. McClellan,
having learned that Stonewall Jackson was
approaching Porter's rear, late at night ordered the withdrawal to another position.
This was on Boatswain Creek, not far
from New Cold Harbor. *Hanover Co.:
Rte. 156, 1.7 miles s. of Mechanicsville.*

PA-9*   SEVEN DAYS' BATTLES—
         GAINES'S MILL

Stonewall Jackson, coming from the
Shenandoah Valley to join Lee, crossed
the road here in the morning of June 27,
1862. He met Lee at Walnut Grove Church
not far to the south. That afternoon Jackson joined in the attack that carried the position held by Porter of McClellan's army
on Boatswain Creek. *Hanover Co.: Rte.
360, 1.8 miles n.e. of Mechanicsville.*

PA-10   SEVEN DAYS' BATTLES—
         GAINES'S MILL

Here Lee and Stonewall Jackson conferred in the morning of June 27, 1862.
Jackson's troops halted here until A. P. Hill
arrived from Beaver Dam Creek. Hill then
moved southward by Gaines's Mill and
Longstreet along a road near the river;
Jackson turned to the east. All three columns approached the Union position on
Boatswain Creek. *Hanover Co.: Rte.
156, 2.7 miles s. of Mechanicsville.*

PA-12*   SEVEN DAYS' BATTLES—
          NEW BRIDGE

The road to the south is the New Bridge
road leading to Old Tavern (Highland
Springs). In the 1862 campaign bridge and
road played an important part in the movements of both armies. The Unionists
moved from New Bridge to Mechanicsville on May 24, 1862. Longstreet and
A. P. Hill crossed the bridge on June 29
going to the battle of Glendale. *Hanover
Co.: Rte. 156, 4.3 miles s. of Mechanicsville.*

PA-16 SEVEN DAYS' BATTLES—
GAINES'S MILL

This is the site of Gaines's Mill, which gave its name to the battle of June 27, 1862. Here A. P. Hill's advance guard, following Porter, came in contact with the Union rear guard. After a short action the Unionists withdrew to a position on Boatswain Creek, closely pursued by the Confederates. *Hanover Co.: Rte. 156, 5 miles s. of Mechanicsville.*

PA-20* SEVEN DAYS' BATTLES—
GAINES'S MILL

Half a mile south is Boatswain Creek. The battle that was begun at Gaines's Mill by A. P. Hill, following Porter's rear guard, culminated at the Union position on Boatswain Creek. There A. P. Hill and Longstreet, moving eastward, and Jackson coming from the north converged to attack Unionists. *Hanover Co.: Rte. 156, 5.7 miles s. of Mechanicsville.*

PA-23* SEVEN DAYS' BATTLES—
GAINES'S MILL

A. P. Hill, in the afternoon of June 27, 1862, moved down this slope, crossed the creek and repeatedly charged the hill to the east, only to be driven back. Lee sent in Longstreet on Hill's right; but the position was not taken until Jackson, on the north, joined in the attack. *Hanover Co.: Rte. 156, 6.3 miles s. of Mechanicsville.*

PA-25 SEVEN DAYS' BATTLES—
GAINES'S MILL

Along the slopes of Boatswain Creek, facing north and west, extended Porter's position in the afternoon of June 27, 1862. The line was held by Sykes's division facing north, and Morell's facing west. Later McCall was thrown in to assist Morell. At dark Lee broke the Union line, and Porter retreated across the Chickahominy. *Hanover Co.: Rte. 718, 6.5 miles s. of Mechanicsville.*

PA-60 SEVEN DAYS' BATTLES—
GAINES'S MILL

Stonewall Jackson reached this point in the afternoon of June 27, 1862, after a circuit of Gaines's Mill. When he learned that A. P. Hill and Longstreet to the west were hard pressed, he moved south to join in the attack. *Hanover Co.: Rte. 156, 7.8 miles s. of Mechanicsville.*

PA-70 SEVEN DAYS' BATTLES—
GAINES'S MILL

The hill to the south, part of the Union line, was assailed by Stonewall Jackson (with D. H. Hill) in the late afternoon of June 27, 1862, after A. P. Hill's and Longstreet's first assaults on the west had failed. Jackson's men carried the Union position at the bayonet's point, while A. P. Hill and Longstreet were also successful. *Hanover Co.: Rte. 156, 8.2 miles s. of Mechanicsville.*

PA-80 SEVEN DAYS' BATTLES— GAINES'S MILL

On this hill, facing north, Sykes's division was posted in the afternoon of June 27, 1862, holding the eastern end of the Union line. Here Jackson attacked, while to the west A. P. Hill and Longstreet renewed their assaults. When the Union line was broken on their left, Sykes's regulars fell back to the river still fighting. *Hanover Co.: Rte. 156, 8.5 miles s. of Mechanicsville.*

PA-105 SEVEN DAYS' BATTLES— GRAPE VINE BRIDGE

Here Sumner crossed the river to reinforce the part of McClellan's army fighting at Fair Oaks, May 31, 1862. Here a part of Porter's force crossed in the night of June 27, 1862, after the battle of Gaines's Mill. Here Stonewall Jackson, rebuilding the bridges destroyed by the retreating Unionists, crossed in pursuit, June 29. *Hanover Co.: Rte. 156, 11.1 miles s. of Mechanicsville.*

PA-125 SEVEN DAYS' BATTLES— GOLDING'S FARM

Half a mile northwest occurred the action of Golding's Farm at dusk on June 27, 1862, as the battle of Gaines's Mill, on the other side of the river, was ending. The Confederates, sallying from their defenses, attacked Hancock's brigade holding the right of the Union line south of the river. A severe fight followed that was ended by darkness. *Henrico Co.: Rte. 156, 12.8 miles s. of Mechanicsville.*

PA-140* SEVEN DAYS' BATTLES— ALLEN'S FARM

Half a mile north took place the action of Allen's Farm, or Peach Orchard, in the morning of June 29, 1862. There Sumner's Corps, forming the Union rear, was attacked by Magruder at 9 A.M. Fighting lasted until 11 A.M. when the Unionists fell back to Savage's Station on the York River Railroad. *Henrico Co.: Rte. 156, at Seven Pines.*

PA-142 SEVEN DAYS' BATTLE— SAVAGE'S STATION

Here Magruder's line of battle, facing east, formed in the late afternoon of June 29, 1862. Barksdale's, Semmes's and Kershaw's brigades, extending from south of this road to the railroad, made a desperate effort to prevent the Union withdrawal. After a fierce struggle the Confederates fell back. In this battle they made the first known use of railway artillery. *Henrico Co.: Rte. 60, 3.6 miles e. of Seven Pines.*

PA-144 SEVEN DAYS' BATTLES—SAVAGE'S STATION

Here, facing west, stretched the Union line in the afternoon of June 29, 1862. Brook's brigade was south of the road with Gorman's and Burn's brigades to the north. In a furious conflict Burn's line was broken but was restored by Sumner in person. Darkness ended the conflict. The Unionists withdrew southward. *Henrico Co.: Rte. 60, 3.6 miles e. of Seven Pines.*

PA-148 SEVEN DAYS' BATTLES— WHITE OAK SWAMP

In the hill just to the west Stonewall Jackson placed his artillery about midday on June 30, 1862. An artillery duel then began with Franklin, guarding the south side of White Oak Swamp, that lasted until dark. *Henrico Co.: Rte. 156, 6.7 miles s.e. of Seven Pines.*

PA-152   SEVEN DAYS' BATTLES—
    WHITE OAK SWAMP

Here the greater part of McClellan's army and wagon trains crossed the swamp, June 28–30, 1862. Jackson, pursuing, arrived about noon on June 30, to find the bridge destroyed and the Unionists holding the south side. Failing to force a passage that day, Jackson rebuilt the bridge and crossed early on July 1. *Henrico Co.: Rte. 156, 7.1 miles s. of Seven Pines.*

PA-159*   SEVEN DAYS' BATTLES—
    GLENDALE (FRAYSER'S FARM)

Across the road here, June 30, 1862, extended the Union line of battle, facing west. Slocum's and Kearny's divisions were north of the road, McCall's and Hooker's south of it. The battle opened with an attack on Seymour's brigade of McCall's division and raged furiously until after nightfall. In the night the Unionists withdrew to Malvern Hill. *Henrico Co.: Rte. 156, on Darbytown Rd., 10.2 miles s. of Seven Pines.*

PA-163   SEVEN DAYS' BATTLES—
    GLENDALE (FRAYSER'S FARM)

Here stood the center of Longstreet's line of battle in the afternoon of June 30, 1862. The Confederates, coming from the west, attacked the Union line just beyond. The battle lasted all afternoon, with varying fortunes and much hand-to-hand fighting. Near nightfall Longstreet sent in A. P. Hill to relieve his exhausted men. *Henrico Co.: Rte. 156, on Darbytown Rd., 10.5 miles s. of Seven Pines.*

PA-175   SEVEN DAYS' BATTLE—
    GLENDALE (FRAYSER'S FARM)

The possession of this, the Quaker road, on June 30, 1862, saved McClellan's army from destruction. The Confederates, coming from the west, sought to seize the road and block the Union withdrawal to James River. While Longstreet was fighting a rearguard battle at Glendale, the Union wagon trains and artillery passed along this road and another road two miles east. *Henrico Co.: Rte. 156, 10 miles s. of Seven Pines.*

PA-180   SEVEN DAYS' BATTLES—
    MALVERN HILL

Here Lee met Longstreet and Jackson in the morning of July 1, 1862. D. H. Hill reported the strength of the Union position on Malvern Hill; but Lee, having cause to believe the Unionists were weakening, prepared to attack. Jackson and D. H. Hill moved on this road southward to Malvern Hill. *Henrico Co.: Rte. 156, 10.6 miles s. of Seven Pines.*

PA-190   SEVEN DAYS' BATTLES—
    GLENDALE (FRAYSER'S FARM)

This was the extreme left of the Union line at Glendale, and was held by Hooker's division. When McCall (just to the north) was broken, Hooker, supported by Burn's brigade, drove the Confederates back. In the night the Union army moved southward. *Henrico Co.: Rte. 156, 11.1 miles s. of Seven Pines.*

PA-195   SEVEN DAYS' BATTLE—
          MALVERN HILL

Across the road here stretched the Confederate line of battle, facing south, in the afternoon of July 1, 1862. Jackson commanded here, Magruder to the west. Longstreet and A. P. Hill were in reserve. The battle lasted intermittently from morning to night, reaching its crisis late in the afternoon. The disjointed Confederate attacks were repulsed with heavy loss. *Henrico Co.: Rte. 156, 12.3 miles s. of Seven Pines.*

PA-220   SEVEN DAYS' BATTLES—
          MALVERN HILL

Here from east to west, Berdan's sharpshooters of Morell's division were strung out in the afternoon of July 1, 1862. Their rapid and accurate fire harassed the Confederates as they emerged from the woods and charged up the hill. *Henrico Co.: Rte. 156, 12.5 miles s. of Seven Pines.*

PA-230   SEVEN DAYS' BATTLES—
          MALVERN HILL

Across the hill here from east to west the Union artillery was in position in the afternoon of July 1, 1862. The Union batteries overpowered the few cannon the Confederates were able to bring up. When the Southern infantry charged from the woods, they were met by a terrible artillery fire but continued to advance until they came under the fire of the Union infantry. *Henrico Co.: Rte. 156, 12.6 miles s. of Seven Pines.*

PA-235   SEVEN DAYS' BATTLES—
          MALVERN HILL

Across the road here stretched the Union line of battle in the afternoon of July 1, 1862. Couch's, Kearney's and Hooker's divisions were to the east of the road, Morell to the west, with Sykes in reserve. The Confederates made several attacks and, for a time, the battle trembled in the balance; but the assailants were finally repulsed. In the night the Union army withdrew to James River. *Henrico Co.: Rte. 156, 12.7 miles s. of Seven Pines.*

PA-240*   SEVEN DAYS' BATTLES—
           MALVERN HILL

The troops of T. H. H. Holmes reached this point on June 30, 1862. It was Holmes' part in Lee's plan to take Malvern Hill; but the fire of the Union artillery there and the Gunboats in the river held him here, inactive. He remained here the next day, July 1, while the battle of Malvern Hill was being fought. *Henrico Co.: Rte. 156, 13.8 miles s. of Seven Pines.*

PA-250*   BENJAMIN HARRISON BRIDGE

Benjamin Harrison (1726–1791), a signer of the Declaration of Independence, was born at Berkeley (2 miles east). He served in the Virginia General Assembly, the Continental Congress, as Governor, and in the Virginia Convention which ratified the U.S. Constitution. *Charles City Co.: Rte. 156, at bridge.*

PA-251 SAD REUNION

On 16 August 1864 Confederate Brig. Gen. John R. Chambliss, Jr., was killed near here attempting to evade capture during the Second Battle of Deep Bottom. As troops of the 16th Pennsylvania Cavalry removed his epaulets, sash, and saber, Union Brig. Gen. David M. Gregg rode by and recognized Chambliss, his schoolmate at West Point in the early 1850s. He took charge of the body and sent it through the lines to Chambliss's widow in Hicksford (now Emporia). By his actions, Gregg adhered to the spirit of the West Point hymn, to "grip hands though it be from the shadows." *Henrico Co.: Rte. 5, .9 mile e. of Turner Rd.*

PB-4 STATE FISH HATCHERY

Half a mile north. This fish cultural station was established in 1937 for hatching and rearing largemouth bass and other species of sunfish for the stocking of the public waters of Virginia. *King and Queen Co.: Rte. 14, 1 mile n.w. of Stevensville.*

PH-6 ACTION OF NANCE'S SHOP

In this vicinity the Union cavalryman, Gregg, guarding army trains moving to Petersburg, was attacked by Wade Hampton, June 24, 1864. Gregg was driven back toward Charles City Courthouse, but the wagon trains crossed the James safely. This action closed the cavalry campaign that began at Trevillians, June 11–12, 1864. *Charles City Co.: Rte. 603, 13.4 miles s.e. of Seven Pines.*

Q-1-1 TARLETON'S OAK

Tradition says that under this oak the British cavalryman, Banastre Tarleton, pitched his tent on his raid to Charlottesville, June 4, 1781. He attempted to capture Governor Jefferson and the legislature, but Captain Jack Jouett, by taking a shorter route, arrived in time to warn the patriots of their danger. *Charlottesville: High St. and Lexington Ave.*

Q-1-a-b-d CHARLOTTESVILLE

The site was patented by William Taylor in 1737. The town was established by a law in 1762, and was named for Queen Charlotte, wife of George III. Burgoyne's army, captured at Saratoga in 1777, was long quartered near here. The legislature was in session here, in June, 1781, but retired westward to escape Tarleton's raid on the town. Jefferson, who lived at Monticello, founded the University of Virginia in 1819. *Charlottesville: a. High St. near Hazel St. b. Rte. 20 and Carlton St. d. Rte. 29 near Piedmont Ave.*

Q-2-a-b WAYNESBORO

Here, on one of the first roads west of the Blue Ridge, a hamlet stood in colonial times. The Walker exploring expedition started from this vicinity in 1748. Here, in June, 1781, the Augusta militia assembled to join Lafayette in the East. A town was founded in 1797. It was established by law in 1801 and named for General Anthony Wayne. *Waynesboro: a. Rte. 250 at e. entrance of Waynesboro. b. Rte. 250 at w. entrance of Waynesboro.*

Q-2-c VIRGINIA METALCRAFTERS

Virginia Metalcrafters had its first beginnings with the founding of the Waynesboro Stove Company in 1890 by William J. Loth. The company, which made ornately cast cookstoves, heaters and all accoutrements for kitchens of the period, later developed the electric Hotpoint Range. It merged with Rife Ram Pump Works, inventors in 1884 of the ram pump widely used to pump water in rural areas before electrification. In 1938, the Rife-Loth Corporation began selling finely crafted brass accessories under the name Virginia Metalcrafters. *Waynesboro: Rte. 250, .3 mile e. of Rte. 340.*

Q-3-a-b-c-d* BERRYVILLE

The town was laid out in 1798 on land of Benjamin Berry and was first known as Battletown. Here at "Audley" lived Nellie Custis, Washington's adopted daughter. Here at "Soldier's Rest" lived General Daniel Morgan, who built "Saratoga." Here Lee's army camped on the way to Gettysburg. Near here many engagements occurred, 1862–64. *Clarke Co.: a. and c. Rte. 7, at e. and w. entrance of Berryville. b. Rte. 340, at n. entrance of Berryville. d. Rte. 12, at s. entrance of Berryville.*

Q-4-a GENERAL DANIEL MORGAN

Morgan used this road in traveling from his home, "Saratoga," to Winchester. He was a frontiersman, Indian fighter and the commander of Morgan's famous riflemen in the Revolution. He won glory at Quebec and Saratoga, and defeated Tarleton at the Cowpens. He died in 1802 and is buried in Winchester. *Winchester: Rte. 50, at e. limits.*

Q-4-a WINCHESTER (back of marker)

At first called Fredericktown, it was founded in 1744, near a Shawnee Indian village, by Colonel James Wood, a native of the English city of Winchester. The town was situated in Lord Fairfax's proprietary of the Northern Neck. It was chartered in 1752. *Winchester: Rte. 50, at e. limits.*

Q-4-b* JOIST HITE AND BRADDOCK

By this road, then an Indian trail, Joist Hite and his followers came to make the first permanent settlement in this section, 1732. In 1755, General Edward Braddock of the British army, accompanied by George Washington, passed here on his way to defeat and death at Fort Duquesne. *Winchester: Rte. 7, at e. limits.*

Q-4-b* WINCHESTER (back of marker)

At first called Fredericktown, it was founded in 1744, near a Shawnee Indian village, by Colonel James Wood, a native of the English city of Winchester. The town was situated in Lord Fairfax's proprietary of the Northern Neck. It was chartered in 1752. *Winchester: Rte. 7, at e. limits.*

Q-4-c* GEORGE WASHINGTON

George Washington began his career here in 1748 as surveyor to Lord Fairfax. Here he had his headquarters as commander on the Virginia frontier against the French and Indians, 1755–1758. Here he built Fort Loudoun, and he was a member of the House of Burgesses for this county, 1758–1761. *Winchester: Rte. 11, at n. limits.*

Q-4-c*   WINCHESTER (back of marker)

At first called Fredericktown, it was founded in 1744, near a Shawnee Indian village, by Colonel James Wood, a native of the English city of Winchester. The town was situated in Lord Fairfax's proprietary of the Northern Neck. It was chartered in 1752. *Winchester: Rte. 11, at n. limits.*

Q-4-d*   LORD FAIRFAX

By this road Thomas Lord Fairfax, proprietor of the Northern Neck of Virginia, was accustomed to pass from his home, "Greenway Court" to preside over the sessions of the justices' court at Winchester, 1749–1769. His tomb is in the crypt of Christ Church, Winchester. *Winchester: Rte. 522, at n. limits.*

Q-4-d*   WINCHESTER (back of marker)

At first called Fredericktown, it was founded in 1744, near a Shawnee Indian village, by Colonel James Wood, a native of the English city of Winchester. The town was situated in Lord Fairfax's proprietary of the Northern Neck. It was chartered in 1752. *Winchester: Rte. 522, at n. limits.*

Q-4-e   COLONEL JAMES WOOD

James Wood, founder of Winchester, named for his native city in England, was the first clerk of Frederick County Court, which was organized in 1743 at the house on his estate, "Glen Burnie," His son, General James Wood, was Governor of Virginia, 1796–1799. *Winchester: Rte. 50, just w. of Rte. 11.*

Q-4-e   WINCHESTER (back of marker)

At first called Fredericktown, it was founded in 1744, near a Shawnee Indian village, by Colonel James Wood, a native of the English city of Winchester. The town was situated in Lord Fairfax's proprietary of the Northern Neck. It was chartered in 1752. *Winchester: Rte. 50, just w. of Rte. 11.*

Q-4-f   JACKSON'S HEADQUARTERS

This house was used by Major General Thomas J. Jackson, then commanding the valley district, department of Northern Virginia, as his official headquarters from November 1861, to March, 1862 when he left Winchester to begin his famous valley campaign. *Winchester: 415 N. Braddock St.*

Q-5   FORT DINWIDDIE

Known as Byrd's Fort and Warwick's Fort. Probably built in 1755, it was visited in that year by George Washington. *Bath Co.: Rte. 39, 5 miles w. of Warm Springs.*

Q-5-a   LAST CONFEDERATE CAPITOL

This, the former home of Major W. T. Sutherlin, is regarded as the last capitol of the Confederacy, April 3–10, 1865. Here President Davis stayed and here was held the last full cabinet meeting, Breckinridge alone being absent. The establishment of the Confederate government in Danville ended when the news of Lee's surrender arrived on April 10. *Danville: at Sutherlin Ave. and Main St.*

Q-5-b WRECK OF THE OLD 97

Here, on September 27, 1903, occurred the railroad wreck that inspired the popular ballad, "The Wreck of the Old 97." The southbound mail express train on the Southern Railroad left the tracks on a trestle and plunged into the ravine below. Nine persons were killed and seven injured, one of the worst train wrecks in Virginia history. *Danville: between Pickett and Farrar sts.*

Q-5-c LADY ASTOR

Here stood the residence in which Nancy Langhorne, Viscountess Astor, 1879–1964, was born. Lady Astor, noted for her wit, advocacy of Women's Rights, strong views on temperance, and articulate affection for her native state, was the first woman to sit, 1919–1945, in the British House of Commons. *Danville: corner of Main and Broad sts.*

Q-5-c THE GIBSON GIRL

Here stood the residence in which Irene Langhorne Gibson, 1873–1956 was born. Her beauty, charm, and vivacity captivated the artist Charles Dana Gibson who, following their marriage in 1895, cast his celebrated, style-setting "Gibson Girl" illustrations in her image. *Danville: Main and Broad sts.*

Q-5-c* LOYAL BAPTIST CHURCH

In 1870 the Loyal Street Baptist Church, organized between 1865–66 by a group of former slaves on "Old Hospital-Dance Hill," was built. Worship continued here until 1924 when the church moved to Holbrook Street. The name was then changed to Loyal Baptist Church. *Danville: 400 Block of Loyal St.*

Q-5-c LOYAL BAPTIST CHURCH

The Loyal Street Baptist Church congregation, which was organized between 1865 and 1866 on Old Hospital-Dance Hill by former slaves, built its church here in 1870. Worship continued at this site until 1924 when the congregation moved to Holbrook Street. The name was then changed to Loyal Baptist Church. *Danville: 400 block of Loyal St.*

Q-5-d DANVILLE SYSTEM

On this site stood Neal's Warehouse where the "Danville System" of selling tobacco began in 1858. Previously tobacco had been sold by sample from hogsheads, but under the new system it was sold at auction in open, loose piles so buyers could examine the whole lot. It is in general use today. *Danville: 126 N. Union St.*

Q-5-e STRATFORD COLLEGE

Stratford College (1930–1974) and its constituent preparatory school, Stratford Hall (1930–1954), maintained the tradition of liberal arts education for women begun in 1854 at the Danville Female College. Main hall was built in 1883 to house the Danville College for Young Ladies (1883–1897) and is a landmark also of its successors Randolph-Macon Institute (1897–1930) and Stratford. *Danville: 1125 W. Main St.*

Q-5-f CALVARY UNITED METHODIST CHURCH

An outgrowth of the mother church on Lynn Street in Danville, the North Danville Methodist Episcopal Church, South, was founded by 47 devoted members at the corner of Church and Keen streets on November 14, 1879. This was the first organized religious group in North Danville. On November 14, 1887, a new sanctuary on this site was dedicated and known as Calvary Methodist Episcopal Church, South. In 1968 the name was changed to Calvary United Methodist Church. *Danville: 924 N. Main St.*

Q-5-g FREDERICK DELIUS (1862–1934)

One block west on Church Street is the site of the Henry P. Richardson house where Frederick Delius lived while teaching music at Roanoke Female College, now Averett. An unsuccessful orange grower in Florida, the Britisher Delius worked in Danville in 1885–1886 to earn return passage to Europe where he pursued a musical career, becoming an internationally acclaimed composer. *Danville: N. Main St. at Keen St.*

Q-5-h CONFEDERATE PRISON #6

Constructed in 1855 as a tobacco factory by Major William T. Sutherlin, this renovated structure housed Union prisoners during the Civil War, 1861–1865. It was one of six Danville Confederate prisons in which as many as 7,000 Union soldiers were confined. *Danville: Loyal St. at Lynn St.*

Q-5-k SCHOOLFIELD

Schoolfield, established in 1903 as a textile mill village, was named for three brothers who founded Riverside Cotton Mills, later Dan River Mills. By the 1920s, this company town—complete with a school, churches, stores, a theatre, and other recreational facilities—was home to over 4,500 residents, mostly mill employees and their families, living in some 800 rental houses. A strike in 1930–31 ended a decade of employer/employee cooperation known as "Industrial Democracy," yet the community's tradition of neighborhood and family life continued to flourish. Danville annexed Schoolfield in 1951. *Danville: W. Main St. at Baltimore Ave.*

Q-6 TERRILL HILL

Nearby is the site of Terrill Hill, home of the Terrill brothers of Bath County. Brigadier General William R. Terrill, a graduate of West Point, commanded a Union Brigade and was killed in the Battle of Perryville, Kentucky, October 8, 1862. His brother, Brigadier General James B. Terrill, a graduate of the Virginia Military Institute, served with General A. P. Hill's 13th Regiment, Virginia Infantry, and died in the Battle of the Wilderness, May 31, 1864. Legend says their father erected a monument to his sons with the inscription "God alone knows which was right." *Bath Co.: Rte. 39 at Rte. 220.*

Q-6-1 FORT EARLY

The redoubt is part of the outer Lynchburg defenses, June, 1864. General Early arrived with the Second Corps of Lee's army in the afternoon of June 17. The redoubt (erected by Early) was occupied by part of Ramseur's and Gordon's divisions. The Union General Hunter attacked in the afternoon of June 18. Repulsed, he began to retreat in the night of June 18–19, followed by Early. *Lynchburg: Fort Ave., near Early Monument.*

Q-6-2 FORT McCAUSLAND

The fort on the hill here was constructed by General J. A. Early to protect the approach to Lynchburg from the west. Union cavalry skirmished with the Confederates along the road immediately west of the fort. The Unionists, driven back by General McCausland, were unable to enter the city from this direction. *Lynchburg: Langhorne Rd., about 1200 feet w. of Clifton St.*

Q-6-3 INNER DEFENSES, 1864

Here ran the inner line of Lynchburg defenses thrown up by General D. H. Hill in June, 1864. General John C. Breckinridge, confronting General Hunter in the Shenandoah Valley, made a forced march to forestall Hunter. Hill constructed a shallow line of trenches, occupied by Breckinridge, and hospital convalescents and home guards. It became a reserve line when General Early arrived. *Lynchburg: Twelfth St., between Fillmore and Floyd sts.*

Q-6-4 INNER DEFENSES

A line of shallow entrenchments extended across Bedford Avenue near this spot, making connection with other trenches crossing the present Southern Railroad. These works protected Lynchburg from entrance by the Lexington Turnpike (now the Hollins Mill road). They were occupied by General Breckinridge's troops. *Lynchburg: Bedford Ave. and Holly St.*

Q-6-5 DEFENSE WORKS

On the crest of the hill just to the south was a redoubt forming part of the defenses thrown up by General D. H. Hill, June, 1864. These works were held by General Imboden's cavalry. A military road was constructed to conduct this point with Fort McCausland. Signs of this road may still be seen in old Rivermont Park. *Lynchburg: Rivermont Ave. and Langhorne Rd.*

Q-6-6 MUSTERED AND DISBANDED, 1861–1865

At this point the Second Virginia Cavalry was mustered into service, May 10, 1861. At the same place the remnant of this regiment was disbanded, April 10, 1865, completing a service of four years lacking one month. The regiment participated in many campaigns and engagements. *Lynchburg: between Rivermont Ave. and Monsview Dr.*

Q-6-7 INNER DEFENSES, 1864

A line of shallow entrenchments extended from near this point along the crest of the hill to the east. These works were occupied by the cadets of the Virginia Military Institute, who had marched here with General Breckinridge after the Institute at Lexington was burned by General Hunter. *Lynchburg: Ninth and Polk sts.*

Q-6-8 INNER DEFENSES

Here, facing west, ran the inner defenses of the city, located by General D. H. Hill. They were constructed by convalescents and home guards. General Early, after an inspection of the system, moved most of the men to the outer works well to the westward. *Lynchburg: between Ninth and Polk sts.*

Q-6-9 INNER DEFENSES

Near here ran the line of inner defenses located by General D. H. Hill, June, 1864. He had been sent from Petersburg by General Beauregard to assist General Breckinridge, then in command. On General Early's arrival troops were moved to the outer works. *Lynchburg: between Wise and Floyd sts.*

Q-6-10 MILLER-CLAYTOR HOUSE

This building formerly stood at Eighth and Church streets. It now stands one block north. It was built by John Miller about 1791. Thoma Wiatt bought the house, long known as the "Mansion House." Samuel Claytor purchased it in 1825. For many years doctors' officers were here. For ninety years the house was owned by the Page family. The Lynchburg Historical Society moved and restored it. *Lynchburg: Rivermont Ave. and Treasure Island Rd.*

Q-6-11 LYNCHBURG

In 1757 John Lynch opened a ferry here; in 1765 a church was built. In 1786 Lynchburg was established by act of assembly; in 1791 the first tobacco warehouse was built. Lynchburg was incorporated as a town in 1805. In 1840 the James River and Kanawha Canal, from Richmond to Lynchburg, was opened; the section of Buchanan, in 1851. Lynchburg became a city in 1852. *Lynchburg: Ninth and Church sts.*

Q-6-11 LYNCHBURG (back of marker)

Trains began running on the first railroad, the Virginia and Tennessee, in 1852. Lynchburg was a main military supply center, 1862–65. Here the Confederates under General Early defeated the Union General Hunter, June 18, 1864. In 1893 Randolph-Macon Woman's College opened; in 1903, Lynchburg College. In 1920 the council manager form of government was adopted. *Lynchburg: Ninth and Church sts.*

Q-6-12 CARTER GLASS

Born January 4, 1858, in a house which stood on this site. Newspaper publisher; member of the State Senate and Delegate to the State Constitutional Convention of 1901–1902; member of the United States House of Representatives, 1902–1918, and principal author of the Federal Reserve Act; Secretary of the Treasury, 1918–1920; member of the United States Senate from 1920 until his death in 1946. *Lynchburg: 829 Church St.*

Q-6-13 LYNCHBURG COLLEGE

Situated on the hill to the southeast, this institution was established in 1903 by Dr. Josephus Hopwood and eight associates to promote Christian Higher Education. It was originally chartered as Virginia Christian College. The name was changed to Lynchburg College in 1919. This College is an educational institution of the churches of the Disciples of Christ. *Lynchburg: Lakeside Dr. (Rte. 221), w. of Old Forest Rd.*

Q-6-14 RANDOLPH-MACON WOMAN'S COLLEGE

Founded by Dr. William Waugh Smith in 1891 and opened in 1893 as a member of the Randolph-Macon System of Educational Institutions, this Liberal Arts College has been recognized from its opening year for its high standards of scholarship. The scenic campus of 100 acres extends to the James River. *Lynchburg: Rivermont Ave. and Princeton Cir.*

Q-6-15 VIRGINIA SEMINARY AND COLLEGE

This college, one block to the southwest, was organized by the Virginia Baptist State Convention, May 1886, as a Negro College of "Self-Help" and "Spiritual Independence." The Charter was granted by an act of the Legislature, February 1888. It was opened January 1890 with 33 students. The College is the outgrowth of Gregory Willis Hayes' "Do-For-Thy-Self" philosophy. *Lynchburg: Campbell Ave. and DeWitt St.*

Q-6-16* ALLEN WEIR FREEMAN, M.D. 1881–1954

Born at 416 Main Street, he was a pioneer in public health administration and education. He served as First Assistant Commissioner of Health, Virginia; Epidemiologist, United States Public Health Service; Health Commissioner, Ohio; Professor and Dean, School of Hygiene and Public Health, Johns Hopkins University; and Consultant to Foreign Governments in Developing Health Programs. *Lynchburg: in front of 416 Main St.*

Q-6-17 DOUGLAS SOUTHALL FREEMAN, Ph.D. (1886–1953)

Born at 416 Main Street, he moved to Richmond at an early age and became a distinguished editor and historian. Editor of the Richmond News Leader, 1915–1959; Rector and President of The Board of Trustees, University of Richmond, 1934–1949; Professor of Journalism, Columbia University, 1935–1941; and Author of Pulitzer Prize biographies of both Robert E. Lee and George Washington, as well as other standard historical works. *Lynchburg: s. end of Rivermont Bridge.*

Q-6-18 SAMUEL D. ROCKENBACH (1869–1952) BRIGADIER GENERAL, U.S. ARMY CAVALRY

Nearby at 805 Madison St. is the birthplace of General Rockenbach, "Father of the U.S. Army Tank Corps." He began his education in Lynchburg schools and was a honor graduate of Virginia Military Institute in 1889. As first chief of the Army's tank corps in 1917, he pioneered training schools and field organization for tank warfare in World War I. *Lynchburg: Eighth and Court sts.*

Q-6-20 THE ANNE SPENCER HOUSE

This was the home of Edward Alexander and Anne Bannister Spencer from 1903 until her death on July 25, 1975. Born on February 6, 1882, in Henry County, Virginia, Anne Spencer was to receive national and international recognition as a poet. Published extensively between 1920 and 1935, she belonged to the Harlem Renaissance school of writers. *Lynchburg: 1313 Pierce St.*

Q-7-a TANGIER ISLAND

The island was visited in 1608 by Captain John Smith, who gave it the name. A part was patented by Ambrose White in 1670. It was settled in 1686 by John Crockett and his sons' families. In 1814, it was the headquarters of a British fleet ravaging Chesapeake Bay. From here the fleet sailed to attack Fort McHenry near Baltimore. The Rev. Joshua Thomas, in a prayer, predicted the failure of the expedition. It was in this attack that the Star-Spangled Banner was written. *Accomack Co.: on Tangier Island.*

Q-7-e 750 MAIN STREET—DANVILLE

On this site stood the residence of James E. Schoolfield. In the parlor of his house were held the meetings to organize both Dan River, Inc. on July 20, 1882 and the Young Women's Christian Association of Danville on December 19, 1904. *Danville: 750 Main St.*

Q-8-a TRINITY CHURCH

Built in 1762 as the parish church of Portsmouth parish, established in 1761. Later named Trinity; enlarged in 1829; remodeled in 1893. Colonel William Crawford, founder of Portsmouth in 1752, was a member of the first vestry. Buried here is Commodore James Barron, commander of the U.S. frigate Chesapeake when attacked by H.M.S. Leopard in 1807; the result was his celebrated duel with Stephen Decatur in 1820. The graves of many Revolutionary patriots are here. *Portsmouth: High and Court sts.*

Q-8-b MONUMENTAL METHODIST CHURCH

This church, founded 1772, is one of the oldest Methodist churches in Virginia. The first building was erected, 1775, at South and Effingham streets. The church was moved to Glasgow Street near Court in 1792. It established the first Sunday School in Portsmouth in 1818. Monumental was moved to this site, Dinwiddie Street, in 1831. *Portsmouth: Dinwiddie St. near High St.*

Q-8-c WATTS HOUSE

Built by Colonel Dempsey Watts in 1799 and inherited by his son, Captain Samuel Watts, who lived here until his death in 1878. Here Chief Black Hawk, of the Black Hawk Indian War, was entertained in 1820, and Henry Clay in 1844. *Portsmouth: 517 North St.*

Q-8-d BALL HOUSE

Built about 1784 by John Nivison at the corner of Crawford and Glasgow streets and moved to this site in 1869. It served as a barracks in the War of 1812. Lafayette was entertained here in 1824 and President Andrew Jackson in 1833. The Ball family acquired the property in 1870. *Portsmouth: 213 Middle St.*

Q-8-e BENEDICT ARNOLD AT PORTSMOUTH

Arnold, after going over to the British, was sent to Virginia to make war on the state. He reached Hampton Roads in December, 1780, raided to Richmond and came to Portsmouth, January 19, 1781. Establishing his headquarters in Patrick Robinson's house, and using the old sugar house on Crawford Street as a prison and barracks, Arnold remained here until spring. Then again he went up the James to open the fateful campaign of 1781 that won the war for America. *Portsmouth: Bayview and Maryland aves.*

Q-8-f CORNWALLIS AT PORTSMOUTH

Lord Cornwallis, commanding the British troops in the South, reached Portsmouth, July, 1781. He prepared to send a portion of his force to New York. Before the movement was made, orders came for him to take up a position at Old Point. Cornwallis selected Yorktown, however, and Portsmouth was abandoned. *Portsmouth: Crawford Pkwy. e. of Court St.*

Q-8-g* COLLIER'S RAID

A British fleet under Sir George Collier sailed up Elizabeth River and captured Fort Nelson, May, 1779. British troops commanded by General Matthews took possession of Portsmouth and destroyed quantities of tobacco and naval stores. Suffolk was burned. The troops then returned by sea to New York. *Portsmouth: Bayview and Maryland aves.*

Q-8-h PORTSMOUTH NAVAL HOSPITAL

This was begun in 1827 and opened in 1830. The hospital was taxed to its capacity in the great yellow fever epidemic of 1855 which decimated Portsmouth and Norfolk. This hospital has cared for the sick and wounded of the Navy in all wars of the United States since its establishment. It is the oldest hospital of the Navy. *Portsmouth: On hospital grounds.*

Q-8-k ELIZABETH RIVER

The Elizabeth River, explored by Captain John Smith in 1608, was named for Princess Elizabeth. Shipbuilding activity began in 1620 when John Wood, a shipbuilder, requested a land grant. Many historic ships were built at the naval shipyard here, including the USS Delaware, first ship dry-docked in America, and CCS Virginia, (Ex-Merrimac), first ironclad to engage in battle. *Portsmouth: Crawford Pkwy. at Court St.*

Q-8-l CITY OF PORTSMOUTH

The site of this city was patented in 1659 by Captain William Carver. Established as a town in 1752 and named by its founder, Lt. Col. William Crawford. Chartered as a city in 1858, it has the country's oldest naval shipyard, established in 1767, the nation's oldest naval hospital, commenced in 1827, and is the birthplace of the world's largest naval installation. *Portsmouth: Rte. 17 at Churchland Bridge.*

Q-8-m CRAWFORD HOUSE

Erected 1835 by J. W. Collins, Portsmouth's first five-story building and for many years a leading hotel. Presidents Van Buren, Tyler, and Fillmore were entertained here. *Portsmouth: Crawford and Queen sts.*

Q-8-n NORFOLK COUNTY COURT HOUSE, 1845–1962

Begun 1845, occupied 20 July 1846. The architect, William R. Singleton, a Portsmouth native, also designed the old Norfolk City Court House. This building stands on one of the four corners dedicated for public use in 1752 by Lt. Col. William Crawford, founder of Portsmouth. The site was formerly occupied by the clerk's office when an earlier court house, occupied in 1803, stood on the northeast corner, opposite. *Portsmouth: High and Court sts.*

Q-8-o ARNOLD'S BRITISH DEFENSE, 1781

This marks a line of British redoubts erected in March 1781 by order of Brigadier General Benedict Arnold who, under Major William Phillips, commanded British troops occupying Portsmouth. The line of fortifications extended in an arc along Washington Street from the northern waterfront to Gosport Creek and defended Portsmouth from American attack from the west. *Portsmouth: Washington and King sts.*

Q-8-p ARNOLD'S BRITISH DEFENSES, 1781

This marks the Northern limit of a line of British redoubts erected in March 1781 by order of Brigadier General Benedict Arnold who, under Major General William Phillips, commanded British troops occupying Portsmouth. This line of fortifications extended in an arc south along Dinwiddie and Washington Streets to Gosport Creek and defended Portsmouth from American attack from the West. *Portsmouth: Crawford Pkwy. at Court St.*

Q-8-q* ARNOLD'S BRITISH DEFENSES, 1781

A brick windmill near here was close to the southern limit of a line of British redoubts erected in March 1781 by order of Brigadier General Benedict Arnold who, under Major General William Phillips commanded British troops occupying Portsmouth. This line of fortifications extended north in an arc along Washington Street to the waterfront near Court Street. *Portsmouth: Washington and Brighton sts.*

Q-9 WARRENTON

Chosen as county seat in 1759, and first called Fauquier Court House, Warrenton was laid out as a town in 1790. John Marshall began law practice here. In the War Between the States it was the center of operations north of the Rappahannock and many wounded were hospitalized here. Union General Pope headquartered here in the Second Manassas Campaign. Seizing the local press, the Unionists edited the newspaper as "The New York Ninth." Mosby, the ranger, made forays in this vicinity. *Fauquier Co.: Rte. 802, at Warrenton.*

Q-10-a CAPPAHOSIC

Seven and one-half miles southwest is Cappahosic, where a ferry was established early in the eighteenth century. On the old charts, this Indian district lay between Werowocomoco and Timberneck Creek. Powhatan is said to have offered it to Capt. John Smith for "two great guns and a grindstone." John Stubbs patented the Cappahosic tract in 1652 and 1702 and a few years later built "Cappahosic House," which has clipped gables and inside chimneys with eight unique corner fireplaces. *Gloucester Co.: Rte. 17, at Gloucester.*

Q-11-a* STONEWALL JACKSON'S HOME

This house was purchased late in 1858 by Thomas Jonathan Jackson, then of the V.M.I. faculty. He and his wife lived here, in the only home he ever owned, from early 1859 to April, 1861, when he entered the service of the Confederacy. *Lexington: Washington and Main sts.*

Q-12-a   CLERK'S OFFICE

Site of first county seat of Pittsylvania County. The building that served as the debtor's prison, 1767–1771, and later as the clerk's office, 1771–1777, remains. Nearby stands the debtor's gaol, built in 1773. It later served as Samuel Calland's store and in 1803 became the post office for Callands. *Pittsylvania Co.: Rte. 969, at Callands.*

QA-1   FOLLY CASTLE

This house was the town home of Peter Jones, who built it in 1763. It was called "Folly Castle" because it was a large house for a childless man, but Jones later had offspring. Major Erasmus Gill, Revolutionary soldier, also lived here. *Petersburg: W. Washington St.*

QA-2   TRADING STATION AND TAVERN

One block north and one block west is the traditional site of the station where Peter Jones, for whom Petersburg probably was named, traded with the Indians. It was established before 1675. There also is the colonial Durell's, or Golden Ball, Tavern, where British officers were quartered in the occupation of 1781. *Petersburg: Sycamore and Bollingbrook sts.*

QA-3*   WORLD WAR MEMORIALS

West on Wythe Street from this corner the trees were planted as memorials to the Petersburg men who died in the World War. Each tree bears the name of a soldier. The street was first known as Week's Cut, from ancient Week's Tavern. *Petersburg: Wythe St. and Crater Rd.*

QA-4   WORLD WAR MEMORIALS

Two blocks east on Wythe Street begin the trees planted as memorials to Petersburg men who died in the World War. Each tree bears the name of a soldier. Wythe Street was first known as Weeks's Cut and on it, diagonally opposite this spot, stood ancient Weeks's Tavern. *Petersburg: Sycamore and Wythe sts.*

QA-5   POPLAR LAWN

Poplar Lawn is now known as Central Park. Here the Petersburg volunteers camped in October, 1812, before leaving for the Canadian border. Here Lafayette was greeted with music and speeches in 1824. The place was bought by the city in 1844. Volunteer companies enlisted here, April 19, 1861. In the siege of 1864–65 a hospital stood here. *Petersburg: Filmore and S. Sycamore sts.*

QA-6   FORT HENRY

Four blocks north is the traditional site of Fort Henry, established under the act of 1645. In 1646 the fort was leased by Abraham Wood. From it, in 1650, Abraham Wood and Edmund Bland set out on an exploring expedition; and, in 1671 Batts and Fallam, on the first expedition known to have crossed the Appalachian Mountains. The fort was garrisoned again in 1675, with Peter Jones as commander. *Petersburg: W. Washington and N. South sts.*

QA-7   GENERAL LEE'S HEADQUARTERS

Three blocks north and a half block west is the Beasley house where General Robert E. Lee had his headquarters in 1864 during the siege of Petersburg. He moved thence to Edge Hill to be in closer touch with his right wing. *Petersburg: W. Washington and Lafayette sts.*

QA-8 NIBLO'S TAVERN

On the northeast corner stood a famous colonial tavern. Lafayette was entertained there in 1824. It was replaced in 1828 by Niblo's Hotel, built by William Niblo. Later it was known as the Bollingbrook Hotel. It was a favorite resort of generals in the siege of 1864–65. *Petersburg: Bollingbrook and Second sts.*

QA-9* BATTERSEA

Four blocks north is Battersea, home of John Banister, Revolutionary soldier, who was elected the first mayor of Petersburg in 1784. In 1781 British officers were quartered there. In the same year the noted French traveler Chastellux visited it, and later the Italian Count Castiglioni. *Petersburg: W. Washington St. and Battersea Ln.*

QA-10 ST. PAUL'S CHURCH

St. Paul's Church was built in 1856. Here Robert E. Lee and his staff worshiped during the siege of Petersburg, 1864–65. Lee attended the wedding of his son, W. H. F. Lee, in this church in 1867. *Petersburg: W. Washington St.*

QA-11 BLANDFORD CHURCH AND CEMETERY

The Brick Church on Well's Hill, now known as Old Blandford Church, was built between 1734 and 1737. The British General Phillips was buried in the churchyard in 1781. In the cemetery is a monument to Captain McRae and the Petersburg volunteers, who at Fort Meigs in 1813 won for Petersburg the name of the "Cockade City of the Union." Soldiers of six wars rest here, among them 30,000 Confederates. *Petersburg: Crater Rd. near Cameron St.*

QA-12 BATTLE OF PETERSBURG

Here was fought the Battle of Petersburg, April 25, 1781. The Southside militia, 1,000 strong and commanded by Baron Steuben and General Muhlenberg, made a brave resistance to 2,500 British regulars under Phillips and Arnold. *Petersburg: Crater Rd. at Cameron St.*

QA-13 EAST HILL

On the hilltop to the south is the site of East Hill, also known as Bollingbrook. There the British General Phillips, Benedict Arnold and Lord Cornwallis stayed in April and May, 1781. The house was bombarded by Lafayette, May 10, 1781. There Phillips died, May 13, 1781. *Petersburg: E. Bank and Fourth sts.*

QA-14 TWO NOTED HOMES

Half a block south is the home of Major General William Mahone, famed for his gallant conduct at the Battle of the Crater, July 30, 1864. Two blocks south is the Wallace home, where Abraham Lincoln conferred with General Grant, April 3, 1865, preceding Grant's march to Appomattox. *Petersburg: W. Washington and S. Market sts.*

QA-15 FORMATION OF THE SOUTHERN METHODIST CHURCH

One block west stood the Union Street Methodist Church, completed in 1820. There was held the first general conference of the Methodist Episcopal Church South, May 1–23, 1846. At this meeting the Southern Methodist Church, which had separated from the Northern Church, effected its organization. *Petersburg: N. Sycamore St. near Washington St.*

QA-16 GRAHAM ROAD

On June 9, 1864, Kautz's Union cavalry, 1300 men, after overwhelming Archer's militia, one mile south, moved westward on this road to attack the city. Upon the hillside, one mile west, they were repulsed by the battery of Captain Edward Graham, and later driven to retreat by General James Dearing's cavalry. This attack, in conjunction with an infantry force that did not come up, was the first attempt to capture Petersburg. *Petersburg: Crater and Graham rds.*

QA-17 GRAHAM ROAD

Upon this site, on June 9, 1864, Captain Edward Graham, commanding two guns of the Petersburg artillery, repulsed the attack of Kautz's cavalry, 1300 men, and by this gallant defense the city was saved. Later the Union forces were driven to retreat by the supporting cavalry of General James Dearing. *Petersburg: Graham Rd. and Clinton St.*

QA-18 THE FIRST METHODIST MEETING HOUSE

The first Methodist Meeting House in Petersburg was a theatre on West Old Street near the river rented by Gressett Davis. Robert Williams, a follower of John Wesley, came to Petersburg to preach in 1773 at the invitation of Davis and Nathaniel Young, local businessmen. From this humble beginning, Methodism became firmly established in Petersburg and spread throughout the surrounding countryside. Petersburg served as Williams' headquarters and later was made part of the Brunswick circuit. *Petersburg: Grove Ave. and Fleet St.*

QA-19 GRACE EPISCOPAL CHURCH

The third home of Grace Church, a brick Gothic Revival-style building, stood on this site from 1859 to 1960. The congregation was founded in 1841 by Dr. Churchill Jones Gibson, rector until 1892. In 1928 a majority of the members, led by the rector, Dr. Edwin Royall Carter, left to form Christ Episcopal Church at 1545 South Sycamore Street. The two congregations reunited in 1953 at the Sycamore Street site as Christ and Grace Episcopal Church. *Petersburg: High St. and Cross St.*

QB-1 FIRST SUFFOLK CHURCH

Here stood the Colonial Suffolk Church, a large, cross-shaped brick building erected in 1753 as the second parish church of Upper Parish, Nansemond County, and the first house of worship in the town of Suffolk. It survived the burning of Suffolk by the British in 1779 but fell to ruin and was torn down by 1802. *Suffolk: Western Ave., 200 feet w. of Church St.*

QC-1 TRINITY CHURCH

Known originally as Augusta Parish Church, it was founded in 1746 as the County Parish. The Virginia General Assembly met here in June 1781 to avoid capture by British Raiders. The present church was erected in 1855 and was used by the Virginia Theological Seminary during the War Between the States. The first Bishop of Virginia, James Madison, was a member of the church. *Staunton: 214 W. Beverley St.*

R-4* LYNCHBURG DEFENSES

Half a mile southeast, on Madison Heights, are two large earthworks forming part of the Confederate defense system, 1861–65. *Amherst Co.: Rte. 29, 1 mile n. of Lynchburg.*

R-15* PATRICK HENRY'S GRAVE

Five miles east is Red Hill, last home and grave of Patrick Henry, orator of the Revolution. He moved there in 1796 and died there, June 6, 1799. Henry is especially famous for his "Liberty or Death" speech made in 1775 at the beginning of the Revolution. *Campbell Co.: Rte. 501, at Brookneal.*

R-20 SWEET BRIAR COLLEGE CHARTERED 1901

This Liberal Arts College for women, opened in 1906, granted its first Bachelor of Arts Degrees in 1910. Established under the will of Indiana Fletcher Williams as a memorial to her only daughter, Daisy, the College is located on a 2800-acre tract of land acquired by Elijah Fletcher before 1830. The eighteenth-century homestead, remodeled and named "Sweet Briar House" by the Fletchers, is set in a boxwood garden. *Amherst Co.: Rte. 29, 2 miles s. of Amherst.*

R-50 BOYHOOD HOME OF COLONEL MOSBY

Five miles south near the "Thoroughfare Gap" was the early boyhood home of Colonel John Singleton Mosby (1833–1916), famous Confederate Ranger. He attended the school near Murrell's Shop, east of Elmington. *Nelson Co.: Rte. 6, 3 miles n. of Woods Mill.*

R-51 HURRICANE CAMILLE

On August 20, 1969, torrential rains, following remnants of Hurricane Camille, devastated this area. A rainfall in excess of 25 inches largely within a 5-hour period, swept away or buried many miles of roads, over 100 bridges, and over 900 buildings. 114 people died and 37 remain missing. The damage totalled more than $100,000,000 and Virginia was declared a disaster area. *Nelson Co.: Rte. 29, at Woods Mill Wayside.*

R-56 LOVINGSTON

This place became the county seat of Nelson when it was formed from Amherst in 1807. It was named for James Loving, Jr., who gave the land for the courthouse, built in 1808–09. The town was incorporated in 1807 and again in 1871, and deincorporated in 1938. *Nelson Co.: Rte. 250, at Lovingston.*

R-58 BIRTHPLACE OF RIVES

Two miles east, at Oak Ridge, was born William Cabell Rives, May 4, 1792. He was minister to France, 1829–32 and 1849–53; United States Senator, 1832–45; member of the Peace convention of 1861 and of the Confederate Congress. He died, April 25, 1868. Later, Oak Ridge was owned by Thomas Fortune Ryan. *Nelson Co.: Rte. 29, 4 miles s. of Lovingston.*

R-59 CONSTITUTION FOREST

In 1938, in celebration of the 150th anniversary of the United States Constitution, the Virginia Daughters of the American Revolution sponsored the planting of Constitution Forest in this area. With the help of the Civilian Conservation Corps and the United States Forest Service, the memorial forest commemorates the Virginia framers of the Constitution. In 1987, the 45 acres of red and white pine seedlings have matured to a forest that provides protection for birds and other wildlife as well as for the watershed of the James River. *Amherst Co.: Rte. 60, at Rockbridge Co. line.*

R-60 GRAVE OF PATRICK HENRY'S MOTHER

In the grove of trees some hundreds of yards to the west is the grave of Sarah Winston (Henry), mother of Patrick Henry, who died in November, 1784. *Amherst Co.: Rte. 151, just s. of Clifford.*

R-61 ACTION AT TYE RIVER

About 800 yards east, on June 11, 1864, the Botetourt Battery, C.S.A., prevented Federal Raiders from burning the Orange and Alexandria Railroad Bridge, thus enabling General Jubal Early to reach Lynchburg in time to save it from capture by General Hunter. *Amherst Co.: Rte. 29, s. of Tye River Bridge.*

R-62 OLD RUSTBURG

The place was named for Jeremiah Rust, who patented land here in 1780. The first courthouse of Campbell County was built here, in 1783; the present building was erected about 1848. The old "Fountain Hotel" was built in 1795 and has been conducted by the Finch family ever since. *Campbell Co.: Rte. 501, at Rustburg.*

R-63 FALLING SPRING PRESBYTERIAN CHURCH

The oldest congregation in the Fincastle Presbytery, the Falling Spring Presbyterian Church, was organized before 1748. The Hanover Presbytery met here in October, 1780. The present Gothic Revival Church was constructed of slave-made brick during the Civil War. At the time of its dedication in April, 1864, General Thomas L. Rosser's Cavalry Brigade was camped here. The first burial in the present cemetery was that of John Grigsby of Fruit Hill (1720–1794). Erected by the National Grigsby Family Society, 1981. *Rockbridge Co.: Rte. 11, 7 miles s. of Lexington.*

R-77* HISTORY AT HALIFAX

A part of Greene's army was here in February, 1781, just after Cornwallis's pursuit. Here Washington stopped, June 4, 1791, in his tour of the Southern States. Here John Randolph of Roanoke in 1827 made one of his great speeches. Here General Custer camped in April, 1865. *Halifax Co.: Rte. 360, at Halifax.*

R-78 HALIFAX CHURCH

Halifax Church is the oldest Presbyterian church in Halifax County. The Congregation was formed in June, 1830, from Cub Creek Church in Charlotte County. The organizational group included the Reverend Clement Read of Cub Creek and twenty-six local communicants including sixteen black members, mostly slaves. Visiting ministers preached occasionally at the church until June, 1831, when the Reverend Thomas A. Ogden began four years of service as the congregation's first pastor. The building was restored in 1983 and placed on the Virginia Landmarks Register in 1987. *Halifax Co.: Rte. 624 at Rte. 623.*

R-79 GREEN'S FOLLY

Built about 1789 by Captain Berryman Green, a quartermaster in Washington's army at Valley Forge and later a deputy clerk of Halifax County. *Halifax Co.: Rte. 501, 2 miles s. of Halifax.*

R-80 MINISTER WHO MARRIED LINCOLN

Here lived Rev. Charles A. Dresser, rector of Antrim Parish and builder of St. Mark's Church, 1828. Dresser left this parish in 1835 for Peoria, Illinois, whence he moved to Springfield. There he married Abraham Lincoln to Mary Todd, November 4, 1842. *Halifax Co.: Rte. 501, 2 miles s. of Halifax.*

RA-4 ROCKFISH CHURCH

This Presbyterian church was established in 1746; James McCann conveyed the land for the church and school. Samuel Black became the first pastor in 1747. The first building was erected in 1771 by Thomas Mason. The church was reorganized in 1849. The present church was built in 1853. *Nelson Co.: Rte. 151, 10.6 miles s. of Afton.*

RA-6 WILLIAM H. CRAWFORD

William Harris Crawford was born in this vicinity, February 24, 1772. Early in life he was taken to Georgia and became a leading politician of the era. He was United States Senator; Minister to France; Secretary of War and of the Treasury; candidate, 1824, for the Presidency, which was decided by the House of Representatives. *Nelson Co.: Rte. 151, 12.7 miles s. of Afton.*

RG-5 JOHN WEATHERFORD'S GRAVE

One half mile west is the grave of Elder John Weatherford (1740–1833) Baptist preacher for 70 years and early advocate of religious liberty. Jailed five months in Chesterfield in 1773 for unlicensed preaching, his release was secured by Patrick Henry. *Pittsylvania Co.: Rte. 29, 9 miles s.e. of Chatham.*

S-1* STEUBEN AND LAFAYETTE

Steuben's militia here, on January 6, 1781, kept the British in Richmond from crossing the James. On April 30, 1781, the British (then south of the river) were kept from crossing to Richmond by Lafayette. *Richmond: Rte. 1, at s. entrance to city.*

S-2* ARNOLD AT WARWICK

Warwick was on the James just to the east, Benedict Arnold burned it, with some ships, on April 30, 1781. *Chesterfield Co.: Rte. 1, 1.5 miles s. of Richmond.*

S-2 WARWICK

Located eight miles downstream from Richmond, Warwick was an important 18th-century James River port and manufacturing center. During the Revolutionary War, Warwick's craftsmen turned out clothing and shoes, and its mills ground flour and meal for the Continental troops stationed at Chesterfield Courthouse. On April 30, 1781, British troops under Benedict Arnold burned the town, destroying ships, warehouses, mills, tannery storehouses, and ropewalks. *Chesterfield Co.: Rte. 1, 1.5 miles s. of Richmond at Falling Creek Wayside.*

S-3 AMPTHILL ESTATE

Built before 1732 by Henry Cary, this was the home of Colonel Archibald Cary, a Revolutionary leader of Virginia. The house was moved, 1929–30, to its present location off Cary Street Road in Richmond's West End. *Chesterfield Co.: Rte. 1, .7 mile s. of Richmond.*

S-4 FIRST IRON FURNACE

On the creek nearby stood the first iron furnace in English America, built in 1619. It was destroyed by the Indians in the massacre of 1622. *Chesterfield Co.: Rte. 1, 1.5 miles s. of Richmond.*

S-5 DREWRY'S BLUFF

This bluff on the James River, a mile east, was fortified by Captain A. H. Drewry in 1862. A Union fleet, attempting to pass it, was driven back, May 15, 1862; and thereafter it served as a bar to attacks on Richmond by water. On June 16, 1864, Longstreet's Corps of Lee's army crossed the river there going to the defense of Petersburg. *Chesterfield Co.: Rte. 1, 2.5 miles s. of Richmond.*

S-6* MAIN CONFEDERATE LINE

The main line of Confederate earthworks, 1864–65, ran from the creek here to Drewry's Bluff on James River. *Chesterfield Co.: Rte. 1, 8 miles s. of Richmond.*

S-6 THE HOWLETT LINE

Just east of this point running from the James River to the Appomattox River, was the Confederate defense line known as the Howlett line, named for the Howlett House that stood at the north end of the line. Established in May, 1864, by General Beauregard's troops after the Battle of Drewry's Bluff, the line became famous as the "Cork in the Bottle" by keeping General Butler's Army of the James at bay. The Union line was one mile to the east. Parker's Virginia Battery was one-half mile to the south. *Chesterfield Co.: Rte. 10, 1.08 miles e. of Chester.*

S-7* CHESTERFIELD COURTHOUSE

It was several miles to the west. Here Steuben had his militia camp in 1780–81. The barracks were burned by the British General Phillips on April 27, 1781. *Chesterfield Co.: Rte. 1, 3.9 miles s. of Richmond.*

S-7 CHESTERFIELD COUNTY COURTHOUSE

This area, known originally as "Cold Water Run," is the site of the first Chesterfield County courthouse, erected in 1750. In 1917 it was demolished and replaced by a larger Georgian Revival brick building that served the county until the 1960s. The most famous trial here was that of seven Baptist preachers for breach of ecclesiastical law in 1773. In 1780–81, Governor Thomas Jefferson designated the courthouse village as a training post and encampment of all reinforcements for the Continental armies from the southern states. *Chesterfield Co.: Rte. 10, at Chesterfield Court House.*

S-8 BATTLE OF DREWRY'S BLUFF

From this point the Confederates, on May 16, 1864, moved to attack the Union Army of the James under Butler advancing northward on Richmond. *Chesterfield Co.: Rte. 1, 3.9 miles s. of Richmond.*

S-9* BATTLE OF DREWRY'S BLUFF

Here ran the line of battle of the Union army on the morning of May 16, 1864. The earthworks, taken by the Unionists on May 14, were given up by them on May 16. *Chesterfield Co.: Rte. 1, 4.5 miles s. of Richmond.*

S-10 HALF-WAY HOUSE

Headquarters of the Union Army of the James, this old inn was a central point in the battle of Drewry's Bluff, May 16, 1864. *Chesterfield Co.: Rte. 1, 5.4 miles s. of Richmond.*

S-11* PROCTOR'S CREEK FIGHT

To the west of the road here the Army of the James, on May 13–14, 1864, attacked the outer line of the Drewry's Bluff defenses. The Confederates withdrew to their second line on Kingsland Creek. *Chesterfield Co.: Rte. 301, at Proctor's Creek.*

S-12 INTO THE BOTTLE

The Union Army of the James, retiring across Proctor's Creek in this vicinity after the battle of Drewry's Bluff, May 16, 1864, turned east into the Peninsula between the James and Appomattox Rivers, where it was "Bottled" by Confederate forces. *Chesterfield Co.: Rte. 1, 6.5 miles s. of Richmond.*

S-12* INTO THE "BOTTLE"

The Union army, retiring across Proctor's Creek after the battle of May 16, 1864, in this vicinity turned east into the "bottle" between the James and Appomattox Rivers. *Chesterfield Co.: Rte. 1, 6 miles s. of Richmond.*

S-13 DUTCH GAP

This great bend in the James River lies due east. The town of Henrico was established here in 1611. In August, 1864, B. F. Butler cut a canal through the neck, shortening the river five miles. *Chesterfield Co.: Rte. 1, 6.7 miles s. of Richmond.*

S-14* OSBORNE'S WHARF

This old wharf lay to the east. Here Benedict Arnold burned state warships on April 27, 1781, and was here joined by Phillips. Lafayette, crossing the James, camped here, May 8–10, 1781, on his way to Petersburg. *Chesterfield Co.: Rte. 1, 6.7 miles s. of Richmond.*

S-14 OSBORNES

The town of Osbornes was named for Captain Thomas Osborne who settled nearby at Coxendale in 1616. During the 17th and 18th centuries, Osbornes plantation wharf was a tobacco inspection station and local shipping center. Thomas Jefferson, grandfather of the President, was born here in 1677. On April 21, 1781, British General Benedict Arnold destroyed nine ships of the American fleet and burned the town's warehouses and stores. George Washington visited Osbornes in 1791 during a national tour designed to afford citizens the opportunity to see their first national hero. *Chesterfield Co.: Rte. 1, 6.33 miles s. of Richmond.*

S-15 DREWRY'S BLUFF

A mile east is Drewry's Bluff, James River fortification of Richmond, 1862–65. Earthworks remain. *Chesterfield Co.: Rte. 1, 2.5 miles s. of Richmond.*

S-16 POCAHONTAS STATE PARK

This park of 7604 acres was originally known as the Swift Creek Recreational Area. Its purchase in 1934 and subsequent development by the federal government were with the understanding that eventually the State would accept and maintain the property, incorporating it into its Park System. On June 6, 1946 the Virginia Conservation Commission dedicated the park, naming it for the Indian princess Pocahontas. *Chesterfield Co.: Rte. 655, 4.1 miles w. of Chesterfield.*

S-16* REDWATER CREEK

Here, on May 12, 1864, the Union Army, advancing northward, formed line of battle across the road and drove the Confederates back on Proctor's Creek. *Chesterfield Co.: Rte. 1, 4.5 miles n. of Petersburg.*

S-17 CHESTER STATION FIGHT

At this station, two miles west, the Union army of the James, turning toward Richmond, fought an action on May 10, 1864, and tore up the railroad. *Chesterfield Co.: Rte. 1, 7.8 miles s. of Richmond.*

S-18* THE "BOTTLE"

This is the peninsula between the James and Appomattox Rivers in which the Army of the James was "bottled" by Beauregard in 1864–65. The line of Union earthworks was enclosed by a line of Confederate works. *Chesterfield Co.: Rte. 1, 6.2 miles n. of Petersburg.*

S-19* FEELING OUT FIGHT

The Confederates, feeling out the Union lines, attacked them just to the east on June 2, 1864, but soon withdrew. *Chesterfield Co.: Rte. 1, 6.9 miles n. of Petersburg.*

S-20* A RAILROAD RAID

The Union Army of the James drove off the defenders and destroyed the railroad here for several miles, May 6–12, 1864. *Chesterfield Co.: Rte. 1, 4.25 miles n. of Petersburg.*

S-21 BERMUDA HUNDRED

This place, some miles to the east, is on the James at the mouth of the Appomattox. A town was established there in 1613. Phillips and Arnold sailed from there in May, 1781. In May, 1864, it became the base of operations of the Army of the James. *Chesterfield Co.: Rte. 1, 7.8 miles s. of Richmond.*

S-22* PORT WALTHALL JUNCTION

This is on the railroad just to the east. Here the Union army, coming from the James River on May 7, 1864, began to tear up the railroad. *Chesterfield Co.: Rte. 1, 5.4 miles n. of Petersburg.*

S-22 PORT WALTHALL

Port Walthall, which stood on the banks of the Appomattox River several miles to the south, was a major shipping and passenger embarkation point prior to the Civil War. The railroad tracks leading to the port were melted down to manufacture Confederate cannon. *Chesterfield Co.: Rte. 10, 2.25 miles w. of Hopewell at Enon.*

S-23* LEE'S HEADQUARTERS

At the Clay house to the east Lee, going to the defense of Petersburg, had his headquarters on June 17, 1864. *Chesterfield Co.: Rte. 1, 7.5 miles n. of Petersburg.*

S-23 POINT OF ROCKS

Point of Rocks is located two miles south on the Appomattox River. In 1608, Captain John Smith wrote about this high rock cliff which projected out to the channel of the river. Known to all as Point of Rocks, it was severely damaged during a battle between Confederate artillery and Federal gunboats on June 26, 1862. Rock from the point was used to build the wall of the City Point National Cemetery shortly after the Civil War. *Chesterfield Co.: Rte. 10, 2.25 miles w. of Hopewell at Enon.*

S-24* ADVANCE ON PETERSBURG

Here the Union Army of the James, on May 9, 1864, turned southward toward Petersburg. *Chesterfield Co.: Rte. 1, 4.1 miles n. of Petersburg.*

S-25 UNION ARMY CHECKED

Here the Army of the James, moving on Petersburg, May 9, 1864, was checked by the Confederate defenses on the creek and turned northward. *Chesterfield Co.: Rte. 1, 3.4 miles n. of Petersburg.*

S-26 LAFAYETTE AT PETERSBURG

From this hill Lafayette, on May 10, 1781, shelled the British in Petersburg. *Chesterfield Co.: Rte. 1, at Colonial Heights.*

S-27 LEE'S HEADQUARTERS

Lee's headquarters from the latter part of June, 1864, to September, 1864, were here. *Chesterfield Co.: Rte. 1, at Colonial Heights.*

S-28 JOHN BAPTIST PIERCE (1875–1942)

A Cooperative Extension Service pioneer, innovator, and educator, John Baptist Pierce was appointed in 1906 by Seaman Knapp and H. B. Frissell of Hampton Institute as the first Negro farm demonstration agent for Virginia. Pierce served for 35 years as district agent for Virginia and North Carolina and as the United States Department of Agriculture field agent for the upper southern states. Pierce's "Live-at-Home and Community Improvement Program" was a unique innovation which helped many rural Virginians raise their standards of living. *Hampton: Rte. 60 between I-64 and Emancipation Dr.*

S-29 MAGNOLIA GRANGE

Built in 1822 by William Winfree, this Federal style house was named for the large stand of magnolia trees in the front yard. It was originally surrounded by a 600 acre farm. A nearby tavern provided lodging for persons with business at the Courthouse; a grist mill formerly stood on nearby Cold Water Run. From 1881 to 1969 it was the residence of the Cogbill family whose members figured prominently in the political history of Chesterfield County. *Chesterfield Co.: Rte. 10, at Chesterfield Court House.*

S-29 CIVILIAN CONSERVATION CORPS COMPANY 2386

Located north of this marker is the site of the camp of CCC Company 2386, Beach, Virginia. The camp was organized in 1935 and disbanded in 1942. The company consisted of 2 to 3 military officers, a civilian technical service staff, and approximately 200 enrollees. During its existence, the company built Swift Creek Recreational Area, the forerunner of Pocahontas State Park, and reforested 7,604 acres of land now known as Pocahontas State Forest. *Chesterfield Co.: Rte. 655, at entrance to Pocahontas State Park.*

S-30 FIRST RAILROAD IN VIRGINIA

Just south of here are the earthen remains and stone culvert of the Chesterfield Railroad, the first railroad in Virginia and the second in the United States. The tramway's trains were operated both by gravity and by horse and mule power. Built in 1831 to haul coal from the Midlothian Mines to the wharves at Manchester, the tramway remained in operation until the Richmond-Danville Railroad opened in 1851. *Chesterfield Co.: Rte. 60, 3.78 miles w. of Richmond.*

S-40* SAPONEY CHURCH

Five miles southeast stands Saponey Church, built in 1728. This church, the oldest in Dinwiddie County, is still in use. *Dinwiddie Co.: Rte. 1, at Dewitt.*

S-41* DINWIDDIE TAVERN

This is the site of old Dinwiddie Tavern, famous stopping-place in the latter part of the eighteenth century. It was burned in 1865. *Dinwiddie Co.: Rte. 1, at Dinwiddie.*

S-42* QUAKER SETTLEMENT

Two miles east was a Quaker settlement, founded about 1794. Some of the houses still stand. *Dinwiddie Co.: Rte. 1, 6 miles s.w. of Petersburg.*

S-43 COTTAGE FARM

A little south stood the home of Robert D. McIlwaine, where on the afternoon of April 2, 1865, General Lee ordered the evacuation of Richmond and Petersburg by the Confederates and the westward march which ended at Appomattox. *Dinwiddie Co.: Rte. 1 at s. limits of Petersburg.*

S-45 SCOTT'S LAW OFFICE

Just to the west stands the law office occupied in early life by Lieutenant-General Winfield Scott, commander of the United States Army, 1841–1861. Scott, born here, June 13, 1786 was admitted to the bar in 1806 and entered the army in 1808. He died, May 29, 1866. *Dinwiddie Co.: Rte. 1, at Dinwiddie.*

S-46* RACELAND

Six miles east is Raceland, where the famous race horse, Timoleon, was born. The oldest part of the house was built in 1707. A museum, cotton gin and slave quarters are there. *Dinwiddie Co.: Rte. 1, n. entrance of Dinwiddie.*

S-47 EDGE HILL

To the right stood the Turnbull House, headquarters of General Robert E. Lee from November 23, 1864, until April 2, 1865. After Lee's departure to Cottage Farm, Federal artillery destroyed the house. The present residence was one of the detached buildings. *Dinwiddie Co.: Rte. 1, at s. limits of Petersburg.*

S-48 THE CATTLE (BEEFSTEAK) RAID

In a field here were penned the cattle herd captured near City Point September 16, 1864 by Confederate Cavalry under General Wade Hampton. The herd was penned here after Hampton's return within his own lines. *Dinwiddie Co.: Rtes. 1 and 613, 5 miles s. of Petersburg.*

S-49   WHERE HILL FELL

In the field a short distance north of this road, the Confederate General A. P. Hill was killed, April 2, 1865. Hill, not knowing that Lee's lines had been broken, rode into a party of Union soldiers advancing on Petersburg. *Dinwiddie Co.: Rte. 1, 2.8 miles s. of Petersburg.*

S-50   HATCHER'S RUN

Lee's right wing was defended by earthworks on this stream, here and to the east. These works were unsuccessfully attacked by Union forces, February 5–7, 1865. On the morning of April 2, 1865, they were stormed by Union troops. *Dinwiddie Co.: Rte. 1, 6.4 miles s. of Petersburg.*

S-51   BURGESS MILL

An old mill stood here, with earthworks. On October 27, 1864, General Hancock, coming from the south, attempted to cross the run here and reach the Southside Railroad. He was supported on the east by Warren's (Fifth) Corps. The Confederates, crossing the run from the north side, intervened between the two Union forces and drove them back. *Dinwiddie Co.: Rte. 1, 6.4 miles s. of Petersburg.*

S-52   WHITE OAK ROAD

The extreme right of Lee's line rested on this road, which was entrenched. General Warren, advancing against Lee's works here, March 31, 1865, was driven back. Reinforced, Warren advanced again, forcing the Confederates to retire to the road. On it, six miles west, the battle of Five Forks was fought next day, April 1, 1865. *Dinwiddie Co.: Rte. 1, 6.8 miles s. of Petersburg.*

S-53*   ACTION OF MARCH 29, 1865

Just south of the junction here of the Boydton Plank Road and Quaker Road, General Warren, moving northward, came into conflict with Anderson's Corps of Lee's army. After a sharp action, Anderson fell back to the trenches on the White Oak Road, March 29, 1865. *Dinwiddie Co.: Rte. 1, 7.7 miles s. of Petersburg.*

S-54   DINWIDDIE COURTHOUSE

Sheridan advanced to this place on March 29, 1865, while Warren was attacking Anderson about three miles north. On March 31 Sheridan moved south but was checked by Pickett and driven back to the courthouse. That night Pickett withdrew to Five Forks. *Dinwiddie Co.: Rte. 1, at Dinwiddie.*

S-55   VAUGHAN ROAD

Hancock moved by it to his defeat at Burgess Mill, October 27, 1864, and in 1865, Grant moved his forces on it from the east to attack Lee's right wing. On March 29, 1865, Sheridan came to Dinwiddie Court House over it in the operations preceding the Battle of Five Forks. *Dinwiddie Co.: Rte. 1, at Dinwiddie.*

S-56   CHAMBERLAIN'S BED

That stream flows into Stony Creek a mile west. On March 31, 1865, Pickett and W. H. F. Lee, coming from Five Forks, forced a passage of Chamberlain's Bed in the face of Sheridan's troops, who were driven back to Dinwiddie Courthouse. *Dinwiddie Co.: Rte. 1, 1.1 miles s. of Dinwiddie.*

S-57 BIRCH'S BRIDGE

At Birch's Bridge (very near this bridge) the second William Byrd and his party crossed the river, in September, 1733, on their way to inspect Byrd's land holdings in North Carolina. Byrd wrote an account of this trip which he called "A Journey to the Land of Eden." On his return, he "laid the foundation" of Richmond and Petersburg. *Brunswick Co.: Rte. 1, 2.8 miles s. of McKenney.*

S-58 EBENEZER ACADEMY

A few hundred yards east is the site of Ebenezer Academy, founded in 1793 by Bishop Asbury, the first Methodist school established in Virginia. It passed out of the hands of the church but remained a noted school for many years. *Brunswick Co.: Rte. 1, 6.8 miles n. of Cochran.*

S-60 STURGEON CREEK

A branch of the Nottoway, named for the huge fish once caught in it. William Byrd, returning from the expedition to survey the Virginia–North Carolina boundary line, camped on this stream in November, 1729. *Brunswick Co.: Rte. 1, 5.7 miles n. of Cochran.*

S-62 CAMPAIGN OF 1781

The British cavalryman Tarleton, returning to Cornwallis from a raid to Bedford, passed near here, July, 1781. *Dinwiddie Co.: Rte. 1, 1.5 miles s. of Dinwiddie.*

S-63 BATTLE OF HATCHER'S RUN, 5–7 FEBRUARY 1865

Hoping to cut Lee's supply route into Petersburg, in February 1865 Grant ordered two army corps led by Major Generals Gouverneur K. Warren and Andrew A. Humphreys to seize the Boydton Plank Road. The Confederate corps commanded by Maj. Gen. John B. Gordon successfully blocked Warren's attacks at nearby Dabney's Mill on 6–7 February, and Warren's corps withdrew to its previous position. The brief Union campaign enabled Grant to extend his lines, and cost the Confederates the life of Brig. Gen. John Pegram on 6 February. *Dinwiddie Co.: Rte. 613, 2.2 miles e. of Rte. 1.*

S-65 OLD BRUNSWICK COURTHOUSE

Here the first courthouse of Brunswick County was built about 1732. In 1746, when the county was divided, the county seat was moved east near Thomasburg. In 1783, after Greensville County had been formed, the courthouse was moved to Lawrenceville. *Brunswick Co.: Rte. 1, at Cochran.*

S-66 FORT CHRISTANNA

Nine miles south is the site of Fort Christanna, built in 1714 by Governor Alexander Spotswood as a protection to settlers and tributary Indians. Under its shelter several tribes dwelt and an Indian school was established there. When settlements spread beyond it to the west, the fort was abandoned. *Brunswick Co.: Rte. 1, at Cochran.*

S-70 SALEM CHAPEL

A mile south is the site of Salem Chapel, one of the pioneer Methodist churches of the state. Of it Francis Asbury wrote, "the best house we have in the country part of Virginia." There he held four sessions of the Virginia Annual conference: November, 1795; April, 1798; March, 1802; April, 1804. The building was burned about 1870. *Mecklenburg Co.: Rte. 1, at South Hill.*

S-72* MEHERRIN HISTORY

Meherrin River was named for an Iroquoian tribe of Indians that long dwelt in this region. In 1669, there were about 200 of them. William Byrd, on his "Journey to the Land of Eden," crossed the river near here, September 13, 1733. *Brunswick Co.: Rte. 1, 7.3 miles s. of Cochran.*

S-76 EARLY EXPLORATION

Near here Edward Bland and Abraham Wood passed, August, 1650, going westward on an exploring expedition. They reached the site of Clarksville. *Mecklenburg Co.: Rte. 1, 1.6 miles n. of South Hill.*

S-79* CAMPAIGN OF 1865

Sheridan, raiding to South Boston, crossed this river at the old bridge, April 24, 1865. *Brunswick Co.: Rte. 1, 7.3 miles s. of Cochran.*

S-80 QUAKER ROAD ENGAGEMENT, 29 MARCH 1865

This was the first in a series of attempts by Grant's army to cut Lee's final supply line—the South Side Railroad—in spring 1865. Here at the Lewis farm, Union forces led by Brig. Gen. Joshua L. Chamberlain engaged Confederates under Maj. Gen. Bushrod R. Johnson. After sharp fighting, the Union troops entrenched nearby along the Boydton Plank Road and Johnson withdrew to his lines at White Oak Road. The Union army cut the rail line four days later, after capturing Five Forks on 1 April. *Dinwiddie Co.: Rte. 660, .78 mile e. of Rte. 1.*

S-81 WHITE OAK ROAD ENGAGEMENT, 31 MARCH 1865

Union forces belonging to the V Corps, under Maj. Gen. Gouverneur K. Warren, sought to seize the White Oak Road and sever the Confederate line of communication with Maj. Gen. George E. Pickett's detachment near Five Forks, four miles west. From here Gen. Robert E. Lee personally supervised the counterattack to Gravelly Run by Lt. Gen. Richard H. Anderson's corps. After a brief success, the Confederates were forced back into these entrenchments as Warren's men gained the important roadway. *Dinwiddie Co.: Rte. 613, 1.63 miles w. of Rte. 1.*

SA-5 ELK HILL

Two miles south is Elk Hill, once owned by Thomas Jefferson. Lord Cornwallis made his headquarters there, June 7–15, 1781; this was the western limit of his invasion. On June 15 he turned eastward, leaving the place pillaged and carrying off slaves. *Goochland Co.: Rte. 6, 1 mile w. of George's Tavern.*

SA-10 GOOCHLAND COURTHOUSE

Near here the ancient trail used by the Iroquois Indians in their raids crossed James River. This trail later became the main north-south road through Virginia. In 1781, Lord Cornwallis, in his invasion of Virginia, marched by this point and his cavalry, under Simcoe, passed here going to Point of Fork. A cavalry skirmish took place here, March 11, 1865. *Goochland Co.: Rte. 6, at Goochland.*

SA-11 DUNGENESS

Seven miles south once stood Dungeness, built about 1730 by Isham Randolph (1685–1742), who was the grandfather of Thomas Jefferson, President of the United States, and of James Pleasants, Governor of Virginia. Sea captain, merchant and planter, Randolph also served as Virginia's agent in London and Adjutant General of the Colony. *Goochland Co.: Rte. 6 at the courthouse.*

SA-14 DAHLGREN'S RAID

Here Colonel Ulric Dahlgren, Union cavalryman, coming from the north, turned east. Dahlgren, who acted in concert with Kilpatrick, left Stevensburg, Culpeper County, on February 28, 1864, and moved toward the James River, tearing up the Virginia Central Railroad near Frederick's Hall. He went on toward Richmond, burning mills and barns. *Goochland Co.: Rte. 6, 2.1 miles e. of Crozier.*

SA-18 SABOT HILL

This is Sabot Hill, home of James A. Seddon, member of Congress and Confederate Secretary of War, 1862–65, who built the house in 1855. On March 1, 1864, the Union cavalryman, Colonel Ulric Dahlgren, raiding to Richmond, burned the barn and plundered the place. *Goochland Co.: Rte. 6, 2.6 miles e. of Crozier.*

SA-20 THE HUGUENOT SETTLEMENT

In this vicinity, though mainly on the south side of James River, Huguenot refugees from France settled, 1699–1701 and later. These industrious settlers left an enduring mark on the community. Manakin is a corruption of the name of the Monocan Indian tribe, which once occupied this region. *Goochland Co.: Rte. 6, 5.9 miles e. of Crozier.*

SA-22 WILLIAM WEBBER

Three miles north are the home site and grave of William Webber, pastor of Dover Baptist Church, 1773–1808. As an early Baptist leader before the Revolution, he was imprisoned in the jails of Chesterfield and Middlesex. He aided in organizing the Baptist General Association of Virginia; he was moderator in 1778. He was moderator of the Dover Association, 1783–1806; of the Baptist General Committee and of the General Meeting of Correspondence until his death in 1808. *Goochland Co.: Rte. 6, 6 miles e. of Crozier at Manakin.*

SA-24 TUCKAHOE

Perhaps the oldest frame residence on James River west of Richmond, Tuckahoe was begun about 1715 by Thomas Randolph. The little schoolhouse still stands here where Thomas Jefferson began his childhood studies. Famous guests here have included William Byrd of Westover, Lord Cornwallis and George Washington. Virginia's Governor Thomas Mann Randolph was born here. *Goochland Co.: Rte. 650, w. of Henrico Co. line.*

SA-25 FIRST TROLLEY CAR SYSTEM IN RICHMOND

In 1888, the world's first successful electric railway, the Richmond Union Passenger Railway, branched at this point to link downtown and Jackson Ward with the suburbs. This system, designed by Frank Julian Sprague (1857–1934), contained 12 miles of track with 40 trolley cars running to Byrd Park in the West End and to 29th and Broad streets in the East End. This model system that revolutionized urban transportation ceased operation in November, 1949. *Richmond: 5th St. between Marshall St. and the Coliseum.*

SA-26 TRINITY METHODIST CHURCH

Erected in 1860, this building housed Trinity Methodist Church until 1945 when the congregation moved to Henrico County. It was designed by noted Richmond architect Albert West, who was also a leading Methodist. The roots of the Trinity congregation date from 1790 when a small group of converts first met at the foot of Church Hill, marking the founding of organized Methodism in Richmond. *Richmond: Broad St. at 20th St.*

SA-27 DAHLGREN'S RAID

Here Colonel Ulric Dahlgren, Union cavalryman, raiding to Richmond, hanged a Negro on a tree beside the road, March 1, 1864. Dahlgren planned to cross the James River in this vicinity and enter Richmond from the south. A Negro guided the raiders to a ford but the water was too high for crossing. Dahlgren thought the guide had deceived him. *Goochland Co.: Rte. 650, 9 miles w. of Richmond.*

SA-28 WINDSOR

Windsor was part of a 600 acre tract that was conveyed to Daniel S. Hylton by Charles Carter, trustee, in the William Byrd lottery of 1776. In the early years of the 19th century Windsor was owned and farmed by William Dandridge, nephew of Martha Washington, who was married to Susan Armistead. Charles F. Gillette, noted landscape architect, worked on the gardens for a period of fifty years beginning in 1919. The present house was built in 1945. *Richmond: 4601 Lilac Ln.*

SA-29 WILTON

A short distance south is Wilton, built by William Randolph and completed in 1753. The house, which originally stood on the north side of James River below Richmond, was removed to this place by the Virginia Society of Colonial Dames, 1934. *Richmond: Cary St. Rd. and Wilton Rd.*

SA-30 AMPTHILL

A short distance south is Ampthill House, built by Henry Cary about 1730 on the south side of James River. It was the home of Colonel Archibald Cary, Revolutionary leader, and was removed to its present site by a member of the Cary family. *Richmond: Cary St. Rd. and Ampthill Rd.*

SA-31* DAHLGREN'S RAID

In this vicinity Colonel Ulric Dahlgren, Union cavalryman, raiding to Richmond, fought an action with the force defending the city in the early evening of March 1, 1864. Dahlgren, unable to cross to the southside of the river as planned, attempted to break through the defenses on this road but was repulsed. He then turned off to the east and was killed. *Henrico Co.: Rte. 650, 1.25 miles w. of Richmond.*

SA-32 SITE OF J. E. B. STUART'S DEATH

Major General James Ewell Brown Stuart, C.S.A., Commander of the cavalry of the Army of Northern Virginia, died here on May 12, 1864, in the home of his brother-in-law, Dr. Charles Brewer. Cause of his death was a wound received the previous day in the defense of Richmond at the Battle of Yellow Tavern. Dr. Brewer's house was demolished in 1893. *Richmond: 206 W. Grace St.*

SA-33 VIRGINIA HISTORICAL SOCIETY

Founded in 1831, the Virginia Historical Society is the oldest such institution in the South. It was located in the Stewart-Lee house in downtown Richmond until 1958, when it moved to its present quarters in Battle Abbey. The Society's extensive collections of Virginiana—manuscripts, rare books, portraits, photographs, and museum objects—form the basis of a research library, museum exhibitions, publications, lectures, and other public educational programs. *Richmond: Boulevard at Kensington Ave.*

SA-34 CRAIG HOUSE

The Craig House, perhaps Richmond's second oldest structure, was built between 1784 and 1787 by Adam Craig (b. ca. 1760–d. 1808). He was clerk of the Richmond Hustings Court, the Henrico County Court, and the General Court. To save the house, a group of Richmond citizens in 1935 formed the William Byrd Branch of the Association for the Preservation of Virginia Antiquities. The house served Richmond's black community as the Craig House Art Center from 1938 to 1941. *Richmond: Grace St. near 19th St.*

SA-35 BOLLING HALL

Bolling Hall, to the south, was built in the late 18th century for William Bolling on land patented by his grandfather in 1714. Col. Bolling served as a county justice, militia officer, and legislator, and founded a pioneer school there for the education of deaf children. Remodeled extensively in the mid-19th and mid-20th centuries, Bolling Hall retains its elegant woodwork, its rural setting on the James River, and its historical function as a farm. *Goochland Co.: Rte. 6, 4 miles w. of Goochland Court House.*

SA-36 BOLLING ISLAND

Bolling Island mansion, overlooking an island of that name, stands at a bend of the James River to the south. John Bolling purchased the land in 1717. Begun about 1771, the house was completed in the late 1830s by Thomas Bolling, son of Col. William Bolling, of Bolling Hall. The principal features of the house are a two-story, Greek Revival–style portico on its south front, and several original outbuildings that stand behind it. Bolling Island remained in the Bolling family until 1870. *Goochland Co.: Rte. 6, 4 miles w. of Goochland Court House.*

SA-37 SAINT JOHN'S EPISCOPAL CHURCH

Here on 23 March 1775 Patrick Henry delivered his "Liberty or Death" speech, calling for American independence, during the second Virginia revolutionary convention that included as members George Washington, Thomas Jefferson, Peyton Randolph, and Richard Henry Lee. Saint John's Church was built in 1741 by Richard Randolph on land donated by Richmond's founder, William Byrd II. It continues to serve Henrico Parish (founded 1611). Buried in its churchyard are George Wythe and Elizabeth Arnold Poe, mother of Edgar Allan Poe. *Richmond: Broad St. near 24th St.*

SA-38   MONUMENTAL CHURCH

The church is a memorial to the 72 people, including Virginia Governor George W. Smith, who died when the Richmond Theatre burned here in 1811. Several survivors owed their lives to the bravery of Gilbert Hunt, a slave blacksmith. A committee chaired by Supreme Court Chief Justice John Marshall raised funds for the church's construction. Designed by Robert Mills and completed in 1814, the octagonal building served as an Episcopal church until 1965 and later as a chapel for the adjacent Medical College of Virginia. *Richmond: Broad St. near College St.*

SA-39   ORIGINS OF RICHMOND

There was "no place so strong, so pleasant, and delightful in Virginia, for which we called it None-such." So wrote Captain John Smith about the site he chose in 1609 when he established the first English settlement near the falls of the James River. It stood a few miles south until 1610. William Byrd I founded the second settlement when he patented land here in 1676. He soon built a fortified community, trading post, and warehouses just across the river near the mouth of Goode Creek. In 1737 his son, William Byrd II, laid out Richmond—which he named for Richmond upon Thames, now a borough of London—here in the Shockoe valley. *Richmond: Franklin St. between 17th and 18th sts.*

SM-2   UNION ACADEMY

Near here stood Union Academy, conducted by Hardy and Crenshaw from 1861 to about 1869. Dr. Walter Reed, who discovered the carrier of yellow fever, and Dr. Robert E. Blackwell, long President of Randolph-Macon College, attended school here. Nearby was an iron foundry, established in 1855 by Captain Richard Irby. *Nottoway Co.: Rte. 42, at s. entrance of Blackstone.*

SM-2   LOTTIE MOON

Lottie Moon, a native of Charlottesville, was appointed by the Southern Baptist Foreign Mission Board as a missionary to China in 1873 where she served for forty years. She died on her trip home in Kobe, Japan, on Christmas Eve, 1912, and her ashes were buried in her brother's plot in the Crewe Cemetery in 1913. The Lottie Moon Christmas offering is the largest mission offering taken during the year in all Southern Baptist churches. *Nottoway Co.: Rte. 49, .4 mile s. of Crewe.*

SN-45   CRAIG'S MILL

Two miles south of Kenbridge stood Craig's Mill on Flat Rock Creek. There flour was ground and supplies were stored for the Revolutionary army. Tarleton, the British cavalryman, burned the mill in July, 1781, when raiding through the Southside. Rev. James Craig, the owner, is said to have been forced to help kill hogs for the troopers. *Lunenburg Co.: Rte. 40, .3 mile n. of Kenbridge.*

SN-60   MASON'S CHAPEL

Near here stood Mason's Chapel, one of the earliest Methodist churches in southern Virginia. The first Virginia conference, May, 1785, was held here or nearby; Bishop Asbury presided. The conference of 1801 was held here. The present Olive Branch church is four miles west. *Brunswick Co.: Rte. 46, 8 miles s. of Brunswick.*

SN-61 SMOKY ORDINARY

The ordinary that stood on this site catered to travelers on the north-south stage road as early as 1750. During the American Revolution local warehouses were burned by British Colonel Tarleton, and legend says that it was from that occurrence that the ordinary derived its name. During the Civil War the post office (1832–1964) and inn were spared when a Union officer recognized the inn's owner, Dr. George M. Raney, as being a former classmate at the University of Pennsylvania. *Brunswick Co.: Rte. 712, 4.2 miles n. of Rte. 58.*

SN-62 HOME OF THE REVEREND JAMES CRAIG

To the south is the site of the late-18th-century home of the Reverend James Craig, minister of Cumberland Parish (1759–1795), physician, and Revolutionary patriot. During the Revolutionary War his nearby mill was burned by Colonel Banastre Tarleton, and Craig was taken prisoner and paroled. John Orgain, Jr. married Reverend Craig's granddaughter. A member of the House of Delegates (1838–1840; 1859–1863), and county judge (1850), he operated a school, the Flat Rock Female Seminary, on the property from 1834 until his death in 1871. *Lunenburg Co.: Rte. 40, 2.3 miles w. of Kenbridge.*

T-1 CARTER HALL

The house was completed about 1792 by Nathaniel Burwell. Edmund Randolph, Governor of Virginia and Secretary of State, died here. General Stonewall Jackson had his headquarters here, October, 1862. *Clarke Co.: Rte. 255, just n. of Millwood.*

T-2 OLD CHAPEL

This place was called "Old Chapel" in 1773. The present building was erected in 1796. Bishop Meade was minister here. Edmund Randolph, Governor of Virginia and Secretary of State, was buried here. *Clarke Co.: Rte. 255, 3.2 miles s. of Berryville.*

T-3 GREENWAY COURT

Three miles south is Greenway Court, residence of Thomas, sixth Lord Fairfax, proprietor of the vast Northern Neck grant, which he inherited. Born in Leeds Castle, England, in 1693, Fairfax settled in Virginia, in 1747, for the rest of his life. He made Greenway Court his home in 1751. George Washington, employed as a surveyor on this grant, was there frequently in his youth. Fairfax died there, December 9, 1781. *Clarke Co.: Rte. 340, 2 miles n.w. of Millwood.*

T-4 AUDLEY

The house to the north is the home of Nellie Parke Custis, George Washington's ward, who married his nephew, Major Lawrence Lewis. After her husband's death in 1839, Nellie Custis Lewis settled here, and here she died in 1852. *Clarke Co.: Rte. 7, .7 mile e. of Berryville.*

T-5 MOTHER OF THE WRIGHT BROTHERS

Six miles north, at Hillsboro, was born in 1831 Susan Koemer, mother of Wilbur and Orville Wright, inventors of the airplane. *Loudoun Co.: Rte. 7, at Purcellville.*

T-6 THE BURWELL-MORGAN MILL

This grist mill, built in 1782–85 by General Daniel Morgan of Saratoga and Colonel Nathaniel Burwell of Carter Hall, was in continuous operation until 1943. Now owned by the Clarke County Historical Association. *Clarke Co.: Rte. 255, at Millwood.*

T-7* WHITE POST

The original white post on this spot was erected by Lord Fairfax as a guide post to Greenway Court, about 1760. *Clarke Co.: Rte. 255, at White Post.*

T-8 COLONIAL HIGHWAY

This is one of the oldest roads leading from the east to the Shenandoah Valley; it crosses the Blue Ridge at Snicker's Gap. The ferry right over the Shenandoah River was granted, 1766. Washington used this road many times. Some distance to the east the first aerial telegraph signals were sent from the roadside, 1868. *Clarke Co.: Rte. 7, 3.7 miles e. of Berryville.*

T-9 CASTLEMAN'S FERRY FIGHT

Three miles north in July 1864, General Jubal Early's Army, returning from his raid on Washington, was attacked by Federal units which forced a passage of the river. On July 18, Colonel Joseph Thoburn led his troops against the Confederates but was driven back across the river. Rutherford B. Hayes, 19th President of the United States, commanded a Federal brigade in the action. *Clarke Co.: Rte. 7 at Rte. 603.*

T-9* CASTLEMAN'S FERRY FIGHT

Near here General Early, in July, 1864, returning from his Washington raid, was attacked by Crook, who forced a passage of the Shenandoah. Early, counterattacking, drove the Unionists back across the river. Rutherford B. Hayes, later President of the United States, commanded a brigade of Union troops. *Clarke Co.: Rte. 7, 4.5 miles e. of Berryville.*

T-10 CROOK AND EARLY

Early, while passing through this gap on his return from his Washington raid, was attacked by Crook's cavalry, July 16, 1864. Crook destroyed a few wagons. Early captured a cannon. *Clarke Co.: Rte. 7, 7.7 miles e. of Berryville.*

T-11 FORERUNNER OF WIRELESS TELEGRAPHY

From nearby Bear's Den Mountain to the Catoctin Ridge, a distance of fourteen miles, Dr. Mahlon Loomis, dentist, sent the first aerial wireless signals, 1866–73, using kites flown by copper wires. Loomis received a patent in 1872 and his company was chartered by Congress in 1873, but lack of capital frustrated his experiments. He died in 1886. *Clarke Co.: Rte. 7, 7.7 miles e. of Berryville.*

T-12 LONG BRANCH

This Classical Revival mansion built for Robert Carter Burwell is one of the few remaining residential works in which B. Henry Latrobe, father of the American architectural profession, played a role in design. Latrobe offered suggestions to Burwell for a staircase and piazza in 1811, a few months after workmen had laid the foundations. Hugh Mortimer Nelson added the porticoes and castellated east wing after 1842, as well as the Greek Revival–style interior trim based on designs published by the architect Minard Lafever. The late Harry Z. Isaacs renovated the mansion in 1989. *Clarke Co.: Rte. 626, .2 mile w. of Rte. 624.*

T-22 EARLY'S WASHINGTON CAMPAIGN

Jubal A. Early passed over this road on his return to the Shenandoah Valley, July 16, 1864. After leaving Lee before Richmond, June 13, Early traveled 450 miles, defeating Hunter at Lynchburg and Wallace on the Monocacy River, and threatening the city of Washington. On the approach of large Union forces he withdrew this way. *Loudoun Co.: Rte. 7, 2.1 miles w. of Leesburg.*

T-23 OLD STONE CHURCH SITE

One block north on Cornwall Street is the site of the first Methodist-owned property in America. Lot 50 was deeded to the Methodist Society in Leesburg on May 11, 1766. In 1778, the Sixth American Conference of Methodists met there, the first such gathering in Virginia. At least two church buildings occupied the site before 1902, when the "Old Stone Church" was demolished. The churchyard is maintained as a national historic shrine of the United Methodist Church. *Loudoun Co.: Bus. Rte. 7, one block w. of Bus. Rte. 15, in Leesburg.*

T-30 BELMONT

Belmont was patented early in the eighteenth century by Thomas Lee, of Stratford. About 1800, Ludwell Lee, an officer in the Revolutionary army, built the house and he lived here until his death in 1836. Here he entertained Lafayette in 1825. In 1931, Belmont became the home of Patrick J. Hurley, Secretary of War, 1929–1933. *Loudoun Co.: Rte. 7, 4.3 miles e. of Leesburg.*

T-36 ACTION AT DRANESVILLE

Near here two foraging expeditions came in conflict, December 20, 1861. The Union force was commanded by General Ord, the Confederate by J. E. B. Stuart. Stuart attacked in order to protect his foraging parties, but was forced to retire after a sharp fight. The next day he returned, reinforced, and carried off his wounded. *Fairfax Co.: Rte. 7, at Dranesville.*

T-37 SHARPSBURG (ANTIETAM) CAMPAIGN

Here Lee entered this road from Ox Hill, September 3, 1862, and turned west toward Leesburg. Crossing the Potomac at White's Ford, the army entered Maryland, September 5–6, 1862. *Fairfax Co.: Rte. 7, at Dranesville.*

T-38 GETTYSBURG CAMPAIGN

J. E. B. Stuart, operating on Lee's right, passed here on his way to the fords of the Potomac north of Dranesville, June 27, 1863. Crossing the river, he became separated from Lee's army and did not rejoin it until July 2, at Gettysburg. *Loudoun Co.: Rte. 7, 2.6 miles w. of Dranesville.*

T-39   J. E. B. STUART AT MUNSON'S HILL

Following the First Battle of Manassas on 21 July 1861, Col. James Ewell Brown Stuart, commander of the 1st Virginia Cavalry, moved his troopers to Fairfax Court House and then here to Munson's Hill, the Confederate position closest to the city of Washington. From his camp Stuart watched Union observers ascend in balloons to study him. Stuart built "Quaker cannons" of logs and marched his men before large campfires to confound the Federals. On 24 September, while still encamped here, he was promoted to the rank of brigadier general. *Fairfax Co.: Rte. 7, 3.03 miles w. of I-395.*

T-40   LINCOLN REVIEWS TROOPS AT
BAILEY'S CROSSROADS

After the Union defeat on 21 July 1861 at the First Battle of Manassas, Lincoln appointed Maj. Gen. George B. McClellan as commander of the demoralized army. A superb organizer, McClellan rebuilt the army and on 20 November 1861 staged a formal military review here, between Munson's Hill and Bailey's Crossroads. Lincoln and his entire cabinet attended. Occupying nearly 200 acres, some 50,000 troops, "including seven divisions—seven regiments of cavalry, ninety regiments of infantry, [and] twenty batteries of artillery," took part in the review, at that time the largest ever held in America. *Fairfax Co.: Rte. 7, 2.48 miles w. of I-395.*

T-41   LITTLE RIVER TURNPIKE

The earliest private turnpike charter in Virginia was granted by the General Assembly to the Company of the Fairfax and Loudoun Turnpike Road in 1796. By 1806 the 34-mile-long road connected Alexandria with Aldie on the Little River in Loudoun County. The company placed wooden tollhouses along the road at five-mile intervals, and one stood near here until 1954. The Little River Turnpike became a free road in 1896. In Fairfax County, only this portion of the road in Annandale retains its original name. *Fairfax Co.: Rte. 650, .01 mile n. of Rte. 236 (Little River Turnpike).*

T-42   RAVENSWORTH

Near here stood Ravensworth, a Fitzhugh and Lee family home. Built about 1796 by William Fitzhugh, the mansion stood on the largest single land grant in Fairfax County, the 21,966 acres acquired by Fitzhugh's great-grandfather in 1685. During the Civil War the house was not molested by either side. After the war Ravensworth came into the possession of Robert E. Lee's second son, Maj. Gen. W. H. F. ("Rooney") Lee. Ravensworth, a frame Palladian-style mansion, was one of the most imposing residences in Fairfax County until it burned in 1926. *Fairfax Co.: Rte. 3090, .11 mile s. of Rte. 620 (Braddock Rd.).*

T-44   VIRGINIA THEOLOGICAL
SEMINARY—FOUNDED 1823

Half mile to the southeast. The idea for such an institution was conceived by a group of Alexandria and Washington clergymen in 1818. Among those interested was Francis Scott Key, author of the Star Spangled Banner. Originally at corner of Washington and King Streets in Alexandria, moved to present location in 1827. Closed in 1861 when occupied as a hospital for Union troops. *Alexandria: Rte. 7, w. of Quaker Ln.*

T-45 EPISCOPAL HIGH SCHOOL—FOUNDED 1839

On the hill to the Southwest. One of the oldest preparatory schools for boys in the South. Taken over by Union Troops in 1861 for use as a Military Hospital. Reopened in 1866, the School was a pioneer in establishing the Honor Code in Education. *Alexandria: Rte. 7, w. of Quaker Ln.*

TA-1 FIRST GERMAN REFORMED CHURCH SITE AND CEMETERY

This is the church site and cemetery of the oldest continuous German Reformed congregation in Virginia. Founded before 1748 by Elder William Wenner, the congregation met in members' houses until the first log meetinghouse was constructed sometime before the American Revolution. About 1819 a brick church was built here; it was demolished in 1901 and its bricks were used to construct the congregation's new church, the St. James United Church of Christ, in Lovettsville. *Loudoun Co.: Rte. 672/673, .6 mile e. of Rte. 287.*

U-22 INDEPENDENCE

This place became the county seat of Grayson County in 1850; the first case was tried in the newly erected courthouse in 1851. The present court-house was built in 1908. Independence was incorporated in 1934. *Grayson Co.: Rte. 58, at Independence.*

U-23 PEYTON GUYN HALE

Born in Elk Creek, Virginia, June 29, 1821, Member of the House of Delegates, 1874–1877. Member State Senate, 1879–1882. One of the "Big Four," a group which resisted many of the proposals of the Readjusters. Died in Elk Creek, December 25, 1885. *Grayson Co.: Rte. 21, at Elks Creek.*

U-25 FIRST COUNTY SEAT

Here at Old Tavern, in 1794, was built the first courthouse of Grayson County. The land was donated by Flower Swift. A second courthouse was built in 1838. The county seat was removed to Independence about 1850. *Grayson Co.: Rte. 640, 3 miles w. of Galax.*

U-26 GALAX

The town is on the dividing line between Grayson and Carroll counties. Its original name was Bonaparte, which was changed to Galax, the name of a mountain shrub abundant in the vicinity. In 1904 a spur of the Norfolk and Western Railroad came here, bringing the town into existence. It was incorporated in 1906. *Grayson Co.: Rte. 89 (Main St.), in Galax.*

U-28 BLUE RIDGE MISSION SCHOOL

The Blue Ridge Mission School was established by the Virginia Baptist General Convention in 1916 at a site just to the southeast. It provided general education and religious training, on both the elementary and secondary level, to day and boarding students. Its program was increasingly coordinated with, and in 1941 superseded by, that of the newly-developed public school system. *Patrick Co.: Rte. 8, at Rte. 613.*

U-30 STUART

This place, first known as Taylorsville for George Taylor, early settler, was established in 1792 after the formation of Patrick County. In 1849 it contained about fifty dwellings. The name was changed to Stuart for General J. E. B. Stuart, C.S.A., who was born in the county. The courthouse was built in 1852 and remodeled in 1928. *Patrick Co.: Rte. 58, at Stuart.*

U-32 FRONTIER FORT

About three miles north stood Fort Mayo, commanded by Captain Samuel Harris in 1756 and visited in that year by Washington. This fort was the southernmost of the line of stockade forts built from the Potomac River to North Carolina as a frontier defense in the French and Indian War. *Patrick Co.: Rte. 58, 14 miles e. of Stuart.*

U-34 REYNOLDS HOMESTEAD

Four miles to the north is Rock Spring Plantation, the boyhood home of Industrialist R. J. Reynolds. The land was settled in 1814 by Abram Reynolds and his wife Mary Harbour. About 1843 their son Hardin William Reynolds built the present brick house for his bride Nancy Jane Cox. The couple had 16 children, including Richard Joshua Reynolds, who founded R. J. Reynolds Tobacco Company. In 1970 the house was restored by Hardin's granddaughter, Nancy Susan Reynolds. *Patrick Co.: Rte. 58, at Critz.*

U-36 WILLIAM BYRD'S SURVEY OF 1728

This was the westernmost point of the survey of the Virginia–North Carolina border run in 1728 by a Joint Commission from both colonies led by Col. William Byrd II of Westover. The exact end of the line was marked on October 16, 1728, by a blazed red oak tree on the east bank of Peter's Creek. *Patrick Co.: Rte. 660, 4 miles s. of Rte. 8, at North Carolina line.*

U-40 BERRY HILL

Berry Hill is situated 7 miles to the south on the Dan River. The original portion of the main house was built in 1745 and there have been several additions. The property was used as a hospital for General Nathaniel Greene's army during the spring of 1781, following the Revolutionary War battle of Guilford Court House. *Pittsylvania Co.: Rte. 58 and Rte. 863.*

U-40 PATRICK HENRY'S LEATHERWOOD HOME

Leatherwood, 1/4 mile to the south, was the home plantation of Patrick Henry from June 1779 until December 1784, when he left to serve his fourth term as governor of Virginia. Henry was one of the largest landowners of the area and served five terms as a member of the House of Delegates from Henry County. *Henry Co.: Rte. 57, .1 mile e. of Rte. 628.*

U-47 CARTERS TAVERN

Samuel and Elizabeth Carter operated an ordinary here from about 1808 until the 1840s. It is one of many historic buildings remaining along River Road, which, as the then principal roadway between Halifax Court House and Danville, formed a link in the main stage road between New York and New Orleans. The smaller and earliest section of Carter's Tavern was built by Joseph Dodson, who died in 1773. *Halifax Co.: Rte. 659, 3.3 miles e. of Pittsylvania Co. line.*

U-48 STAUNTON RIVER STATE PARK

This park was developed by the National Park Service, Interior Department, through the Civilian Conservation Commission in conjunction with the Virginia Conservation Commission. It covers 1200 acres and was opened, June 15, 1936. Nearby is Occaneechee Island where Nathaniel Bacon defeated the Indians in 1676. *Halifax Co.: Rte. 360, 7.1 miles e. of Halifax.*

U-50 NATHANIEL TERRY'S GRAVE

A short distance south is the grave of Nathaniel Terry, colonial soldier and statesman. Terry served as sheriff of Halifax County, 1752, and captain of Rangers, 1755. He was a member of the House of Burgesses, 1755–1765, 1771–1775, and also sat in the convention of 1776 that framed the Constitution of Virginia. Terry died in 1780. *Halifax Co.: Rte. 304, 6 miles n.e. of South Boston.*

U-51 WILLIAM MUNFORD TUCK
(1896–1983)

William M. Tuck was born near High Hill, Halifax County, Virginia. After service in the U.S. Marine Corps in World War I, he attended the College of William and Mary and earned a law degree from Washington and Lee University. Governor Tuck served three terms in the Virginia House of Delegates, followed by service in the Virginia Senate (1932–1942) and as Lieutenant Governor (1942–1946). As Governor of Virginia (1946–1950), Governor Tuck worked for passage of Virginia's Right-to-Work Act. Tuck served in the United States House of Representatives from 1953–1969. He died in South Boston, June 9, 1983. *Halifax Co.: Rte. 58 at Rte. 601.*

U-60* OCCANEECHEE INDIANS

Nearby, on an island now inundated by the lake, the Occaneechee Indians lived and traded furs. About 1672 the Saponi and Tutelo moved to neighboring islands. Nathaniel Bacon, the rebel, killed many of them in 1676 and broke their power. *Mecklenburg Co.: Rte. 58, 1.5 miles e. of Clarksville.*

U-80 A REVOLUTIONARY SOLDIER

Richard Kennon of Mecklenburg served as an officer in the 5th Virginia Regiment, 1776–1778 and later in the State Militia. He served in both houses of the General Assembly and was Presiding Officer of the Senate, 1800–1802. He died in 1805. *Mecklenburg Co.: Rte. 58, at Boydton.*

U-90th FORT CHRISTANNA

Three miles south is the site of Fort Christanna, which was built in 1714 by Governor Alexander Spotswood for the protection of friendly Indians from hostile tribes. A school for Indian children was also established there. *Brunswick Co.: Rte. 58, w. of Lawrenceville.*

U-102 TARLETON'S MOVEMENTS

Near this point Tarleton, the British cavalryman, entered the road from the south and moved westward to clear the fords for Cornwallis's army, May 14, 1781. Cornwallis was moving north on Petersburg. *Southampton Co.: Rte. 58, 8.2 miles e. of Emporia.*

U-105 JOHN Y. MASON'S HOME

Four miles west stood the home of John Y. Mason, statesman. Mason was a member of the House of Representatives; United States district judge; twice Secretary of the Navy; United States Attorney General, and Minister to France. He took part in the famous "Ostend Manifesto," 1854. Mason died in Paris, October 3, 1859. *Southampton Co.: Rte. 58, 8.2 miles e. of Emporia.*

U-115 BUCKHORN QUARTERS

One mile north was the estate of Major Thomas Ridley. In the servile [*sic*] insurrection of August, 1831, the houses were fortified by faithful slaves and made a place of refuge for fugitive whites. In this vicinity Nat Turner, the leader of the insurrection, spent the night after his defeat near Courtland, August 28, 1831. *Southampton Co.: Rte. 58, 4.5 miles w. of Courtland.*

U-120 GENERAL THOMAS'S BIRTHPLACE

General George H. Thomas, "The Rock of Chickamauga," was born on July 31, 1816, about five miles to the south. A graduate of West Point, Thomas sided with the Union during the Civil War and won distinction in the campaigns in Tennessee. *Southampton Co.: Rte. 58, 1.7 miles s.e. of Courtland.*

U-120* GENERAL THOMAS'S BIRTHPLACE

Five miles southwest George H. Thomas was born, July 31, 1816. A graduate of West Point, Thomas served in the Mexican War and remained in the United States service in 1861. In saving Rosecrans' army from destruction, September 20, 1863, he won the name of "The Rock of Chickamauga." Commanding in Tennessee, he defeated Hood at Nashville, December 16, 1864. *Southampton Co.: Rte. 58, 1.7 miles s.e. of Courtland.*

U-122* SOUTHAMPTON INSURRECTION

Seven miles southwest Nat Turner, a Negro, inaugurated, August 21, 1831, a slave insurrection that lasted two days and cost the lives of about sixty whites. The slaves began the massacre near Cross Keys and moved eastward toward Courtland (Jerusalem). In meeting resistance, the insurrection speedily collapsed. *Southampton Co.: Rte. 58, 2 miles w. of Courtland.*

U-122 NAT TURNER'S INSURRECTION

On the night of 21–22 August 1831, Nat Turner, a slave preacher, began an insurrection some seven miles west with a band that grew to about 70. They moved northeast toward the Southampton County seat, Jerusalem (now Courtland), killing about 60 whites. After two days militiamen and armed civilians quelled the revolt. Turner was captured on 30 October, tried and convicted, and hanged on 11 November; some 30 blacks were hanged or expelled from Virginia. In response to the revolt, the General Assembly passed harsher slave laws and censored abolitionists. *Southampton Co.: Rte. 35 near Rte. 665.*

U-123 MAJOR JOSEPH E. GILLETTE

The "Southampton Cavalry" was formed just north of this site in May, 1861 at what was the Gillette Farm, Cedar Lawn. Joseph E. Gillette was elected captain. The Company eventually became Company A of the 13th Virginia Cavalry. Gillette was promoted to major in the regiment. He died here November 1, 1863, after being wounded at Brandy Station. The company served gallantly until the end of the Civil War as part of General J. E. B. Stuart's cavalry in General Robert E. Lee's Army of Northern Virginia. *Southampton Co.: Rte. 58, .9 mile w. of Franklin.*

U-124 OLD INDIAN RESERVATION

Just to the north was the Nottoway Indian Reservation. William Byrd, while running the boundary line between Virginia and North Carolina, visited these Indians, April 7, 1729. Indians were living here as late as 1825. *Southampton Co.: Rte. 58, .8 mile w. of Courtland.*

U-125 CAMP MANUFACTURING COMPANY

This industrial complex evolved from a sawmill that operated here prior to the Civil War. In 1887, three brothers, Paul D. Camp, James L. Camp, and Robert J. Camp, founded Camp Manufacturing Company, later Union Camp Corporation. The lumbering enterprise pioneered a program to purchase land as well as timber rights, allowing extensive reforestation efforts. The facility is a major producer of paper, paperboard, lumber, and particleboard. The Blackwater River and the railroads have traditionally provided transportation for raw materials and manufactured products for the western Virginia Tidewater area. *Isle of Wight Co.: Bus. Rte. 58 near Blackwater River.*

U-126 FRANKLIN

Incorporated as a town in 1876, Franklin began as a Southampton County village in the 1830s. In October, 1862, during the Civil War, Union gunboats on the Blackwater River shelled the town and the railroad station. Several skirmishes occurred nearby in 1862 and 1863. A major fire destroyed 43 buildings in the town on February 26, 1881. The Camp Brothers' lumber mill and later their paper mill, as well as the peanut industry, helped Franklin prosper in this century. Franklin became an incorporated city in 1960. *Franklin: Main St. at South St.*

U-127 FIRST RURITAN CLUB

The first Ruritan Club was founded here in Holland, Va. on May 21, 1928. Ruritan is an organization of rural leaders striving through community service, fellowship and good will to make the rural community a better place in which to live. *Suffolk ("old" Nansemond Co.): Rte. 58, at Holland.*

U-130 DISMAL SWAMP

This swamp was visited by William Byrd in 1728. In 1763, George Washington made explorations in it and organized a company to drain it for farm land. Lake Drummond is in its midst. *Suffolk ("old" Nansemond Co.): Rte. 58, 4.7 miles e. of Suffolk.*

UC-5 STATE FISH HATCHERY

This fish cultural [*sic*] station was established in 1930 for hatching and rearing trout for the trout waters of Virginia. *Smyth Co.: Rte. 16, 5 miles s.e. of Marion.*

UE-2* FRIES

Center of early recorded country music. On March 1, 1923, in New York City Henry Whitter of Fries, Virginia recorded two songs "The Wreck of the Old 97" and "Lonesome Road Blues." These were among the first successful country recordings by a country artist. His recordings inspired many other local artists to record, including E. V. "Pop" Stoneman and Kelly Harrell. All three men were employees of the Fries Textile Plant. *Grayson Co.: Rte. 94, at Carroll Co. line.*

UE-5 FIRST COURT OF GRAYSON COUNTY

Near here, in the barn of William Bourne, was held the first court of this county, May 21, 1793. *Grayson Co.: Rte. 805, 5 miles s.w. of Fries.*

UE-6 FRIES—CENTER OF EARLY RECORDED COUNTRY MUSIC

On March 1, 1928, in New York City Henry Whitter of Fries, Virginia recorded two songs "The Wreck of the Old Southern 97" and "Lonesome Road Blues." These were among the first successful country recordings by a country artist. His records inspired many other local artists to record, including E. V. "Pop" Stoneman and Kelly Harrell. All three men were employees of the Fries Textile Plant. *Grayson Co.: Rte. 94, at Fries.*

UE-7 "NEW RIVER TRAIN" SONG

The original "New River Train" song was claimed by the Ward family of Galax as part of their repertoire as early as 1895. The song was believed to refer to the train that ran on the New River Line in 1883 as part of the Norfolk and Western system serving the town of Fries until 1985. It was first recorded in December 1923 by Henry Whitter. It has since been recorded by a number of artists, including local residents Kelly Harrell in 1925 and E. V. "Pop" Stoneman in 1928. *Grayson Co.: Rte. 94 at Rte. 1001 in Fries.*

UK-4 OLD NOTTOWAY MEETING HOUSE

This is the site of the Old Nottoway Meeting House, built in 1769, the second Baptist church established south of James River. Jeremiah Walker was the first minister. *Nottoway Co.: Rte. 723, 2 miles s. of Burkeville.*

UL-2 CAMPAIGN OF 1781

Boyd's and Irwin's ferries to the north were used by Nathanael Greene in his passage of Dan River, in mid-February, 1781, while Cornwallis was in close pursuit. Edward Carrington collected the boats for the crossing. *Halifax Co.: Rte. 501, .4 mile s. of South Boston.*

UL-4* OLD RANDOLPH-MACON COLLEGE

The large building to the north is old Randolph-Macon College, one of the first Methodist colleges in America. It was named for John Randolph of Roanoke and Nathaniel Macon, and was opened for instruction on October 9, 1832. The college was moved to Ashland in 1868. *Mecklenburg Co.: Rte. 58, .3 mile w. of Boydton.*

UL-5 TAYLOR'S FERRY

Seven miles south. There a detachment of Virginia militia crossed the Roanoke River in February, 1781, on the way to join Greene in North Carolina. There Baron Steuben, commanding the forces in Virginia, had a depot of supplies. *Mecklenburg Co.: Rte. 58, .3 mile w. of Boydton.*

UM-12* JARRATT'S STATION

Half a mile south is Jarratt's Station, a depot on the old Weldon Railroad. The Union cavalryman, Kautz, acting with Butler's Army of the James, burned the place, May 8, 1864. The Union General Wilson, retreating from Reams Station, camped here, June 29, 1864. Warren on his raid to destroy the Weldon Railroad camped here in December, 1864. *Sussex Co.: Rte. 301, at Jarratt.*

UM-12 JARRATT'S STATION

On 8 May 1864 Jarratt's Station, a nearby depot on the Petersburg Railroad, was the subject of a Union cavalry raid. Brig. Gen. August V. Kautz led his division on a series of raids in early May to cut the railroad from Petersburg to Weldon, North Carolina. Kautz's cavalry tore up the road in several locations, destroyed bridges, and burned the depot at Jarratt's Station on 8 May. The raids slowed the flow of supplies to Lee's army in Richmond and Petersburg. *Sussex Co.: Rte. 139 in Jarratt.*

UM-14 OLD HALIFAX ROAD

Here the highway merges with the Halifax Road, the ancient road from Petersburg to Halifax, North Carolina. Over this road Cornwallis marched in May, 1781, from Halifax to Petersburg in his invasion of Virginia. Over this road the Confederates hauled supplies during the siege of Petersburg, 1864–65, and over it parts of the Union and Confederate armies constantly passed. *Sussex Co.: Rte. 301, at Jarratt.*

UM-16* NOTTOWAY RIVER

Near here the British cavalryman, Simcoe, crossed the river going south to join Cornwallis, May 11, 1781. Here Cornwallis, moving northward, was met by Benedict Arnold, coming from Petersburg, May 19, 1781. Here the Union General Wilson crossed the river, June 28, 1864, and recrossed, June 29, 1864. *Sussex Co.: Rte. 301, 3.4 miles s. of Stony Creek.*

UM-18 HISTORY AT STONY CREEK

In 1864, supplies for Lee's army were carted from the Weldon railroad here to Petersburg. Here the Union cavalryman, Wilson, returning from his raid to Burkeville, fought an action with Lee's cavalry, June 28–29, 1864. The place was raided by the Union cavalryman, Gregg, on December 1, 1864. *Sussex Co.: Rte. 301, at Stony Creek.*

UM-20 REAMS STATION

Three miles north. There, the Union cavalryman, Kautz, in Wilson's raid, destroyed the station, June 22, 1864. Returning from Burkeville, Kautz reached there again June 29, and was joined by Wilson. Attacked by Hampton, Wilson and Kautz hastily retreated to Grant's army. Hancock, while destroying the Weldon railroad, was attacked at Reams Station by A. P. Hill and Hampton, August 25, 1864, and driven back to Grant's army. *Prince George Co.: Rte. 301, 12.6 miles s. of Petersburg.*

UM-38 GRAVE OF GEN. JOHN R. CHAMBLISS, JR.

Brig. Gen. John Randolph Chambliss, Jr., C.S.A., is buried just west of here. Born in Hicksford (present-day Emporia) on 23 January 1833, Chambliss graduated from the U.S. Military Academy at West Point in 1853. During the Civil War, he commanded the 41st Virginia Infantry Regiment in the Seven Days' campaign. He next led the 13th Virginia Cavalry and served under J. E. B. Stuart. Chambliss was killed in an engagement on the Charles City Road east of Richmond on 16 August 1864. His former West Point schoolmate, Union Brig. Gen. David M. Gregg, took charge of the body and sent it home. *Emporia: Rte. 301 (S. Main St.), 350 ft. s. of Brunswick Ave.*

UM-39 BENJAMIN D. TILLAR, JR.

Benjamin Donaldson Tillar, Jr. (1853–1887), a Greensville County native, president of the Atlantic and Danville Railroad, and member of the House of Delegates, is known as "the man who named Emporia." Two villages, Hicksford and Belfield, merged in 1887 to form the town. Tillar named the town after Emporia, Kansas, the hometown of his friend, United States Senator Preston B. Plumb. Emporia comes from the Latin word meaning a place of plenty where business is transacted. The town became a city in 1967. *Emporia: Rte. 301, at Main and Battery sts.*

UM-40 TARLETON'S MOVEMENTS

At this point Tarleton, the British cavalryman, crossed the Meherrin River, May 14, 1781. Sent ahead of Cornwallis's army, he had raided through Southampton and Greensville counties. *Greensville Co.: Rte. 301, at Emporia.*

UM-41 SITE OF "HOMESTEAD"

Near this site stood "Homestead," home of James Mason (1744–1784), officer in the continental army. Here was located the first clerk's office of Greensville County. This was the home of Edmunds Mason, county clerk 1807–1834, and birthplace of his sons John Y. Mason, statesman, and Dr. George Mason whose school, Homestead Seminary, occupied the house. *Greensville Co.: Rte. 58 and Chapman's Ford Rd.*

UO-5 THE CATTLE (BEEFSTEAK) RAID

One mile southwest, on September 16, 1864, General Wade Hampton's Confederate Cavalry herded about 2,500 head of captured cattle across the Nottoway River, while two miles northwest, at Belsches' Mill, Federal troops sent to recapture the cattle were intercepted and repulsed. *Sussex Co.: Rtes. 35 and 626.*

US-3 WILLIAM MAHONE'S BIRTHPLACE

Three and a half miles southwest, at Monroe, Major-General William Mahone was born, December 1, 1826. He served brilliantly in the Confederate army throughout the war, and won the title, "Hero of the Crater," at Petersburg, July 30, 1864. He was United States Senator, 1881–1887. Mahone died in Washington, October 8, 1895. *Southampton Co.: Rte. 258, 2.2 miles s. of Franklin.*

US-6* SOUTH QUAY

Two miles southeast is South Quay on the Blackwater, a port into which supplies and military stores were brought from Europe in the Revolution. A British force from Portsmouth burned stores there, July 16, 1781. At the ferry there, Confederates fought a skirmish with Union raiders, March 10, 1865. *Southampton Co.: Rte. 258, 4.8 miles s. of Franklin.*

UT-20 SUFFOLK CAMPAIGN

Longstreet crossed the river here and advanced on Suffolk, held by a Union garrison, April 10, 1863. The siege of Suffolk followed. *Isle of Wight Co.: Rte. 460, 6.3 miles n.w. of Windsor.*

UT-28* CAVALRY SKIRMISH

Near here, December 28, 1862, Confederate cavalry attacked Union vedettes and drove them in. The Unionists, reinforced, repulsed the attack. *Suffolk ("old" Nansemond Co.): Rte. 460, 4.6 miles n.w. of Suffolk.*

V-1 WILTON

Five miles southwest. The house was built by William Randolph, son of William Randolph of Turkey Island, early in the eighteenth century. It was Lafayette's headquarters, May 15–20, 1781, just before Cornwallis crossed the James in pursuit of him. *Henrico Co.: Rte. 5, 2 miles s.e. of Richmond.*

V-2 VARINA AND FORT HARRISON

At Varina, a short distance south, John Rolfe and Pocahontas lived after their marriage in 1614. The place became the first county seat of Henrico County, and here also was the glebe house of Rev. James Blair, founder of William and Mary College. Under the name of Aiken's Landing, Varina was a point of exchange for prisoners in 1862. Fort Harrison near by was one of the principal works in the Richmond defenses, 1862–64. It was captured on September 29, 1864. *Henrico Co.: Rte. 5, 4.5 miles s.e. of Richmond.*

V-3* CURLES NECK AND BREMO

Named for the curves made here by James River, Curles Neck was patented in 1617. It was the home of Nathaniel Bacon, the Rebel, in 1676. In 1698, William Randolph of Turkey Island obtained the estate, which he left to his son, Richard Randolph, grandfather of John Randolph of Roanoke. Just beyond is Bremo, patented by Richard Cocke in 1639. *Henrico Co.: Rte. 5, 9.3 miles s.e. of Richmond.*

V-4* MALVERN HILL

A colonial dwelling of the Cocke family was here. Lafayette camped here in July–August, 1781, watching Cornwallis. Here McClellan's army retiring from Richmond was attacked by Lee on July 1, 1862. Lee did not storm the hill, but that night McClellan fell back to James River at Harrison's Landing. *Henrico Co.: Rte. 5, 13.3 miles s.e. of Richmond.*

V-5* TURKEY ISLAND

So named in 1607 by Captain Christopher Newport on his voyage of discovery up James River. In 1684 it became the property of William Randolph, founder of the Randolph family in Virginia and ancestor of Jefferson, Marshall and Lee. The colonial house was destroyed by Union gunboats in 1862. An action took place near the creek between Union and Confederate forces, June 30, 1862. *Henrico Co.: Rte. 5, 12.3 miles s.e. of Richmond.*

V-6 SHIRLEY

The house is a short distance south. Shirley was first occupied in 1613 and was known as West-and-Shirley Hundred. In 1664, Edward Hill patented the place, which was left by the third Edward Hill to his sister, Elizabeth Carter, in 1720. Here was born Anne Hill Carter, mother of Robert E. Lee, who often visited Shirley. The present house was built about 1740. *Charles City Co.: Rte. 5, 17.1 miles s.e. of Richmond.*

A short distance south. The place was first settled in 1619 but was abandoned. It was repatented in 1636. Benjamin Harrison, signer of the Declaration of Independence, lived here; his son, William Henry Harrison, President of the United States, was born here, 1773. In July–August, 1862, General McClellan had his headquarters at Berkeley while the Army of the Potomac was here. *Charles City Co.: Rte. 5, 7.2 miles w. of Charles City.*

V-8*   WESTOVER

Two miles southeast. In 1619 the first settlement was made there; settlers were killed there in the Indian massacre of 1622. In 1666, Theodoric Bland bought Westover; in 1688 it passed to William Byrd. His son, Colonel William Byrd, built the present house about 1730. In January, 1781, Cornwallis crossed the river there in pursuit of Lafayette. *Charles City Co.: Rte. 5, 7.2 miles w. of Charles City.*

V-8   WESTOVER

In 1619 the first settlement was made at Westover, about two miles southeast. Two settlers died in the Powhatan uprising of 1622. Theodorick Bland bought Westover in 1666; William Byrd I acquired it in 1688. About 1730 his son, Colonel William Byrd II, built the present house, which exemplifies the high level of architectural quality attained during the colonial era. In January 1781 the British army under General Charles Cornwallis crossed the James River at Westover in pursuit of the Marquis de Lafayette. *Charles City Co.: Rte. 5, 6.71 miles w. of Charles City.*

V-9*   GRANT'S CROSSING

A mile south, at Wilcox's Wharf, a part of Grant's army going to Petersburg was ferried over James River to Windmill Point, June 14–16, 1864. The rest of the army crossed a little lower on a pontoon bridge. *Charles City Co.: Rte. 5, 2.4 miles w. of Charles City.*

V-10   GREENWAY

This was the home of John Tyler, Governor of Virginia, 1808–1811. His son, John Tyler, President of the United States, was born here, March 29, 1790. *Charles City Co.: Rte. 5, .7 mile w. of Charles City.*

V-11   CHARLES CITY COURTHOUSE

In 1702 Charles City County, which then included both sides of James River, was divided; the courthouse here was built about 1730. Here Simcoe's British cavalry surprised a party of militia, January 8, 1781. Here Grant's army passed on its way to the river, June, 1864. *Charles City Co.: Rte. 5, at Charles City.*

V-12   UPPER WEYANOKE

Five miles due south. In 1617, the Indian chief, Opechancanough, gave Governor Yeardley land there. In 1665, the place passed to Joseph Harwood, whose descendants, the Douthats, still own it. In June, 1864, most of Grant's army crossed the James River at Weyanoke on a pontoon bridge nearly half a mile long. *Charles City Co.: Rte. 5, at Charles City.*

V-13 SALEM CHURCH

This church, four miles north, was used as a field hospital, June, 1864, following the action at Nance's Shop, where the Union cavalryman Gregg, guarding a wagon train, was attacked by Wade Hampton. Gregg was driven from the field but saved the wagons. Wounded soldiers were brought to the church and some of the dead were buried there. *Charles City Co.: Rte. 5, 5.9 miles w. of Charles City.*

V-14 WESTOVER CHURCH

A short distance south is Westover Church. It was first built on the James River near Westover House early in the eighteenth century. About 1730 the site was changed and the present building erected. Defaced in the Campaign of 1862, the church was reopened for worship in 1867. *Charles City Co.: Rte. 5, 6.5 miles w. of Charles City.*

V-15 SCENE OF JEFFERSON'S WEDDING

Two miles east is the site of "The Forest," home of Martha Wayles Skelton, widow of Bathurst Skelton. There she was married to Thomas Jefferson, January 1, 1772. The bridal couple drove in the snow to Jefferson's home, "Monticello." *Charles City Co.: Rte. 5, 15.1 miles s.e. of Richmond.*

V-16 CAMPAIGN OF 1781

Tarleton, British cavalryman, moving eastward to join Cornwallis at Richmond, passed near here, June 15, 1781. *Henrico Co.: Rte. 250, 8.5 miles w. of Richmond.*

V-17* OUTER DEFENSES

The outer line of Richmond defenses, 1862–65, here crossed the road. To the east were the intermediate defenses; the inner line lay well within the limits of the present city. *Henrico Co.: Rte. 250, 1.9 miles w. of Richmond.*

V-18 REUBEN FORD

A mile north are the home and grave of Reuben Ford, pastor of Goochland Baptist Church, 1771–1823. He was an advocate of equal religious rights for all, a leader in securing separation of church and state in Virginia. *Goochland Co.: Rte. 250, 1.9 miles e. of Oilville.*

V-19 PROVIDENCE CHURCH

Half a mile northeast stands Providence Presbyterian church, built probably in 1749 and little altered since. John Todd, Senior, a founder of Hampden-Sydney College, was pastor for forty years (1753–1793). Hanover Presbytery met there in October, 1762. *Louisa Co.: Rte. 250, .4 mile n.w. of Gum Spring.*

V-20 CAMPAIGN OF 1781

Here Lafayette, moving west to protect a supply depot in Albemarle from Cornwallis, entered this road, June 13, 1781. *Louisa Co.: Rte. 250, at Ferncliff.*

V-21 PRESIDENT TYLER'S HOME

Just to the south is Sherwood Forest, where President John Tyler lived after his retirement from the presidency until his death in 1862. He bought the place in 1842 and came to it as his home in March, 1845. Here Tyler, with his young second wife, entertained much and raised another large family. The house, well-furnished, was damaged in the war period, 1862–65. *Charles City Co.: Rte. 5, 3.5 miles e. of Charles City.*

V-22 EVELYNTON

Originally part of William Byrd's Westover, Evelynton has been occupied by the Ruffin family since 1847, when it was purchased by Edmund Ruffin, Jr. Fierce skirmishes took place on the property during the 1862 Peninsula Campaign. Confederate troops were led by generals J. E. B. Stuart and James Longstreet. The breastworks are still visible near the house. The dwelling and dependencies of the plantation were much damaged during the fighting. The Georgian-Revival house, built on the foundation of an earlier structure, was designed by noted architect, Duncan Lee, in 1935. *Charles City Co.: Rte. 5, 4.73 miles w. of Charles City.*

V-23 PINEY GROVE AND E. A. SAUNDERS

Eight miles west on "The Old Main Road" is Piney Grove. The original portion, built ca. 1800 on Southall's Plantation, is a rare survival of Tidewater log architecture. Edmund Archer Saunders, a successful Richmond businessman, operated a store at Piney Grove between 1857 and 1874 when he sold it to Thomas Harwood. Saunders later returned to Charles City County and purchased Upper Shirley and Weyanoke plantations. Harwood enlarged the building for his home in 1910. *Charles City Co.: Rte. 5, 9.05 miles e. of Charles City.*

V-24 NORTH BEND

Three miles south is North Bend, a Greek Revival residence built in 1819. Sarah Minge, sister of President William Henry Harrison, and her husband, John, built the original portion of the house located on Kittiewan Creek. Thomas H. Wilcox greatly enlarged the dwelling in 1853. General Sheridan established his Union headquarters here while his 30,000 men crossed the James River on a pontoon bridge at Weyanoke. *Charles City Co.: Rte. 5, 1.27 miles e. of Charles City.*

V-25 FIRST SUCCESSFUL COLONIAL TOBACCO CROP

In 1611 John Rolfe became the first Englishman to cultivate tobacco nearby at Varina Farm, on the James River. Rolfe planted seeds bred in Varinas, Spain, and experimented with curing methods to produce a tobacco milder than the native variety. The success of tobacco as a cash crop encouraged the Virginia Company of London and renewed the spirit of confidence among the colonists. It supported a wealthy planter class and enriched shippers and merchants. Tobacco thereby contributed to the economic security and survival of the Virginia colony, and thus the nation. *Henrico Co.: Rte. 5, 5 miles e. of Richmond.*

V-26 BATTLE OF NEW MARKET HEIGHTS

On 28 September 1864, elements of Maj. Gen. Benjamin F. Butler's Army of the James crossed the James River to assault the Confederate defenses of Richmond. At dawn on 29 September, 6 regiments of U.S. Colored Troops fought with exceptional valor during their attack along New Market Road. Despite heavy casualties, they carried the earthworks there and succeeded in capturing New Market Heights, north of the road. Of the 20 Medals of Honor awarded to "Negro" soldiers and sailors during the Civil War, 14 were bestowed for this battle. Butler wrote that "the capacity of the negro race for soldiers had then and there been fully settled forever." *Henrico Co.: Rte. 5, 8.5 miles e. of Richmond.*

W-1* TO FRAZIER'S FARM

Over this road Longstreet's and A. P. Hill's divisions moved, on June 29, 1862, to attack McClellan at Frazier's Farm. *Henrico Co.: Rte. 60, Williamsburg Ave. at Darbytown Rd.*

W-2 WILLIAMSBURG ROAD

Over the road here D. H. Hill's and Longstreet's divisions moved, on May 31, 1862, to the battle of Seven Pines and over it, on June 29, 1862, Magruder moved to the battle of Savage's Station. *Henrico Co.: Rte. 60, .4 mile e. of Richmond.*

W-3* CHARLES CITY ROAD

Over this road Ruger's division moved, on June 29, 1862, to attack McClellan at Frazier's Farm. *Henrico Co.: Rte. 60, 1 mile e. of Richmond.*

W-4 McCLELLAN'S PICKET LINE

The picket line of McClellan's army crossed the road here on the morning of May 31, 1862. *Henrico Co.: Rte. 60, at Sandston.*

W-5 McCLELLAN'S FIRST LINE

Here was McClellan's first line of defense, held by Casey. The Confederates, advancing eastward on May 31, 1862, stormed the earthworks. *Henrico Co.: Rte. 60, at Sandston.*

W-6* MUNITIONS PLANT

Here stood a large munitions plant of the World War, 1918. *Henrico Co.: Rte. 60, e. entrance of Sandston.*

W-7* FAIR OAKS BATTLE

At Fair Oaks Station, a mile north, McClellan's right wing stayed the advance of the Confederates on May 31, 1862. *Henrico Co.: Rte. 60, .5 mile e. of Sandston.*

W-8 McCLELLAN'S WITHDRAWAL

In this vicinity a part of McClellan's army remained for several weeks after the battle of Seven Pines. The part of his army north of the Chickahominy was attacked by Lee, June 26–27, 1862. McClellan then began to withdraw to the James, June 28–29, 1862. *Henrico Co.: Rte. 60, 3.6 miles e. of Seven Pines.*

W-9 McCLELLAN'S SECOND LINE

Here, at Seven Pines, was McClellan's second and main line of defense. The Confederates under D. H. Hill, having taken the first line, attacked this position, held by Casey and Couch reinforced by Kearny, May 31, 1862. The battle was bitterly contested until Longstreet sent in fresh troops. The Union line was broken; the Unionists fell back a mile and a half east. *Henrico Co.: Rte. 60, at Seven Pines.*

W-10* SECOND DAY AT SEVEN PINES

The Confederates attacked McClellan's army along the railroad north of this road but soon withdrew, ending the battle, June 1, 1862. On the same day Robert E. Lee assumed command of the Army of Northern Virginia, replacing Johnston. *Henrico Co.: Rte. 60, .3 mile e. of Seven Pines.*

W-11 McCLELLAN'S THIRD LINE

Here ran McClellan's third line of defense, May 31–June 1, 1862. The Confederates, taking the first and second lines on this road, did not reach the third. *Henrico Co.: Rte. 60, 1.3 miles e. of Seven Pines.*

W-12* BATTLE OF SAVAGE'S STATION

Near here, on June 29, 1862, Magruder attacked the rear of McClellan's army withdrawing to the James and fought an indecisive action. McClellan continued his withdrawal. *Henrico Co.: Rte. 60, 2 miles e. of Seven Pines.*

W-13* TO WHITE OAK SWAMP AND MALVERN HILL

This road was used, on June 29, 1862, by McClellan's army moving to the James, and by Stonewall Jackson, following, on June 30. *Henrico Co.: Rte. 60, 2 miles e. of Sandston.*

W-14 McCLELLAN'S CROSSING

Here a part of McClellan's army crossed the Chickahominy on May 23, 1862, advancing on Richmond. It was attacked by the Confederates at Seven Pines. *New Kent Co.: Rte. 60, at Bottoms Bridge.*

W-15* CAMP BOTTOM'S BRIDGE

Here, in 1814, was a large camp of militia mustered to resist British invasion. *Henrico Co.: Rte. 60, 15 miles e. of Richmond.*

W-16 LAFAYETTE AND CORNWALLIS

Lafayette camped near here, on May 4, 1781. On May 28, 1781, Cornwallis camped here in pursuit of Lafayette and camped here again on June 21, 1781, while retiring eastward before Lafayette and Wayne. *New Kent Co.: Rte. 60, at Bottoms Bridge.*

W-17 NEW KENT ROAD

This was the main road to Williamsburg in early days. Cornwallis, retiring eastward, used this road in June, 1781. The Confederates, retreating westward, passed over it in May, 1862. *New Kent Co.: Rte. 60, at Bottoms Bridge.*

W-18 LONG BRIDGE

One mile south is Long Bridge over the Chickahominy River. Benedict Arnold sent Simcoe there in the British invasion of 1781. Longstreet crossed there in the Peninsular Campaign, May, 1862. Grant's Fifth and Second Corps crossed there, in June, 1864, on the way to Petersburg. *New Kent Co.: Rte. 60, 4.9 miles s.e. of Bottoms Bridge.*

W-19* SOANE'S BRIDGE

Half a mile south is Soane's Bridge over the Chickahominy. Here Stuart crossed, on June 14, 1862, in his famous ride around McClellan; here the Ninth and Sixth Corps of Grant's army crossed, June 13–14, 1864. *New Kent Co.: Rte. 60, at Bottoms Bridge.*

W-20 PROVIDENCE FORGE

Here about 1770, Charles Jeffery Smith, a Presbyterian minister, settled and, with William Holt, built a forge for making farm implements. Francis Jerdone became a partner in 1771. A militia camp was established here in 1781, and Lafayette was here in July and August, 1781. *New Kent Co.: Rte. 60, at Providence Forge.*

W-21 STATE GAME FARM

Established, 1920, for breeding partridges in captivity on a large scale. The first institution of the kind in the world. Game sanctuaries are stocked from this plant. *New Kent Co.: Rte. 60, 2.8 miles s.e. of Providence Forge.*

W-21 STATE GAME FARM

Established, 1920, for breeding partridges in captivity on a large scale. The first institution of the kind in the world. Game sanctuaries are stocked from this plant. *Cumberland Co.: Rte. 45, 6 miles s. of Cartersville at Rte. 615.*

W-22 CHICKAHOMINY INDIANS

One mile south is the home of descendants of the Chickahominy Indians, a powerful tribe at the time of the settlement of Jamestown. Chickahominies were among the Indians who took Captain John Smith prisoner in December, 1607. *New Kent Co.: Rte. 60, 4.2 miles s.e. of Providence Forge.*

W-23 FORT JAMES

A mile and a half south stood Moysonec, an Indian village occupied in 1607. This was the region of the Chickahominy tribe, members of which took part, in 1607, in the capture of Captain John Smith. There Fort James was established in 1645 after the great Indian massacre of 1644 in which several hundred colonists perished. *New Kent Co.: Rte. 60, 7.6 miles s.e. of Providence Forge.*

W-24 DIASCUND BRIDGE

Naval stores for the Virginia navy were destroyed here by British troops, April 22, 1781. *New Kent Co.: Rte. 60, 6.7 miles n.w. of Toano.*

W-25* COOPER'S MILL

One-half mile north up Diascund Creek stood Cooper's Mill at which Cornwallis obtained supplies, June 23–24, 1781. *New Kent Co.: Rte. 60, 7.25 miles e. of Providence Forge.*

W-26* NEW KENT ROAD

Cornwallis camped about a mile north of this point on June 24, 1781. A part of Lafayette's army, following, camped at the same place on June 27, 1781. *James City Co.: Rte. 60, 3 miles n.w. of Toano.*

W-27 WHITE HALL TAVERN

This was a station on the old stage road between Williamsburg and Richmond, before 1860. *James City Co.: Rte. 60, 1.3 miles n.w. of Toano.*

W-28* OLIVE BRANCH CHRISTIAN CHURCH

This church was built in 1835 on land granted to Leonard Henley in 1661, and is one of the oldest churches of the Disciples of Christ in this part of the State. In 1862–65, it was occupied by Union soldiers; with that exception the church has been continuously in use since its erection. *James City Co.: Rte. 60, .9 mile s.e. of Toano.*

W-29* TYREE'S PLANTATION

North of the road was Tyree's Plantation, Lafayette's headquarters, June 28–July 5, 1781, in his campaign against Cornwallis. *New Kent Co.: Rte. 60, 6.7 miles n.w. of Toano.*

W-30 HICKORY NECK CHURCH

Hickory Neck Church was built about 1740. Militia opposing the British camped here on April 21, 1781. A few miles north is the foundation of an ancient stone house, dating possibly from about 1650. *James City Co.: Rte. 60, .8 mile n.w. of Toano.*

W-31 STATE SHIPYARD

On this road five miles west was the State shipyard on Chickahominy River, burned by the British General Phillips on April 21–22, 1781. *James City Co.: Rte. 60, at Toano.*

W-32 CHICKAHOMINY CHURCH

Two miles south is the site of the colonial Chickahominy Church, now destroyed. Lafayette's forces camped there, July 6–8, 1781. The church was used as a hospital after the battle of Green Spring, July 6, 1781. *James City Co.: Rte. 60, at Toano.*

W-33* BURNT ORDINARY

Here was a colonial tavern which, after its destruction by fire, was known as "Burnt Ordinary." Cornwallis passed here on his way to Williamsburg, June 25, 1781. *James City Co.: Rte. 60, at Toano.*

W-34* SIX-MILE ORDINARY

Near this spot was Allen's Ordinary, sometimes called "Six-Mile Ordinary." An early settlement of Quakers was east of this point, near Scimino Creek. Militia under Colonel James Innes camped here on April 20, 1781. Colonel Thomas Mathews and his militia were attacked here by Tarleton, August 22, 1781. *James City Co.: Rte. 60, 4.3 miles s.e. of Toano.*

W-35 SPENCER'S ORDINARY

On this road, four miles south, the action of Spencer's Ordinary was fought, June 24, 1781, between detachments from Lafayette's and Cornwallis's armies. *James City Co.: Rte. 60, 4.3 miles s.e. of Toano.*

W-36 GREEN SPRING

On this road, five miles south, is Green Spring, home of Governor Sir William Berkeley. Bacon, the Rebel, occupied it in 1676. Cornwallis, after moving from Williamsburg by this road on July 4, 1781, was attacked by Lafayette at Green Spring on July 6, 1781. Anthony Wayne was the hero of this fight. *James City Co.: Rte. 60, 4.3 miles s.e. of Toano.*

W-37* PENINSULAR CAMPAIGN

In the Peninsular Campaign, Johnston's army marched over this road toward Richmond, May 4–6, 1862. McClellan's army followed May 6–10, 1862. *James City Co.: Rte. 60, n.w. entrance of Williamsburg.*

W-38*   IRON-BOUND ROAD

The Iron-Bound Road, the oldest road between Williamsburg and Jamestown, dates from the seventeenth century. *James City Co.: Rte. 60, 3 miles n.w. of Williamsburg.*

W-40   FIRST BALLOON FLIGHT IN VIRGINIA

On May 7, 1801, J. S. Watson, a student at William and Mary, wrote a letter detailing attempts at flying hot air balloons on the Court House Green. The third balloon, decorated with sixteen stars, one for each of the existing states, and fueled with spirits of wine, was successful. Watson wrote, "I never saw so great and so universal delight as it gave to the spectators." This is the earliest recorded evidence of aeronautics in the Commonwealth. *Williamsburg: Rte. 162, at entrance to Cary Field.*

W-42*   QUARTER PATH

The first quarter mile of this side road was known as the "Quarter Path," a colonial race track. *James City Co.: Rte. 60, s.e. entrance of Williamsburg.*

W-43   BATTLE OF WILLIAMSBURG

To the east of the road here, centering at Fort Magruder, was fought the battle of Williamsburg on May 5, 1862. The Union General McClellan was pursuing General Johnston's retiring army, the rearguard of which was commanded by General Longstreet. Johnston ordered Longstreet to hold off McClellan's attacking forces until the Confederate wagon trains, bogged down in mud, were out of danger. This mission was accomplished and Johnston continued his retirement. *James City Co.: Rte. 60, .3 mile s.e. of Williamsburg.*

W-44   MAGRUDER'S DEFENSES

Here is a redoubt in the Line of Confederate defenses, built across the James-York peninsula in 1861–62 by General John B. Magruder. *James City Co.: Rte. 60, .3 mile s.e. of Williamsburg.*

W-45   WHITAKER'S HOUSE

A mile north of the road is Whitaker's House, headquarters of General W. F. Smith, battle of Williamsburg, May 5, 1862. *James City Co.: Rte. 60, 1.4 miles s.e. of Williamsburg.*

W-46   VINEYARD TRACT

One mile north of the highway, an experimental farm for the culture of grapes was established by the Virginia government in 1769. On this tract stood a hospital of the French-American army, 1781. *York Co.: Rte. 641, 1.4 miles e. of Williamsburg, on secondary road.*

W-47*   KINGSMILL

Kingsmill Plantation is two miles south. Burwell's Ferry, a river landing, was there. In January, 1781, General Thomas Nelson, with militia, prevented Benedict Arnold from landing at the ferry. On April 20, 1781, Arnold and Phillips landed there and marched to Williamsburg. *James City Co.: Rte. 60, 2.4 miles s.e. of Williamsburg.*

W-48*   LITTLETOWN

Here was Littletown, the plantation of George Menefie, occupied by him as early as 1633. Camp Wallace, an artillery camp of the World War, 1917–1918, was here. *James City Co.: Rte. 60, 2.8 miles s.e. of Williamsburg.*

W-49* TREBELL'S LANDING

At Trebell's Landing, one mile southwest, the artillery and stores of the French and American armies for the siege of Yorktown were landed, September, 1781. These were conveyed by land (six miles) to Yorktown. The troops disembarked at the landings near Williamsburg. *James City Co.: Rte. 60, 5.1 miles s.e. of Williamsburg.*

W-50* CARTER'S GROVE

Carter's Grove was owned by the Burwell family. Carter Burwell, who built the mansion in 1751, was the grandson of Robert ("King") Carter. *James City Co.: Rte. 60, 3.25 miles s.e. of Williamsburg.*

W-51* MARTIN'S HUNDRED

On both sides of this road and extending west was the plantation known as Martin's Hundred, originally of 80,000 acres. Settled in 1619, this hundred sent delegates to the first legislative assembly in America, 1619. In the Indian massacre of 1622, seventy-eight persons were slain here. *James City Co.: Rte. 60, 6.7 miles s.e. of Williamsburg.*

W-51 MARTIN'S HUNDRED

This plantation was founded by the London-based Society of Martin's Hundred in 1617 and later was assigned 21,500 acres; it was settled in 1619. The site of Wolstenholme Town, its administrative center, was discovered by archaeologists in 1977. They located the graves of several victims of the Indian massacre of 22 March 1622, when 78 colonists here—half the plantation's population—were reported slain. The area soon was resettled but the town was never rebuilt. *James City Co.: Rte. 60, at entrance to Carter's Grove.*

W-52* MARTIN'S HUNDRED CHURCH

A mile south is the site of the early colonial church of Martin's Hundred. *James City Co.: Rte. 60, 6.7 miles s.e. of Williamsburg.*

W-53* SKIFFES CREEK

Skiffes, or Keith's Creek was named for Rev. George Keith, minister of Martin's Hundred parish in 1624. *Newport News ("old" Warwick Co.): Rte. 60, 1 mile n.w. of LeeHall.*

W-54* LEE HALL

Lee Hall was the headquarters of John B. Magruder, Confederate general, in April and May, 1862. *Newport News ("old" Warwick Co.): Rte. 60, at Lee Hall.*

W-55* TO YORKTOWN

On this road, seven miles north, is Yorktown, where Cornwallis surrendered to Washington and Rochambeau on October 19, 1781. *Newport News ("Old" Warwick Co.): Rte. 60, at Lee Hall.*

W-56* FORT EUSTIS

Fort Eustis, half a mile south, was a cantonment of the World War and is now an artillery post. Within the fort grounds are the Jones House, built about 1660 and rebuilt in 1727; and Fort Crawford, a Confederate work. Here also was Stanley Hundred, granted to Sir George Yeardley in 1626. *Newport News ("old" Warwick Co.): Rte. 337, 1 mile s. of Lee Hall.*

W-57* MULBERRY POINT

Five miles through Fort Eustis grounds is Mulberry Point on James River. Near this spot, on June 8, 1610, the starving colonists, who had abandoned Jamestown, met a messenger bearing tidings of relief and returned to the settlement. *Newport News ("old" Warwick Co.): Rte. 337, 1 mile s. of Lee Hall.*

W-58* LEE'S MILL

A short distance north of this road across the reservoir is the site of the ancient Lee's Mill. The side road leads to the Miles Curtis farm, where, in April and May, 1862, officers of McClellan's army made balloon observations. *Newport News ("old" Warwick Co.): Rte. 337, 2 miles s.e. of Lee Hall.*

W-59* BATTLE OF DAM NO. 1

One mile east of this road is the battlefield of Dam No. 1 (or Lee's Mill), fought April 16, 1862, the opening engagement of the Peninsular Campaign. *Newport News ("old" Warwick Co.): Rte. 60, 1.9 miles s.e. of Lee Hall.*

W-60 WARWICK COURTHOUSE

The clerk's office was built in 1810, when Warwick Courthouse was moved here. *Newport News ("old" Warwick Co.): Rte. 60, at Denbigh (14421 Old Courthouse Way).*

W-61 DENBIGH PLANTATION

Two miles to the southwest was Denbigh, plantation of Samuel Matthews, who came to Virginia in 1622 and was governor in 1658. A public storehouse was built there in 1633 and Warwick Courthouse in 1691. *Newport News ("old" Warwick Co.): Rte. 60, 2.2 miles s.e. of Denbigh, at Menchville Rd.*

W-62* WARWICK RIVER

A short distance west of this road is Warwick River, on the west side of which, extending to Yorktown, John B. Magruder built fortifications in January and February, 1862. *Newport News ("old" Warwick Co.): Rte. 337, 4 miles s.e. of Denbigh.*

W-63* YOUNG'S MILL

Here ran a line of Confederate fortifications, built in 1861 to oppose the Union advance from Fortress Monroe. *Newport News ("old" Warwick Co.): Rte. 337, .75 mile s.e. of Denbigh.*

W-64* WATERS CREEK

In 1624 Captain Edward Waters obtained a patent on this creek. He was living here in 1625. *Newport News ("old" Warwick Co.): Rte. 60, 6.5 miles s.e. of Denbigh.*

W-65* DENBIGH BAPTIST CHURCH

This church is near the site of the colonial church of Upper Denbigh Parish. *Newport News ("old" Warwick Co.): Rte. 60, 2.6 miles s.e. of Denbigh.*

W-66* BATTLE OF BIG BETHEL

Five miles east is Big Bethel, where a battle was fought on June 10, 1861. *Newport News ("old" Warwick Co.): Rte. 60, at Morrison.*

W-66* BATTLE OF BIG BETHEL

Five miles east was Big Bethel Church. On June 10, 1861, General Ebenezer W. Peirce attacked a numerically inferior confederate force under Colonel John B. Magruder. The assault was repulsed, and Peirce withdrew to Hampton and Newport News. *Newport News ("old" Warwick Co.): Rte. 60, at Rte. 306.*

W-67* MARY'S MOUNT

Two and one-half miles east is Mary's Mount (present Merry Point), settled by Daniel Gookin, Jr., before 1630. *Newport News: Rte. 337, 1 mile n.w. of Hilton Village.*

W-68* CAMP HILL

This was a World War Aeration camp, 1918. *Newport News: Rte. 337, near Hilton Village.*

W-69* BLUNT POINT

Four miles south on James River is Blunt Point, named for Humphrey Blount, who was killed by the Indians in 1610. *Newport News: Rte. 337, 1 mile n.w. of Hilton Village.*

W-70* NEWPORT NEWS

This community was known to Captain John Smith as Point Hope, but it was called "Newportes Newes" as early as 1619. The name may commemorate Captain Christopher Newport, Commander of five expeditions to Jamestown during 1606–1612. *Newport News: Twenty-seventh St. at the waterfront.*

W-70* NEWPORT NEWS

Daniel Gookin, Sr., settled a colony of eighty people here in November, 1621. The place was named for Sir William Newce. *Newport News: Rte. 337, w. entrance of Newport News.*

W-70* SETTLEMENT OF NEWPORT NEWS

The place appears on Captain John Smith's map as Point Hope. In 1621, Sir William Newce, marshal of Virginia, his brother, Captain Thomas Newce, and Daniel Gookin came here from Newcestown, Ireland, and made a settlement. It was known as Newport Newce, later Newport News. *Newport News: s. end of Twenty-sixth St.*

W-71 LEE'S MILL EARTHWORKS

These earthworks were part of General John B. Magruder's second line of defense. At this site on April 5, 1862, Confederate General Lafayette McLaw's [*sic*] four companies of the Tenth Georgia with Captain Joseph B. Cosnahan's two batteries stopped the advance of Union General William F. "Baldy" Smith's two divisions of the Fourth Army Corps and Captain Charles C. Wheeler's six batteries. Several skirmishes and engagements occurred here between April 5 and May 4, 1862, at which time the Confederate forces abandoned the earthworks and withdrew to Williamsburg. *Newport News: Rte. 60, .2 mile e. of Rte. 105.*

W-79 LAST INDIAN RAID

Near this spot, in 1764, John Tremble was killed by Indians in the last raid in Augusta County. *Augusta Co.: Rte. 250, 4 miles w. of Staunton.*

W-84 FIRST BATTLE OF IRONCLADS

In Hampton Roads, southward and a mile or two offshore, the Virginia (Merrimac) and the Monitor fought their engagement, March 9, 1862. The day before the Virginia destroyed the Cumberland and Congress, wooden ships of the Union navy. *Hampton ("old" Elizabeth City Co.): Chesapeake Ave. between La Salle and East aves.*

Eight miles north George Wythe, Revolutionary leader and Signer of the Declaration of Independence, was born, 1726. *Hampton ("old" Elizabeth City Co.): Rte. 60, .5 mile west of Hampton.*

A short distance to the east are the sites of Fort Henry and Fort Charles, built in 1610 by Sir Thomas Gates after the expulsion of the Indians living here. In 1637, Fort Henry was abandoned. *Hampton ("old" Elizabeth City Co.): Rte. 60, .5 mile s.w. of Hampton proper.*

The Indian village of Kecoughtan stood here in 1607. An English village was built on its site in 1610. In 1630 William Claiborne set up a trading post here. The town of Hampton was established by law in 1680 and named for the Earl of Southampton. The first Revolutionary engagement in Virginia took place here, October 25, 1775. British sacked the town in June, 1813. Confederates burned it in August, 1861, to prevent its use by Union troops. *Hampton ("old" Elizabeth City Co.): Sunset and Kecoughtan rds.*

To the west, on the grounds of Hampton Institute, is the tree under which Mrs. Mary Peake, a Freedwoman, taught children of former slaves in 1861. Nearby stood the Butler School, a free school established in 1863 for colored children. *Hampton: East Tyler St. and ramp to I-64.*

This point, patented by William Capps about 1634, was known for a century as Capps Point. In June, 1813, a small militia garrison here was forced to retreat before a British invasion. *Hampton: Rte. 60, at Newport News line.*

Near here Captain John Ratcliffe built Fort Algernourne, 1609. In 1614, it was a stockade containing fifty people and seven cannon. In 1632, the fort was rebuilt. It was discontinued after 1667. In 1727, a new fort, Fort George, was ordered built here. This fort was destroyed by a hurricane in 1749. *Hampton ("old" Elizabeth City Co.): Rte. 60 at Fort Monroe, near Old Point Comfort.*

The fort was begun in 1819 and named for President James Monroe. It remained in possession of the Union forces, 1861–65, and from it as a base McClellan began the Peninsular Campaign, 1862. Jefferson Davis was imprisoned here, 1865–67. *Hampton ("old" Elizabeth City Co.): Rte. 60, at Fort Monroe, near Old Point Comfort.*

This zero mile post is a replica of the original post that stood here at the end of the track on the Chesapeake and Ohio Railway, from which point all main line distances have been measured for the 664.9 miles to Cincinnati, Ohio, since 1889. The Fort Monroe (Old Point Comfort) station located here ceased operation in December, 1939. *Hampton ("old" Elizabeth City Co.): Rte. 258, at Fort Monroe.*

W-92 CONFINEMENT OF JEFFERSON DAVIS

In this casemate Jefferson Davis, President of the Confederate States, was confined, May 22–October 2, 1865. As his health suffered in the casemate, he was removed to Carroll Hall in the fortress, where he remained from October, 1865, until May, 1867, when he was released on bail. He was never brought to trial. *Hampton ("old" Elizabeth City Co.): Rte. 60, at Fort Monroe, near Old Point Comfort.*

W-93 OLD POINT COMFORT LIGHT

The lighthouse, built in 1802, is the oldest standing structure at Fort Monroe. It remains an active navigational aid, the property of the U.S. Coast Guard. During the War of 1812, the tower was used as a lookout by a British invasion force while they attacked Washington. The adjacent house was the lightkeepers' quarters until the light was automated in 1973 when the house became Army property. *Hampton: Rte. 60, at Fort Monroe, near Old Point Comfort.*

W-94 FREEDOM'S FORTRESS

Fort Monroe was the site of Major General Benjamin F. Butler's decision in 1861 to accept escaping slaves as "contrabands of war." Thousands of former slaves who cast off their bondage and sought sanctuary here called this "The Freedom Fort." The First and Second Regiments of U.S. Colored Cavalry and Battery B, Second U.S. Colored Light Artillery, were raised here during the Civil War. In 1865 the Bureau for the Relief of Freedmen and Refugees ("Freedmen's Bureau") established its state headquarters here. *Hampton: Ruckman Rd., at Fort Monroe.*

W-148 FORT GEORGE ON THE BULLPASTURE RIVER

Fort George was built in the spring of 1757 by Captain William Preston, acting on orders of Major Andrew Lewis. Local residents assisted in construction of the 80-foot-square log fort located on the land of Wallace Estill. It was never attacked directly by Indians, although arrows were shot at it from a ridge across the Bullpasture River. The fort site is located in the meadow southeast of this marker. *Highland Co.: Rte. 678, 6 miles s. of McDowell.*

W-149* FORT EDWARD JOHNSON

This earthwork was made by the Confederate General Edward Johnson about April 1, 1862. He withdrew from it to occupy Shenandoah Mountain near Staunton, where he prepared to resist invasion from the west. *Highland Co.: Rte. 250, 5 miles w. of West Augusta.*

W-150 BATTLE OF McDOWELL

Stonewall Jackson, to prevent a junction of Fremont and Banks, took position on the hills just to the south and beat off the attacks of Fremont's advance under Milroy, May 8, 1862. Milroy retreated that night. *Highland Co.: Rte. 250, 1 mile e. of McDowell.*

W-155 TINKLING SPRING CHURCH

This was first the southern branch of the "Triple Forks of Shenandoah" congregation, which called John Craig as pastor in 1741. A church was completed here about 1748; two other buildings have succeeded it. Beginning with 1777, James Waddel, the noted blind preacher, was supply [*sic*] for some years. R. L. Dabney, of Stonewall Jackson's staff, was the minister here, 1847–1852. *Augusta Co.: Rte. 608, 1.3 miles s. of Fishersville.*

W-159 FIRST SETTLERS' GRAVE

One mile north is the grave of John Lewis, first settler in this region, who came here in 1732 and died in 1762. He chose the site of the town of Staunton. His four sons, Thomas, Andrew, William and Charles, took an important part in the Indian and Revolutionary wars. *Augusta Co.: Rte. 250, at e. entrance of Staunton.*

W-160* EARLY'S LAST BATTLE

Sheridan attacked Early on the ridge west of this city, driving him from his position and capturing many of his men, March 2, 1865. This was the last important battle in northern Virginia. *Augusta Co.: Rte. 250, at w. entrance of Waynesboro.*

W-161 BIRTHPLACE OF MERIWETHER LEWIS

Half a mile north was born, 1774, Meriwether Lewis, of the Lewis and Clark Expedition, sent by Jefferson to explore the Far West, 1804–1806. The expedition reached the mouth of the Columbia River, November 15, 1805. *Albemarle Co.: Rte. 250, 5 miles w. of Charlottesville.*

W-162 JACKSON'S VALLEY CAMPAIGN

Near here, Stonewall Jackson's troops entrained, May 4, 1862, to go west to Staunton in the move that led to the battle of McDowell, May 8, 1862. *Albemarle Co.: Rte. 250, at Mechums River.*

W-163 REVOLUTIONARY SOLDIERS GRAVES

Jesse Pitman Lewis (d. March 8, 1849), of the Virginia Militia, and Taliaferro Lewis (d. July 12, 1810), of the Continental Line, two of several brothers who fought in the war for independence, are buried in the Lewis family cemetery 100 yards south of this marker. *Albemarle Co.: Rte. 250, w. entrance to Charlottesville.*

W-173 CROZET

The town grew around a rail stop established on Wayland's farm in 1876. It was named for Col. B. Claudius Crozet, (1789–1864)—Napoleonic army officer, and the state's engineer and cartographer. He built this pioneer railway through the Blue Ridge. The 4273' tunnel through the rocksolid mountain below Rockfish Gap carried traffic from 1858–1944. His talents were tested in solving safety, drainage and ventilation problems posed by the construction of this tunnel. *Albemarle Co.: Rte. 240, in Crozet.*

W-197 SKIRMISH AT RIO HILL

On February 29, 1864, General George A. Custer and 1500 cavalrymen made a diversionary raid into Albemarle County. Here, north of Charlottesville, he attacked the winter camp of four batteries of the Stuart Horse Artillery commanded by Captain Marcellus N. Moorman. Despite the destruction to the camp, 200 Confederates rallied in a counterattack which forced Custer's withdrawal. Few casualties were reported. *Albemarle Co.: Rte. 15, 3.5 miles n. of Charlottesville.*

W-198* SHADWELL—THOMAS JEFFERSON'S BIRTHPLACE

To the south stands a representation of the house in which Thomas Jefferson was born. It stands on the original foundations, which were identified in 1955. It was completed in 1960. *Albemarle Co.: Rte. 250, 3 miles e. of Charlottesville.*

W-199 CLARK'S BIRTHPLACE

A mile north was born George Rogers Clark, defender of Kentucky and conqueror of the Northwest, November 19, 1752. *Albemarle Co.: Rte. 250, .2 mile e. of Charlottesville.*

W-200 MONTICELLO

Three miles to the southeast. Thomas Jefferson began the house in 1770 and finished it in 1802. He brought his bride to it in 1772. Lafayette visited it in 1825. Jefferson spent his last years there and died there, July 4, 1826. His tomb is there. The place was raided by British cavalry, June 4, 1781. *Charlottesville: at courthouse.*

W-201 COLLE

The house was built about 1770 by workmen engaged in building Monticello. Mazzei, an Italian, lived here for some years adapting grape culture to Virginia. Baron de Reidesel, captured at Saratoga in 1777, lived here with his family, 1779–1780. Scenes in Ford's novel, Janice Meredith, are laid here. *Albemarle Co.: Rte. 250, 4.2 miles e. of Charlottesville.*

W-202 SHADWELL ESTATE

Peter Jefferson acquired the land in 1735, and built the house about 1737. Thomas Jefferson was born here, April 13, 1743. He lived here, 1743–1745, and 1752–1770. The house burned in 1770, and Jefferson then moved to Monticello. *Albemarle Co.: Rte. 250, 2.9 miles e. of Charlottesville.*

W-203 EDGEHILL

The land was patented in 1735. The old house was built in 1790; the new in 1828. Here lived Thomas Mann Randolph, Governor of Virginia, 1819–1822, who married Martha, daughter of Thomas Jefferson. *Albemarle Co.: Rte. 250, 4.2 miles e. of Charlottesville.*

W-204 CASTLE HILL

The original house was built in 1765 by Doctor Thomas Walker, explorer and pioneer. Tarleton, raiding to Charlottesville to capture Jefferson and the legislature, stopped here for breakfast, June 4, 1781. This delay aided the patriots to escape. Castle Hill was long the home of Senator William Cabell Rives, who built the present house. *Albemarle Co.: Rte. 231, e. of Shadwell.*

W-205* MECHUNK CREEK

Two miles south of this place Lafayette camped, June 13–14, 1781. He had come from the Rapidan River to throw himself between Cornwallis on the east and military stores in Albemarle County. *Albemarle Co.: Rte. 22, 6 miles e. of Shadwell.*

W-206 THE MARQUIS ROAD

Lafayette reopened this road in June, 1781, when moving south to intervene between Cornwallis and military stores in Albemarle County. The road has ever since been known as "The Marquis Road." *Louisa Co.: Rte. 22, at Boswell's Tavern.*

W-207 BOSWELL'S TAVERN

At this old tavern Lafayette camped, on June 12, 1781, while moving southward to intervene between Cornwallis and military stores in Albemarle County. *Louisa Co.: Rte. 22, at Boswell's Tavern.*

W-208 GREEN SPRINGS

Near here Wade Hampton's Confederate cavalry camped the night of June 10, 1864, just before the battle of Trevilians. *Louisa Co.: Rte. 33, 7 miles w. of Louisa.*

W-209 BATTLE OF TREVILIANS

Here, on June 12, 1864, Sheridan's cavalry, coming from Trevilians, attacked Wade Hampton, who had taken position across the road. A bloody engagement followed. Fitz Lee joined Hampton, and the Union cavalry was driven back. That night Sheridan retired eastward. *Louisa Co.: Rte. 33, 4.5 miles w. of Louisa.*

W-210* BATTLE OF TREVILIANS

Near here Custer of Sheridan's cavalry, raiding westward, got between Fitz Lee's division and the rest of Wade Hampton's cavalry, capturing wagons. The Confederates recaptured the wagons but withdrew to the west after a fierce conflict, June 11, 1864. *Louisa Co.: Rte. 33, 4.5 miles w. of Louisa.*

W-211 PATRICK HENRY'S HOME

At Roundabout Plantation, eight miles southwest, Patrick Henry lived from 1765 to 1768, when he sat for Louisa County in the House of Burgesses. This was the beginning of his political career. *Louisa Co.: Rte. 33, at Louisa.*

W-212 HISTORIC LOUISA

Here the county seat was established in 1742. The British Cavalryman, Tarleton, stopped here on his raid to Charlottesville, June 3, 1781. Stoneman raided the place and destroyed the railroad, May 2, 1863. Near here Fitz Lee camped, June 10, 1864, just before the Battle of Trevilians. *Louisa: Rtes. 33 and 22, e. of Louisa.*

W-213 JACK JOUETT'S RIDE

From the tavern that stood here, Jack Jouett rode to Charlottesville, by the Old Mountain Road, in time to warn the members of the Virginia government of the coming of Tarleton's British cavalry, June 3, 1781. *Louisa Co.: Rte. 33, at Cuckoo.*

W-214 SCOTCHTOWN

A mile north is Scotchtown, Patrick Henry's home, 1771–1777. Dolly Madison, President James Madison's wife, lived here in her girlhood. Lafayette was here in May, 1781, retreating northward before Cornwallis. Cornwallis passed here in June, 1781, moving westward. *Hanover Co.: Rte. 54, 8 miles n.w. of Ashland.*

W-218   ROCKFISH GAP MEETING

The commission appointed to select a site for the University of Virginia met 1–4 August 1818 in the tavern that stood nearby. Among the 21 members present were former presidents Thomas Jefferson and James Madison, as well as judges Spencer Roane, Archibald Stuart, and Creed Taylor. The commissioners chose Charlottesville over Lexington and Staunton for the site of the university. The tavern at which they met was owned by Samuel Leake (1790–1858) and Walter Leake (1792–1859). Enlarged later, as part of the Mountain Top Hotel and Springs, the popular tavern burned in 1909. *Nelson Co.: Rte. 250, 2 miles n.w. of Afton.*

W-218*   ROCKFISH GAP MEETING

In the tavern near here the commission appointed to select a site for the University of Virginia met, August 14, 1818. Ex-Presidents Thomas Jefferson and James Monroe and Judge Spencer Roane were the most distinguished members. After considering several places, Charlottesville was chosen. *Nelson Co.: Rte. 250, 2 miles n.w. of Afton.*

W-219   FLIGHT OF RICHARD C. DUPONT

Near this site on September 21, 1933, Richard C. duPont was launched from Afton Mountain in his Bowlus sailplane, Albatross. Four hours and fifty minutes later he landed at Frederick, Maryland, establishing a United States distance record for sail planing of 121.6 miles, almost double the previous U.S. record of 66 miles. *Nelson Co.: I-64 overlook on Afton Mountain.*

W-220   GEORGE CALEB BINGHAM

George Caleb Bingham, a renowned American genre painter of the 19th century, was born in a frame house just north of here on 20 March 1811. Bingham moved to Missouri in 1819, where he began painting portraits in the 1830s and later specialized in paintings of the American West. He died in July 1879 in Kansas City, Missouri. *Augusta Co.: Rtes. 256 and 668, near Grottoes bridge.*

W-221   VIRGINIA ESTELLE RANDOLPH

The daughter of parents born in slavery, Virginia Randolph (1874–1958) taught in a one-room schoolhouse beginning in 1892. A gifted teacher, she became in 1908 the nation's first Jeanes Supervising Industrial Teacher, a position sponsored by the Anna T. Jeanes Fund of Philadelphia for black Southern education. Randolph developed the Henrico Plan, teaching both traditional subjects and vocational skills. Henrico County named two schools in her honor here in 1915 and 1957. In 1969 the schools were merged to form the Virginia Randolph Education Center; Randolph is buried here. *Henrico Co.: 2200 Mountain Rd., at Virginia Randolph Education Center.*

WO-12   THE WHITE HOUSE

This place, six miles northeast, was the home of Martha Custis. According to tradition, George Washington first met her at Poplar Grove, near by, in 1758. On January 6, 1759, Washington and Martha Custis were married, it is believed at the White House. The house was burned by Union troops when McClellan made the White House his base of operations in May, 1862. *New Kent Co.: Rte. 249, at Talleysville.*

WO-13 ST. PETER'S CHURCH

Two miles northeast is St. Peter's Church, built in 1703 in English bond. David Mossom, rector there for forty years, was the minister who married George Washington. According to one tradition, the wedding took place at St. Peter's Church. *NewKent Co.:ʼ Rte. 249, at Talleysville.*

WO-14 STUART'S RIDE AROUND McCLELLAN

J. E. B. Stuart, on his famous ride around McClellan's army, June 12–15, 1862, arrived here in the early night of June 13, coming from Hanover Courthouse. He rested here several hours and then pressed on to the Chickahominy River, rejoining Lee's army on June 15. *New Kent Co.: Rte. 33, at Talleysville.*

WO-16 NEW KENT COURTHOUSE

Lord Cornwallis's army was here, moving eastward, June 22, 1781; Lafayette, in pursuit, June 25; Washington, Rochambeau and Chastellux, on their way to Yorktown, September 14, 1781. A part of Joseph E. Johnston's army, retiring to Richmond, passed through, May, 1862. *New Kent Co.: Rte. 249, at New Kent.*

WO-18 MARTHA WASHINGTON'S BIRTHPLACE

About two miles northeast is the site of Chestnut Grove. Here Martha Dandridge was born June 2, 1731. The house here burned in 1927. Her first marriage was to Daniel Parke Custis in 1749, her second to George Washington on January 6, 1769. They honeymooned at the White House, her plantation in this county, later moving to Mount Vernon. *New Kent Co.: Rte. 249, 7 miles e. of New Kent.*

WO-30 ELTHAM

Eltham, a mile north, was long the home of the Bassett family and one of the largest and finest colonial houses in Virginia. Burwell Bassett, the owner at the time of the Revolution, was a patriot leader. Washington was a frequent visitor at Eltham and was there in November, 1781, at the deathbed of his stepson, John Parke Custis, a soldier of Yorktown. The old house was burned in 1875; the foundation remains. *New Kent Co.: Rte. 33, 1.9 miles w. of West Point.*

WO-31 PENINSULAR CAMPAIGN

A mile north, at Eltham Landing on the Pamunkey River, Franklin's division of McClellan's army disembarked on May 6, 1862. The next morning the Union troops came in contact with the Confederates retiring toward Richmond. The Confederate wagon trains were in danger; but Gustavus W. Smith drove Franklin back to the river. The action occurred in this vicinity, May 7, 1862. *New Kent Co.: Rte. 33, 1.5 miles w. of West Point.*

WO-33 THE BRICK HOUSE

A short distance south stood the Brick House. In 1677, at the end of Bacon's Rebellion, the rebel leaders, Drummond and Lawrence, were at Brick House when West Point surrendered to Berkeley. They fled, Drummond to be caught and executed, Lawrence never to be heard of again. In August, 1716, Governor Alexander Spotswood crossed the river there on his western expedition. *New Kent Co.: Rte. 33, 1.5 miles w. of West Point.*

WO-37 SCOTTISH FACTORS STORE

Two miles to the north, in the colonial port of entry of Urbanna, is a restored eighteenth century storehouse. Scottish merchants became active commercial factors in the colony subsequent to the Act of Union of England and Scotland. Urbanna was established as a town in 1706. *Middlesex Co.: Rte. 33, 1.5 miles e. of Saluda.*

WP-5* GREAT BRIDGE CHAPEL

Here stood the second Southern Branch Chapel, or Great Bridge Chapel. It was built in 1701 as a Chapel of Ease for Elizabeth River Parish and in 1761 became a Chapel of St. Bride's Parish. The building was torn down about 1845. *Chesapeake ("old" Norfolk Co.): Rte. 168, in Great Bridge.*

WP-7* NORFOLK COUNTY COURTHOUSE

One-half mile west is the last courthouse of Norfolk County. It was built in 1962 and is now the Courthouse of the City of Chesapeake. Continuous court records beginning in 1637 are preserved here. *Chesapeake ("old" Norfolk Co.): Rte. 168, in Great Bridge.*

WP-10 ST. BRIDE'S CHURCH

At this point stood St. Bride's Church, the Parish Church of St. Bride's Parish which was established in 1761. The church, sometimes known as Northwest Church, was built in 1762 and survived until 1853. *Chesapeake ("old" Norfolk Co.): Rte. 168, 4 miles n. of North Carolina line.*

WT-1 FIRST AFRICANS IN ENGLISH AMERICA

The first documented Africans in English America arrived at Jamestown in August 1619. A Dutch man-of-war captured them from the Spanish, who had enslaved them, and sold them to the Virginia colonists. The "twenty and odd" Africans, some of whom had been given Spanish names, may have been treated like indentured servants and later freed after their periods of servitude expired. From this beginning the institution of slavery evolved during the 17th century as the Virginia colonists extended the length of service for Africans from a fixed term to life. The United States abolished slavery in 1865. *James City Co.: Rte. 31, .2 mile s. of Rte. 614.*

WY-2 SITE OF TIDEWATER INSTITUTE

Tidewater Institute was incorporated in 1903 with the stated purpose of establishing an industrial, academic, collegiate, and seminary boarding school for the education of black youth. Founded by the Rev. George E. Reid, and supported by the Northampton/Accomack Baptist Association, the institute attracted students from both Virginia and other Atlantic seaboard states. For twenty-eight years, the school was dedicated to the education and molding of lives of young black men and women of Virginia's Eastern Shore. *Northampton Co.: Rte. 636, .75 mile e. of Rte. 13.*

WY-3 SALEM METHODIST CHURCH

1.8 miles east of here stood Salem Methodist Church (1836–1918) scene of the initial violence resulting from the schism between northern and southern Methodists in 1846. A northern circuit preacher was dragged from the pulpit by members of the congregation. The building burned in 1870 and was replaced. Salem was the mother church of congregations at Cheriton and Oyster and five Eastern Shore Methodist ministers. *Northampton Co.: Rte. 13, at Rte. 636.*

WY-4 CAPE CHARLES

Two miles west of here, the town of Cape Charles was founded in 1884 as the Eastern Shore terminus of the New York, Philadelphia, and Norfolk Railroad, connecting the northeast with Norfolk by car float. Enjoying rapid growth, the planned community established itself as the commercial and residential center of Northampton County. No longer a railroad center, the business district and many of the railroad-era residences are listed on the Virginia Landmarks Register and the National Register of Historic Places. *Northampton Co.: Rte. 13 near Rte. 184.*

WY-5 ARLINGTON

Two miles west stood Arlington, original home of the Custis Family, built by John Custis. The family tombs are still preserved there. Governor William Berkeley made his headquarters there during Bacon's Rebellion in 1676. Arlington on the Potomac was named for this Arlington. *Northampton Co.: Rte. 13, 3 miles n. of Cape Charles.*

WY-5* ARLINGTON

Five miles southeast, on the south side of Old Plantation Creek, is Arlington, built by John Custis before 1680. There Sir William Berkeley, when driven from Jamestown by Bacon in 1676, made his headquarters and thence he sailed back to Jamestown. *Northampton Co.: Rte. 13, 3 miles n. of Cape Charles.*

WY-6* OLD PLACES

Two miles south is Stratton Manor, built by Thomas Stratton about 1657 and remodeled in 1764. Five and a half miles south, on the east side of Old Plantation Creek, is the site of Magothy Bay Church, built about 1690. *Northampton Co.: Rte. 13, 3 miles n. of Cape Charles.*

WY-7 TOWNE FIELDS

This site, two and a half miles west was the first seat of local government on the Eastern Shore. Francis Bolton preached there in 1623, and the first church was built before 1632. The oldest continuous county records in the English Colonies began there in 1632. The first courthouse (built for that purpose) on the Eastern Shore was erected in 1664 and used until Court moved to the Eastville area in 1677. *Northampton Co.: Rte. 13, at Cheriton.*

WY-7* FIRST COURTHOUSE

Two and a half miles west, at Town Fields, the first courthouse on the Eastern Shore was built, 1664. Court was held here until 1677, when the courthouse was moved to Eastville. In the Revolution a fort stood at Town Fields. *Northampton Co.: Rte. 13, at Cheriton.*

WY-8 HOME OF FIRST SETTLER

Here, in Savages Neck, was the home of Ensign Thomas Savage, who came to Virginia in 1608. Granted a tract of land by Debedeavon, the "Laughing King" of the Indians, in 1619, Savage became the first permanent English settler on the Eastern Shore. A mile west is Old Castle, built in 1721. *Northampton Co.: Rte. 13, 1 mile s. of Eastville.*

WY-9 INDIAN VILLAGE

Three miles east, on Pocahontas farm, was the main village of the Gingaskin Indians, one of the largest tribes on the Eastern Shore. Survivors of this tribe were found here as late as 1860. *Northampton Co.: Rte. 13, at Eastville.*

WY-10 OLD COURTHOUSE

The courthouse was moved to Eastville in 1677, and court has been held here ever since. The old courthouse was built about 1731; from its door the Declaration of Independence was read, August 13, 1776. Militia Barracks were here during the Revolution. Just behind the courthouse is the debtors' prison. *Northampton Co.: Rte. 13, at Eastville.*

WY-11* HUNGARS CHURCH AND VAUCLUSE

Three miles west is Hungers Church, built by 1742. Two and a half miles west of the church is the Glebe farm, which was church property until 1840. Four and a half miles south of the Glebe is Vaucluse, birthplace of Abel Parker Upshur, Secretary of State, killed in the explosion on the Princeton, 1844. *Northampton Co.: Rte. 13, 2.8 miles s. of Nassawadox.*

WY-12* BATTLE OF PUNGOTEAGUE

Seven miles west. On May 30, 1814, the British Admiral Cockburn landed at Pungoteague Creek with 500 marines and fought a battle with the Eastern Shore militia under Major Finney. Cockburn, seeing that he would be surrounded, withdrew to Tangier Island, where the British had landed on April 5, 1814. *Accomack Co.: Rte. 13, at Melfa.*

WY-13 OCCAHANNOCK

Five miles west is "Hedra Cottage," site of the home of Colonel Edmund Scarborough (Scarburgh), Surveyor General of the Colony. Beyond, at the end of Scarborough's Neck, was the village of the Occahannock Indians, the seat of Debedeavon, the "Laughing King." *Accomack Co.: Rte. 13, at Belle Haven.*

WY-14 ONANCOCK

Two miles west is Onancock, founded in 1680. A courthouse was then built and used for a few years. Militia barracks were there in the Revolution. From Onancock, Colonel John Cropper went to the aid of Commodore Whaley in the last naval action of the Revolution, November 30, 1782. Near by is Onley, home of Henry A. Wise, Governor of Virginia, 1856–60. *Accomack Co.: Rte. 13, 2 miles s. of Accomac.*

WY-15 FOUNDER OF PRESBYTERIANISM

Five miles west was the home of Rev. Francis Makemie, founder of Presbyterianism in the United States. About 1684, Makemie established in Maryland the first Presbyterian church. Later he moved to Accomac and married. He died here in 1708. *Accomack Co.: Rte. 13, at Temperanceville.*

WY-16 OAK GROVE METHODIST CHURCH

Two miles east, on Rte. 600, meets what is possibly the nation's oldest continuous Sunday School. Begun by William Elliott in his home in 1785, it was moved in 1818 to Burton's Chapel and in 1870 to the present church. *Accomack Co.: Rte. 13, in Keller.*

WY-17 THE BEAR AND THE CUB

This first play recorded in the United States was presented August 27, 1665. The Accomack County Court at Pungoteague heard charges against three men "For Acting a Play," ordered inspection of costumes and script, but found men "Not Guilty." *Accomack Co.: Rte. 13, at Keller.*

WY-18 "THE BEAR AND THE CUB"

Probable site of Fowkes' Tavern where the first recorded play in English America was performed August 27, 1665. *Accomack Co.: Rte. 178, .5 mile n. of Pungoteague.*

WY-19 DEBTOR'S PRISON

Built in 1783 in one corner of the jail yard wall to serve as residence for the jailer. Iron bars, oak batten doors and locks were added in 1824 when the building was converted into a debtor's prison, the purpose it served until 1849. *Accomack Co.: Rte. 764, in town of Accomac.*

WY-88 THIRD ELIZABETH CITY PARISH CHURCH

Here is the site of "the New Church of Kecoughtan," built before 1667 on Pembroke Farm as the third church of Elizabeth City Parish, established in 1610. It was a frame building and its brick foundation and some early colonial tombstones remain. When the town of Hampton was founded in 1691, this church lay outside it, and in 1727 was ordered to be replaced by a fourth parish church within the town, the existing St. John's Church, Hampton. *Hampton: Rte. 351 (Pembroke Ave. and Parkdale St.).*

WY-89 SECOND CHURCH AT KECOUGHTAN

Nearby a monument marks the site of the second church at Kecoughtan (later Hampton), built in 1624 for Elizabeth City Parish, established 1610 and now the oldest Protestant parish in continuous existence in America. This building was replaced before 1667 by a third parish church west of the town and was pulled down in 1698. *Hampton: Tyler St., at Exit 267 of I-64.*

WY-90 FIRST CHURCH AT KECOUGHTAN

Near here on the church creek stood the first church at Kecoughtan (later Hampton). Built on the Parish Glebe Farm about 1616, as the first church of the oldest continuous settlement of English origin in America, William Mease was the first known minister of the Parish from 1613 until about 1620. *Hampton: LaSalle and Kenmore sts.*

WY-91 CAMP HAMILTON

In this vicinity was situated Camp Hamilton, a large camp of Union troops first occupied in May, 1861. A great military hospital, Hampton Hospital, was here. *Hampton: College Pl. and E. Queen St.*

WY-92 BUCKROE

In 1620, Frenchmen sent over to plant mulberry trees and grape vines settled here. The name was taken from a place in England. *Hampton ("old" Elizabeth City Co.): at Buckroe Beach (Atlantic Ave. and Mallo St.).*

WY-93 PHOEBUS

Settled as Mill Creek and Strawberry Banks by English Colonists, the Town of Phoebus was "Roseland Farm" until 1871 when it was divided into lots and became known as Chesapeake City. When the town was incorporated in 1900, it was named PHOEBUS in honor of its leading citizen, Harrison Phoebus. *Hampton Co.: County St. and Woodland Rd.*

WY-94 PHOEBUS

Settled as Mill Creek and Strawberry Banks by English Colonists, the Town of Phoebus was "Roseland Farm" until 1871 when it was divided into lots and became known as Chesapeake City. When the town was incorporated in 1900, it was named PHOEBUS in honor of its leading citizen, Harrison Phoebus. *Hampton: Mallory St., at Exit 268 of I-64.*

X-3 FRANCES DICKENSON SCOTT JOHNSON

Near this site is the grave of Frances Dickenson Scott Johnson (died 1796), sister of Henry Dickenson who was the first clerk of Russell County. In 1785, while living in Powell's Valley in Scott County, her first husband, Archibald Scott, and their four children were murdered by Indians, and she was taken captive. She utimately escaped, and after wandering in the rugged mountains of Kentucky for nearly a month, made her way back to Russell County. She later married Thomas Johnson. *Russell Co.: Rte. 80 and Rte. 619, 3.8 miles e. of Rte. 19/460.*

X-4 OLD RUSSELL COUNTY COURTHOUSE

This building, erected in 1799, served as the second courthouse of Russell County and is one of the earliest public buildings still standing in Southwest Virginia. Russell County was formed in 1786 from Washington County and originally encompassed the greater part of what is now Lee, Scott, Dickenson, Buchanan, and Tazewell counties. The county sold the building when the county seat was moved to the town of Lebanon in 1818. *Russell Co.: Rte. 19, .5 mile e. of Rte. 71/82 in Lebanon.*

X-5 EARLY SETTLERS IN RUSSELL COUNTY

In 1787, Isaiah Salyer (1752–1818), son of Zachariah Salyer (1730–1789) of North Carolina, settled on Copper Creek, two miles southeast of here. Isaiah's brothers John Benjamin, and Zachariah, and sisters Sarah, wife of Solomon Saylor, and Rebecca, wife of Stephen Kilgore, settled on nearby land. The Salyer land was officially surveyed in 1790. The Salyers intermarried with other Virginia pioneer families—Castle, Isaacs, Nickels, Stapleton, Vicars, and Byerley. *Russell Co.: Rte. 71, at Grassy Creek Church.*

X-6 RUSSELL COURTHOUSE

The county government was organized at Russell's Fort, May 9, 1786, with the following officers: Alexander Barnett, County Lieutenant; David Ward, Sheriff; Henry Dickenson, Clerk. Justices: Alexander Barnett, Thomas Carter, Henry Smith, Henry Dickenson, David Ward, John Thompson, Samuel Ritchie. The present courthouse was built in 1874. *Russell Co.: Rte. 19, at Lebanon.*

X-7 RUSSELL'S FORT

On the hill to the north stood Russell's Fort, an important link in the chain of forts built to protect settlers on Clinch River in the Indian War of 1774. William Russell, who established it, was a prominent soldier of the Revolution. *Russell Co.: Rte. 615, at Castlewood.*

X-8 GLADE HOLLOW FORT

A short distance south stood Glade Hollow Fort, garrisoned by twenty-one men in 1774. From Witten's to Blackmore's these Clinch Valley forts were the frontier defenses in Dunmore's War, 1774. *Russell Co.: Rte. 71, 1 mile w. of Lebanon.*

X-9* ELK GARDEN FORT

A short distance south stood the fort commanded by John Kinkead, 1774. It was then the center of Elk Garden community, later the homestead of William A. Stuart. The house was built near the site of the fort. *Russell Co.: Rte. 19, 8 miles e. of Lebanon.*

X-9 ELK GARDEN FORT

This fort was one of a string of defensive posts and protective forts that served the community of Elk Garden and isolated homes in the Clinch Valley in the 18th century. There is no known date of construction, but it is believed to have been a large and well-stockaded fort. An important outpost during the Indian wars of the frontier period, it was garrisoned by 1774 under the command of Captain John Kinkead. The site was later the homestead of Governor Henry Carter Stuart (1914–1918). *Russell Co.: Rte. 19, 8 miles e. of Lebanon.*

X-10 WILLIAM WYNNE'S FORT

On the hillside to the north stood Wynne's Fort. A settlement was made here as early as 1752. Some years later William Wynne obtained land here and built a neighborhood fort. After 1776 the State government built a fort and garrisoned it. *Tazewell Co.: Bus. Rte. 19, in Tazewell.*

X-11 TAZEWELL

The town was laid off as the county seat in 1800, when Tazewell County was formed, on land given by William Peery and Samuel Ferguson. First known as Jeffersonville, the name was changed to Tazewell, for Senator Henry Tazewell. Averell was here in May, 1864, and the town was occupied in other raids. It was incorporated in 1866. *Tazewell Co.: Bus. Rte. 19, at Tazewell.*

X-12 BURKE'S GARDEN

Eight miles east is Burke's Garden, discovered by James Burke in 1749. Major Lewis's expedition against the Indians, 1756, camped there, and Burke's fort was there in 1774. In 1781 Indians raided into Burke's Garden, carrying off the wife and children of Thomas Ingles. *Tazewell Co.: Rte. 61, 1.8 miles e. of Tazewell.*

X-12-a BURKE'S GARDEN

Known for its fertility and great natural beauty, the bowl-shaped Burke's Garden is the highest valley in Virginia. James Burke discovered it during the 1740s while hunting and settled here about 1754. After four years Burke and his family moved to North Carolina, where he died in 1783. The threat of Indian attack and the remoteness of the area discouraged permanent white settlement until the early 19th century. *Tazewell Co.: Rtes. 666 and 623.*

X-12-a*   BURKE'S GARDEN

Burke's Garden was first settled about 1754 by James Burke who had been hunting in the area during the previous decade. Burke lived here until 1774 when he and his wife were killed by the Indians. Two years later a fort was erected here as a defense from the Indians. The area around Burke's Garden is known for its great natural beauty. *Tazewell Co.: Rtes. 666 and 623.*

X-13   MAIDEN SPRINGS FORT

On the hillside to the west stood Maiden Springs Fort, also known as Reese Bowen's Fort. It was garrisoned in Dunmore's War, 1774. Reese Bowen, the founder, fought at Point Pleasant, 1774, and was killed at King's Mountain, 1780. *Tazewell Co.: Rte. 91, 12 miles s.w. of Tazewell.*

X-14   BIG CRAB ORCHARD OR WITTEN'S
        FORT

On the hillside to the south stood Big Crab Orchard Fort, also known as Witten's Fort. Thomas Witten obtained land here in 1771 and built the fort as a neighborhood place of refuge. It was garrisoned in Dunmore's War, 1774. *Tazewell Co.: Rte. 19/460 and Bus. Rte. 19, at Tazewell.*

X-15   BLUEFIELD, VIRGINIA

The place was first known as "Pin Hook." In 1883 the New River branch of the N. & W. Railroad was completed here and the first coal shipped from the Pocahontas mines. The town of Graham was incorporated in 1884 and named for Thomas Graham of Philadelphia. The town was reincorporated and the name changed to Bluefield, 1924, to conform to its sister city. *Tazewell Co.: Rte. 19, at w. entrance to Bluefield.*

X-16   INDIAN OUTRAGES

Four miles south the first Indian attack in the Upper Clinch Valley took place, September 8, 1774. John Henry was wounded and his wife and children were carried into captivity. In 1781, Indians attacked the house of Robert Maxwell, near here, and killed two girls. *Tazewell Co.: Bus. Rte. 19, 2 miles w. of Tazewell.*

X-17   SMITH'S FORT

Near here, in 1774, stood Daniel Smith's Fort, also known as Fort Christian. The fort was named for Smith, who was a surveyor and captain of the military company on upper Clinch River. *Russell Co.: Rte. 19, 17.5 miles e. of Lebanon.*

X-18   MOORE'S FORT

Near here, on Clinch River, stood Moore's Fort. Daniel Boone, on his way to Kentucky with a party of settlers, stopped here for some time. On September 29, 1774, Indians made an attack here from ambush, killing John Duncan. *Russell Co.: Alt. Rte. 58, e. entrance of St. Paul.*

X-20   COEBURN

The town stands on the site of one of Christopher Gist's camps when he was returning from his exploration of the Ohio Valley about 1750. Big Tom and Little Tom creeks are named for him and his son. The name of the town comes from W. W. Coe, chief engineer of the N. & W. Railroad, and Judge W. E. Burns of Lebanon. Coeburn was incorporated in 1894. *Wise Co.: Rte. 58 at Rte. 72, in Coeburn.*

X-21 NORTON

As early as 1750 Christopher Gist explored in this vicinity. The first house here was built about 1785 by William Prince, for whom the settlement was called Prince's Flat. It was later named Norton for Eckstein Norton, president of the Louisville and Nashville Railroad, and was incorporated in 1894. Norton is the center of a bituminous coal region. High Knob, National Forest area, is nearby. *Wise Co.: Rte. 23, at Norton.*

X-22* BENGE'S GAP

The pass to the south was a secret route named Benge's Gap for an Indian half-breed who used it in making surprise attacks on settlers. The latter discovered the gap. When Benge was returning to it after his last raid, 1794, his party was attacked by settlers and exterminated. *Wise Co.: Alt. Rte. 58, at Norton.*

X-23 APPALACHIA

The town sprang up after the Louisville and Nashville Railroad and Southern Railroad made a junction here in 1890. Named for the Appalachian Mountains, in the heart of which it stands, it was incorporated in 1906; the streets were laid out in 1907. Appalachia, in the Jefferson National Forest area, is the trading center of the Wise coal fields. *Wise Co.: Rte. 78 and Bus. Rte. 23.*

X-24 SEMINARY METHODIST CHURCH

The foundation of this Methodist Church was laid in 1851 and built from brick made near the church. The first Board of Trustees: Henry C. Slemp, W. N. G. Barron, James F. Jones, John W. Slemp, John Snodgrass. First Circuit Rider: W. W. Farthing. *Lee Co.: Alt. Rte. 58, 5 miles s.w. of Big Stone Gap.*

X-25 PISGAH UNITED METHODIST CHURCH

The Reverend John Kobler preached the first sermon by a Methodist in Tazewell County here in 1793 and received eleven members into the church. The church building, constructed on a parcel of land donated by Thomas Peery, was the first church of any denomination in the county. The construction of the Clinch Valley Railroad in 1889 necessitated the relocation of the church to its present site. Pisgah is the mother church of numerous Methodist and later United Methodist congregations and ministers. *Tazewell Co.: Rte. 19/460 and Bus. Rte. 19.*

X-26* MEMBERS OF CONGRESS

Within one mile of this point three men were born who afterwards became members of Congress: James B. Richmond, 46th Congress, March 4, 1879–March 4, 1881. Campbell Slemp, 58th, 59th and 60th Congresses, March 4, 1903–October 13, 1907. Campbell Bascom Slemp, 61st–67th Congresses, October 13, 1907–March 3, 1923. Also: Jonathan Richmond (1805–1871), Brigadier General Virginia Militia. *Lee Co.: Alt. Rte. 58, 6 miles s.w. of Big Stone Gap.*

X-27 MATHIAS HARMAN, SR.

Just east of here is the last home site and grave of Mathias Harman, Sr. (1736–1832), early explorer, hunter and Revolutionary War veteran. Harman helped establish the first permanent English settlement in eastern Kentucky in 1755. In 1789 he founded Harman's Station on the Levisa River near John's Creek in present-day Johnson County. He and his wife, Lydia, settled in this area in 1803. *Tazewell Co.: Rte. 637, 7 miles n. of Rte. 460.*

X-28 FIRST COURT FOR TAZEWELL COUNTY

The first court for Tazewell County was held June 1800 at the residence of Henry Harman, Jr. The house site is located two tenths of a mile to the northeast. Harman's grave is to the north. In the same burying ground is the marked grave of his brother Daniel Harman who was killed by Indians in 1791. *Tazewell Co.: Rte. 19 and Bus. Rte. 460.*

X-30 PENNINGTON GAP

Pennington Gap is a mountain pass named for an early settler. The town came into existence with the extension of the Louisville and Nashville Railroad, 1890. It was incorporated in 1891. Standing on a shortcut highway to eastern Kentucky, it is a center for an extensive coal-mining region. *Lee Co.: Alt. Rte. 58, at Pennington Gap.*

X-31 BLUEFIELD COLLEGE

Bluefield College was chartered in May 1920 as "an institution of learning for the instruction of boys and men and girls and women in literature, philosophy and the liberal and useful arts." Opened as a junior college in 1922 with three buildings and strong support from the Baptist General Association of Virginia and citizens of the area, Bluefield College was accredited by the Southern Association of Colleges and Schools as a four-year institution in 1977. *Tazewell Co.: Rte. 102, .3 mile w. of West Virginia line.*

XB-4 WISE

This town, one of the highest in Virginia, was built on land first owned by Pierre de Tarbeau, French nobleman. Originally known as Big Glades, it became Gladesville in 1856. A first courthouse, built in 1858, was burned by Union troops. An action was fought here, July 7, 1863, between Confederates and Union raiders. The name was changed to Wise when the town was rechartered in 1928. *Wise Co.: Bus. Rte. 23 (Main St.), at Wise.*

XB-7* POUND GAP

Christopher Gist, returning from the Ohio River, crossed this gap in 1751. James A. Garfield (afterward President) with Union troops forced this gap in March, 1862. In June, 1864, John H. Morgan, on his Kentucky raid, forced it from the Virginia side, capturing and destroying much property. *Wise Co.: Rte. 23, 4 miles n. of Pound.*

XB-10 OLD BUFFALO SCHOOL

Established in 1875 on land given by Simpson Dyer, the Old Buffalo School became the first free school of Dickenson County in 1880. Alexander Johnson Skeen served as first teacher. The school remained in operation for twenty-five years. During which time it educated many future leaders in the area. *Dickenson Co.: Rte. 63, at Nora.*

XB-11 CLINTWOOD

The name originally was Holly Creek. In 1882 the county seat of Dickenson County was moved from Ervington to this place, which was named Clintwood for Major Henry Clinton Wood. The town was incorporated in 1894. With the coming of the railroad to the county in 1915, the population rapidly increased as the mineral and timber resources were opened. *Dickenson Co.: Rte. 83, at Clintwood.*

XB-12* EARLY SETTLER

Near here, on Holly Creek, John Mullins settled in 1829; becoming the second settler in this county. The county seat was moved from Nora to Clintwood in 1882. *Dickenson Co.: Rte. 83, at Clintwood.*

XB-13 JOHN MULLINS

Near here on Holly Creek, John Mullins settled in 1829, becoming the second settler in Dickenson County. His father John Mullins, the only known Revolutionary War soldier resting in this county, spent his last years here with his son. He died in 1849 and is buried nearby. *Dickenson Co.: Rte. T-1009, at Clintwood.*

XB-20* FIRST SETTLER

Near here "Fighting" Dick Colley, from Clinch River, built, in 1816, his three-walled cabin and became the first permanent settler in this section. *Dickenson Co.: Rte. 83, at Haysi.*

XB-23 INDIAN OUTRAGE

In 1792, Indians attacked the home of David Musick, near Honaker, Russell County, killing him and capturing his wife and five children. Near here the Indians were overtaken by pursuing settlers and the captives were retaken. *Dickenson Co.: Rte. 83, at Haysi.*

XB-24 COLLEY'S CABIN

Near here stood the cabin of Richard "Fighting Dick" Colley who was one of the earliest settlers in what is now Dickenson County. *Dickenson Co.: Rte. 80, 3 miles s. of Haysi.*

XB-25 GRUNDY

This place became the county seat when Buchanan County was formed, in 1858, and was probably named for Felix Grundy of Tennessee, statesman. In October, 1864, the Union General Burbridge passed through Grundy on his raid to Saltville. The town was incorporated in 1876. *Buchanan Co.: Buchanan Co. Courthouse.*

XC-4* DORTOR'S FORT

The old building just to the east is Dortor's Fort, built as a protection for the early settlers from Indian attacks. Robin Kilgore lived here. *Scott Co.: Rte. 71, 1.5 miles w. of Nickelsville.*

XH-1 MOLLY TYNES' RIDE

To the north was "Rocky Dell," the home of Samuel Tynes. From here on July 17, 1863, his daughter Molly rode across the mountains to Wytheville to warn the town of an attack by Federal forces under Colonel J. T. Toland. *Tazewell Co.: Rte. 61, 1.8 miles e. of Tazewell.*

XH-2 SHAWVER MILL

The Shawver Mill community grew up here around the gristmill that George Shawver built before 1860. William Leffel and Adam Britts soon built sawmills, and the community developed like many in Virginia during the 19th century. By 1911 it sustained a general store, Odd Fellows hall, post office, cemetery, two churches, and a baseball team. The end of milling operations in 1947, together with new road construction, diminished the community. By 1992 only the mill dam, the cemetery on the hill, and Chestnut Grove Church survived. *Tazewell Co.: Rte. 61 at Rte. 614.*

XL-4 RICHLANDS

This fertile region was known as Richlands from an early period. In 1782 and later Richlands was a militia station for frontier defense. The town was laid off in 1890, with the coming of the Norfolk and Western Railroad, and was incorporated in 1891. It is the center of an agricultural section. *Tazewell Co.: Rte. 460, at Richlands.*

XL-5 SITE OF JAMES BURKE'S GARDEN

In this fertile soil James Burke, who discovered this "hunter's paradise," planted potato peelings by the campfire of a 1748 surveying party led by Col. James Patton. The next year a fine crop of potatoes was found here; so, the name "Burke's Garden" was jokingly given. On the bluff east of Station Creek, Burke built a cabin where he lived from 1753 to 1756, when he was driven out by the Shawnees. *Tazewell Co.: Rte. 623, in Burke's Garden.*

XP-4 POCAHONTAS

This region was visited by the explorer, Dr. Thomas Walker, in 1750. Following a report by Captain I. A. Welch in 1873, the first coal mine was opened here in 1882. Shipment of coal followed in 1883, when the Norfolk and Western Railroad reached this point from Radford. First known as "Powell's Bottom," the town was incorporated in 1884 and named for the Indian princess Pocahontas. *Tazewell Co.: Rte. 102, just e. of Pocahontas.*

XP-5 ABB'S VALLEY

Five miles southwest is Abb's Valley, discovered by Absalom Looney. James Moore and Robert Poage were the first settlers, about 1770. In July, 1786, Shawnee Indians raided the valley, killing or carrying into captivity the Moore family. Mary (Polly) Moore, Martha Evans and James Moore (captured earlier) finally returned. They are known as "The Captives of Abb's Valley." *Tazewell Co.: Rte. 102, just e. of Pocahontas.*

XP-6 ENGAGEMENT AT FALLS MILLS

Here at dawn on 20 July 1863 the Confederate cavalry of Maj. Andrew J. May surprised a Union raiding party led by Lt. Col. Freeman E. Franklin. Aroused from its bivouac in Brown's Meadow, where it was preparing to burn the Falls Mill, the Union cavalry fled north toward Abb's Valley. Brig. Gen. John S. Williams's Confederate cavalry struck the raiders as they withdrew up the valley, compelling them to abandon captured livestock and contraband slaves. *Tazewell Co.: Rte. 102 at Rte. 643.*

Markers Without Letter-Number Symbols

The markers that follow were never assigned a letter and number designation and are therefore listed in alphabetical order.

BATTLE OF SEAWELL'S POINT

Confederate batteries at Seawall's Point were located near here. These batteries mounting twenty 32-pounders, three 42-pounder carronades, and six 9-inch rifles, successfully repulsed an attack by the Federal fleet, May 19, 1861. This was the first engagement fought in Virginia in the War between the States. These batteries, under fire many times, were never silenced or captured. They were abandoned when Norfolk was evacuated May 10, 1862. *Norfolk: inside naval base grounds.*

BUCKINGHAM COURTHOUSE

Designed by Thomas Jefferson in 1821, burned in 1869, rebuilt in 1873. The exterior follows Jefferson's plan with the interior redesigned. Copy of original plan and specifications on display in courthouse. Registered in 1969 as a National and Virginia historic landmark. Renovated in 1976. *Buckingham Co.: Rte. 60, at Buckingham Court House.*

THE BURNING OF NORFOLK

Lord Dunmore's fleet of seven vessels, extending in line of battle in the Elizabeth River from the eastern to the western end of Main Street, bombarded the Borough of Norfolk January 1, 1776. H.M.S. Liverpool lay off the end of Church Street. Much damage was done and many houses were burned. Nearly all remaining houses were later destroyed by the Virginia militia to prevent Dunmore's return. *Norfolk: St. Paul's Blvd. and City Hall Ave.*

CAMP TALBOT

Half a mile west is site of Confederate Camp. Georgia and Virginia troops defending Norfolk were encamped there from April, 1861, until the evacuation of the city, May 10, 1862. *Norfolk: Oak Grove Rd. and Granby St.*

CRANEY ISLAND

is two miles down, and across the Elizabeth River from this point. There on June 22, 1813, the Virginia militia under General Robert B. Taylor of Norfolk, without losing a man, defeated 4,000 British troops. They had come to destroy Norfolk and Portsmouth. Repulsed at Craney Island, they wreaked their vengeance on Hampton, which was taken, pillaged, and well-nigh destroyed. *Norfolk: Norfolk-Southern R.R. Piers, Old Dominion Wharf.*

EASTERN TOWN LIMIT

The eastern limit of the fifty acres constituting the original town of Norfolk, established by Act of June, 1680, is a few feet east of this point. The land was purchased as a port for Lower Norfolk County from Nicholas Wise, Jr., for "Tenn thousand pounds of tobacco and caske." It was deeded by him August 16, 1682, to Capt. William Robinson and Lt. Col. Anthony Lawson feoffees in trust for Lower Norfolk County. *Norfolk: East Main St.*

FATHER RYAN'S HOME

On Chapel Street south of this point stood the home of Father Abram J. Ryan, beloved poet of the Confederacy.
"But their memories e'er shall
    remain for us
And their names, bright names,
    without stain for us;
The glory they won shall not wane
    for us,
In legend and lay-our heroes in
    Gray
Shall forever live over again for
    us."
Norfolk: Tidewater Dr. and Lafayette Blvd.

THE FIRST CONFEDERATE FLAG

flown in the City of Norfolk was unfurled from a house-top about a block and a half east of this corner, April 2, 1861, two weeks before the secession of Virginia from the Union. *Norfolk: Market St. at Monticello Ave.*

FORT BARBOUR

This is the site of Fort Barbour, which, with Forts Tar, Norfolk, and Nelson, constituted the outer defenses of Norfolk and Portsmouth against the British in the War of 1812. Fort Barbour guarded against hostile advances from the north and east. *Norfolk: Princess Anne Rd. and Church St.*

FORT FARTHING OR TOWN POINT

Here at a cedar tree was the western limit of the fifty acres constituting the original town of Norfolk. The land was bought in 1682 as a port for Lower Norfolk County from Nicholas Wise, Jr., for "tenn thousand pounds of tobacco and caske." It was deeded to Capt. Wm. Robinson and Lt. Col. Anthony Lawson as feoffees in trust for the county. *Norfolk: near end of West Main St.*

FORT TAR

This is the site of Fort Tar, built to guard the approach to the city from the west. Situated on the outskirts of Norfolk, near Armistead's Bridge, which spanned Glebe Creek near by, it served with Forts Barbour, Norfolk, and Nelson to protect Norfolk and Portsmouth from invasion by the British in the War of 1812. *Norfolk: Monticello Ave. n. of Virginia Beach Blvd.*

INDIAN POOL BRIDGE*

A bridge has spanned Tanner's Creek (now called Lafayette River) at this—the ancient Indian Pool Point—since 1851. The bridge was burned by the Confederates to retard the advance of the Federal forces upon Norfolk, May 10, 1862. *Norfolk: New Granby St. Bridge.*

JOHN HUNTER HOLT

Norfolk's first newspaper, The Virginia Gazette or Norfolk Intelligencer, was put out of business when its press was seized by British troops near this spot on September 30, 1775. The editor, John Hunter Holt, who had defied Governor Dunmore, then volunteered for service in the Revolutionary Army. He died in Richmond June 8, 1787. *Norfolk: Main St., s. of Commercial Pl.*

MAIN STREET

This street followed a ridge of high land in the original town site, which was almost an island. It was laid out in the division of the fifty acres of Town Lands in 1682, and the angles in it were made to avoid the two creeks. Dunmore's ships lay along Main Street when they bombarded Norfolk, January 1, 1776. *Norfolk: Main St. facing Granby St.*

THE NATIONAL HOTEL

originally French's, stood on this site. In it were entertained Prince Louis Napoleon (later Napoleon III) of France, 1837; General Winfield Scott, 1858; G. P. R. James, 1863; and President Tyler, 1859. It was later known as the Purcell House. *Norfolk: St. Paul's Blvd. opposite Courts Building.*

NORTHERN LIMIT OF OLD NORFOLK

This marks the northern limit of the fifty acres constituting the original town of Norfolk. It was bounded on the north by Town Back Creek and Dun-in-the-Mire Creek. The land was purchased as a port for Lower Norfolk County for "tenn thousand pounds of tobacco and caske," being deeded to feoffees in trust for the county in 1682. It was divided into streets and sold in half-acre lots. *Norfolk: City Hall Ave. and St. Paul's Blvd.*

OLD ACADEMIC BUILDING SITE

On this site September 21, 1930, the first classes for 206 students were held at the Norfolk Division of the College of William and Mary, now Old Dominion University. That year the Norfolk School Board gave the building, constructed in 1912 as the Larchmont Elementary School, to William and Mary to establish the Division. The building served the institution until 1975 when it was razed. *Norfolk: on grounds of Old Dominion University.*

OLD NORFOLK COUNTY COURT HOUSE

The red brick house one block east was the courthouse of Norfolk County from 1784 to 1858. In the latter year the court was transferred to Portsmouth. *Norfolk: Chestnut and Pine sts.*

SALISBURY

Only a few yards from here stood Salisbury. Here Patrick Henry lived during his fourth and fifth terms as Governor of Virginia, 1784–1786. The Confederate Major General Edward Johnson lived here in his later years and died here. *Chesterfield Co.: Rte. 902, on Salisbury Rd.*

SELDEN'S HOME

This house was built in 1807 as the country residence of Dr. William B. Selden. During the Federal occupation of Norfolk (1862–1865) it was seized and occupied as the headquarters of the Federal commanders. On his last visit to Norfolk, April, 1870, General Robert E. Lee was the guest here of his friend, Dr. William Selden, Surgeon, C.S.A. *Norfolk: Freemason and Botetourt sts.*

SITE OF LOWER NORFOLK COUNTY COURT

This was the site of the courthouse from 1689–1776. A debtor's prison, jail, ducking stool and pillory were in the rear. The Hustings Court of the Borough of Norfolk, erected on adjoining property in 1752, was moved in 1799 to Main and Nebraska streets, and in 1850 to the present courthouse on Bank Street. *Norfolk: Main St. facing Commercial Place.*

TAZEWELL'S HOME

On this site stood the residence of Littleton Waller Tazewell (1774–1860), Lawyer, Congressman, United States Senator, Governor of Virginia. His life was spent in the service of his native Virginia. *Norfolk: Tazewell St. near Granby St.*

TRIPOLI STREET

Monticello Avenue, south of Market Street, was formerly Tripoli Street. It was named in honor of Commodore Stephen Decatur's victory over the Barbary pirates, after he had requested that his own name should not be used. *Norfolk: City Hall Ave. and Monticello Ave.*

VIRGINIA AND MONITOR

Across Hampton Roads from this point the C.S.S. Virginia (Merrimac) and the U.S.S. Monitor fought, March 9, 1862. This was the first combat between ironclad vessels in the history of the world. After a severe engagement in which each vessel failed to pierce the other's armour, the Monitor retired. On the previous day, the Virginia had destroyed the U.S.S. Congress and the U.S.S. Cumberland, and dispersed the remainder of the Federal fleet. *Norfolk: W. Ocean View Ave. between Thirteenth View and Fourteenth View sts.*

WHITTLE HOME

This house was built about 1791 and bought in 1803 by Richard Taylor, whose descendants still occupy it (1931). It was the home of Richard Lucien Page, Lieut. U.S.N., Capt. C.S.N., Brig. Gen. C.S.A.; of William Conway Whittle, Jr., executive officer of the C.S.S. Shenandoah; the birthplace of Walter H. Taylor, Lt. Col. C.S.A., who served on Lee's staff for the whole period of the war. *Norfolk: 227 W. Freemason St., at Duke St.*

YOUEL-CONDON HOUSE

Built in 1819 by William Youel, Scottish immigrant who fought in the American Revolution. William, who died in 1834 at age 100, and his wife are buried in the family cemetery up the hill. The house, later owned by William's son and grandson, was bought by David Condon in 1863 and has been owned since then by the Condon family. *Rockbridge Co.: Rte. 39, 3.5 miles e. of Goshen.*

The following markers were a special gift from the French Government, Committee of the Bicentennial, to the Commonwealth of Virginia in 1976. Although not numbered in the state's marker system, they are the property of the Commonwealth and carry significant and interesting historical information.

WASHINGTON-ROCHAMBEAU ROUTE

Generals Washington and Rochambeau slept here the night of September 12, 1781. Having learned that Admiral de Grasse had put to sea to fight the British fleet under Admiral Graves, Washington and Rochambeau with their staffs hastened to Williamsburg. *Spotsylvania Co.: Bus. Rte. 17, 200 ft. from Rte. 1.*

WASHINGTON-ROCHAMBEAU ROUTE

General Washington, in 1781, rode 60 miles in one day from Baltimore to Mount Vernon which he had not visited for over 6 years. General Rochambeau arrived the next day with his and Washington's staff. They spent September 10 and 11 at Mount Vernon before going on to Fredericksburg. *Fairfax Co.: Rte. 235, 800 ft. from Mount Vernon entrance.*

WASHINGTON-ROCHAMBEAU ROUTE

General Washington and General Rochambeau passed here on September 13, 1781 on their way to victory at Yorktown. One mile south, they turned east on State Route 605. *Hanover Co.: Rte. 301, at Hanover Courthouse.*

WASHINGTON-ROCHAMBEAU ROUTE

Generals Washington and Rochambeau and their staffs arrived in Williamsburg on September 14, 1781. Here they gathered their troops and supplies prior to laying siege to Cornwallis at Yorktown 12 miles away on September 28, 1781. *James City Co.: Rte. 60, .4 mile w. of Williamsburg town limits.*

WASHINGTON-ROCHAMBEAU ROUTE

General Washington, in 1781, rode 60 miles in one day from Baltimore to Mount Vernon which he had not visited for over 6 years. General Rochambeau arrived the next day with his and Washington's staff. They spent September 10 and 11 at Mount Vernon before going on to Fredericksburg. *Fairfax Co.: Rte. 235, 800 ft. from Mount Vernon entrance.*

Alphabetical Index

First Synagogue of Beth El Hebrew Congregation, Site of, E-92
First Trolley Car System in Richmond, SA-25
Fisher's Hill, Battle of, A-22*, A-23
Fitchett's Wharf, N-86
Five Forks, Battle of, K-307
Fleming, Dr. William, A-64
Flight of Richard C. duPont, W-219
Flippo's, Doctor, E-29*
Flowerdew Hundred, K-214
Floyd, KG-5
Floyd, Governor, Grave, KH-1
Fluvanna County Courthouse, F-49
Flying Point, K-223
Folly Castle, QA-1
Fonthill, N-20, N-20*
Ford, Reuben, V-18
Forerunner of Wireless Telegraphy, T-11
Fork Church, E-5
Fork Union Academy, GA-33
Formation of the Southern Methodist Church, QA-15
Fort Algernourne, W-89
Fort Barbour, p. 203
Fort Blackmore, K-13
Fort Blackwater, A-93
Fort Bowman, A-55*
Fort Breckenridge, D-26
Fort Christanna, S-66, U-90*
Fort Collier, A-4*
Fort Dickinson, KB-75
Fort Dinwiddie, Q-5
Fort Early, Q-6-1
Fort Edward Johnson, W-159*
Fort Eustis, W-56*
Fort Farthing or Town Point, p. 203
Fort George on the Bullpasture River, W-148
Fort Harrison, D-1
Fort Harrison, Varina and, V-2
Fort Henry, QA-6
Fort Humphreys, E-64*
Fort James, W-23
Fort Lewis, D-24
Fort Long, C-31*
Fort Lowry, N-29
Fort Lowry—Camp Byron, N-24

Fort McCausland, Q-6-2
Fort Monroe, W-90
Fort Nelson, K-265*
Fort Pickett, K-173
Forts Henry and Charles, W-86*
Fort Tar, p. 203
Fort Trial, A-54
Fort Vause, K-73
Fort William, D-29
Fort Young, D-27
"Fotheringay," K-67
Founder of Presbyterianism, WY-15
Francisco's Fight, M-18
Franklin, U-126
Frazier's Farm, To, W-1*
Fredericksburg, E-45*, E-46-a, E-46-b*
Fredericksburg, Battles of, E-44*
Fredericksburg Campaign, C-56*, N-4
Fredericksville Furnace, EM-1
Freedom's Fortress, W-94
Freeman, Allen Weir, M.D., 1881–1954, Q-6-16*
Freeman, Douglas Southall, Ph.D., 1886–1953, Q-6-17
Fries, UE-2
Fries—Center of Early Recorded Country Music, UE-6
Frontier Fort, A-20, U-32

Galax, U-26
Gallant Pelham, The, N-3
Gate City, K-11
Geographical Center of Virginia, O-39
Germanna, J-34, J-34*
Germanna Ford, J-35
Gettysburg Campaign, B-32*, FF-4*, J-14*, J-25, T-38
Gettysburg Campaign, Opening of, F-13
Gibson Girl, Q-5-c
Giles County, First Court of, KG-20
Giles's Home, O-31
Gillette, Major Joseph E., U-123
Glade Hollow Fort, X-8
Glass, Carter, Q-6-12
Glebe, The, JT-3
Glebe Burying Ground, AL-5
Glebe Church, K-258

Subject Index

CHURCHES AND OTHER RELIGIOUS BUILDINGS AND SITES

The church has played a major role in Virginia's history since the settlement period. The great majority of markers note the sites of church buildings and cemeteries; many markers point out church buildings that are still standing. A few deal with the history and leaders of Virginia's religious institutions.

THE CIVIL WAR IN VIRGINIA

Many significant battles and campaigns in the American Civil War, 1861–65, were fought in Virginia, with few areas of the Commonwealth escaping its scars. The first group of markers includes information on Lee and his lieutenants. The next four groups are divided geographically: Fredericksburg and the campaign in northern Virginia; the Valley campaign and southwest Virginia; Richmond and the campaign in southeastern Virginia; and Lee's retreat to Appomattox. Today these markers are often the only visible sign of the military strategy and maneuvers of the Civil War.

COURTHOUSES AND OTHER PUBLIC BUILDINGS

The courthouse served as the center of Virginia's political life in the colonial and antebellum periods; throughout the nineteenth century and to the present day, the county courthouses have remained significant local landmarks. Other markers note the sites of institutional structures that have contributed to Virginia's history.

EXPLORATION AND EARLY SETTLEMENTS IN VIRGINIA'S TIDEWATER AND MOUNTAIN REGIONS

Early settlements include buildings, sites, and events associated with Virginia's early European settlers. Many of the seventeenth-century sites are located in the Tidewater region; a number of the eighteenth-century sites relate to the transmontane settlements.

FORTS

Forts played a major role in the defense of colonial Virginia. Many forts, particularly in the mountain regions of the state, were designed to protect settlements from Indians attacks. Few colonial fort structures exist today.

HOMES AND HOMESITES OF COLONIAL VIRGINIA

These markers include residential structures and plantations dating from before the American Revolution. Virginia, as the earliest and one of the largest of the British colonies, boasts a large number of such sites. Although the texts of these markers are basically accurate, more recent research has assigned later construction dates to a number of these houses. Many of the plantations are associated with Virginia's colonial leadership.

HOMES OF FAMOUS VIRGINIANS IN THE NINETEENTH CENTURY

This section includes birthplaces as well as major residences associated with notable citizens of the Commonwealth. All structures date from after the American Revolution.

INDUSTRY AND AGRICULTURE IN VIRGINIA

These markers point out sites of early industrial efforts in Virginia, such as grist mills, mines, and furnaces. Several other markers explain aspects of Virginia's agricultural history.

NATIVE AMERICANS

Landmarks associated with Virginia's native population are scattered throughout the state. Important sites include towns, burial grounds, and locations of Indian trails.

NATURAL FEATURES

"Natural Features" include creeks, capes, islands, points, rivers, mountains, and fords in Virginia. Many of these features are associated with events in Virginia history.

Tangier Island, Q-7-a
Upper Chippokes Creek, K-211*
Urbanna Creek, OC-40, OC-40*
Ward's Creek, K-216
Warwick River, W-62*
Waters Creek, W-64*
Windmill Point, J-87

NOTABLE PERSONS IN VIRGINIA

Markers for "Notable Persons in Virginia" include biographical data on many Virginians who attained prominence during the seventeenth through nineteenth centuries.

Asbury, Francis (Asbury's Deathplace),
  EH-8
Atkinson, Sallie Jones, K-304
Austin, Stephen F., KD-8
Ball, Mary, J-80, JT-4, JT-16
Barbee, William Randolph, C-56
Barbour, James (Barboursville), D-22
Bennett, Jessee, A-59
Bingham, George Caleb, W-220
Blow, Michael, K-230
Bocock, Thomas S., MG-3
Booth, John Wilkes, EP-9, EP-20, N-16
Bowman, Joseph (Fort Bowman), A-55*
Bowser, James, K-310
Bowyer, John (Thorn Hill Estate), A-49
Byrd, William, II, A-57
Cabell, William, OQ-5
Campbell, William, K-20
Carrington, Paul, M-9
Chambliss, John R., Jr., UM-38
Champe, John (A Revolutionary War
  Hero), B-33
Clark, George Rogers, W-199
Clay, Henry (Ashland), E-16*, ND-6
Clayton, John, NN-3
Colley, Dick, XB-20*
Colter, John, JD-15
Cooke, John Esten, B-2*
Craig, James, SN-62
Crawford, William H., RA-6

Crozet, B. Claudius (Crozet), W-173
Custis, Martha, WO-12
Decatur, Stephen (Tripoli Street), p. 205
Delius, Frederick, Q-5-g
Dresser, Charles A., R-80
Early, Jubal, Birthplace of, A-95
Eppes, John Wayles, O-38
Fairfax, Thomas Lord, Q-4-d*
Fleming, William, A-64
Floyd, John, KH-1
Ford, Reuben, V-18
Francisco, Peter, M-18
Gibbs, J. A. E., A-51
Gillette, Joseph E., U-123
Goode, John, K-132
Griffin, Cyrus, J-78
Hagan, Patrick, KA-16
Hale, Peyton Guyn, U-23
Hall, Henrietta, J-89
Harman, Mathias, Sr., X-27
Harrison, Benjamin, PA-25*
Henry, Patrick, FR-25, ND-4, R-15*,
  U-40, W-211
Henry, Sarah Winston, R-60
Holt, John Hunter, p. 204
Houston, Sam, A-52
Humphreys, Alexander, A-63
Jackson, Stonewall, Mother of, F-15
Johnson, Frances Dickenson Scott, X-3
Kemper, James Lawson, F-17
Kennon, Richard, U-80
Kenton, Simon, F-14
Lee, Richard Bland, C-18
Lee, Richard Henry, JT-6
Lewis, Andrew, K-75, K-77
Lewis, Jesse Pitman, W-163
Lewis, John, W-159
Lewis, Meriwether, W-161
Lewis, Taliaferro, W-163
Lincoln, Thomas, A-18, KB-65*
Lygon, Thomas, K-203
McCormick, Cyrus H., A-51
McDowell, John, A-40*, A-43, A-45*
McDowell, Ephraim (Red House Estate),
  A-45*
McDowell, James (Cherry Grove Estate),
  A-47
Madison, James, EP-8

SITES OF SOME NOTABLE EVENTS IN VIRGINIA'S HISTORY

A small group of markers in the Virginia system notes certain interesting events in Virginia's history.

Civilian Conservation Corps Company
2386, S-29
Constitution Forest, R-59
Douthat State Park, L-3
Fairy Stone State Park, AS-1
First Ruritan Club, U-127
Fort Eustis, W-56*
Fort Pickett, K-173
Freeman, Allen Weir, M.D., Q-6-16*
Freeman, Douglas Southall, Q-6-17
Fries, UE-2
Fries—Center of Early Recorded Coun-
try Music, UE-6
Gibson Girl, Q-5-c
Glass, Carter, L-21, Q-6-12
Hospital of St. Vincent Depaul, KN-1
Hungry Mother State Park, K-33
Hurricane Camille, R-51
Lady Astor, Q-5-c
Leesylvania State Park, JQ-1
Lewis, John L., E-93
McConnell, John Preston, K-14
Meadow Farm—Birthplace of Secre-
tariat, ND-10
Montview, L-21
Moton, Robert Russa, NW-12
Munitions Plant, W-6*
"New River Train" Song, UE-7
Norfolk Botanical Gardens, KN-2
Occoquan Workhouse, E-61
Operation Torch, 1942, KV-7
Pick, General, Birthplace of, FR-27
Pierce, John Baptist, S-28
Pocahontas State Park, S-16
Puller, Tomb of, N-49
Recreational Center of Front Royal, J-12
Robert Russa Moton High School, M-1
Rockenbach, Samuel D., Q-6-18
Sandy, T. O., M-20
Seashore State Park, KV-4
750 Main Street (Danville), Q-7-e
Slemp, Campbell, X-26*
Slemp, Campbell Bascom, X-26*
Southwest Virginia Museum, I-2
Spencer, Anne, House, Q-6-20
State Colony, I-5*
State Fish Hatchery, FF-2, PB-4, UC-5
State Game Farm, W-21

Staunton River State Park, U-48
Swanson, Claude A., L-49
Tuck, William Munford, U-51
Westmoreland State Park, J-75
Wilson, Woodrow, A-61, A-62
Woodrow Wilson Rehabilitation Center,
I-18
Woodson, Carter G., F-53, F-57
Wreck of the Old 97, Q-5-b
World War Memorials, QA-3*, QA-4

VIRGINIA'S COMMUNITIES, CITIES, AND TOWNS

Markers for Virginia's communities, cities, and towns include information on the founding of these towns, together with significant historical events associated with them. Several towns noted no longer exist. Some markers indicate original boundaries of cities that have long since expanded.

Abingdon, K-49
Alexandria, Historic, E-71*
Appalachia, X-23
Ashland, E-16*
Bedford, K-134
Berryville, Q-3-a-b-c-d*
Big Stone Gap, KA-11
Blackstone, K-172
Bland, KC-1
Bluefield, Virginia, X-15
Bristol, Virginia, K-42, K-43
Buchanan, A-58
Burkeville, Historic, M-17
Callands, LT-1
Cape Charles, WY-4
Charlottesville, Q-1-a-b-d
Chilhowie, K-22
Chuckatauck, K-248
Christiansburg, K-72
City Point and Hopewell, K-205
Clintwood, XB-11
Coeburn, X-20
Crozet, W-173

VIRGINIA'S EDUCATIONAL INSTITUTIONS AND EDUCATORS

Markers in this section relate to Virginia's colleges and universities, together with secondary and primary schools. Several markers commemorate noted Virginia educators.

WARS WITH THE BRITISH—THE REVOLUTION AND THE WAR OF 1812

Two major wars were fought against the British on Virginia soil: the American Revolution and the War of 1812, both of which assured American independence. Markers note the leaders, events, sites, and battles of the wars.

Geographical Index

COUNTIES

ACCOMACK COUNTY
Area: 502 square miles

The Eastern Shore was called Accomack, the Indian name meaning the "across-the-water-place." It was one of the original shires formed in 1643. The name was changed to Northampton in 1643. In 1663 the present Accomack county was made from Northampton.

Birthplace of Governor Wise, EP-21	Bus. Rte. 13, town of Accomac
Mary Nottingham Smith High School, EP-22	Bus. Rte. 13, .5 mile e. of Rte. 13
Tangier Island, Q-7-a	on Tangier Island
Battle of Pungoteague, WY-12*	Rte. 13, at Melfa
Occahannock, WY-13	Rte. 13, at Belle Haven
Onancock, WY-14	Rte. 13, 2 miles s. of Accomac
Founder of Presbyterianism, WY-15	Rte. 13, at Temperanceville
Oak Grove Methodist Church, WY-16	Rte. 13, in Keller
The Bear and the Cub, WY-17	Rte. 13, at Keller
"The Bear and the Cub," WY-18	Rte. 178, .5 mile n. of Pungoteague
Debtor's Prison, WY-19	Rte. 764, in town of Accomac

ALBEMARLE COUNTY
Area: 751 square miles

Formed in 1744 from Goochland and named for the Earl of Albemarle, titular governor of Virginia, 1734–54. In 1761 Albemarle was divided and Buckingham and Amherst formed, and a part of Louisa was added to Albemarle. Thomas Jefferson was born in this county and lived in it.

Ash Lawn, FL-8	Rte. 695, 4 miles s. of Charlottesville
General Sumter's Boyhood, G-25*	Rte. 29, 5 miles s. of Ruckersville
Rio Mills, G-26	Rte. 29, 5.75 miles n. of Charlottesville
Barclay House and Scottsville Museum, GA-35	Rte. 6, at Scottsville
Historic Scottsville, GA-36	Rte. 20, Int. Rte. 6 in Scottsville
Hatton Ferry, GA-37	Rte. 625, 5.75 miles w. of Scottsville
Hatton Ferry, GA-38	Rte. 6, at Rte. 726, .38 mile n.w. of Scottsville
Maury's School, JE-6	Rte. 231, 4.5 miles s.e. of Gordonsville
Birthplace of Meriwether Lewis, W-161	Rte. 250, 5 miles w. of Charlottesville
Jackson's Valley Campaign, W-162	Rte. 250, at Mechums River
Revolutionary Soldiers Graves, W-163	Rte. 250, w. entrance to Charlottesville
Crozet, W-173	Rte. 240, in Crozet

Skirmish at Rio Hill, W-197	Rte. 15, 3.5 miles n. of Charlottesville
Shadwell—Thomas Jefferson's Birthplace, W-198*	Rte. 250, 3 miles e. of Charlottesville
Clark's Birthplace, W-199	Rte. 250, .2 mile e. of Charlottesville
Monticello, W-200	Charlottesville: at courthouse
Colle, W-201	Rte. 250, 4.2 miles e. of Charlottesville
Shadwell Estate, W-202	Rte. 250, 2.9 miles e. of Charlottesville
Edgehill, W-203	Rte. 250, 4.2 miles e. of Charlottesville
Castle Hill, W-204	Rte. 231, e. of Shadwell
Mechunk Creek, W-205*	Rte. 22, 6 miles e. of Shadwell

ALLEGHANY COUNTY
Area: 458 square miles

Formed in 1822 from Bath, Botetourt, and Monroe, and named for the Alleghany Mountains. At Fort Mann in this county a battle took place between settlers and Indians led by Cornstalk, 1763.

Fort Breckenbrudge, D-26	Rte. 220, 3 miles n. of Covington
Low Moor Iron Company Coke Ovens, D-33	Rte. 1101, .04 mile e. of Rte. 696
Governor Floyd's Grave, KH-1	Rte. 311, just s. of Sweet Chalybeate
Douthat State Park, L-3	Rte. 60, 1.5 miles e. of Clifton Forge
Lucy Selina Furnace, L-5	Rte. 60, at Longdale

AMELIA COUNTY
Area: 371 square miles

Formed in 1734 from Prince George and Brunswick, and named for Princess Amelia, daughter of King George II. William B. Giles, Governor of Virginia 1827–30, lived in this county.

Lee's Retreat, M-11	Rte. 360, at Amelia
Lee's Retreat, M-12	Rte. 360, 4.8 miles s.w. of Amelia
Lee's Retreat, M-13	Rte. 360, 5.3 miles s.w. of Amelia
Lee's Retreat, M-14	Rte. 360, .7 mile s.w. of Jetersville
Lee's Retreat, M-15	Rte. 360, at Jetersville
Lee's Retreat, M-19	Rte. 360, at Jetersville
Battle of Sailors (Sayler's) Creek, M-26	Rte. 617, 5 miles n.e. of Rice
Lee's Retreat, OL-10	Rte. 38, 7 miles e. of Mannboro

AMHERST COUNTY
Area: 470 square miles

Formed in 1761 from Albemarle, and named for Jeffrey, Lord Amherst, British commander in the French and Indian War. Balcony Falls are in this county.

State Colony, I-5*	Rte. 29, 1 mile n. of Lynchburg
Lynchburg Defenses, R-4*	Rte. 29, 1 mile n. of Lynchburg
Sweet Briar College Chartered 1901, R-20	Rte. 29, 2 miles s. of Amherst
Constitution Forest, R-59	Rte. 60, at Rockbridge County line
Grave of Patrick Henry's Mother, R-60	Rte. 151, just s. of Clifford
Action at Tye River, R-61	Rte. 29, s. of Tye River Bridge

APPOMATTOX COUNTY
Area: 342 square miles

Formed in 1845 from Buckingham, Prince Edward, Charlotte, and Campbell, and named for an Indian tribe. This county was the scene of Lee's surrender, April 9, 1865.

The Last Fight, K-156	Rte. 460, at Rte. 131, in Appomattox
Surrender at Appomattox, D-157	Rte. 460, at Rte. 131, in Appomattox
Appomattox Court House, New and Old, K-158, K-158*	Rte. 131, at town of Appomattox
Battle of Appomattox Station—1865, K-159	Main and Church sts. in Appomattox
Eldon, M-66	Rte. 460, at 131, in Appomattox
Eldon, M-66*	Rte. 24, 1.1 miles n. of Appomattox
Inventor of the Banjo, M-66	Rte. 24, 3.2 miles e. of Appomattox
Clay Smoking Pipes, M-67	Rte. 460, at Pamplin
Appomattox Court House Confederate Cemetery, MG-1	Rte. 24, .2 miles e. of Appomattox
The Last Positions, MG-2*	Rte. 24, 2 miles n. of Appomattox
Wildway, MG-3	Rte. 24, at Vera

ARLINGTON COUNTY
Area: 31 square miles

This county, formerly Alexandria County, was formed in 1847 from the part of the District of Columbia retroceded to Virginia. It was renamed Arlington in 1920 for Arlington estate.

Clay and Randolph Duel, C-1*	Rte. 123, near Fairfax Co. line
World's First Public Passenger Flight, C-2	Rte. 50 and Pershing Dr. at Fort Myer
First Heavier-than-Air Flight in Virginia, C-7	Rte. 50, at entrance to Fort Myer

AUGUSTA COUNTY
Area: 1,006 square miles

Formed in 1738 from Orange, and named for Augusta, Princess of Wales and mother of King George III. Originally it included a large part of the Middle West. President Woodrow Wilson was born in Staunton.

Old Providence Church, A-31	Rte. 11, 1.4 miles n. of Steeles Tavern
New Providence Church, A-39	Rte. 11, at Steeles Tavern
First Settler's Camp, A-40*	Rte. 11, at Steeles Tavern
Virginia Inventors, A-51	Rte. 11, at Steeles Tavern
Bethel Church, A-53	Rte. 11, 2.1 miles n. of Greenville
Birthplace of Woodrow Wilson, A-61	Rte. 11, 3.5 miles n. of Rte. 275
Bellefont, A-62*	Rte. 254, 1 mile e. of Rte. 11
Willow Spout, A-99	Rte. 11, .03 mile s. of Rte. 742
Glebe Burying Ground, AL-5	Rte. 876, 12 miles s.w. of Staunton
Roanoke College, I-11-a	Rte. 11, 2.1 miles n. of Greenville
Woodrow Wilson Rehabilitation Center, I-18	Rte. 250 at Rte. 358, .88 mile w. of Fishersville
Jarman's Gap, JD-14	Rte. 340, 1.2 miles n. of Waynesboro
John Colter, JD-15	Rte. 340, 2.5 miles s. of I-64
Walnut Grove, JF-15	Rte. 340, .3 mile s. of Waynesboro city limits
Last Indian Raid, W-79	Rte. 250, 4 miles w. of Staunton
Tinkling Spring Church, W-155	Rte. 608, 1.3 miles s. of Fishersville
First Settler's Grave, W-159	Rte. 250, at e. entrance of Staunton
Early's Last Battle, W-160*	Rte. 250, at w. entrance of Waynesboro
George Caleb Bingham, W-220	Rte. 256 at Rte. 668, near Grottoes bridge

BATH COUNTY
Area: 545 square miles

Formed in 1790 from Augusta, Greenbrier, and Botetourt, and probably named for the town of Bath in England. The Warm Springs and Hot Springs are in this county.

Fort Lewis, D-24	Rte. 220, 11 miles n. of Warm Springs
Fort Dickinson, KB-75	Rte. 42, 3 miles s.e. of Milboro Springs
Fort Dinwiddie, Q-5	Rte. 39, 5 miles w. of Warm Springs
Terrill Hill, Q-6	Rte. 39 at Rte. 220

BEDFORD COUNTY
Area: 790 square miles

Formed in 1753 from Lunenburg and Albemarle, and named for the fourth Duke of Bedford, English statesman. The Peaks of Otter are in this county.

Indian Remains, K-119*	Rte. 460, 12 miles w. of Bedford
Colonial Fort, K-121*	Rte. 460, 11 miles w. of Bedford

Hunter's Bivouac, K-130	Rte. 460, 3 miles w. of Bedford
Home of John Goode, K-132	Rte. 460, at Bedford
Bedford, K-134	Rte. 460, at Bedford
Peaks of Otter Road, K-136	Rte. 460, at Bedford
Poplar Forest, K-138	Rte. 460, 6.5 miles w. of Lynchburg
St. Stephen's Church, K-140	Rte. 460, 8 miles w. of Lynchburg
New London Academy, K-141	Rte. 460, at New London Academy
Quaker Baptist Church, KM-5	Rte. 24, 3 miles e. of Rtes. 122 and 24

BLAND COUNTY
Area: 360 square miles

Formed in 1861 from Wythe, Tazewell, and Giles. Named for Richard Bland, Revolutionary leader. This county is rich in coal.

Bland, KC-1	Rte. 52, .35 mile s. of Rte. 98
A Great Preacher, KC-2*	Rte. 52, 2 miles s. of Rocky Gap
One of the "Big Four," KC-3	Rte. 52, 7 miles s. of Bland

BOTETOURT COUNTY
Area: 360 square miles

Formed in 1769 from Augusta, and named for Lord Botetourt, Governor of Virginia 1768–70. Buchanan was the western terminus of the noted James River and Kanawha Canal.

Audley Paul's Fort, A-48	Rte. 11, 4.5 miles s. of Natural Bridge
Indian Massacre, A-50	Rte. 11, .9 mile n. of Buchanan
Buchanan, A-58	Rte. 11, at Buchanan
Coming of the Railroad, A-80	Rte. 11, 4.2 miles n. of Troutville
Old Carolina Road, A-81	Rte. 11, 8 miles n. of Roanoke
Cloverdale Furnace, A-82	Rte. 11, 8.2 miles n. of Roanoke
Looney's Ferry, A-91	Rte. 11, .7 mile s. of Buchanan
Cartmill's Gap, A-92	Rte. 11, 1.4 miles n. of Buchanan
Fincastle, D-28	Rte. 220, at Fincastle
Fort William, D-29	Rte. 220, 3 miles s. of Fincastle
Greenfield, D-30*	Rte. 220, 5 miles s. of Fincastle
Roanoke Valley Baptist Association, D-31	Rte. 220, near Rte. 681
Santillane, D-32	Rte. 220 at Rte. 1211, .25 mile s. of Fincastle

BRUNSWICK COUNTY
Area: 557 square miles

Formed in 1720 from Prince George, Surry, and Isle of Wight. Named for the House of Brunswick, which came to the throne of England in 1714, when George I was crowned king. Colonial Fort Christanna was in this county.

Birch's Bridge, S-57	Rte. 1, 2.8 miles s. of McKenney
Ebenezer Academy, S-58	Rte. 1, 6.8 miles n. of Cochran
Sturgeon Creek, S-60	Rte. 1, 5.7 miles n. of Cochran
Old Brunswick Courthouse, S-65	Rte. 1, at Cochran
Fort Christanna, S-66	Rte. 1, at Cochran
Meherrin History, S-72*	Rte. 1, 7.3 miles s. of Cochran
Campaign of 1865, S-79*	Rte. 1, 7.3 miles s. of Cochran
Mason's Chapel, SN-60	Rte. 46, 8 miles s. of Brunswick
Smoky Ordinary, SN-61	Rte. 712, 4.2 miles n. of Rte. 58
Fort Christanna, U-90*	Rte. 58, w. of Lawrenceville

BUCHANAN COUNTY
Area: 514 square miles

Formed in 1858 from Tazewell and Russell and named for James Buchanan, President of the United States 1857–61.

Grundy, XB-25	Buchanan County Courthouse

BUCKINGHAM COUNTY
Area:584 square miles

Formed in 1761 from Albemarle, and named for Buckinghamshire, England. Peter Francisco, noted Revolutionary soldier, lived in this county.

Carter G. Woodson, F-53	Rte. 15, 10 miles n. of Dillwyn
Female Collegiate Institute, F-54	Rte. 15, 5 miles n. of Dillwyn
Gold Mines, F-55	Rte. 15, at Dillwyn
Old Buckingham Church, F-56	Rte. 15, .75 mile s.w. of Rte. 610
Carter G. Woodson Birthplace, F-57	Rte. 15, at Rte. 670
March to Appomattox, F-59	Rte. 15, 8.8 miles s. of Sprouses
Eve of Appomattox, F-60	Rte. 15, 11.3 miles s. of Sprouses
New Store Village, F-61	Rte. 15, 11.3 miles s. of Sprouses
Millbrook—Home of John Wayles Eppes, O-38	Rte. 15, 6.5 miles s. of Rte. 60
Geographical Center of Virginia, O-39	Rtes. 60 and 24 at Mount Rush
After Appomattox, O-42	Rte. 60, 1.1 miles e. of Buckingham
Buckingham Courthouse, p. 202	Rte. 60, at Buckingham Court House

CAMPBELL COUNTY
Area: 557 square miles

Formed in 1781 from Bedford, and named for General William Campbell, hero of the battle of King's Mountain, 1780. Tarleton passed through the county in 1781. The Union General Hunter was defeated near Lynchburg, 1864.

Hat Creek Church, FR-16	Rte. 40, 2.1 miles e. of Brookneal
Patrick Henry's Grave, FR-25	Rte. 40, 2.5 miles e. of Brookneal
Birthplace of General Pick, FR-27	Rte. 40, in Brookneal
New London, K-139	Rte. 858, 4 miles w. of Lynchburg
Chestnut Hill, K-146	Rte. 501, 4 miles e. of Lynchburg
Mount Athos, K-148*	Rte. 460, 6 miles e. of Lynchburg
Oxford Furnace, K-150*	Rte. 460, 2.5 miles e. of Lynchburg
Concord Station, K-152	Rte. 460, at Concord
Shady Grove, L-12	Rte. 501, at Gladys
Origin of Lynch Law, L-30*	Rte. 29, 1 mile n. of Alta Vista
Patrick Henry's Grave, R-15*	Rte. 501, at Brookneal
Old Rustburg, R-62	Rte. 501, at Rustburg

CAROLINE COUNTY
Area: 529 square miles

Formed in 1727 from Essex, King and Queen, and King William. Named for Queen Caroline, wife of King George II. George Rogers Clark, conqueror of the Northwest, passed his youth in this county.

Lee and Grant, E-23	Rte. 1, 2.8 miles s. of Carmel Church
Long Creek Action, E-24	Rte. 1, 2.4 miles s. of Carmel Church
Grant's Operations, E-25	Rte. 1, at Carmel Church
Dickinson's Mill, E-26	Rte. 1, 2.2 miles s. of Ladysmith
Bull Church, E-27*	Rte. 1, at Ladysmith
Nancy Wright's, E-28	Rte. 1, 5.1 miles n. of Ladysmith
Doctor Flippo's, E-29*	Rte. 1, 1.6 miles n. of Ladysmith
John Wilkes Booth, EP-20	Rte. 301, 9.1 miles n.e. of Bowling Green
Lederer Expedition, N-8	Rte. 17, 12.5 miles s.e. of Fredericksburg
Jackson's Headquarters, N-11	Rte. 17, 5.7 miles s.e. of New Post
Windsor, N-12	Rte. 17, 6.9 miles s.e. of New Post
Skinker's Neck, N-13	Rte. 17, 6.9 miles s.e. of New Post
Hazelwood, N-14	Rte. 17, 12.7 miles s.e. of New Post
Rappahannock Academy, N-15	Rte. 17, 10 miles s.e. of New Post
Where Booth Died, N-16	Rte. 301, at Port Royal Cross Roads
Old Port Royal, N-17	Rte. 1002, Port Royal
Edmund Pendleton's Home, ND-5	Rte. 2, 2.5 miles s. of Bowling Green
Campaign of 1781, ND-7	Rte. 2, at Bowling Green
Meadow Farm—Birthplace of Secretariat, ND-10	Rte. 301, .4 mile e. of Hanover Co. line

CARROLL COUNTY
Area: 458 square miles

Formed in 1842 from Grayson, and named for Charles Carroll of Carrollton, signer of the Declaration of Independence. New River runs through this county.

Hillsville, KD-12   Rte. 52, at Hillsville

CHARLES CITY COUNTY
Area: 188 square miles

One of the original eight shires formed in 1634, and named for Charles City at Bermuda Hundred. William Henry Harrison and John Tyler, presidents of the United States, were born in this county.

Benjamin Harrison Bridge, PA-250*	Rte. 156, at bridge
Action of Nance's Shop, PH-6	Rte. 603, 13.4 miles s.e. of Seven Pines
Shirley, V-6	Rte. 5, 17.1 miles s.e. of Richmond
Berkeley and Harrison's Landing, V-7	Rte. 5, 7.2 miles w. of Charles City
Westover, V-8	Rte. 5, 6.71 miles w. of Charles City
Westover, V-8*	Rte. 5, 7.2 miles w. of Charles City
Grant's Crossing, V-9	Rte. 5, 2.4 miles w. of Charles City
Greenway, V-10	Rte. 5, .7 mile w. of Charles City
Charles City Courthouse, V-11	Rte. 5, at Charles City
Upper Weyanoke, V-12	Rte. 5, at Charles City
Salem Church, V-13	Rte. 5, 5.9 miles w. of Charles City
Westover Church, V-14	Rte. 5, 6.5 miles w. of Charles City
Scene of Jefferson's Wedding, V-15	Rte. 5, 15.1 miles s.e. of Richmond
President Tyler's Home, V-21	Rte. 5, 3.5 miles e. of Charles City
Evelynton, V-22	Rte. 5, 4.73 miles w. of Charles City
Piney Grove and E. A. Saunders, V-23	Rte. 5, 9.05 miles e. of Charles City
North Bend, V-24	Rte. 5, 1.27 miles e. of Charles City

CHARLOTTE COUNTY
Area: 496 square miles

Formed in 1764 from Lunenburg, and named for Queen Charlotte, wife of King George III. Patrick Henry and John Randolph of Roanoke lived in this county, and Henry is buried here.

Colonial Home, F-8	Rte. 15, 2.4 miles n. of Keysville
Early Exploration, F-77	Rte. 15, .2 mile n. of Keysville
Campaign of 1781, F-78	Rte. 15, at s. entrance of Keysville
Roanoke Plantation, F-80	Rte. 15, at Wylliesburg
Staunton Bridge Action, F-82	Rte. 15, at Wylliesburg
Red House, FR-3	Rte. 727, at Red House

Edgehill, FR-6   Rte. 40, 2 miles e. of Charlotte
Greenfield, FR-7   Rte. 40, 2 miles e. of Charlotte
Colonial Home, FR-8*   Rte. 40, 2 miles e. of Charlotte Court House
Henry and Randolph's Debate, FR-10   Rte. 40, at Charlotte
Campaign of 1781, FR-12   Rte. 40, at Charlotte
Cub Creek Church, FR-14   Rte. 40, 2 miles e. of Phenix
Rough Creek Church, FR-15   Rte. 727, n. of Phenix
Paul Carrington, M-9   Rte. 360, at Rte. 607 in Wylliesburg

CHESTERFIELD COUNTY
Area: 468 square miles

Formed in 1748 from Henrico, and named for the Earl of Chesterfield, noted courtier. The first iron furnace in America, 1619, was in this county. The battle of Drewry's Bluff, 1864, took place here.

Colonel Thomas Lygon, K-203   Rte. 10, 1 mile w. of Hopewell
Ettrick, K-204   Rte. 36, .2 mile w. of Petersburg
Trabue's Tavern, M-7   Rte. 677, . 6 mile w. of Rte. 147
Eppington, M-8   Rte. 602, 4.5 miles e. of Amelia Co. line
Goode's Bridge, M-10   Rte. 360, 7.8 miles e. of Amelia Co. line
Mattoax, O-26   Rte. 36, 1.9 miles w. of Ettrick
Bethlehem Baptist Church, O-27*   Rte. 60, 5.4 miles w. of Richmond
Huguenot Settlement, O-28   Rte. 60, 1.7 miles e. of Midlothian
Salisbury, O-29   Rte. 60, at Midlothian
Black Heath, O-34   Rte. 60, 1.7 miles e. of Midlothian
Midlothian Coal Mines, O-35, O-35*   Rte. 60, at Midlothian
Providence United Methodist Church, O-37   Rte. 678, .86 mile s. of Rte. 60
Bellona Arsenal, O-40   Rte. 60, 3.22 miles w. of Richmond
Bellona Arsenal, O-40*   Rte. 60, 5.7 miles w. of Richmond
Bethel Baptist Church, O-50   Rte. 607, .1 mile n. of Rte. 60
Warwick, S-2   Rte. 1, 1.5 miles s. of Richmond at Falling Creek Wayside

Arnold at Warwick, S-2*   Rte. 1, 1.5 miles s. of Richmond
Ampthill Estate, S-3   Rte. 1, .7 mile s. of Richmond
First Iron Furnace, S-4   Rte. 1, 1.5 miles s. of Richmond
Drewry's Bluff, S-5   Rte. 1, 2.5 miles s. of Richmond
The Howlett Line, S-6   Rte. 10, 1.08 miles e. of Chester
Main Confederate Line, S-6*   Rte. 1, 8 miles s. of Richmond
Chesterfield County Courthouse, S-7   Rte. 10, at Chesterfield Court House
Chesterfield Courthouse, S-7*   Rte. 1, 3.9 miles s. of Richmond
Battle of Drewry's Bluff, S-8   Rte. 1, 3.9 miles s. of Richmond
Battle of Drewry's Bluff, S-9*   Rte. 1, 4.5 miles s. of Richmond
Half-Way House, S-10   Rte. 1, 5.4 miles s. of Richmond
Proctor's Creek Fight, S-11*   Rte. 301, at Proctor's Creek
Into the Bottle, S-12   Rte. 1, 6.5 miles s. of Richmond
Into the "Bottle," S-12*   Rte. 1, 6 miles s. of Richmond

Dutch Gap, S-13	Rte. 1, 6.7 miles s. of Richmond
Osbornes, S-14	Rte. 1, 6.33 miles s. of Richmond
Osborne's Wharf, S-14*	Rte. 1, 6.7 miles s. of Richmond
Drewry's Bluff, S-15	Rte. 1, 2.5 miles s. of Richmond
Pocahontas State Park, S-16	Rte. 655, 4.1 miles w. of Chesterfield
Redwater Creek, S-16*	Rte. 1, 4.5 miles n. of Petersburg
Chester Station Fight, S-17	Rte. 1, 7.8 miles s. of Richmond
The "Bottle," S 18*	Rte. 1, 6.2 miles n. of Petersburg
Feeling Out Fight, S-19*	Rte. 1, 6.9 miles n. of Petersburg
A Railroad Raid, S-20*	Rte. 1, 4.25 miles n. of Petersburg
Bermuda Hundred, S-21	Rte. 1, 7.8 miles s. of Richmond
Port Walthall, S-22	Rte. 10, 2.25 miles w. of Hopewell at Enon
Port Walthall Junction, S-22*	Rte. 1, 5.4 miles n. of Petersburg
Point of Rocks, S-23	Rte. 10, 2.25 miles w. of Hopewell at Enon
Lee's Headquarters, S-23*	Rte. 1, 7.5 miles n. of Petersburg
Advance on Petersburg, S-24*	Rte. 1, 4.1 miles n. of Petersburg
Union Army Checked, S-25	Rte. 1, 3.4 miles n. of Petersburg
Lafayette at Petersburg, S-26	Rte. 1, at Colonial Heights
Lee's Headquarters, S-27	Rte. 1, at Colonial Heights
Salisbury, p. 00	Rte. 902, on Salisbury Road
Magnolia Grange, S-29	Rte. 10, at Chesterfield Court House
Civilian Conservation Corps Company 2386, S-29	Rte. 655, at entrance to Pocahontas State Park
First Railroad in Virginia, S-30	Rte. 60, 3.78 miles w. of Richmond

CLARKE COUNTY
Area: 171 square miles

Formed in 1836 from Frederick, and added to from Warren. Named for George Rogers Clark, conqueror of the Northwest. Lord Fairfax and General Daniel Morgan, Revolutionary hero lived in this county.

The Briars, B-2*	Rte. 50, 3 miles n.w. of Boyce
Saratoga, B-4*	Rte. 50, at Boyce
Signal Station, B-7	Rte. 50, .7 mile w. of Paris
Ashby's Tavern, B-23*	Rte. 50, 2 miles n.w. of Paris
A Raid of Mosby's, J-1*	Rte. 340, 1 mile n. of Berryville
Buck March Baptist Church, J-1-a	Rte. 340, n. of Berryville
Buck Marsh, J-2*	Rte. 340, 1.5 miles n. of Berryville
Gettysburg Campaign, J-14*	Rte. 340, 1 mile n. of Berryville
Anderson and Crook, J-30*	Rte. 7, .7 mile w. of Berryville
Berryville, Q-3-a-b-c-d*	*a* and *c:* Rte. 7, at e. and w. entrance of Berryville. *b:* Rte. 340, at n. entrance of Berryville. *d*:* Rte. 12, at s. entrance of Berryville
Carter Hall, T-1	Rte. 255, just n. of Millwood
Old Chapel, T-2	Rte. 255, 3.2 miles s. of Berryville

Greenway Court, T-3   Rte. 340, 2 miles n.w. of Millwood
Audley, T-4   Rte. 7, .7 mile e. of Berryville
The Burwell-Morgan Mill, T-6   Rte. 255, at Millwood
White Post, T-7*   Rte. 255, at White Post
Colonial Highway, T-8   Rte. 7, 3.7 miles e. of Berryville
Castleman's Ferry Fight, T-9   Rte. 7 at Rte. 603
Castleman's Ferry Fight, T-9*   Rte. 7, 4.5 miles e. of Berryville
Crook and Early, T-10   Rte. 7, 7.7 miles e. of Berryville
Forerunner of Wireless Telegraphy, T-11   Rte. 7, 7.7 miles e. of Berryville
Long Branch, T-12   Rte. 626, .2 mile w. of Rte. 624

CRAIG COUNTY
Area: 333 square miles

Formed in 1851 from Botetourt, Roanoke, Giles, and Monroe. Named for Robert Craig, member of Congress. Craig Healing Springs are in this county.

Great Eastern Divide—Elevation 2704 Feet, KH-2   Rte. 42, 8.1 miles w. of Rte. 311
New Castle, KH-4   Rte. 311, at New Castle

CULPEPER COUNTY
Area: 384 square miles

Formed in 1748 from Orange, and named for Lord Culpeper, Governor of Virginia 1680–83. The battle of Cedar Mountain, 1862, was fought in this county.

Stuart's Ride around Pope, C-8   Rte. 613, 6 miles w. of Warrenton
Greenwood, F-3   Rte. 15, .8 mile s. of Culpeper
Where Pelham Fell, F-10   Rte. 15, at Elkwood
Battle of Brandy Station, F-11   Rte. 29, 1 mile n. of Brandy
Battle of Brandy Station, F-11   Rtes. 15 and 29, .7 mile n.e. of Brandy
Betty Washington, F-12*   Rte. 15, 3.1 miles n.e. of Culpeper
Opening of Gettysburg Campaign, F-13   Rte. 15, .5 mile s.w. of Brandy
Signal Station, F-15*   Rte. 15, 2 miles s. of Culpeper
Lee and Pope, F-16   Rte. 15, 4.7 miles s. of Culpeper
Battle of Cedar Mountain, F-19*   Rte. 15, 3 miles s. of Culpeper
Battle of Cedar Mountain, F-20   Rte. 15, 6.1 miles s. of Culpeper
Crooked Run Baptist Church, F-21*   Rte. 15, 9.7 miles s. of Culpeper
Mitchells Presbyterian Church, F-25   Rte. 652, .28 mile e. of Rte. 615
Mitchells Presbyterian Church, F-25A   Rte. 522 at Rte. 615, .25 mile s. of Winston
Campaign of Second Manassas, G-9   Rte. 211, 7 miles n.w. of Warrenton
Little Fork Church, G-9   Rte. 229, 6 miles s. of Rte. 211
General Edward Stevens, G-10   Rte. 229, at n. entrance of Culpeper
George Washington Carver Regional High School, J-5   Rte. 15, 8 miles s. of Culpeper

John S. Barbour's Birthplace, J-6*   Rte. 522, at w. entrance of Culpeper
Culpeper Minute Men, J-10   Rte. 522, at w. entrance of Culpeper
Signal Stations, J-15   Rte. 3, 3.6 miles e. of Culpeper
Opening of the Wilderness Campaign, J-33   Rte. 3, at Stevensburg

CUMBERLAND COUNTY
Area: 293 square miles

Formed in 1748 from Goochland, and named for the Duke of Cumberland, second son of King George II. The earliest call for independence came from this county, April 22, 1776.

Lee's Stopping Place, JE-35   Rte. 690 at 612, 8.8 miles s. of Columbia
Clifton, JE-36   Rte. 690 at 605, 11 miles s. of Columbia
Bizarre, MJ-1   Rte. 45, at n. entrance of Farmville
Campaign of 1781, O-44   Rte. 60, 1.8 miles w. of Cumberland
Campaign of 1781, ON-5   Rte. 45, at Cartersville
Campaign of 1781, ON-7   Rte. 45, 1.8 miles s. of Cartersville
State Game Farm, W-21   Rte. 45, 6 miles s. of Cartersville

DICKENSON COUNTY
Area: 325 square miles

Formed in 1880 from Russell, Wise, and Buchanan, and named for W. J. Dickenson, prominent public man.

Old Buffalo School, XB-10   Rte. 63, at Nora
Clintwood, XB-11   Rte. 83, at Clintwood
Early Settler, XB-12*   Rte. 83, at Clintwood
John Mullins, XB-13   Rte. T-1009, at Clintwood
First Settler, XB-20*   Rte. 83, at Haysi
Indian Outrage, XB-23   Rte. 83, at Haysi
Colley's Cabin, XB-24   Rte. 80, 3 miles s. of Haysi

DINWIDDIE COUNTY
Area: 521 square miles

Formed in 1752 from Prince George, and named for Robert Dinwiddie, Governor of Virginia 1751–56. General Winfield Scott was born in this county, and in it took place the battle of Five Forks, 1865.

Central State Hospital, I-6   Rte. 1, .4 mile w. of Peterburg
Sallie Jones Atkinson, K-304   Rte. 40, 2.5 miles w. of McKenney
Lee's Retreat, K-305*   Rte. 460, .2 mile e. of Sutherland
Battle of Five Forks, K-307   Rte. 460, 4.9 miles w. of Sutherland
Saponey Church, S-40*   Rte. 1, at Dewitt
Dinwiddie Tavern, S-41*   Rte. 1, at Dinwiddie

Quaker Settlement, S-42*   Rte. 1, 6 miles s.w. of Petersburg
Cottage Farm, S-43   Rte. 1, at s. limits of Petersburg
Scott's Law Office, S-45   Rte. 1, at Dinwiddie
Raceland, S-46*   Rte. 1, n. entrance of Dinwiddie
Edge Hill, S-47   Rte. 1, at s. limits of Petersburg
The Cattle (Beefsteak) Raid, S-48   Rtes. 1 and 613, 5 miles s. of Petersburg
Where Hill Fell, S-49   Rte. 1, 2.8 miles s. of Petersburg
Hatcher's Run, S-50   Rte. 1, 6.4 miles s. of Petersburg
Burgess Mill, S-51   Rte. 1, 6.4 miles s. of Petersburg
White Oak Road, S-52   Rte. 1, 6.8 miles s. of Petersburg
Action of March 29, 1865, S-53*   Rte. 1, 7.7 miles s. of Petersburg
Dinwiddie Courthouse, S-54   Rte. 1, at Dinwiddie
Vaughan Road, S-55   Rte. 1, at Dinwiddie
Chamberlain's Bed, S-56   Rte. 1, 1.1 miles s. of Dinwiddie
Campaign of 1781, S-62   Rte. 1, 1.5 miles s. of Dinwiddie
Battle of Hatcher's Run,   Rte. 613, 2.2 miles e. of Rte. 1
5–7 February 1865, S-63
Quaker Road Engagement, 29 March 1865, S-80   Rte. 660, .78 mile e. of Rte. 1
White Oak Road Engagement,   Rte. 613, 1.63 miles w. of Rte. 1
31 March 1865, S-81

ESSEX COUNTY
Area: 258 square miles

Formed in 1691 from Old Rappahannock County, and named for Essex County, England. R. M. T. Hunter, United States Senator and Confederate Secretary of State, lived in this county.

Early Settlement, N-9   Rte. 17, 7 miles n.w. of Caret
Old Rappahannock Courthouse, N-18   Rte. 17, at Caret
Portobago Indian Towns, N-19   Rte. 17, 11.8 miles n.w. of Caret
Fonthill, N-20, N-20*   Rte. 17, 3 miles n.w. of Caret
Historic Tappahannock, N-21   Rte. 360, at Tappahannock
Ritchie's Birthplace, N-22   Cross St., at Tappahannock
Vauter's Church, N-23   Rte. 17, 10.7 miles n.w. of Caret
Fort Lowry—Camp Byron, N-24   Rte. 17 at Rte. 611
Ancient Indian Town, N-25   Rte. 17, 1.75 miles w. of Tappahannock
Mann Meeting House, N-26   Rte. 17, 12.4 miles s.e. of Tappahannock
Gouldborough Plantation, N-27   Rte. 17, 2.27 miles s. of Caret
Departure of the Indians, N-28   Rte. 17, 2.8 miles n.w. of Tappahannock
Fort Lowry, N-29   Rte. 646 at fort site
Mattapony Indian Town, O-22   Rte. 360, at Millers Tavern
Bacon's Northern Force, O-23   Rte. 360, at Millers Tavern

FAIRFAX COUNTY
Area: 417 square miles

> Formed in 1742 from Prince William and Loudoun, and
> named for Lord Fairfax, proprietor of the Northern Neck.
> Mount Vernon, George Washington's home, is in this county.

Battle of Chantilly (Ox Hill), B-11	Rte. 50, 1.6 miles w. of I-66
Colonel John Singleton Mosby, B-12	Rte. 50, 4. miles w. of Fairfax near Rte. 645
Action of Ox Hill, B-13*	Rte. 50, 6.9 miles w. of Fairfax
Burke Station, BW-3	Rte. 645 at Rte. 652, 3.11 miles n.e. of Rte. 123
Sully Plantation, C-18	Rte. 28, at milepost 350
First Battle of Manassas, C-20	Rte. 211, . 5 mile s. of Centerville
Confederate Defenses, C-21	Rte. 29, .5 mile s. of Centerville
Second Battle of Manassas, C-22	Rte. 29, .5 mile s. of Centerville
Campaign of Second Manassas, C-40	Rte. 29, .5 mile s. of Centerville
First Battle of Manassas, C-42*	Rte. 211, 1.8 miles w. of Centerville
The Falls Church, C-90	At Falls Church, s. of Rte. 7
Events on Pohick Creek, E-60*	Rte. 1, 3.2 miles n. of Woodbridge
Occoquan Workhouse, E-61	Rte. 123, at Lorton Penitentiary Youth Center
Old Telegraph Line, E-62	Rte. 1, 4.1 miles n. of Woodbridge
Early Land Patents, E-63*	Rte. 1, 5.6 miles n. of Woodbridge
Fort Humphreys, E-64*	Rte. 1, .7 mile n. of Woodbridge
Gunston Hall, E-65	Rte. 1, 2.4 miles n. of Woodbridge
Woodlawn, E-66*	Rte. 1, 7.4 miles s. of Alexandria
History On Dogue Run, E-67*	Rte. 1, 7.1 miles s. of Alexandria
Mount Vernon Estate, E-68*	Rte. 1, 4.5 miles s. of Alexandria
Little Hunting Creek, E-69*	Rte. 1, 4.5 miles s. of Alexandria
Colonial Fort, E-70*	Rte. 1, at Alexandria
Lewis Chapel/Cranford Memorial Methodist Church, E-71	Rte. 242 at Rte. 611, .7 mile e. of Rte. 1
Pohick Church, E-72	Rte. 1, 4.3 miles n. of Woodbridge
Old Road to West, E-72*	Rte. 50, at n. entrance of Alexandria
Washington's Mill, E-73	Rte. 1, 7.4 miles s. of Alexandria at Rte. 235
Indian Massacre, E-80*	Rte. 1, 8.25 miles s. of Alexandria
Defenses of Washington, E-81*	Rte. 1, .8 mile s. of Alexandria
Gum Springs, E-94	Rte. 626, .27 mile e. of Rte. 1
Silas Burke House, E-95	Rte. 645, 2.5 miles n. of Rte. 123
Action at Dranesville, T-36	Rte. 7, at Dranesville
Sharpsburg (Antietam) Campaign, T-37	Rte. 7, at Dranesville
J. E. B. Stuart at Munson's Hill, T-39	Rte. 7, 3.03 miles w. of I-395
Lincoln Reviews Troops at Bailey's Crossroads, T-40	Rte. 7, 2.48 miles w. of I-395
Little River Turnpike, T-41	Rte. 650, .01 mile n. of Rte. 236 (Little River Turnpike)
Ravensworth, T-42	Rte. 3090, .11 mile s. of Rte. 620 (Braddock Rd.)

FAUQUIER COUNTY
Area: 666 square miles

Formed in 1759 from Prince William, and named for Frances Fauquier, Governor of Virginia, 1758–1768. Chief Justice John Marshall was born in this county.

Jackson's Bivouac, B-20	Rtes. 50 and 17, at Paris
Delaplane, B-21	Rte. 17, 6.5 miles s. of Paris
Ancient Highway, B-24*	Rte. 17, 1 mile s. of Paris
Mosby's Rangers, B-25	Rte. 50, 4 miles w. of Middleburg
Stuart and Gregg, B-31	Rte. 50, .4 mile e. of Upperville
Stuart and Mosby, B-36	Rte. 28, 3.1 miles w. of Prince William Co. line
Brent Town, BX-2*	Rte. 806, 5 miles s. of Catlett
Neavil's Ordinary, BX-7	Rte. 670, 6.1 miles e. of Warrenton
McClellan's Farewell, C-5*	Rte. 211, 3 miles w. of Buckland
Colonial Road, C-29	Rte. 211, 2.6 miles e. of Warrenton
Campaign of Second Manassas, C-54*	Rte. 211, 4.5 miles w. of Gainsville
Fredericksburg Campaign, C-56*	Rte. 211, 2.6 miles e. of Warrenton
Black Horse Cavalry, C-57	Rte. 17/211 Bus. at Rte. 211, in Warrenton
Campaign of Second Manassas, C-58*	Rte. 211, 4 miles w. of Warrenton
Campaign of Second Manassas, C-60	Rte. 211, 5.1 miles w. of Warrenton
Campaign of Second Manassas, CB-1	Rte. 688, 12 miles w. of Warrenton
Ashland Farm, CB-2	Rte. 211, 4.4 miles w. of Warrenton
John Marshall's Birthplace, CL-3	Rte. 28, .8 mile e. of Midland
Campaign of Second Manassas, F-9	Rte. 55, at The Plains
Goldvein, F-18	Rte. 17, at Goldvein
John Marshall's Home, FB-2	Rte. 55, 4 miles w. of Marshall
Campaign of Second Manassas, FB-4	Rte. 55, at Marshall
Gettysburg Campaign, FF-4*	Rte. 55, at Markham
Lee's Escape, FF-5*	Rte. 55, 2 miles w. of Marshall
McClellan Relieved from Command, FF-8	Rte. 55, at Marshall
Manassas Gap, FF-9	Rte. 55, .57 mile e. of Linden
Leeton Forest, G-2	Rte. 802, .5 mile s. of Warrenton
Warrenton, Q-9	Rte. 802, at Warrenton

FLOYD COUNTY
Area: 376 square miles

Formed in 1831 from Montgomery, and added to from Franklin. Named for John Floyd, Governor of Virginia 1830–34. Buffalo Knob is in this county.

Floyd, KG-5	Rte. 8, at Floyd

FLUVANNA COUNTY
Area: 285 square miles

Formed in 1777 from Albemarle. Named (in Latin) Anne's River, the early name of the Upper James given in honor of Queen Anne. Point of Fork was an important supply depot in 1781.

Fluvanna County Courthouse, F-49	Rte. 15, at the courthouse
Point of Fork, F-50	Rte. 15, at Dixie
"Texas Jack" Omohundro Birthplace, F-51	Rte. 15, 1 mile s. of Palmyra
Bremo, F-52	Rte. 15, 3.2 miles s. of Fork Union
Point of Fork, GA-32	Rte. 6, .8 mile w. of Columbia
Fork Union Academy, GA-33	Rte. 6, at Rte. 15
Rassawek, GA-34	Rte. 6, .8 mile w. of Columbia

FRANKLIN COUNTY
Area: 697 square miles

Formed in 1785 from Henry and Bedford and added to from Patrick. Named for Benjamin Franklin. General Jubal A. Early lived in this county.

Rocky Mount, A-60	Rte. 220, at Rocky Mount
Fort Blackwater, A-93	Rte. 220, 3 miles n. of Rocky Mount
Booker T. Washington's Birthplace, KP-4, KP-4*	Rte. 122, just w. of Hales Ford Church
Birthplace of General Jubal Early, A-95	Rte. 116, 5.2 miles n. of Rte. 122
Carolina Road, A-96	Rte. 220, .7 mile s. of Roanoke-Franklin Co. line
Washington Iron Works, A-97	Rte. 220 Bus., .5 mile s. of Franklin Co. courthouse in Rocky Mount
Taylor's Store, A-98	Rte. 122, 1.6 miles e. of Rte. 116

FREDERICK COUNTY
Area: 435 square miles

Formed in 1738 from Orange, and named for Frederick, Prince of Wales, father of King George III. Several battles were fought in the vicinity of Winchester, 1862–64.

Action at Stephenson's Depot, A-1	Rte. 11 at Rte. 664
Action at Stephenson's Depot, A-1*	Rte. 11, 4 miles n. of Winchester
Action of Rutherford's Farm, A-2	Rte. 11 at Rte. 664
Action of Carter's Farm, A-2*	Rte. 11, 2.75 miles n. of Winchester
Capture of Star Fort, A-3	Rte. 11, .8 mile n. of Winchester
Fort Collier, A-4, A-4*	Rte. 11, .1 mile s. of Rte. 764
First Battle of Winchester, A-5	Rte. 11, .1 mile s. of Handley Blvd.
First Battle of Winchester, A-6*	Rte. 11, s. of Winchester
First Battle of Winchester, A-7	Rte. 11, .6 mile s. of Winchester

Second Battle of Winchester, A-8	Rte. 11, .18 mile s. of Rte. 37
Second Battle of Winchester, A-8*	Rte. 11, .6 mile s. of Winchester
Battle of Kernstown, A-9	Rte. 11, 5.3 miles n. of Stephens City
Early and Crook, A-10	Rte. 11, 1 mile n. of Kernstown
First Battle of Winchester, A-11	Rte. 11, 3.2 miles n. of Stephens City
House of First Settler, A-12	Rte. 11, 2.3 miles n. of Stephens City
Stephens City, A-12	Rte. 11, .16 mile s. of Rte. T1017
Stephens City, A-13*	Rte. 11, center of Stephens City
End of Sheridan's Ride, A-14	Rte. 11, 3.2 miles s. of Stephens City
Battle of Cedar Creek, A-15	Rte. 11, .2 mile n. of Middletown
Engagement of Middletown, A-16	Rte. 11, at Middletown
Tomb of an Unknown Soldier, A-17	Rte. 11, 1 mile s. of Middletown
Old Stone Fort, A-37	Rte. 11, at Middletown
Hackwood Park, A-38	Rte. 11, .19 mile e. of Rte. 661
Hackwood Park, A-38*	Rte. 11, 1.7 miles n. of Winchester
Chrisman's Spring, A-42*	Rte. 11, 2 miles s. of Stephens City
Battle of Cedar Creek, A-56	Rte. 11, 1.3 miles s. of Middletown
Colonel John Singleton Mosby, B-16	Rte. 50 at Rte. 723
Willow Shade, B-17	Rte. 50, .71 mile e. of Gore
Willa Cather Birthplace, B-18	Rte. 50, at Gore
Second Battle of Winchester, B-19	Rte. 50, 2.5 miles w. of Winchester
Third Battle of Winchester, J-3	Rte. 7 at Rte. 656
Third Battle of Winchester, J-3*	Rte. 522 at e. entrance of Winchester
Third Battle of Winchester, J-13	Rte. 7, .41 mile e. of Rte. 716
Third Battle of Winchester, J-13*	Rte. 50, at Winchester
Defenses of Winchester, J-16	Rte. 522, 4 miles s. of Winchester

GILES COUNTY
Area: 369 square miles

Formed in 1806 from Montgomery, Tazewell, and Monroe, and named for William B. Giles, United States Senator and Governor of Virginia 1827–30. Mountain Lake is in this county.

Eggleston's Springs, KB-56	Rte. 730, at Eggleston
Camp John J. Pershing, Civilian Conservation Corps, Company 1370–2386, KG-14	Rte. 460 at Rte. 1404, in Pembroke
Mountain Evangelist, KG-15	Rte. 100, at Rte. 730
Old-Fashioned Camp Meeting, KG-16	Rte. 100, .6 mile n. of Rte. 659
Snidow's Ferry, KG-17	Rte. 460, 3 miles e. of Pearisburg
Discovery of New River, KG-19	Rte. 460, 3 miles e. of Pearisburg
First Court of Giles County, KG-20	Rte. 460, 1 mile n. of Pearisburg
Pearisburg, KG-21	Rte. 460, at Pearisburg
Narrows, KG-22	Rte. 460, at Narrows

GLOUCESTER COUNTY
Area: 223 square miles

Formed in 1651 from York, and named for Gloucester County, England. Bacon the Rebel died in this county, 1676. Gloucester Point was the outpost of Cornwallis at Yorktown, 1781.

Marlfield, M-66	Rte. 17 at Rte. 613
Poplar Spring Church, N-61	Rte. 17, 5 miles n.w. of Gloucester
Marlfield, N-66	Rte. 17, 4.5 miles n.w. of Gloucester
Gloucester Courthouse, NW-1	Rte. 17, at Gloucester
Ware Church, NW-2	Rte. 17, at e. entrance of Gloucester
To Gwynn's Island, NW-3	Rte. 17, at e. entrance of Gloucester
Warner Hall, NW-4	Rte. 17, 4.2 miles s. of Gloucester
Abingdon Church, NW-5	Rte. 17, 6.2 miles s. of Gloucester
White Marsh and Reed's Birthplace, NW-6	Rte. 17, 5.3 miles s. of Gloucester
Tarleton's Last Fight, NW-7	Rte. 1216, 2.1 miles n. of Gloucester Point
Rosewell and Werowocomoco, NW-8	Rte. 17, 5.3 miles s. of Gloucester
Gloucester Point, NW-9	Rte. 17, at Gloucester Point
Early Land Patent, NW-10	Rte. 17, at Gloucester Point
Thomas Calhoun Walker, NW-11	Rte. 17, .1 mile n. of Rtes. 3 and 14
Robert Russa Moton, NW-12	Rte. 17, .04 mile s. of Rte. 614
United Negro College Fund, NW-12	Rte. 17, .04 mile s. of Rte. 614
Cappahosic, Q-10-a	Rte. 17, at Gloucester

GOOCHLAND COUNTY
Area: 287 square miles

Formed in 1727 from Henrico, and named for William Gooch, Governor of Virginia 1727–49. Cornwallis and Lafayette passed through this county in 1781.

Elk Hill, SA-5	Rte. 6, 1 mile w. of George's Tavern
Goochland Courthouse, SA-10	Rte. 6, at Goochland
Dungeness, SA-11	Rte. 6 at the courthouse
Dahlgren's Raid, SA-14	Rte. 6, 2.1 miles e. of Crozier
Sabot Hill, SA-18	Rte. 6, 2.6 miles e. of Crozier
The Huguenot Settlement, SA-20	Rte. 6, 5.9 miles e. of Crozier
William Webber, SA-22	Rte. 6, 6 miles e. of Crozier at Manakin
Tuckahoe, SA-24	Rte. 650, w. of Henrico Co. line
Dahlgren's Raid, SA-27	Rte. 650, 9 miles w. of Richmond
Bolling Hall, SA-35	Rte. 6, 4 miles w. of Goochland Court House
Bolling Island, SA-36	Rte. 6, 4 miles w. of Goochland Court House
Reuben Ford, V-18	Rte. 250, 1.9 miles e. of Oilville

GRAYSON COUNTY
Area: 425 square miles

Formed in 1792 from Wythe, and named for William Grayson, one of the first two United States Senators from Virginia. Headwaters of New River are in this county.

Caty Sage, KC-10	Rte. 21, 4 miles s. of Wythe Co. line
Independence, U-22	Rte. 58, at Independence
Peyton Guyn Hale, U-23	Rte. 21, at Elks Creek
First County Seat, U-25	Rte. 640, 3 miles w. of Galax
Galax, U-26	Rte. 89 (Main St.), in Galax
Fries, UE-2*	Rte. 94, at Carroll Co. line
First Court of Grayson County, UE-5	Rte. 805, 5 miles s.w. of Fries
Fries—Center of Early Recorded Country Music, UE-6	Rte. 94, at Fries
"New River Train" Song, UE-7	Rte. 94 at Rte. 1001 in Fries

GREENE COUNTY
Area: 155 square miles

Formed in 1838 from Orange, and named for General Nathanael Greene, commander of the Army of the South in the Revolutionary War.

Ruckersville, D-11	Rtes. 29 and 33, in Ruckersville

GREENSVILLE COUNTY
Area: 307 square miles

Formed in 1780 from Brunswick, and probably named for Sir Richard Grenville, leader of the settlement on Roanoke Island, 1585. Cornwallis passed through this county in 1781.

Tarleton's Movements, UM-40	Rte. 301, at Emporia
Site of "Homestead," UM-41	Rte. 58 and Chapman's Ford Road

HALIFAX COUNTY
Area: 814 square miles

Formed in 1752 from Lunenburg, and named for George Montague Dunk, Earl of Halifax, British statesman. Berry Hill, old home, is in this county.

History at Halifax, R-77*	Rte. 360, at Halifax
Halifax Church, R-78	Rte. 624 at Rte. 623
Green's Folly, R-79	Rte. 501, 2 miles s. of Halifax
Minister Who Married Lincoln, R-80	Rte. 501, 2 miles s. of Halifax
Carters Tavern, U-47	Rte. 659, 3.3 miles e. of Pittsylvania Co. line

HANOVER COUNTY
Area: 512 square miles

Formed in 1720 from New Kent, and named for the Elector-
ate of Hanover. Patrick Henry and Henry Clay were born in
this county. In it were fought the battles of Gaines's Mill,
1862, and Cold Harbor, 1864.

HENRICO COUNTY
Area: 280 square miles

An original shire formed in 1634. Named for Henrico Town, founded in 1611, which was named for Henry, Prince of Wales. The battles of Seven Pines, Savage's Station, Glendale, and Malvern Hill took place in this county in 1862.

Seven Days' Battles, Glendale (Frayser's Farm), PA-175	Rte. 156, 10 miles s. of Seven Pines
Seven Days' Battles, Malvern Hill, PA-180	Rte. 156, 10.6 miles s. of Seven Pines
Seven Days' Battles, Glendale (Frayser's Farm), PA-190	Rte. 156, 11.1 miles s. of Seven Pines
Seven Days' Battles, Malvern Hill, PA-195	Rte. 156, 12.3 miles s. of Seven Pines
Seven Days' Battles, Malvern Hill PA-220	Rte. 156, 12.5 miles s. of Seven Pines
Seven Days' Battles, Malvern Hill, PA-230	Rte. 156, 12.6 miles s. of Seven Pines
Seven Days' Battles, Malvern Hill, PA-235	Rte. 156, 12.7 miles s. of Seven Pines
Seven Days' Battles, Malvern Hill, PA-240*	Rte. 156, 13.8 miles s. of Seven Pines
Sad Reunion, PA-251	Rte. 5, .9 mile e. of Turner Rd.
Dahlgren's Raid, SA-31	Rte. 650, 1.25 miles w. of Richmond
Wilton, V-1	Rte. 5, 2 miles s.e. of Richmond
Varina and Fort Harrison, V-2	Rte. 5, 4.5 miles s.e. of Richmond
Curles Neck and Bremo, V-3*	Rte. 5, 9.3 miles s.e. of Richmond
Malvern Hill, V-4*	Rte. 5, 13.3 miles s.e. of Richmond
Turkey Island, V-5*	Rte. 5, 12.3 miles s.e. of Richmond
Campaign of 1781, V-16	Rte. 250, 8.5 miles w. of Richmond
Outer Defenses, V-17*	Rte. 250, 1.9 miles w. of Richmond
First Successful Colonial Tobacco Crop, V-25	Rte. 5, 5 miles e. of Richmond
Battle of New Market Heights, V-26	Rte. 5, 8.5 miles e. of Richmond
To Frazier's Farm, W-1*	Rte. 60, Williamsburg Ave. at Darbytown Rd.
Williamsburg Road, W-2	Rte. 60, .4 mile e. of Richmond
Charles City Road, W-3*	Rte. 60, 1 mile e. of Richmond
McClellan's Picket Line, W-4	Rte. 60, at Sandston
McClellan's First Line, W-5	Rte. 60, at Sandston
Munitions Plant, W-6*	Rte. 60, e. entrance of Sandston
Fair Oaks Battle, W-7*	Rte. 60, .5 mile e. of Sandston
McClellan's Withdrawal, W-8	Rte. 60, 3.6 miles e. of Seven Pines
McClellan's Second Line, W-9	Rte. 60, at Seven Pines
Second Day at Seven Pines, W-10*	Rte. 60, .3 mile e. of Seven Pines
McClellan's Third Line, W-11	Rte. 60, 1.3 miles e. of Seven Pines
Battle of Savage's Station, W-12*	Rte. 60, 2 miles e. of Seven Pines
To White Oak Swamp and Malvern Hill, W-13*	Rte. 640, 2 miles e. of Sandston
Camp Bottom's Bridge, W-15*	Rte. 60, 15 miles e. of Richmond
Virginia Estelle Randolph, W-221	2200 Mountain Rd., at Virginia Randolph Education Center

HENRY COUNTY
Area: 444 square miles

Formed in 1776 from Pittsylvania, and named for Patrick Henry, Governor of Virginia. Henry lived in this county, 1779–84.

Fort Trial, A-54	Rte. 57, 6 miles n. of Martinsville
William Byrd's Camp, A-57	Rte. 220, 3.5 miles s.w. of Ridgeway
Belleview, A-135	Rte. 220, 4 miles s. of Martinsville
Patrick Henry's Leatherwood Home, U-40	Rte. 57, .1 mile e. of Rte. 628

HIGHLAND COUNTY
Area: 422 square miles

Formed in 1847 from Pendleton and Bath, and given its name because of its mountains. The battle of McDowell, 1862, was fought in this county.

Fort George on the Bullpasture River, W-148	Rte. 678, 6 miles s. of McDowell
Fort Edward Johnson, W-149*	Rte. 250, 5 miles w. of West Augusta
Battle of McDowell, W-150	Rte. 250, 1 mile e. of McDowell

ISLE OF WIGHT COUNTY
Area: 314 square miles

One of the original shires formed in 1634. Its name was at first Warrascoyack, changed in 1637 to Isle of Wight. One of the oldest churches in the United States is in this county.

Old Town, K-238	Rte. 621, .1 mile e. of Rte. 10
Lawne's Creek, K-239	Rte. 10, 8.1 miles n.w. of Smithfield
Wrenn's Mill Site, K-240*	Rte. 10, 4.5 miles n.w. of Smithfield
Wrenn's Mill, K-240-b	Rte. 10, 4.5 miles w. of Smithfield
Bennett's Plantation, K-241*	Rte. 10, 2 miles n.w. of Smithfield
Basses Choice, K-242*	Rte. 10, 2 miles n.w. of Smithfield
Smithfield, K-243	Rte. 10, at Smithfield
Pagan Point, K-244	Rte. 10, .4 mile w. of Smithfield
Saint Luke's Church, K-245	Rte. 10, 4.25 miles s.e. of Smithfield
Saint Luke's Church, K-245*	Rte. 10, .25 mile n.w. of Benn's Church
Benn's Church, K-246	Rte. 10, 4.2 miles s.e. of Smithfield
Macclesfield, K-247*	Rte. 10, 4.2 miles s.e. of Smithfield
James River, K-311	Rte. 17, at s. end of James River Bridge
Camp Manufacturing Company, U-125	Bus. Rte. 58 near Blackwater River
Suffolk Campaign, UT-20	Rte. 460, 6.3 miles n.w. of Windsor

JAMES CITY COUNTY
Area: 164 square miles

One of the original shires formed in 1634, and named for Jamestown, the first settlement in Virginia, 1607. Williamsburg is in this county.

New Kent Road, W-26*	Rte. 60, 3 miles n.w. of Toano
White Hall Tavern, W-27	Rte. 60, 1.3 miles n.w. of Toano
Olive Branch Christian Church, W-28*	Rte. 60, .9 mile s.e. of Toano
Hickory Neck Church, W-30	Rte. 60, .8 mile n.w. of Toano
State Shipyard, W-31	Rte. 60, at Toano
Chickahominy Church, W-32	Rte. 60, at Toano
Burnt Ordinary, W-33*	Rte. 60, at Toano
Six-Mile Ordinary, W-34*	Rte. 60, 4.3 miles s.e. of Toano

Spencer's Ordinary, W-35	Rte. 60, 4.3 miles s.e. of Toano
Green Spring, W-36	Rte. 60, 4.3 miles s.e. of Toano
Peninsular Campaign, W-37*	Rte. 60, n.w. entrance of Williamsburg
Iron-Bound Road, W-38*	Rte. 60, 3 miles n.w. of Williamsburg
Quarter Path, W-42*	Rte. 60, s.e. entrance of Williamsburg
Battle of Williamsburg, W-43	Rte. 60, .3 mile s.e. of Williamsburg
Magruder's Defenses, W-44	Rte. 60, .3 mile s.e. of Williamsburg
Whitaker's House, W-45	Rte. 60, 1.4 miles s.e. of Williamsburg
Kingsmill, W-47*	Rte. 60, 2.4 miles s.e. of Williamsburg
Littletown, W-48*	Rte. 60, 2.8 miles s.e. of Williamsburg
Trebell's Landing, W-49*	Rte. 60, 5.1 miles s.e. of Williamsburg
Carter's Grove, W-50*	Rte. 60, 3.25 miles s.e. of Williamsburg
Martin's Hundred, W-51	Rte. 60, at entrance to Carter's Grove
Martin's Hundred, W-51*	Rte. 60, 6.7 miles s.e. of Williamsburg
Martin's Hundred Church, W-52	Rte. 60, 6.7 miles s.e. of Williamsburg
First Africans in English America, WT-1	Rte. 31, .2 mile s. of Rte. 614

KING AND QUEEN COUNTY
Area: 320 square miles

Formed in 1691 from New Kent, and named for King William III and Queen Mary. The family of George Rogers Clark long lived in this county.

The Servants' Plot, N-58*	Rte. 14, 1.1 miles w. of Adner
Old Places, O-17*	Rte. 631, 2 miles n. of Manquin
Clark Home, O-20	Rte. 360, at Saint Stephens Church
Where Dahlgren Died, O-21*	Rte. 360, at Saint Stephens Church
Piscataway Church, O-41*	Rte. 360, 1.6 miles s.w. of Millers Tavern
Bruington Church, OB-2	Rte. 14, 6.2 miles n.w. of Stevensville
Mattapony Church, OB-3	Rte. 14, 4.1 miles n.w. of King and Queen Courthouse
Hillsboro, OB-5	Rte. 14, 4.7 miles n.w. of Stevensville
Where Dahlgren Died, OB-6	Rte. 631, 2.5 miles n.w. of King and Queen Courthouse
Newtown, OB-9	Rtes. 625 and 721
Newington, OB-10	Rte. 14, 1 mile n.w. of King and Queen Courthouse
Apple Tree Church, OB-11	Rte. 360, .4 mile e. of Rte. 14
Corbin's Church—The New Church, OB-12	Rte. 14, 1 mile n. of Rte. 33
Laneville, OB-16	Rte. 14, 10 miles s.e. of King and Queen Courthouse
Colonial Church, OB-18	Rte. 14, 8.5 miles s.e. of King and Queen Courthouse
Poropotank Creek, OB-50	Rte. 14, 1.1 miles w. of Adner
State Fish Hatchery, PB-4	Rte. 14, 1 mile n.w. of Stevensville

KING GEORGE COUNTY
Area: 180 square miles

Formed in 1720 from Richmond, and named for King George I. James Madison, "Father of the American Constitution" and President of the United States, was born in this county.

Birthplace of Madison, EP-8	Rte. 301, .4 mile n. of Port Royal
Cleydael, EP-9	Rte. 206, 1.35 miles w. of Rte. 218
Lamb's Creek Church, J-62	Rte. 3, 5.5 miles w. of King George
Marmion, J-63	Rte. 3, 2.3 miles w. of King George
St. Paul's Church, J-65	Rte. 3, 1.5 miles w. of King George
Historic Port Conway, J-66*	Rte. 3, 2.7 miles e. of King George

KING WILLIAM COUNTY
Area: 263 square miles

Formed in 1701 from King and Queen, and named for King William III. Here lived Carter Braxton, signer of the Declaration of Independence.

Rumford Academy, O-16	Rte. 360, at Central Garage
Cavalry Raids, O-18	Rte. 360, at Aylett
Montville Estate, O-25*	Rte. 360, 1 mile s.w. of Aylett
Pamunkey Reservation, OC-14	Rte. 30, .6 mile s.e. of King William
Mattapony Reservation, OC-15	Rte. 30, 4.9 miles s.e. of King William
Campaign of 1781, OC-22*	Rte. 30, 6.6 miles n.w. of West Point
Campaign of 1781, OC-25	Rte. 30, 3.4 miles n.w. of West Point
St. John's Church, OC-18	Rte. 30, 8.9 miles n.w. of West Point
Mangohick Church, OC-20	Rte. 30 near Rte. 671
Chericoke (Home of Signer), OC-26	Rte. 33, at West Point

LANCASTER COUNTY
Area: 130 square miles

Formed in 1652, and named for Lancaster, England. Ancient Christ Church and Epping Forest, birthplace of Washington's mother, are in this county.

Birthplace of Washington's Mother, J-80	Rte. 3, 9.3 miles e. of Farnham
Epping Forest, J-80*	Rte. 3, 12 miles e. of Warsaw
Bewdley, J-81	Rte. 354, 2.13 miles e. of Rte. 3
St. Mary's White Chapel, J-82	Rte. 3, at Lively
White Marsh Church, J-83	Rte. 3, 3.6 miles n.w. of Kilmarnock
Corotoman, J-85	Rte. 646, .66 mile w. of Rte. 3
Christ Church, J-86	Rte. 646, .66 mile w. of Rte. 3
Windmill Point, J-87	Rte. 695, 6.5 miles e. of Rte. 3
Ditchley and Cobbs, J-88	Rte. 200, 1.4 miles n. of Kilmarnock

First American Woman Missionary to China, Rte. 3, at Kilmarnock
J-89
Barford, J-90 Rte. 604 at Rte. 611
A. T. Wright High School, J-91 Rte. 637, .19 mile w. of Rte. 3

LEE COUNTY
Area: 446 square miles

Formed in 1792 from Russell, and named for Henry (Light-Horse Harry) Lee, Revolutionary soldier and Governor of Virginia 1791–94. Daniel Boone's son was killed by Indians here.

Cumberland Gap, K-1 Rte. 58, at Cumberland Gap
Indian Mound, K-3 Rte. 58, 2 miles w. of Rose Hill
Colonial Fort, K-4 Rte. 58, at Rose Hill
Indian Massacre, K-5 Rte. 58, at Stickleyville
Thompson Settlement Church, K-6 Rte. 758, 10.2 miles s.w. of Jonesville
Hanging Rock, K-7 Rte. 58, .25 mile w. of Ewing
Doctor Still's Birthplace, K-8 Rte. 58, at w. entrance of Jonesville
Jonesville Methodist Camp Ground, K-9 Rte. 58, 1 mile w. of Jonesville
Jonesville, K-10 Rte. 58, at Jonesville
Death of Boone's Son, K-32 Rte. 58 and Rte. 684, 11 miles e. of Cumberland Gap

Death of Boone's Son, K-32* Rte. 58, 1 mile e. of Stickleyville
Donelson's Indian Line, KA-8 Rte. 23, 5 miles s. of Big Stone Gap
Seminary Methodist Church, X-24 Alt. Rte. 58, 5 miles s.w. of Big Stone Gap
Members of Congress, X-26* Alt. Rte. 58, 6 miles s.w. of Big Stone Gap
Pennington Gap, X-30 Alt. Rte. 58, at Pennington Gap

LOUDOUN COUNTY
Area: 519 square miles

Formed in 1757 from Fairfax, and named for Lord Loudoun, titular governor of Virginia, and head of the British forces in America, 1756–58. Oak Hill, President James Monroe's home, is in this county.

Campaign of Second Manassas, B-11 Rte. 50, .44 mile w. of Fairfax Co. line
Military Movements, B-22* Rte. 50, at Middleburg
Braddock Road, B-27* Rte. 50, at Aldie
Mercer's Home, B-28, B-28* Rte. 50, at Aldie
Stuart and Bayard, B-30* Rte. 50, at Aldie
Gettysburg Campaign, B-32* Rte. 50, at limits of Middleburg
A Revolutionary War Hero, B-33 Rte. 50, 1.1 miles w. of Aldie
Battle of Ball's Bluff, F-1 Rte. 15, .9 mile n. of Leesburg
Potomac Crossings, F-2 Rte. 15, 6.9 miles n. of Leesburg
Oak Hill, F-4 Rte. 15, 3 miles n. of Aldie

Wayne's Crossing, F-5	Rte. 15, 7.2 miles n. of Leesburg
Sharpsburg (Antietam) Campaign, F-6	Rte. 15, 2.7 miles n. of Leesburg
Goose Creek Chapel, F-7	Rte. 15, 2 miles n. of Leesburg
Mother of Stonewall Jackson, F-15	Rte. 15, .9 mile s. of Gilberts Corner
Catoctin Rural Historic District, F-27	Rte. 15, 4.5 miles s. of Maryland line
St. James United Church of Christ, G-3	Rte. 673, .1 mile e. of Rte. 287
Mother of the Wright Brothers, T-5	Rte. 7, at Purcellville
Early's Washington Campaign, T-22	Rte. 7, 2.1 miles w. of Leesburg
Belmont, T-30	Rte. 7, 4.3 miles e. of Leesburg
Gettysburg Campaign, T-38	Rte. 7, 2.6 miles w. of Dranesville
First German Reformed Church Site and Cemetery, TA-1	Rte. 672/673, .6 mile e. of Rte. 287

LOUISA COUNTY
Area: 516 square miles

Formed in 1742 from Hanover, and named for the Queen of
Denmark, daughter of King George II. Patrick Henry lived
in this county for some years. In it was fought the Cavalry
battle of Trevillians, 1864.

Campaign of 1781, F-40	Rte. 15, 3.3 miles s. of Boswell's Tavern
Providence Church, V-19	Rte. 250, .4 mile n.w. of Gum Spring
Campaign of 1781, V-20	Rte. 250, at Ferncliff
The Marquis Road, W-206	Rte. 22, at Boswell's Tavern
Boswell's Tavern, W-207	Rte. 22, at Boswell's Tavern
Green Springs, W-208	Rte. 33, 7 miles w. of Louisa
Battle of Trevilians, W-209	Rte. 33, 4.5 miles w. of Louisa
Battle of Trevilians, W-210*	Rte. 33, 4.5 miles w. of Louisa
Patrick Henry's Home, W-211	Rte. 33, at Louisa
Historic Louisa, W-212	Rtes. 33 and 22, e. of Louisa
Jack Jouett's Ride, W-213	Rte. 33, at Cuckoo

LUNENBURG COUNTY
Area: 430 square miles

Formed in 1746 from Brunswick. Named for King George
II, who was also duke of Brunswick-Lunenburg. Tarleton
passed though the county in 1781.

Craig's Mill, SN-45	Rte. 40, .3 mile n. of Kenbridge
Home of the Reverend James Craig, SN-62	Rte. 40, 2.3 miles w. of Kenbridge

MADISON COUNTY
Area: 324 square miles

Formed in 1792 from Culpeper, and named for James Madison, "Father of the American Constitution" and President of the United States. Governor Spotswood's exploring expedition passed here, 1716.

Jackson's Crossing, F-22	Rte. 15, 7.6 miles n. of Orange
Woodberry Forest School, F-24	Rte. 15, 6 miles n. of Orange
Cavalry Engagement at Jack's Shop, G-11	Rte. 231, 6.5 miles s. of Madison
Cavalry Engagement, G-11*	Rte. 231, 5.5 miles s. of Madison
Joseph Early Home, G-12	Rte. 29, 3 miles s. of Madison
Jackson's March to Fredericksburg, JE-1	Rte. 231, at Madison
Knights of the Golden Horseshoe, JE-2	Rte. 15, 3.3 miles n. of Orange
James L. Kemper Residence, JE-3	Bus. Rte. 29, .1 mile s. of Madison
Hebron Church, JE-4	Rte. 231, 9.5 miles n. of Madison
A Camp of Stonewall Jackson's, JE-15	Rte. 670, 1 mile n. of Criglersville

MATHEWS COUNTY
Area: 94 square miles

Formed in 1790 from Gloucester, and named for Colonel Thomas Mathews, Revolutionary soldier. Gwynn's Island, from which Dunmore was driven in 1776, is here.

Captain Sally L. Tompkins, C.S.A., 1833–1916, N-84	Rte. 611, 2 miles w. of Mathews Court House
Battle of Cricket Hill, N-85	Rte. 223, 4 miles n. of Mathews
Fitchett's Wharf, N-86	Rte. 642, at Moon Post Office
Kingston Parish Glebe, N-87	Rte. 621 near Rte. 611
Mathews County Courthouse Square, N-88	Rte. 611, .2 mile w. of Rte. 14
John Clayton, Botanist, NN-3	Rte. 14 e. of Gloucester Co. line

MECKLENBURG COUNTY
Area: 669 square miles

Formed in 1764 from Lunenburg, and named for Princess Charlotte, of Mecklenburg-Strelitz, queen of George III. Bacon the Rebel defeated the Indians near the present town of Clarksville, 1676.

Prestwould Plantation, F-95	Rte. 15, 3 miles n. of Clarksville
Occaneechee Island, F-98*	Rte. 15, near state line
Salem Chapel, S-70	Rte. 1, at South Hill
Early Exploration, S-76	Rte. 1, 1.6 miles n. of South Hill
Occaneechee Indians, U-60*	Rte. 58, 1.5 miles e. of Clarksville
A Revolutionary Soldier, U-80	Rte. 58, at Boydton
Old Randolph-Macon College, UL-4*	Rte. 58, .3 mile w. of Boydton

Taylor's Ferry, UL-5   Rte. 58, .3 mile w. of Boydton

MIDDLESEX COUNTY
Area: 146 square miles

Formed in 1673 from Lancaster, and named for an English
county. Rosegill, frequented by colonial governors, is here.

Glebe Landing Church, N-40	Rte. 17, 12.1 miles n.w. of Saluda
Hewick, N-45	Rte. 17, 3.1 miles n.w. of Saluda
Christ Church, N-48	Rte. 33, 2.4 miles s. of Urbanna
Tomb of Puller, N-49	Rte. 33, 3 miles e. of Saluda
Lower Methodist Church, N-50	Rte. 33, 9.3 miles s.e. of Saluda
Stingray Point, N-77	Rte. 33, 8.6 miles west of Deltaville
Rosegill, OC-35	Rte. 227, .7 mile s. of Urbanna
Christopher Robinson, OC-36	Rte. 602, 100 ft. n. of Rte. 615, .5 mile w. of Urbanna
Urbanna Creek, OC-40, OC-40*	Rte. 227, at Urbanna
Scottish Factors Store, WO-37	Rte. 33, 1.5 miles e. of Saluda

MONTGOMERY COUNTY
Area: 401 square miles

Formed in 1776 from Fincastle, and named for General
Richard Montgomery, killed at Quebec, 1775. The Virginia
Polytechnic Institute is in this county.

Virginia Polytechnic Institute, I-2-a	Rte. 11, .6 mile e. of Christiansburg
Virginia Polytechnic Institute, I-2-b	Rte. 11, at w. entrance of Christiansburg
Virginia Polytechnic Institute, I-2-c	Rte. 460, at Blacksburg
Solitude, I-20	At VPI&SU on West Campus Dr., .4 mile s. of Rte. 412
Founding of the Future Farmers of Virginia, K-64	Rte. 314 at VPI&SU, .25 mile e. of Rte. 460 Bypass
"Fotheringay," K-67	Rte. 11, 4.5 miles w. of Roanoke County
Christiansburg Industrial Institute, K-68	Rte. 460 Bus., 1 mile w. of Rte. 11, in Christiansburg
Ingles Ferry Road, K-70	Rte. 11, 1.4 miles e. of Radford
Lewis-McHenry Duel, K-71	Rtes. 11 and 460, at Christiansburg
Christiansburg, K-72	Rte. 11, .6 mile e. of Christiansburg
Fort Vause, K-73	Rte. 11, .3 mile w. of Shawsville
Colonel William Preston, KG-8	Rte. 460, at Blacksburg
Draper's Meadow Massacre, KG-10	Rte. 460, at s. entrance of Blacksburg
Montgomery White Sulphur Springs, KG-12	I-81, .75 mile n. of Exit 128 at rest area, northbound lane

NELSON COUNTY
Area: 473 square miles

Formed in 1807 from Amherst, and named for General Thomas Nelson, Governor of Virginia, 1781. Oak Ridge, an old home, is in this county.

Thomas Massie, OQ-4*	Rtes. 56 and 666 at Massie's Mill
William Cabell, OQ-5	Rte. 56, at Wingina
Boyhood Home of Colonel Mosby, R-50	Rte. 6, 3 miles n. of Woods Mill
Hurricane Camille, R-51	Rte. 29, at Woods Mill Wayside
Lovingston, R-56	Rte. 250, at Lovingston
Birthplace of Rives, R-58	Rte. 29, 4 miles s. of Lovingston
Rockfish Church, RA-4	Rte. 151, 10.6 miles s. of Afton
William H. Crawford, RA-6	Rte. 151, 12.7 miles s. of Afton
Rockfish Gap Meeting, W-218, W-218*	Rte. 250, 2 miles n.w. of Afton
Flight of Richard C. duPont, W-219	I-64 overlook on Afton Mountain

NEW KENT COUNTY
Area: 191 square miles

Formed in 1654 from York, and named for an English county. The White House, where Washington's wife lived, was in this county, and here he married her.

McClellan's Crossing, W-14	Rte. 60, at Bottoms Bridge
Lafayette and Cornwallis, W-16	Rte. 60, at Bottoms Bridge
New Kent Road, W-17	Rte. 60, at Bottoms Bridge
Long Bridge, W-18	Rte. 60, 4.9 miles s.e. of Bottoms Bridge
Soane's Bridge, W-19*	Rte. 60, at Bottoms Bridge
Providence Forge, W-20	Rte. 60, at Providence Forge
State Game Farm, W-21	Rte. 60, 2.8 miles s.e. of Providence Forge
Chickahominy Indians, W-22	Rte. 60, 4.2 miles s.e. of Providence Forge
Fort James, W-23	Rte. 60, 7.6 miles s.e. of Providence Forge
Diascund Bridge, W-24	Rte. 60, 6.7 miles n.w. of Toano
Cooper's Mill, W-25*	Rte. 60, 7.25 miles e. of Providence Forge
Tyree's Plantation, W-29*	Rte. 60, 6.7 miles n.w. of Toano
The White House, WO-12	Rte. 249, at Talleysville
St. Peter's Church, WO-13	Rte. 249, at Talleysville
Stuart's Ride around McClellan, WO-14	Rte. 33, at Talleysville
New Kent Courthouse, WO-16	Rte. 249, at New Kent
Martha Washington's Birthplace, WO-18	Rte. 249, 7 miles e. of New Kent
Eltham, WO-30	Rte. 33, 1.9 miles w. of West Point
Peninsular Campaign, WO-31	Rte. 33, 1.5 miles w. of West Point
The Brick House, WO-33	Rte. 33, 1.5 miles w. of West Point

NORTHAMPTON COUNTY
Area: 239 square miles

One of the original shires formed in 1634 and named Accomac. In 1643 the name was changed to Northampton for an
English county. This county was Governor Berkeley's
stronghold in the rebellion of 1676.

Site of Tidewater Institute, WY-2	Rte. 636, .75 mile e. of Rte. 13
Salem Methodist Church, WY-3	Rte. 13, at Rte. 636
Cape Charles, WY-4	Rte. 13 near Rte. 184
Arlington, WY-5, WY-5*	Rte. 13, 3 miles n. of Cape Charles
Old Places, WY-6*	Rte. 13, 3 miles n. of Cape Charles
Towne Fields, WY-7	Rte. 13, at Cheriton
First Courthouse, WY-7*	Rte. 13, at Cheriton
Home of First Settler, WY-8	Rte. 13, 1 mile s. of Eastville
Indian Village, WY-9	Rte. 13, at Eastville
Old Courthouse, WY-10	Rte. 13, at Eastville
Hungers Church and Vaucluse, WY-11*	Rte. 13, 2.8 miles s. of Nassawadox

NORTHUMBERLAND COUNTY
Area: 205 square miles

Originally an Indian district called Chickacoan. In 1648 it
became Northumberland County, named for an English
county. The mouth of the Potomac River is here.

Coan River, JT-9*	Rte. 360, 2.2 miles w. of Heathsville
Northumberland House and Mantua, JT-12	Rte. 360, 1 mile e. of Heathsville
Morattico Baptist Church, JX-5	Rte. 200, 2.8 miles n. of Kilmarnock
St. Stephen's Parish, O-49	Rte. 360, at Heathsville
Reedville, O-51	Rte. 360 at Rte. 726

NOTTOWAY COUNTY
Area: 310 square miles

Formed in 1788 from Amelia, and named for an Indian tribe.
Tarleton passed through this county in 1781. Here lived
William Hodges Mann, Governor of Virginia 1910–14.

Nottoway Courthouse, K-170	Rte. 460, .2 mile w. of Nottoway
Blackstone, K-172	Rte. 460, at Blackstone
Fort Pickett, K-173	Rte. 40, 1 mile s. of Rte. 460
Lee's Retreat, M-16	Rte. 360, at Burkeville
Historic Burkeville, M-17	Rte. 360, at Burkeville
Francisco's Fight, M-18	Rte. 360, 6 miles n.e. of Burkeville
T. O. Sandy (First Co. Agent), M-20	Rte. 460, 2.1 miles e. of Burkeville
Civilian Conservation Corps Company 1370, M-21	Rte. 460, at Crewe e. corp. limits

Union Academy, SM-2	Rte. 42, at s. entrance of Blackstone
Lottie Moon, SM-2	Rte. 49, .4 mile s. of Crewe
Old Nottoway Meeting House, WK-4	Rte. 723, 2 miles s. of Burkeville

ORANGE COUNTY
Area: 359 square miles

Formed in 1734 from Spotsylvania, and named for the prince of Orange, who in that year married Princess Anne, daughter of King George II. President James Madison lived in this county, and President Zachary Taylor was born here.

Montebello, D-20	Rte. 33, 3 miles w. of Gordonsville
Barboursville, D-22	Rte. 33, at Barboursville
Kemper's Grave, F-17	Rte. 15, 2.7 miles n. of Orange
Church of the Blind Preacher, F-23	Rte. 15, .5 mile n. of Gordonsville
Woodberry Forest School, F-24*	1.5 miles n. of Orange
Montpelier and Madison's Tomb, F-26	Rte. 15, at Orange
Campaign of Second Manassas, F-32	Rte. 15, 3.2 miles s. of Orange
Germanna, J-34, J-34*	Rte. 3, 4.8 miles w. of Wilderness
Germanna Ford, J-35	Rte. 3, 4.8 miles w. of Wilderness
Lee's Headquarters, JJ-2*	Rte. 20, 1.6 miles e. of Orange
Bloomsbury, JJ-4	Rte. 20, 3.3 miles e. of Orange
Campaign of Second Manassas, JJ-6	Rte. 20, 5.7 miles e. of Orange
Mine Run Campaign, JJ-10	Rte. 20, 6.6 miles e. of Unionville
Stuart's Escape, JJ-12*	4.1 miles e. of Unionville
Robinson's Tavern, JJ-15	Rte. 20, at Locust Grove
Battle of the Wilderness, JJ-20	Rte. 20, 2.9 miles e. of Locust Grove
Campaign of 1781, JJ-24	Rte. 20, 2.6 miles e. of Unionville (at Rhodesville)

PAGE COUNTY
Area: 322 square miles

Formed in 1831 from Shenandoah and Rockingham, and named for John Page, Governor of Virginia 1802–5. Luray Cave is in this county.

Cavalry Engagement, C-3*	Rte. 211, at Luray
White House, C-30	Rte. 211, 4 miles w. of Luray
Fort Long, C-31*	Rte. 211, 2 miles w. of Luray
William Randolph Barbee, C-56	Rte. 211 and Skyline Drive, at Panoramo

PATRICK COUNTY
Area: 485 square miles

Formed in 1790 from Henry, and named for Patrick Henry, who thus had two counties named for him. General J. E. B. Stuart was born in this county.

Fairy Stone State Park, AS-1	Rte. 623, 6 miles s. of Franklin Co. line
Colonel Abram Penn, HD-1	Rte. 58, 1.86 miles s.e. of Henry Co. line
Stuart's Birthplace, KG-2	Rte. 103, 4 miles s. of Friends Mission
Blue Ridge Mission School, U-28	Rte. 8, at Rte. 613
Stuart, U-30	Rte. 58, at Stuart
Frontier Fort, U-32	Rte. 58, 14 miles e. of Stuart
Reynolds Homestead, U-34	Rte. 58, at Critz
William Byrd's Survey of 1728, U-36	Rte. 660, 4 miles s. of Rte. 8, at North Carolina line

PITTSYLVANIA COUNTY
Area: 1,015 square miles

Formed in 1766 from Halifax, and named for William Pitt, Earl of Chatham, British statesman. This is the largest county in Virginia. The home of Claude A. Swanson, Governor of Virginia 1906–10.

Pittsylvania Court House, KG-23	Rte. 29, in front of court house
Clement Hill, L-32	Rte. 29, 1 mile s. of Alta Vista
Whitmell P. Tunstall, L-48	Rte. 29 at Rte. 703
Claude A. Swanson, L-49	Rte. 29, .5 mile n. of Bus. Rte. 29
Peytonsburg, L-50*	Rte. 29, at Chatham
Markham, L-52	Rte. 29 Chatham Bypass, .25 mile s. of Rte. 685 exit
Beavers Tavern, L-61	Rte. 29, 5 miles n. of Danville
Callands, LT-1	Rte. 57, at Callands
Clerk's Office, Q-12-a	Rte. 969, at Callands
John Weatherford's Grave, RG-5	Rte. 29, 9 miles s.e. of Chatham
Berry Hill, U-40	Rtes. 58 and 863

POWHATAN COUNTY
Area: 273 square miles

Formed in 1777 from Cumberland and Chesterfield and named for Powhatan, the noted Indian ruler. Many Huguenots settled in this county, 1699–1700. Here Robert E. Lee spent the summer of 1865.

Dunlora Academy, O-25	Rte. 60, 5.7 miles w. of Powhatan
Derwent, O-30	Rte. 13, 2 miles e. of Tobaccoville
Giles's Home, O-31	Rte. 60, 1.7 miles w. of Powhatan

Powhatan Courthouse, O-32	Rte. 13, at Powhatan
Huguenot Settlement, O-33	Rte. 711, 2.55 miles w. of Chesterfield Co. line
Huguenot Springs Confederate Cemetery, O-36	Rte. 711, 2.13 miles w. of Chesterfield Co. line
Lee's Last Camp, OH-10	Rte. 711, 9.8 miles w. of Chesterfield Co. line
Lee's Last Camp, OH-10*	Rte. 711, 9.5 miles n. of Powhatan

PRINCE EDWARD COUNTY
Area: 356 square miles

Formed in 1753 from Amelia, and named for Prince Edward, son of Frederick, Prince of Wales, and younger brother of King George III. General Joseph E. Johnston was born in this county; Hampden-Sydney College is in it.

Old Worsham, F-65	Rte. 15, 5.6 miles s. of Farmville
Slate Hill Plantation, F-66*	Rte. 15, 6.5 miles s. of Farmville
Randolph-Macon Medical School, F-69	Rte. 15, 5 miles s. of Farmville
Kingsville, F-70	Rte. 15, 4.5 miles s. of Farmville
Providence, F-71	Rte. 15, 5.6 miles s. of Farmville
Campaign of 1781, F-72	Rte. 15, 5.6 miles s. of Farmville
High Bridge, F-73	Rte. 619 at Rte. 688, 2.25 miles n. of Rte. 460
Old Briery Church, F-75	Rte. 15, 2.4 miles n. of Keysville
Hampden-Sydney College, I-9	Rte. 692, at Hampton Sydney
State Teachers College at Farmville, I-15	Rte. 15, at Farmville
Longwood College, I-15-a*	Rte. 460, at Farmville
Presbyterian Seminary, I-19	Rte. 1001, on campus of Hampden-Sydney College
Robert Russa Moton High School, M-1, M-1*	Rte. 15 and Ely Street in Farmville
Lee's Retreat, M-24	Rte. 307, 3 miles e. of Rice
Battle of Sailor's Creek, M-25	Rte. 460, at Rice
Action of High Bridge, M-30*	Rte. 460, at Rice
Longwood Estate, M-33*	Rte. 460, at Farmville

PRINCE GEORGE COUNTY
Area: 294 square miles

Formed in 1702 from Charles City, and named for Prince George of Denmark, husband of Queen Anne. The battles of the crater, 1864, and Fort Steadman, 1865, took place in this county.

City Point and Hopewell, K-205	Rte. 36, .7 mile e. of Petersburg
Bailey's Creek, K-206*	Rte. 106, 5.5 miles e. of Petersburg
History at Prince George Courthouse, K-207	Rte. 106, at Prince George
Jordan's Point, K-208	Rte. 106, 2.9 miles e. of Prince George
Merchant's Hope Church, K-209	Rte. 10, 8.3 miles n.w. of Burrowsville
Coggins's Point, K-210	Rte. 10, 8.3 miles n.w. of Burrowsville
The Cattle Raid, K-211	Rte. 106, 6.8 miles e. of Prince George

Powell's Creek, K-212	Rte. 10, 5.3 miles n.w. of Burrowsville
Maycock's Plantation, K-213	Rte. 10, 5.3 miles n.w. of Burrowsville
Flowerdew Hundred, K-214	Rte. 10, 5.3 miles n.w. of Burrowsville
Hood's, K-215	Rte. 10, at Burrowsville
Ward's Creek, K-216	Rte. 10, at Burrowsville
Brandon, K-218	Rte. 10, at Burrowsville
Reams Station, UM-20	Rte. 301, 12.6 miles s. of Petersburg

PRINCE WILLIAM COUNTY
Area: 345 square miles

Formed in 1730 from Stafford and King George, and named for William Augustus, Duke of Cumberland, second son of King George II. The first and second battles of Manassas took place in this county.

The Stone Bridge, C-23	Rte. 211, 6 miles e. of Gainesville
Battle of Groveton, C-26*	Rte. 211, 3.5 miles e. of Gainesville
Second Battle of Manassas, C-27	Rte. 211, 1.6 miles e. of Gainesville
Campaign of Second Manassas, C-28*	Rte. 211, at Gainesville
Bull Run Battlefields, C-31	Rte. 211, .4 mile e. of Gainesville
Second Battle of Manassas, C-33*	Rte. 211, 3 miles e. of Gainesville
First Battle of Manassas, C-34	Rte. 211, 4.7 miles e. of Gainesville
First Battle of Manassas, C-44	Rte. 211, 4.7 miles e. of Gainesville
Second Battle of Manassas, C-46	Rte. 211, 4.7 miles e. of Gainesville
Campaign of Second Manassas, C-48	Rte. 211, 4.7 miles e. of Gainesville
Thoroughfare Gap, C-50	Rte. 55, at Gainesville
Chopawamsic, E-52*	Rte. 1, 4.3 miles s. of Dumfries
Campaign of 1781, E-53	Rte. 1, at n. entrance of Dumfries
Early Land Patents, E-53*	Rte. 1, s. of Dumfries
Ancient Road to Valley, E-54*	Rte. 1, s. of Dumfries
History of Dumfries, E-55	Rte. 1, at Dumfries
Early Land Patents, E-56*	Rte. 1, 1.1 miles s. of Woodbridge
Early Land Patents, E-57*	Rte. 1, 4 miles n. of Dumfries
Early Iron Furnace, E-58*	Rte. 1, 3.2 miles n. of Dumfries
The Occoquan, E-59*	Rte. 1, at Woodbridge
Simon Kenton's Birthplace, F-14	Rte. 15, 6.9 miles s. of Gilberts Corner
Campaign of Second Manassas, FA-1*	Rte. 55, 5 miles s.e. of The Plains
Henry House, G-15	Rte. 234, 5.1 miles n.w. of Manassas
James Robinson House, G-16	Rte. 29, .27 mile n. of Rte. 234
Second Prince William County Courthouse, G-17	Rte. 646, 3.55 miles w. of Rte. 234
Leesylvania State Park, JQ-1	Rte. 610, 1153 miles e. of Rte. 1

PULASKI COUNTY
Area: 333 square miles

Formed in 1839 from Wythe and Montgomery, and named for Count Casimir Pulaski, killed at the siege of Savannah, 1779. New River flows through this county.

New River, K-25	Rte. 11, .5 mile n.w. of Radford
First Settlement, K-29	Rte. 11, 1.9 miles w. of Radford
Battle of Cloyd's Mountain, K-38	Rte. 100, 1.4 miles n. of Rte. 627
Battle of Cloyd's Mountain, K-38*	Rte. 100, at Dublin
Draper's Valley, K-40	Rte. 11, 1.9 miles s. of Pulaski
Pulaski, K-41	Rte. 11, at Pulaski
Page's Meeting House, K-45	Rte. 11, 1.25 miles w. of Radford
Battle of Cloyd's Mountain, KE-5	Rte. 100, 5 miles n. of Dublin

RAPPAHANNOCK COUNTY
Area: 274 square miles

Formed in 1833 from Culpeper, and named for the Rappahannock River, headwaters of which are in this county.

Cavalry Engagement, C-4	Rte. 211, at Sperryville
Washington, Virginia, the First of Them All, C-5	Rte. 211, at Washington
Campaign of Second Manassas, C-6	Rte. 211, 7.2 miles e. of Massies Corner
William Randolph Barbee, C-56	Rte. 211 and Skyline Drive, at Panoramo
Campaign of Second Manassas, C-61	Rte. 211, 9.5 miles e. of Massies Corner
Gettysburg Campaign, J-25	Rte. 522, 5 miles s. of Front Royal
Albert Gallatin Willis, J-26	Rte. 522, 5.5 miles n. of Flint Hill
Pope's Army of Virginia, J-29*	Rte. 522, at Sperryville

RICHMOND COUNTY
Area: 204 square miles

Formed in 1692 from Old Rappahannock County, and named for the town of Richmond, Surrey, England. Sabine Hall and Mount Airy, noted old homes, are in this county.

Menokin, J-73	Rte. 690, 4.1 miles n. of Warsaw
North Farnham Church, J-77	Rte. 692, at Farnham
Cyrus Griffin's Birthplace, J-78	Rte. 2, 2.8 miles s.e. of Farnham
Sabine Hall, O-45*	Rte. 360, .3 mile west of Warsaw
Warsaw, O-46	Rte. 360, at Warsaw

ROANOKE COUNTY
Area: 305 square miles

Formed in 1838 from Botetourt and Montgomery, and probably named for the Roanoke River. General Andrew Lewis lived here. The city of Roanoke is known as the Magic City of the South.

Hollins College, A-79	Rte. 11, 5.8 miles n. of Roanoke
Catawba Sanatorium, I-4	Rte. 311, at Catawba
Roanoke College, I-11-b	Rte. 11, .2 mile w. of Salem
Colonial Mansion Site, K-74	Rte. 11, 2.5 miles w. of Salem
Old Lutheran Church, K-76	Rte. 11, .8 mile w. of Roanoke
Old Salem Inns, K-88	Rte. 11, .2 mile of Salem
Hanging Rock, KH-7	Rte. 311, n. of Salem at Rte. 116

ROCKBRIDGE COUNTY
Area: 616 square miles

Formed in 1778 from Augusta and Botetourt, and named for the Natural Bridge. Samuel Houston and Cyrus H. McCormick were born in this county. Robert E. Lee and Stonewall Jackson are buried in Lexington. Washington and Lee University and the Virginia Military Institute are there.

Ruffner's Home, A-42*	Rte. 11, at Lexington
McDowell's Grave, A-43	Rte. 11, 1.1 miles s. of Fairfield
Liberty Hall Academy, A-44	Rte. 11, 5.3 miles n. of Lexington
Red House Estate, A-45*	Rte. 11, 1.1 miles s. of Fairfield
Timber Ridge Church, A-46	Rte. 11, 5.3 miles n. of Lexington (at Sam Houston Wayside)
Cherry Grove Estate, A-47	Rte. 11, .3 mile s. of Fairfield
Thorn Hill Estate, A-49	Rte. 251, .6 mile n. of Lexington
Birthplace of Sam Houston, A-52	Rte. 11, 5.3 miles n. of Lexington
Natural Bridge of Virginia, A-72	Rte. 11, at Natural Bridge
Virginia Military Institute, I-1	Rte. 11, at Lexington
Washington and Lee University, I-8	Rte. 11, at Lexington
New Monmouth Church and Morrison's Birthplace, L-8	Rte. 60, 2 miles w. of Lexington
First Indian Fight, L-10	Rte. 130, at Glasgow
Moomaw's Landing, L-11	Rte. 60, w. end of Buena Vista
Falling Spring Presbyterian Church, R-63	Rte. 11, 7 miles s. of Lexington
Youel-Condon House, p. 205	Rte. 39, 3.5 miles e. of Goshen

ROCKINGHAM COUNTY
Area: 876 square miles

Formed in 1778 from Augusta, and named for the Marquis of Rockingham, British statesman. John Sevier, of Tennessee, was born in this county. In it took place the battles of Cross Keys and Port Republic, 1862.

Abraham Lincoln's Father, A-18	Rte. 11, at Lacy Spring
Cavalry Engagement, A-29	Rte. 11, 7.5 miles n. of Harrisonburg
Where Ashby Fell, A-30	Rte. 11, 1.5 miles s. of Harrisonburg
Sheridan's Last Raid, A-32	Rte. 11, .3 mile s. of Mount Crawford
Dr. Jessee Bennett, A-59	Rte. 11, Rte. 42, at Edom
Fort Harrison, D-1	Bus. Rte. 42 at corp. limits of Dayton
Battle of Cross Keys, D-6	Rte. 33, 5 miles e. of Harrisonburg
First Church in Rockingham County, D-7	Rte. 732, .2 mile w. of Rte. 290
Knights of the Golden Horseshoe, D-10	Rte. 33, 7 miles s.e. of Elkton
Bridgewater College, I-13	Rte. 11, at Va. 257 (Mount Crawford)
Bridgewater College, I-13-a	Rtes. 613 and 748 at Spring Creek
First Settler (Green Meadow), JD-8	Rte. 340, .5 mile n. of Elton
Battle of Port Republic, JD-10	Rte. 340, 3 miles n. of Grottoes
Lincoln's Virginia Ancestors, KB-65*	Rte. 42, 2.5 miles n. of Edom

RUSSELL COUNTY
Area: 496 square miles

Formed in 1786 from Washington, and named for General William Russell, pioneer and Revolutionary soldier. Clinch River runs through the county.

Frances Dickenson Scott Johnson, X-3	Rte. 80 and Rte. 619, 3.8 miles e. of Rte. 19/460
Old Russell County Courthouse, X-4	Rte. 19, .5 mile e. of Rte. 17/82 in Lebanon
Early Settlers in Russell County, X-5	Rte. 71, at Grassy Creek Church
Russell Courthouse, X-6	Rte. 19, at Lebanon
Russell's Fort, X-7	Rte. 615, at Castlewood
Glade Hollow Fort, X-8	Rte. 71, 1 mile e. of Lebanon
Elk Garden Fort, X-9, X-9*	Rte. 19, 8 miles e. of Lebanon
Smith's Fort, X-17	Rte. 19, 17.5 miles e. of Lebanon
Moore's Fort, X-18	Alt. Rte. 58, e. entrance of St. Paul

SCOTT COUNTY
Area: 543 square miles

Formed in 1814 from Lee, Washington, and Russell. Named for General Winfield Scott, later commander of the American army. The Natural Tunnel is in this county.

Gate City, K-11	Rte. 71 and Rte. 23, at Gate City
Faris Station, K-12	Rte. 71 and Rte. 23, at Gate City

Fort Blackmore, K-13	Rte. 71 and Rte. 23, at Gate City
McConnell's Birthplace, K-14	Rte. 23 and Rte. 58, at Weber City
Big Moccasin Gap, K-15	Rte. 23 and Rte. 58, at Weber City
Donelson's Indian Line, K-16	Rte. 23 and Rte. 58, at Weber City
Houston's Fort, K-17	Rte. 613, 6.8 miles s. of Rte. 71
Patrick Porter, K-18	Rte. 65, .5 mile e. of Rte. 72, in Dungannon
Carter's Fort, KA-7	Rte. 23, .5 mile w. of Rte. 871
Kilgore Fort House, KA-9	Rte. 71, 1.2 miles w. of Nickelsville
Carter's Fort, KA-10	Rte. 871, 1 mile e. of Sunbright
First Court of Scott County, KA-15	Rte. 23 and Rte. 58, at Weber City
Patrick Hagan and Dungannon, KA-16	Rte. 65, at Dungannon
Dortor's Fort, XC-4*	Rte. 71, 1.5 miles w. of Nickelsville

SHENANDOAH COUNTY
Area: 510 square miles

Formed in 1772 from Frederick, and first named Dunmore for Lord Dunmore, Governor of Virginia 1771–75. In 1778 the county was renamed for the Shenandoah River.

Trenches on Hupp's Hill, A-19	Rte. 11, .8 mile n. of Strasburg
Frontier Fort, A-20	Rte. 11, at Strasburg
Battle of Cedar Creek, A-21	Rte. 11, at Strasburg
Battle of Fisher's Hill, A-22*	Rte. 11, 1.9 miles s. of Strasburg
Battle of Fisher's Hill, A-23	Rte. 11, 3.1 miles s. of Strasburg
Banks' Fort, A-24	Rte. 11, at Strasburg
Action of Tom's Brook, A-25	Rte. 11, .1 mile s. of Tom's Brook
Cavalry Engagement, A-26*	Rte. 11, 1 mile s. of Mount Jackson
Rude's Hill Action, A-27	Rte. 11, 3.7 miles n. of New Market
Battle of New Market, A-28	Rte. 11, .6 mile n. of New Market
Sevier's Birthplace, A-34	Rte. 11, .7 mile s. of New Market
Fairfax Line, A-36	Rte. 11, .7 mile s. of New Market
Last Indian Outrage, A-41	Rte. 11, 1.9 miles s. of Woodstock
Fort Bowman, A-55*	Rte. 11, 1.9 miles n. of Strasburg
Meem's Bottom Covered Bridge, AB-1	Rte. 11, .2 mile s. of Rte. 720

SMYTH COUNTY
Area: 435 square miles

Formed in 1832 from Washington and Wythe, and named for General Alexander Smyth, member of Congress for many years. Saltworks here were operated at an early date, and at Saltville a battle was fought in 1864.

Seven Mile Ford, K-19	Rte. 11, 2.9 miles e. of Chilhowie
William Campbell's Grave, K-20	Rte. 11, 2 miles e. of Chilhowie
Farthest West, 1750, K-21	Rte. 11, at Chilhowie
Chilhowie, K-22	Rte. 11, at Chilhowie

Early Church, K-24*	Rte. 11, .6 mile e. of Marion
Battle of Marion, K-26	Rte. 11, at Marion e. corp. limits
Site of Colonial Home, K-27	Rte. 11 at Rte. 16, in Marion
Saltville History, K-28	Rte. 107, 1 mile s. of Saltville
Early Settlers, K-30	Rte. 11, 8.5 miles e. of Marion
Hungry Mother State Park, K-33	Rte. 16, at entrance to park, 3.75 miles n. of Rte. 11
Marion, K-34	Smyth County Courthouse, in Marion
Sherwood Anderson, K-46	Rte. 11, at e. corp. limits of Marion
Saltville, KB-6	Rte. 91, at Saltville
State Fish Hatchery, UC-5	Rte. 16, 5 miles s.e. of Marion

SOUTHAMPTON COUNTY
Area: 604 square miles

Formed in 1748 from Isle of Wight and Nansemond. Named
for a locality that was originally named for the Earl of Southampton, active in the first settlement. General William
Mahone was born in this county.

Tarleton's Movements, U-102	Rte. 58, 8.2 miles e. of Emporia
John Y. Mason's Home, U-105	Rte. 58, 8.2 miles e. of Emporia
Buckhorn Quarters, U-115	Rte. 58, 4.5 miles w. of Courtland
General Thomas's Birthplace, U-120, U-120*	Rte. 58, 1.7 miles s.e. of Courtland
Nat Turner's Insurrection, U-122	Rte. 35 near Rte. 665
Southampton Insurrection, U-122*	Rte. 58, 2 miles w. of Courtland
Major Joseph E. Gillette, U-123	Rte. 58, .9 mile w. of Franklin
Old Indian Reservation, U-124	Rte. 58, .8 mile w. of Courtland
William Mahone's Birthplace, US-3	Rte. 258, 2.2 miles s. of Franklin
South Quay, US-6*	Rte. 258, 4.8 miles s. of Franklin

SPOTSYLVANIA COUNTY
Area: 413 square miles

Formed in 1720 from Essex, King and Queen, and King
William, and named for Alexander Spotswood, Governor
of Virginia 1710–22. The battles of Fredericksburg, Chancellorsville, the Wilderness, partly, and Spotsylvania were
fought in this county.

Stuart, E-8	Rte. 1, 5.4 miles s. of Falmouth
Turn in Sheridan's Raid, E-30	Rte. 1, 1.8 miles s. of Thornburg
Jerrell's Mill, E-31	Rte. 1, 1.1 miles s. of Thornburg
Mud Tavern, E-32	Rte. 1, at Thornburg
A Raid's End, E-33*	Rte. 1, 2 miles n. of Thornburg
Where Burnside Turned, E-34*	Rte. 1, 1.3 miles n. of Thornburg
Where Burnside Crossed, E-35*	Rte. 1, 1.3 miles n. of Thornburg
Union Army Route, E-36*	Rte. 1, 3.8 miles n. of Thornburg

Massaponax Church, E-37*	Rte. 1, 4.5 miles n. of Thornburg
Lee's Headquarters, E-38*	Rte. 1, 5.4 miles s. of Falmouth
Start of Sheridan's Raid, E-39	Rte. 1, 5.3 miles s. of Falmouth
Grant's Supply Line, E-40*	Rte. 1, 4 miles s. of Fredericksburg
Longstreet's Headquarters, E-41*	Rte. 1, 3.5 miles s. of Fredericksburg
Early's Line of Battle, E-42*	Rte. 1, 3.5 miles s. of Fredericksburg
Lee's Position, E-43*	Rte. 1, 1 mile s. of Fredericksburg
Battles of Fredericksburg, E-44*	Rte. 1, at s. entrance of Fredericksburg
Fredericksburg, E-45*	Rte. 1, at n. entrance of Fredericksburg
Colonial Fort, E-46*	Rte. 1, at n. entrance of Fredericksburg
Fredericksburg, E-46-a	Alt. Rte. 1, 2 miles s. of Falmouth
Fredericksburg, E-46-b	Rte. 1, 2 miles s. of Falmouth
Fall Hill, E-49-a, and E-49-b	Rte. 1, at Fredericksburg
Massaponax Baptist Church, E-78	Rte. 608 near Rte. 1
Asbury's Deathplace, EH-8	Rte. 738, 5.5 miles s. of Spotsylvania Court House
Fredericksville Furnace, EM-1	Rte. 208, 100 yards s.w. of Furnace
Engagement at Harris Farm (Bloomsbury), EM-2	Rte. 208, .25 mile w. of Rte. 628
Jackson's Amputation, J-37	Rte. 3, e. of Route 20
Ely's Ford, J-38	Rte. 610, .54 mile e. of Culpeper Co. line
Wounding of Jackson, J-39*	Rte. 3, .9 mile w. of Chancellorsville
Battle of Chancellorsville, J-40	Rte. 3, at Chancellorsville
Spotswood's Furnace, J-42	Rte. 3, 5.4 miles w. of Fredericksburg
Gaspar Tochman, JJ-25	Rte. 621, .25 mile s. of Rte. 611
The Gallant Pelham, N-3	Rte. 17, .02 mile s. of Rte. 608
Colonial Post Office, N-10	Rte. 17, .4 mile n.w. of New Post

STAFFORD COUNTY
Area: 274 square miles

Formed in 1664 from Westmoreland, and named for Staffordshire, England. The Army of the Potomac camped in this county, 1862–63.

Historic Aquia Creek, E-41	Rte. 1, 3.6 miles n. of Stafford
Historic Falmouth, E-47	Rte. 1, .95 mile n. of Route 17
Potomac Creek, E-48	Rte. 1, 3.8 miles n. of Falmouth
Potomac Creek, E-48*	Rte. 1, 3 miles n. of Falmouth
Smith and Pocahontas, E-48*	Rte. 1, 1.5 miles n. of Falmouth
Ancient Iron Furnace, E-49*	Rte. 1, 2 miles s. of Stafford Courthouse
Indian Trail, E-50*	Rte. 1, .3 mile n. of Stafford
Marlborough, E-75	Rte. 1, 3.8 miles n. of Falmouth
First Roman Catholic Settlement in Virginia, E-76	Rte. 1, near Rte. 637
Gold Mining in Stafford County, E-77	Rte. 17, .5 mile n. of Hartwood Post Office
Peyton's Ordinary, E-79	Rte. 1, 1.8 miles n. of Stafford
Aquia Church, E-90	Rte. 1, 2.7 miles n. of Stafford

Chatham, J-60	Rte. 3, .2 mile e. of Fredericksburg
Washington's Boyhood Home, J-61	Rte. 3, 1.1 miles e. of Fredericksburg
Fredericksburg Campaign, N-4*	Rte. 17, 4.1 miles n.w. of Falmouth
Cavalry Affairs, N-5	Rte. 17, 8 miles n.w. of Falmouth
The Mud March, N-6*	Rte. 17, 4.1 miles n.w. of Falmouth

SURRY COUNTY
Area: 278 square miles

Formed in 1652 from James City, and named for an English county. Bacon's Castle, a fortress in the rebellion of 1676, is in this county.

Upper Chippokes Creek, K-211*	Rte. 10, 13.5 miles w. of Surry
Historic Cabin Point, K-222	Rte. 10, 4 miles n.w. of Spring Grove
Flying Point, K-223	Rte. 10, 4 miles n.w. of Spring Grove
Pace's Paines, K-224	Rte. 10, 3.5 miles w. of Surry
Claremont, K-225*	Rte. 613, at Claremont
Claremont, K-225*	Rte. 10, 4 miles n.w. of Spring Grove
Wakefield and Pipsico, K-226	Rte. 10, at Spring Grove
Pleasant Point, K-227	Rte. 10, 1.3 miles s.e. of Surry
Glebe House, K-228*	Rte. 10, 4.7 miles w. of Surry
Southwark Church, K-229	Rte. 10, 3.5 miles w. of Surry
Settlement on Gray's Creek, K-230*	Rte. 10, 2 miles n.w. of Surry
Swann's Point, K-231	Rte. 10, at Spring Grove
Cypress Church, K-232*	Rte. 10, 1 mile s. of Surry
Smith's Fort Plantation, K-233	Rte. 10, at Surry
History on Crouch's Creek, K-234*	Rte. 10, at Surry
Bacon's Castle, K-235	Rte. 10, at Bacon's Castle
Organization of the Christian Church, K-236	Rte. 10, 1.5 miles w. of Surry
Hog Island, K-237	Rte. 10, at Bacon's Castle
Historic Claremont, K-255*	Rte. 10, at Spring Grove
Chippokes Plantation, K-279	Rte. 10, 1.3 miles s.e. of Surry
Lawnes Creek Church, K-300	Rte. 10, 7.2 miles s.e. of Surry
James River Ferry, K-301	Rte. 31, at Scotland Wharf

SUSSEX COUNTY
Area: 515 square miles

Formed in 1753 from Surry, and named for an English county. Cornwallis passed through this county in 1781.

Bell Farm (Colonel Michael Blow), K-230	Rte. 460, at Rte. 628
Early Peanut Crop, K-306	Rte. 460, 4 miles s.e. of Waverly
Miles B. Carpenter, K-308	Rte. 460 in Waverly, .11 mile n. of Rte. 40
Jarratt's Station, UM-12	Rte. 139 in Jarratt
Jarratt's Station, UM-12*	Rte. 301, at Jarratt
Old Halifax Road, UM-14	Rte. 301, at Jarratt

Nottoway River, UM-16*   Rte. 301, 3.4 miles s. of Stony Creek
History at Stony Creek, UM-18   Rte. 301, at Stony Creek
The Cattle (Beefsteak) Raid, UO-5   Rte. 35 at Rte. 626

TAZEWELL COUNTY
Area: 531 square miles

Formed in 1799 from Russell and Wythe, and named for
Henry Tazewell, United States Senator 1794–99. Beautiful
Burke's Garden is in this county.

William Wynne's Fort, X-10	Bus. Rte. 19, in Tazewell
Tazewell, X-11	Bus. Rte. 19, at Tazewell
Burke's Garden, X-12	Rte. 61, 1.8 miles e. of Tazewell
Burke's Garden, X-12-a, X-12-a*	Rtes. 666 and 623
Maiden Springs Fort, X-13	Rte. 91, 12 miles s.w. of Tazewell
Big Crab Orchard or Witten's Fort, X-14	Rte. 19/460 and Bus. Rte. 19, at Tazewell
Bluefield, Virginia, X-15	Rte. 19, at w. entrance of Bluefield
Indian Outrages, X-16	Bus. Rte. 19, 2 miles w. of Tazewell
Pisgah United Methodist Church, X-25	Rte. 19/460 and Bus. Rte. 19
Mathias Harman, Sr., X-27	Rte. 637, 7 miles n. of Rte. 460
First Court for Tazewell County, X-28	Rte. 19 and Bus. Rte. 460
Bluefield College, X-31	Rte. 102, .3 mile w. of West Virginia line
Molly Tynes' Ride, XH-1	Rte. 61, 1.8 miles e. of Tazewell
Shawver Mill, XH-2	Rte. 61 at Rte. 64
Richlands, XL-4	Rte. 460, at Richlands
Site of James Burke's Garden, XL-5	Rte. 623, in Burke's Garden
Pocahontas, XP-4	Rte. 102, just e. of Pocahontas
Abb's Valley, XP-5	Rte. 102, just e. of Pocahontas
Engagement at Falls Mills, XP-6	Rte. 102 at Rte. 643

WARREN COUNTY
Area: 216 square miles

Formed in 1836 from Frederick and Shenandoah, and named
for General Joseph Warren, killed at Bunker Hill, 1775.

State Fish Hatchery, FF-2	Rte. 55, 5 miles w. of Riverton
The McKay Home, J-7	Rte. 340, at Cedarville
Capture of Front Royal, J-8	Rte. 340, at Front Royal
Mosby's Men, J-9	Rte. 340, .5 mile n. of Front Royal
Guard's Hill Affair, J-11*	Rte. 340, .2 mile n. of Riverton Recreational Center of Front Royal, J-12 Rte. 340, 1.1 miles n. of Riverton
Brother against Brother, J-17	Rte. 340, at Front Royal
Belle Boyd and Jackson, JD-1	Rte. 340, 3 miles s.w. of Front Royal
William E. Carson, JD-2	Rte. 340, at Front Royal

WASHINGTON COUNTY
Area: 604 square miles

Formed in 1776 from Fincastle, and named for George Washington. This county was the first locality named for him. General William Campbell, hero of King's Mountain, lived in this county. Emory and Henry College is here.

Emory and Henry College, I-7	Rte. 11, 8.3 miles e. of Abingdon
King's Moutain Men, K-47	Rte. 11, at w. entrance of Abingdon
Site of Black's Fort, K-48	Rte. 11, at Abingdon
Abingdon, K-49	Rte. 11, at Abingdon

WESTMORELAND COUNTY
Area: 252 square miles

Formed in 1653 from Northumberland and King George, and named for an English county. In it were born George Washington, James Monroe, and Robert E. Lee.

Bristol Iron Works, J-64	Rte. 3, 2.6 miles w. of Oak Grove
History at Oak Grove, J-67	Rte. 3, at Oak Grove
Westmoreland Association, J-68	Rte. 3, at Oak Grove
Leedstown, J-68*	Rte. 3, s. of Colonial Beach
The Washington Home, J-69*	Rte. 3, 2.8 miles s.e. of Oak Grove
Popes Creek Episcopal Church, J-69-a	Rte. 3, 4.8 miles s.e. of Oak Grove
Washington's Birthplace, J-69-b	Rte. 3, 2.8 miles s.e. of Oak Grove
Lee's Birthplace, J-70*	Rte. 3, 4 miles n.w. of Montross
Old Westmoreland Courthouse, J-71	Rte. 3, at Montross
Nomini Hall, J-72	Rte. 3, at Templemans Cross Roads
Chantilly, J-74*	Rte. 3, 4 miles n.w. of Montross
Westmoreland State Park, J-75	Rte. 3, 4.7 miles n.w. of Montross
Stratford and Chantilly, J-76	Rte. 3, 4 miles n.w. of Montross
Nomini Baptist Church, J-79	Rte. 3 at Rte. 202
Birthplace of Monroe, JP-6	Rte. 205, 1.8 miles s. of Colonial Beach
Nominy Church, JT-2	Rte. 202, 3.7 miles e. of Templemans Cross Roads
The Glebe, JT-3	Rte. 202, 4.4 miles e. of Templemans Cross Roads
Washington's Mother, JT-4	Rte. 202, 4.8 miles n.w. of Callao
Bushfield, JT-5	Rte. 202, 4.4 miles e. of Templemans Cross Roads
Richard Henry Lee's Grave, JT-6	Rte. 202, 8.8 miles s.e. of Templemans Cross Roads
Yeocomico Church, JT-7	Rte. 202, 8.1 miles n.w. of Callao
Kinsale, JT-8	Rte. 202, 4.8 miles n.w. of Callao
Leedstown, JT-15	Rte. 637, at Leedstown
Sandy Point, JT-16	Rte. 604, at Sandy Point

WISE COUNTY
Area: 420 square miles

Formed in 1856 from Lee, Scott, and Russell, and named for Henry A. Wise, Governor of Virginia 1856–60.

Southwest Virginia Museum, I-2	Alt. Rte. 58, at Big Stone Gap
Big Stone Gap, KA-11	Rte. 23, at Powell River Bridge in Big Stone Gap
Coeburn, X-20	Rte. 58 at Rte. 72, in Coeburn
Norton, X-21	Rte. 23, at Norton
Benge's Gap, X-22*	Alt. Rte. 58, at Norton
Appalachia, X-23	Rte. 78 and Bus. Rte. 23
Wise, XB-4	Bus. Rte. 23 (Main St.), at Wise
Pound Gap, XB-7*	Rte. 23, 4 miles n. of Pound

WYTHE COUNTY
Area: 479 square miles

Formed in 1789 from Montgomery, and named for George Wythe, signer of the Declaration of Independence. New River flows through this county.

St. John's Lutheran Church, FR-26	Rte. 21, at Wytheville
A Colonial Soldier's Home, K-23*	Rte. 11, at e. entrance of Wytheville
Site of Mount Airy, K-31	Rte. 11, 12.9 miles w. of Wytheville
Wytheville, K-35	Rte. 11, at Wytheville
Anchor and Hope Plantation, K-36	Rte. 52, at Fort Chiswell
Ingleside, K-37	Rte. 11, at e. entrance of Wytheville
Lead Mines, K-39	Rte. 52, at Fort Chiswell
Toland's Raid, KC-4	Rte. 52, at Bland Co. line
Seat of Fincastle County, KD-5	Rte. 52, 5.5 miles s.e. of Fort Chiswell
Jackson's Ferry and Old Shot Tower, KD-6	Rte. 52, 7.7 miles s.e. of Fort Chiswell
Austin's Birthplace, KD-8	Rte. 52, at Poplar Camp

YORK COUNTY
Area: 136 square miles

One of the eight original shires formed in 1634. First called Charles River, which was named for King Charles I. The name was changed in 1643 to York for Yorkshire, England. Cornwallis's surrender, October 19, 1781, took place at Yorktown.

Charles Church, NP-1	Rtes. 134 and 17 at Tabb
Vineyard Tract, W-46	Rte. 641, 1.4 miles e. of Williamsburg, on secondary road
Seaford, NP-3	Rte. 622, at Seaford
Goodwin Neck, NP-12	Rte. 173, 3.5 miles e. of Rte. 17

INDEPENDENT CITIES

ALEXANDRIA

Land was first patented here in 1657. In 1731 a warehouse was built on Hunting Creek, about which grew up the village of Belhaven. The town of Alexandria was established in 1749 and became one of the main colonial trading centers. It was part of the original District of Columbia but was returned to Virginia in 1847.

Historic Alexandria, E-71*	Rte. 1, at s. entrance to city
Lee's Boyhood Home, E-91	607 Oronoco St.
Virginia Theological Seminary, T-44	Rte. 7, w. of Quaker Lane
Episcopal High School, T-45	Rte. 7, w. of Quaker Lane
First Synagogue of Beth El Hebrew Congregation, Site of, E-92	206 North Washington St.
Lee-Fendall House, E-93	614 Oronoco St.

BEDFORD

Randolph-Macon Academy—Liberty Academy, K-133	College St. near Bedford Primary School

BRISTOL

The Sapling Grove tract (Bristol) was surveyed for John Tayloe in 1749. It was owned by Isaac Baker and Evan Shelby, who built a post about 1770. The Virginia tract was bought by John Goodson, whose son founded the town of Goodson, incorporated as a city.

Bristol, Virginia, K-42	Rte. 11, at n. corp. limits of Bristol
Historic Bristol, K-43	Randall Expwy. at State St., at train station

CHARLOTTESVILLE

The site was patented by William Taylor in 1737. The town was established by law in 1762 and was named for Queen Charlotte, wife of George III. Burgoyne's army, captured at Saratoga in 1777, was long quartered near here. The legislature was in session here in June 1781, but retired westward to escape Tarleton's raid on the town. Jefferson, who lived at Monticello, founded the University of Virginia in 1819.

University of Virginia, I-3	Rte. 29, at Charlottesville
Tarleton's Oak, Q-1-1	High St. and Lexington Ave.
Charlottesville, Q-1-a-b-d	a: High St. near Hazel St. b: Rte. 20 and Carleton St. d: Rte. 29 near Piedmont Ave.

CHESAPEAKE
(Includes old Norfolk County)

Craney Island, K-262	Rte. 17, w. of Churchland bypass
Craney Island, K-262*	Rte. 337, 2.8 miles w. of Portsmouth
Hodges Ferry, K-263*	Rte. 337, 2.3 miles w. of Portsmouth
Dale Point, K-264*	Rte. 460, .25 mile w. of Portsmouth
Fort Nelson, K-265*	Rte. 337, near w. city limits of Portsmouth
Great Bridge, K-275*	Rte. 17, 3 miles s. of Portsmouth
Battle of Great Bridge, KY-4*	Rte. 170, at Great Bridge
Battle of Great Bridge, KY-5	Rte. 168, at Great Bridge
Dismal Swamp Canal, NW-15, NW-15*	Rte. 17, 1 mile s. of Rte. 104
Great Bridge Chapel, WP-5*	Rte. 168 in Great Bridge
Norfolk County Courthouse, WP-7*	Rte. 168 in Great Bridge
St. Bride's Church, WP-10	Rte. 168, 4 miles n. of North Carolina line

COVINGTON

Fort Young, D-27	Rte. 154, on Durant Rd., n. of Jackson River

DANVILLE

Saponi Religious Beliefs Explained, L-53	Rte. 29 at North Carolina line
Last Confederate Capitol, Q-5-a	Sutherlin Ave. and Main St.
Wreck of the Old 97, Q-5-b	between Pickett and Farrar sts.
The Gibson Girl, Q-5-c	Main and Broad sts.
Lady Astor, Q-5-c	Main and Broad sts.
Loyal Baptist Church, Q-5-c, Q-5-c*	400 block of Loyal St.
Danville System, Q-5-d	126 N. Union St.
Stratford College, Q-5-e	1125 W. Main St.
Calvary United Methodist Church, Q-5-f	924 N. Main St.
Frederick Delius, Q-5-g	N. Main St. at Keen St.
Confederate Prison #6, Q-5-h	Loyal St. at Lynn St.
Schoolfield, Q-5-k	W. Main St. at Baltimore Ave.
750 Main Street, Q-7-e	750 Main St.

EMPORIA

Grave of Gen. John R. Chambliss, Jr., UM-38	Rte. 301 (S. Main St.), 350 ft. s. of Brunswick Ave.
Benjamin D. Tillar, Jr., UM-39	Rte. 301, at Main and Battery sts.

FREDERICKSBURG

Captain John Smith was here in 1608; Lederer, the explorer, in 1670. In May, 1671, John Buckner and Thomas Royster patented the Lease Land Grant. The town was established in 1727 and lots were laid out. It was named for Frederick, Prince of Wales, father of George III. The court for Spotsylvania county was moved here in 1732, and the town was enlarged in 1759 and 1769. Fredericksburg was incorporated as a town in 1781, as a city in 1879, and declared a city of first class in 1941.

HAMPTON
(includes Old Elizabeth City County)

Buckroe, WY-92	at Buckroe Beach (Atlantic Ave. and Mallo St.)
Phoebus, WY-93	County St. and Woodland Rd.
Phoebus, WY-94	Mallory St., at Exit 268 of I-64

HARRISONBURG

Harrisonburg, A-33	Rte. 11, at Harrisonburg
End of the Campaign, A-35	Rte. 11, at Harrisonburg

LEXINGTON

Virginia Military Institute, I-1	Letcher Ave., at entrance to VMI, .15 mile w. of Rte. 11
Stonewall Jackson's Home, Q-11-a*	Washington and Main sts.

LYNCHBURG

In 1757 John Lynch opened a ferry here; in 1765 a church was built. In 1786 Lynchburg was established by act of assembly; in 1791 the first tobacco warehouse was built. Lynchburg was incorporated as a town in 1805. In 1840 the James River and Kanawha Canal, from Richmond to Lynchburg, was opened; the section to Buchanan, in 1851. Lynchburg became a city in 1852.

John Daniel's Home, K-142, K-142*	720 Court St.
Quaker Meeting House, L-20	Fort Ave. at Quaker Pkwy.
Montview, L-21	University Blvd., at entrance to Liberty University
Sandusky, L-22	Fort Ave. at Quaker Pkwy.
Lynchburg Defenses, M-60	Rte. 501, e. entrance to Lynchburg
Fort Early, Q-6-1	Fort Ave., near Early Monument
Fort McCausland, Q-6-2	Langhorne Rd., about 1,200 ft. w. of Clifton St.
Inner Defenses, 1864, Q-6-3	Twelfth St., between Fillmore and Floyd sts.
Inner Defenses, Q-6-4	Bedford Ave. and Holly St.
Defense Works, Q-6-5	Rivermont Ave. and Langhorne Rd.
Mustered and Disbanded, 1861–1865, Q-6-6	between Rivermont Ave. and Monsview Dr.
Inner Defenses, 1864, Q-6-7	Ninth and Polk sts.
Inner Defenses, Q-6-8	between Ninth and Polk sts.
Inner Defenses, Q-6-9	between Wise and Floyd sts.
Miller-Claytor House, Q-6-10	Rivermont Ave. and Treasure Island Rd.
Lynchburg, Q-6-11	Ninth and Church sts.
Carter Glass, Q-6-12	829 Church St.
Lynchburg College, Q-6-13	Lakeside Dr. (Rte. 221), w. of Old Forest Rd.
Randolph-Macon Woman's College, Q-6-14	Rivermont Ave. and Princeton Cir.
Virginia Seminary and College, Q-6-15	Campbell Ave. and DeWitt St.

Allen Weir Freeman, M. D. 1881–1954, Q-6-16*   in front of 416 Main St.
Douglas Southall Freeman, Ph.D., Q-6-17   s. end of Rivermont Bridge
Samuel D. Rockenbach, Q-6-18   Eighth and Court sts.
The Anne Spencer House, Q-6-20   1313 Pierce St.

MANASSAS

Ruffner Public School Number 1, CL-2   Rte. 28, .1 mile s. of Rte. 334, in Manassas
Manassas, CL-4   Rte. 28, 5.41 miles n. of Rte. 215, in Manassas

MARTINSVILLE

Named for Joseph Martin, pioneer, who settled here in 1773. In 1793 the courthouse of Henry County was moved here and the town was established. Patrick Henry, for whom the county was named, lived near here once. In 1865, Stoneman, moving south to join Sherman, captured Martinsville. It was incorporated as a town in 1873 and as a city in 1929.

Martinsville, A-94   Rte. 220, at Martinsville

NEWPORT NEWS
(includes old Warwick County)

This community was known to Captain John Smith as Point Hope, but was called Newportes Newes as early as 1619. The name may commemorate Captain Christopher Newport, commander of five expeditions to Jamestown during 1606–12.

Skiffes Creek, W-53*   Rte. 60, 1 mile n.w. of Lee Hall
Lee Hall, W-54*   Rte. 60, at Lee Hall
To Yorktown, W-55*   Rte. 60, at Lee Hall
Fort Eustis, W-56*   Rte. 337, 1 mile s. of Lee Hall
Mulberry Point, W-57*   Rte. 337, 1 mile s. of Lee Hall
Lee's Mill, W-58*   Rte. 337, 2 miles s.e. of Lee Hall
Battle of Dam No. 1, W-59*   Rte. 60, 1.9 miles s.e. of Lee Hall
Warwick Courthouse, W-60   Rte. 60, at Denbigh (14421 Old Courthouse Way)
Denbigh Plantation, W-61   Rte. 60, 2.2 miles e. of Denbigh, at Menchville Rd.
Warwick River, W-62*   Rte. 337, 4 miles s.e. of Denbigh
Young's Mill, W-63*   Rte. 337, .75 mile s.e. of Denbigh
Waters Creek, W-64*   Rte. 60, 6.5 miles s.e. of Denbigh
Denbigh Baptist Church, W-65*   Rte. 60, 2.6 miles s.e. of Denbigh
Battle of Big Bethel, W-66*   Rte. 60, at Morrison
Battle of Big Bethel, W-66*   Rte. 60, at Rte. 306

NORFOLK

This marks the northern limit of the fifty acres constituting the original town of Norfolk. It was bounded on the north by Town Back Creek and Dun-in-the-Mire Creek. The land was purchased as a port for Lower Norfolk County for "tenn thousand pounds of tobacco and caske," being deeded to feoffees [*sic*] in trust for the county in 1682. It was divided into streets and sold in half-acre lots.

PETERSBURG

PORTSMOUTH

The site of this city was patented in 1659 by Captain William Carver. Established as a town in 1752 and named by its founder, Lt. Col. William Crawford. Chartered as a city in 1858, it has the country's oldest naval shipyard, established in 1767, the nation's oldest naval hospital, commenced in 1827, and is the birthplace of the world's largest naval installation.

City of Portsmouth, Q-8-l   Rte. 17 at Churchland Bridge
Crawford House, Q-8-m   Crawford and Queen sts.
Norfolk County Court House, Q-8-n   High and Court sts.
Arnold's British Defense, 1781, Q-8-o   Washington and King Sts.
Arnold's British Defenses, 1781, Q-8-p   Crawford Pkwy. at Court St.
Arnold's British Defenses, 1781, Q-8-q*   Washington and Brighton sts.

RADFORD

It originated as a railroad town in 1856 and was known as
Central. In 1862-65 this section was in the range of Union
raids; Confederates burned the bridge at Ingles Ferry to retard raiders. Incorporated in 1887 as a town, the place was
incorporated as a city in 1892 and named Radford, for Dr.
John B. Radford, prominent citizen. Radford State Teachers
College was established here, 1913.

Radford, K-65   Rte. 11, at Radford
State Teachers College at Radford, K-66   Rte. 11, at Radford

RICHMOND

Bacon's Plantation, E-1*   Chamberlayne Ave., in Richmond
Intermediate Defenses, E-2, E-2*   Laburnam and Chamberlayne aves., in
Richmond
Brook Road, E-4*   Brook Rd. and Rte. 1, in Richmond
Steuben and Lafayette, S-1*   Rte. 1, at s. entrance to Richmond
First Trolley Car System in Richmond, SA-25   5th St. between Marshall St. and the Coliseum
Trinity Methodist Church, SA-26   Broad St. at 20th St.
Windsor, SA-28   4601 Lilac Ln.
Wilton, SA-29   Cary Street Rd. and Wilton Rd.
Ampthill, SA-30   Cary Street Rd. and Ampthill Rd.
Site of J. E. B. Stuart's Death, SA-32   206 W. Grace St.
Virginia Historical Society, SA-33   Boulevard at Kensington Ave.
Craig House, SA-34   Grace St. near 19th St.
Saint John's Episcopal Church, SA-37   Broad St. near 24th St.
Monumental Church, SA-38   Broad St. near College St.
Origins of Richmond, SA-39   Franklin St. between 17th and 18th sts.

ROANOKE

In June 1864, General Hunter passed here retreating from Lynchburg. In 1874 Big Lick was incorporated. In 1881, with the junction of the new Shenandoah Valley Railroad and the N. & W., rapid growth began. In 1882 the name was changed to Roanoke; in 1884 it was incorporated as a city. In 1909 the Virginian Railroad operated its first train. In recent years Roanoke became the third largest city of Virginia.

Roanoke, K-95	East Bullitt and South Jefferson sts.
Roanoke City Market, K-96	Campbell Ave. adjacent to Center in the Square
A Colonial Ford, K-116	Franklin Rd., S.W., between Naval Reserve and Brandon aves.

SALEM

General Andrew Lewis, K-75	Rte. 11, at College Ave. and Eighth St.
General Andrew Lewis's Grave, K-77	Rte. 460, at Park Ave. and Main St.
Sgt. James Walton, Salem Flying Artillery, C.S.A., K-78	Main St. at entrance to East Hill Cemetery

STAUNTON

Birthplace of Woodrow Wilson, A-62	Rte. 11, .05 mile n. of Rte. 261
Dr. Alexander Humphreys, A-63	Augusta St. at Johnson St.
Dr. William Fleming, A-64	Greenville Ave. at New St.
The Virginia School for the Deaf and the Blind, I-16	Rte. 11 Bypass, just e. of the school
Mary Baldwin College, I-17	E. Frederick St., at Mary Baldwin College
Stuart Hall, I-20	W. Frederick and St. Clair sts.
Trinity Church, QC-1	214 W. Beverly St.

SUFFOLK
(includes old Nansemond County)

Chuckatuck, K-248	Rte. 10, 9.2 miles n.w. of Suffolk proper
Dumpling Island, K-249	Rte. 10, 6 miles n.w. of Suffolk proper
Reid's Ferry, K-250	Rte. 10, 5.5 miles n.w. of Suffolk proper
Early History of Suffolk, K-251*	Rte. 10, 1.5 miles n.w. of Suffolk proper
Siege of Suffolk, K-252	Rte. 460, .5 mile w. of old city limits
Dismal Swamp, K-253*	Rte. 58, 4.7 miles e. of Suffolk proper
Revolutionary Camp, K-254*	Rte. 337, 6.2 miles n.e. of Suffolk proper
Yeates School, K-255	Rte. 337, at Driver
Sleepy Hole Ferry, K-256	Rte. 337, at Driver
Bennett's Home, K-257	Rte. 337, at Driver
Glebe Church, K-258	Rte. 337, at Driver

Siege of Suffolk, K-259 — Rte. 10, 1.5 miles n.w. of Suffolk proper
Pig Point, K-261* — Rte. 460, 8 miles w. of Portsmouth
Hargrove's Tavern, K-270* — .8 mile e. of Driver
James Bowser Plantation, K-310 — 1 mile n. of Rtes. 629 and 337
St. John's Church, KO-1 — Rte. 125, 1 mile e. of Chuckatuck
Nansemond Collegiate Institute, KO-2 — E. Washington St. near Fifth St.
First Suffolk Church, QB-1 — Western Ave., 200 ft. w. of Church St.
First Ruritan Club, U-127 — Rte. 58, at Holland
Dismal Swamp, U-130 — Rte. 58, 4.7 miles e. of Suffolk
Cavalry Skirmish, UT-28* — Rte. 460, 4.6 miles n.w. of Suffolk

VIRGINIA BEACH
(includes old Princess Anne County)

Kempsville, K-272* — Rte. 165, at Kempsville
New Town, K-273* — Rte. 58, 3 miles e. of Norfolk
Donation Church and Witch Duck, K-276* — Rte. 58, 5 miles e. of Norfolk
Eastern Shore Chapel, K-278* — Rte. 58, 2.2 miles w. of beachfront
Seashore State Park, KV-4 — Rte. 60, 1 mile e. of Rte. 615
First Landing, KV-15 — Rte. 60, .85 mile w. of Rte. 305, at Cape Henry
Oldest Brick House in Virginia, KW-16* — Rte. 500, 7 miles e. of Norfolk

WAYNESBORO

Here, on one of the first roads west of the Blue Ridge, a hamlet stood in colonial times. The Walker exploring expedition started from this vicinity in 1748. Here, in June, 1781, the Augusta militia assembled to join Lafayette in the east. A town was founded in 1797. It was established by law in 1801 and named for General Anthony Wayne.

Waynesboro, Q-2-a-b — *a:* Rte. 250 at e. entrance of Waynesboro
b: Rte. 250 at w. entrance of Waynesboro
Virginia Metalcrafters, Q-2-c — Rte. 250, .3 mile e. of Rte. 340

WILLIAMSBURG

First Balloon Flight in Virginia, W-40 — Rte. 162, at entrance to Cary Field

WINCHESTER

At first called Frederickstown, it was founded in 1744, near a Shawnee Indian village, by Colonial James Wood, a native of the English city of Winchester. The town was situated in Lord Fairfax's proprietary of the Northern Neck. It was chartered in 1752.

Third Battle of Winchester, J-4	Rte. 522 at national cemetery
General Daniel Morgan, Q-4-a	Rte. 50, at e. limits
Winchester, Q-4-a	Rte. 50, at e. limits
Joist Hite and Braddock, Q-4-b*	Rte. 7, at e. limits
Winchester, Q-4-b*	Rte. 7, at e. limits
George Washington, Q-4-c	Rte. 11, at n. limits
Winchester, Q-4-c*	Rte. 11, at n. limits
Lord Fairfax, Q-4-d*	Rte. 522, at n. limits
Winchester, Q-4-d*	Rte. 522, at n. limits
Colonel James Wood, Q-4-e	Rte. 50, just w. of Rte. 11
Winchester, Q-4-e	Rte. 50, just w. of Rte. 11
Jackson's Headquarters, Q-4-f	415 N. Braddock St.

COUNTIES THAT ARE NO LONGER IN EXISTENCE OR ARE IN BORDERING STATES

ELIZABETH CITY COUNTY
Area: 54 square miles

One of the eight original shires formed in 1634, and named for Elizabeth City, or Hampton. This is the oldest English-settled town in America. *See* Hampton.

NANSEMOND COUNTY
Area: 423 square miles

Formed in 1637 from New Norfolk County. It was first called Upper Norfolk County, but in 1642 it was named Nansemond for an Indian tribe. Dismal Swamp is partly in this county. *See* Suffolk.

NORFOLK COUNTY
Area: 415 square miles

Formed in 1637, when New Norfolk County was divided into Upper Norfolk and Lower Norfolk. The name is that of an English county. The battle of Great Bridge, 1775, took place in this county, and in the waters near its shores the warship *Merrimac* performed her exploits in 1862. *See* Chesapeake.

PRINCESS ANNE COUNTY
Area: 279 square miles

Formed in 1691 by a division of Lower Norfolk County into Norfolk and Princess Anne. Named for Queen Anne (then Princess Anne). The first settlers first landed at Cape Henry, April 26, 1607. *See* Virginia Beach

WARWICK COUNTY

Area: 69 square miles

One of the original shires formed in 1634, it was given the name of the Warwick River. The river itself was named for the Earl of Warwick. *See* Newport News.

KENTUCKY

This first permanent settlement was made at Harrodsburg in 1774. Kentucky County was established in 1776 and was represented in the Virginia legislature by Daniel Boone. Kentucky was admitted to the Union as the fifteenth state in 1792.

MARYLAND

Maryland was one of the original thirteen states. At first a part of Virginia, it became a separate colony under a charter granted Lord Baltimore, and was settled in 1634.

NORTH CAROLINA

North Carolina was one of the original thirteen states. The first settlement was made on Roanoke Island, 1585, but was not permanent. Settlers from Virginia occupied the Albemarle region before 1663, in which year the colony of Carolina was founded.

TENNESSEE

First permanently settled in 1769 and long a part of North Carolina. In 1785, settlers formed the state of Franklin, not recognized by Congress. Tennessee was admitted to the Union as the sixteenth state in 1796.

WEST VIRGINIA

West Virginia was long a part of Virginia. Morgan Morgan began the settlement of the region in 1727. A great battle with the Indians took place at Point Pleasant in 1774. West Virginia became a separate state of the Union in 1863.

The following map shows the boundaries of Virginia's counties and its independent cities. It also includes all interstate highways and all primary roads on which more than twelve markers are located. For highways not shown on this map, please consult the official highway map of Virginia.

COUNTIES

Accomack	I-3
Albemarle	F-3
Alleghany	E-3
Amelia	G-4
Amherst	E-3, F-3
Appomattox	F-4
Arlington	G-2
Augusta	E-3, F-3
Bath	E-3
Bedford	E-4
Bland	C-4, D-4
Botetourt	E-3, E-4
Brunswick	G-4, G-5
Buchanan	B-4, C-4
Buckingham	F-3, F-4
Campbell	F-4
Caroline	G-3, H-3
Carroll	D-4, D-5
Charles City	H-4
Charlotte	F-4
Chesterfield	G-4
Clarke	G-2
Craig	D-4
Culpeper	G-2
Cumberland	G-3, G-4
Dickenson	B-4
Dinwiddie	G-4
Essex	H-3
Fairfax	G-2, H-2
Fauquier	G-2
Floyd	D-4
Fluvanna	F-3
Franklin	E-4
Frederick	F-1, F-2
Giles	D-4
Gloucester	H-3
Goochland	G-3
Grayson	C-5
Greene	F-2, F-3
Greensville	G-4, G-5
Halifax	F-4, F-5
Hanover	G-3
Henrico	G-3
Henry	E-5
Highland	E-2, E-3
Isle of Wight	H-4
James City	H-4
King and Queen	H-3
King George	H-3
King William	H-3
Lancaster	H-3
Lee	A-5
Loudoun	G-2
Louisa	G-3
Lunenburg	F-4, G-4
Madison	F-2
Mathews	I-4
Mecklenburg	F-5, G-5
Middlesex	H-3
Montgomery	D-4
Nelson	F-3
New Kent	H-3
Northampton	I-4
Northumberland-	H-3
Nottoway	G-4
Orange	G-3
Page	F-2
Patrick	D-5
Pittsylvania	E-4, F-5
Powhatan	G-3
Prince Edward	F-4
Prince George	H-4
Prince William	G-2
Pulaski	D-4
Rappahannock	F-2, G-2
Richmond	H-3
Roanoke	E-4
Rockbridge	E-3
Rockingham	F-2
Russell	B-4, C-4
Scott	B-5
Shenandoah	F-2
Smyth	C-4, C-5

Southampton	H-4, H-5	Covington	E-3
Spotsylvania	G-3	Danville	E-5
Stafford	G-2	Fairfax	G-2
Surry	H-4	Hampton	I-4
Sussex	G-4, H-4	Harrisonburg	F-2
Tazewell	C-4	Lexington	E-3
Warren	F-2	Lynchburg	E-4
Washington	B-5, C-5	Manassas	G-2
5Westmoreland	H-3	Martinsville	E-5
Wise	B-4	Newport News	H-4
Wythe	C-4, D-4	Norfolk	I-4
York	H-4	Petersburg	G-4
		Portsmouth	I-4
		Radford	D-4
		Richmond	G-3
INDEPENDENT CITIES WITH		Roanoke	E-4
HISTORICAL MARKERS		Staunton	F-3
		Suffolk	H-4
Alexandria	H-2	Virginia Beach	I-4
Bristol	B-5	Waynesboro	F-3
Charlottesville	F-3	Williamsburg	H-4
Chesapeake	I-5	Winchester	F-1

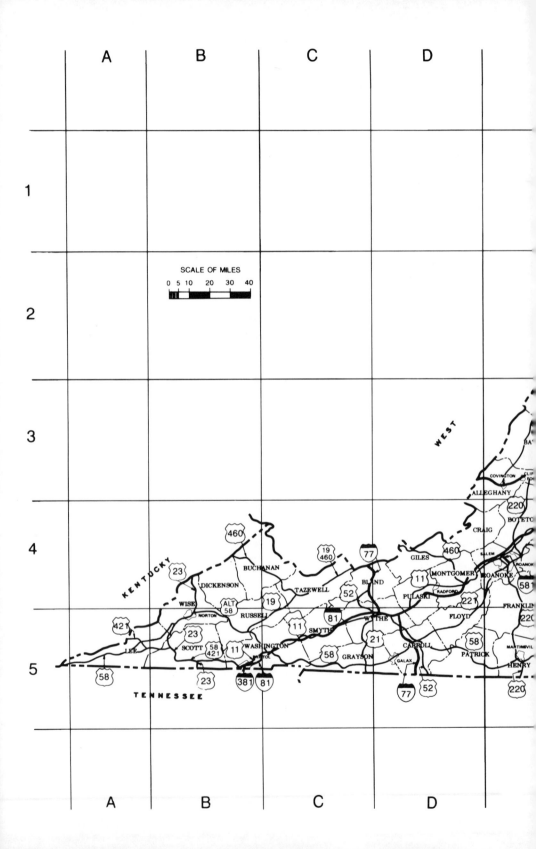